THE GREAT AMERICAN

A Bulfinch Press Book

Little, Brown and Company

Boston   Toronto   London

Comic Strip

Judith O'Sullivan

One Hundred Years of Cartoon Art

The author and publisher gratefully acknowledge the support of King Features Syndicate. For seventy-five years, King Features Syndicate has been one of the major creative influences in comic art.

First edition

Research assistance provided by Mark Johnson.

A substantial portion of the information in the biographical section in this book was originally published in *The Art of the Comic Strip*, a catalog by Judith O'Sullivan that accompanied an exhibition at the University of Maryland Art Gallery, April 1–May 9, 1971. It is used in this publication with permission from the University of Maryland at College Park.

Chapter 2, "Winsor McCay, American Master," is a revised and expanded version of the article originally published in the June 1974 *AFI Report* entitled "In Search of Winsor McCay." Reprinted with permission of The American Film Institute.

Library of Congress Cataloging-in-Publication Data
O'Sullivan, Judith.
   The great American comic strip: one hundred years of cartoon art /Judith O'Sullivan. — 1st ed.
   p. cm.
   "A Bulfinch Press book."
   ISBN 0-8212-1754-2 (hc) — ISBN 0-8212-1756-9 (pb)
   1. Comic books, strips, etc. — United States — History and criticism. 2. Cartoonists — United States — Biography. I. Title.
PN6725.075 1990
741.5'0973 — dc20   90-5752
                                                            CIP

Bulfinch Press is an imprint and trademark of Little, Brown and Company (Inc.)
Designed by Wondriska Associates
Published simultaneously in Canada by Little, Brown & Company (Canada) Limited
PRINTED IN THE UNITED STATES OF AMERICA

ACKNOWLEDGMENTS

I am deeply indebted to the following individuals and organizations for their help with this volume and for their support of *Great American Comics*, the Smithsonian Institution Traveling Exhibition Service show accompanying it: Joseph F. D'Angelo, President, King Features Syndicate, and Ted Hannah, Director of Advertising and Public Relations, King Features Syndicate, who made possible the SITES exhibition on the occasion of the syndicate's seventy-fifth anniversary; collectors Murray A. and Bea Harris, who shared with me their warm hospitality and many cartoon treasures; collector Mark J. Cohen, who generously provided access to his rich collection of artists' self-caricatures; my dear friend Deborah Bennett, and the staff of the Smithsonian Traveling Exhibition Service: Director Anna Cohn, Frederica Adelman, Betty Teller, and interns Rachel Heller and Courtney Braun; Rosemary Regan, Tina Lynch, and the staff of the Smithsonian Institution's Office of Exhibits Central; Smithsonian Institution Assistant Secretary for Museums Tom Freudenheim, special assistant Barbara Schneider, and the Smithsonian Institution Special Exhibitions Fund, which provided funding for the preliminary planning of the show; my co-curator and distinguished associate, Professor Lucy Caswell, Curator of the Ohio State University Cartoon, Graphic, and Photographic Arts Research Library; SITES exhibition scholarly advisory committee members Professor Thomas Inge, Professor Donald Ault, Professor Arthur Asa Berger, Professor Louis Budd, Dr. Robert Harvey, Nicole Hollander, Professor A. J. R. Russell-Wood, and Professor David Smith; Bernie Reilly, Head Curator, Division of Prints and Photographs, the Library of Congress; Curator Emmy Dana of the Busch-Reisinger Museum of Germanic Culture, Harvard University Museums; Margaret Goostray of the Mugar Memorial Library, Boston University; Kathe Todd, Vice President, Rip Off Press; collector and artist Jerry Weist; collector Art Wood; my friends and former associates at The National Museum of American Art — Gaye Brown, Migs Grove, Terry Winch, Audrey Fuller, Richard Murray, Lois Fink, Tina Norelli, Ann Martha Rubin, Rebecca Reynolds, Virginia Tate, Mary Kay Zuravleff, Victoria Jennings, Sarah Gettel, and Cynthia Hodvedt; Barbara Nosanow, Director, The Portland Museum of Art, and Karen Siatras, special assistant; Gwendolyn Owens, Director, the University of Maryland Art Gallery; The American Film Institute; the generous representatives of the syndicates whose strips are represented herein; the selfless artists of all ages who continue to produce the art of the comics; Bill Blackbeard, for his warm hospitality in November 1989; Terry Hackford, senior editor, and Dana Goodall, editorial assistant, Bulfinch Press; David Coen, copy editor, Little, Brown; Jimmy O'Sullivan, who helped to update and expand the "Who's Who in the Comics" section, and who entered the manuscript, in its many forms, into the computer; and my husband of twenty-six years, Jim O'Sullivan.

CONTENTS

Color plates follow page 148

CHAPTER **1**

The Comics, Medium and Message

Detail from Winsor McCay, *Little Nemo in Slumberland*,
November 22, 1908

From time immemorial man the maker has communicated through word and image. Among his works are major monuments of civilization that contain riveting visualizations and compelling narratives. Such masterpieces include the murals of ancient Egypt, which utilized horizontal bands called registers to indicate spatial and temporal progression; classical reliefs, both Greek and Roman, which depicted Homeric epics and actual events through repetition of recognizable types in an unfolding friezelike or spiraling continuum; and medieval embroideries, tapestries, and stained glass, which depicted religious mysteries and national events by means of simplified physiognomic types in emblematic settings. In each of these cases, the implicit message of the image was reinforced by the accompanying text, which itself became an element of the artist's composition.

Within this grand tradition of picture and poetry developed that uniquely American art form, the comics, and its special aesthetic, an aesthetic dictated by the demands of the marketplace and by the sensibilities of its readers. Richly various, comics have communicated over the years through different devices, including continuous narration, whereby a single set of characters appears repeatedly from frame to frame and the action progresses from left to right; calligraphic caricature, which renders the protagonists and their adversaries immediately recognizable; facial and gestural schemata, which express the characters' actions and reactions; action abstraction, a pictorial shorthand, universally understood, in which exploding lines indicate sudden impact, stars unconsciousness, light bulbs ideas, and balloon puffs thoughts; literary legend, conveyed in the balloon, which clarifies the comic's visual message; and specialized vocabularies, such as "Banana Oil!" "Zap!" and "Pow!" which heighten the extreme emotion or action manifested by the characters.

Through such devices comics creators have expressed the highest of human aspirations and the darkest of human fears. From its birth in 1892, the medium has entertained, interpreted, satirized, and shocked, holding an enchanted mirror to American society. At the same time, as the late communications historian Marshall McLuhan observed, comics have, by presenting characters who are at once the readers' beloved familiars and surrogates, provided "a sort of magically recurrent daily ritual . . . serving a very different function from equally popular art forms like the sports page and detective fiction."[1]

From its birth in the pages of the American newspaper through its adaptation in book form, the comic medium has had its undoubted masters. These have worked in distinctive styles, and they have distinguished themselves by the ingenuity exercised in expressing personal social visions while making their work comprehensible to a wide public. Transcending both the inherent limitations of the medium and the external circumstances of its origin, the great practitioners of this graphic art form have taken a simple series of panels and a cast of speakers and through these given voice to the full range of American experience. Moreover, comics have achieved a high level of artistic and literary excellence within an intensely commercial environment and despite a sometimes hostile reception by critics, courts, and lawmakers.

First and foremost, comics were conceived as a medium of entertainment. This function continues today. In the words of Bill Griffith's Zippy the Pinhead, "Are we having fun yet?" But this function has never circumscribed the vision of our greatest comic artists, who have reflected in their work, sometimes obliquely, often explicitly, the issues and events of their day. The themes of corporate greed and environmental destruction have been sounded in the work of comic masters from McCay to Crumb. A panoply of ideologies, from the conservative visions of Harold Gray, Chester Gould, and Al Capp, to the humanistic dreams of Walt Kelly, Jules Feiffer, and Nicole Hollander, to the radical protest of the underground cartoonists, have found expression in the comics. The cataclysmic events of this century, the Great Depression, the two world wars, the Holocaust, have all been fit subjects for the graphic master's potent pen. The great strips are replete with significant issues and historical movements, including civil rights, feminism, and the constitutional guarantee of free expression. In short, a reading of American comics is a reading of twentieth-century social history. It is the purpose of the present volume to examine the achievements of our greatest artists, whose work mirrored and transformed their times, and to introduce a new generation of cartoonists whose work continues that

proud tradition.

The birth of this national art form, the comics, is closely connected with turn-of-the-century American urbanization and with the communications explosion that produced and revolutionized the American newspaper industry. Although weekly illustrated newspapers such as *Gleason's* (1852), *Leslie's* (1855), and *Harper's* (1857) achieved immediate popularity, it was the invention of photoengraving in 1873 that made possible for the first time inexpensive newspaper illustration. Publishers were quick to realize that one picture was worth a thousand words and that illustration could, in fact, significantly expand their readership in cities swollen by newly arrived, often non-English-speaking, Americans. American newspapers, therefore, became at once more pictorial and more plentiful. Thus began the battle of the newspaper titans, who were to employ an infant art form as a lethal weapon. Publishing giants such as William Randolph Hearst, Joseph Pulitzer, James Gordon Bennett, Jr., and Joseph Medill Patterson vied with one another to capture the country's imagination. Ruthlessly competitive, these newspaper magnates sponsored transatlantic races and worldwide explorations, contending with one another for reporters to describe spectacular events and artists to illustrate them.

The gauntlet in the battle for newspaper supremacy was thrown on September 25, 1895, when, challenging his arch-rival, Joseph Pulitzer, Hearst acquired the *New York Morning Journal* from John R. McLean, who had previously purchased it from Pulitzer's brother Albert. Immediately perceiving the potential of the comic strip to increase circulation, Hearst in 1896 raided Pulitzer's *New York World*, securing the services of comic-strip artist Richard Felton Outcault as a contributor to the *American Humorist*, the *Journal's* comic supplement. Outcault was the creator of the popular slum strip *Hogan's Alley*, which featured as its protagonist the Yellow Kid. Historian Stephen Becker asserts that the Kid was conceived when "Charles Saalburgh, foreman of the color press room, needed an open patch of white space which the presses could print yellow. . . . One of the residents of 'Hogan's Alley' was a gap-toothed jug-eared urchin who wore what looked like a white nightgown. Saalburgh chose that nightgown as the test area for his tallow-drying

R. F. Outcault, *Buster Brown*, February 18, 1923

Outcault's second strip, like *The Yellow Kid* utilizing a child protagonist, was designed to appeal to a different audience, that of the leisure class. For decades serving as a guide to children's haute couture, *Buster Brown* — in contrast to the explosive vulgarity and horror of vacuum characteristic of *The Yellow Kid* — was a model of thematic and compositional decorum. In *Buster Brown*, a severely limited cast of characters proceeded in orderly progression from left to right in a single setting. Each Sunday, the episode concluded with an intensive, inscribed, scroll-like proclamation setting forth the strip's moral message.

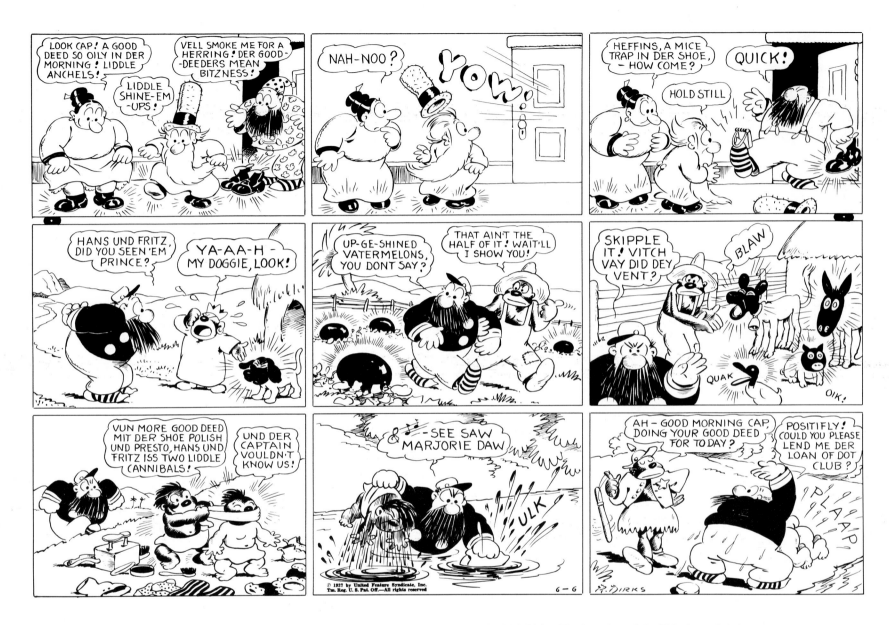

Rudolph Dirks, *The Captain and the Kids*, June 6, 1937

Created by German immigrant Rudolph Dirks, *The Captain and the Kids* chronicled the adventures of mischief-makers Hans and Fritz. Based on Wilhelm Busch's *Max und Moritz*, the strip enjoyed tremendous popularity in the German-American community. In addition to poking fun at its audience, the strip frequently included caricatures of other ethnic groups. In this episode, Hans and Fritz perform in blackface as "two liddle cannibals," with boot polish transforming farm animals as well as "up-ge-shined watermelons." Such stereotyping was to cease only with the entry of African-American cartoonists, among them Morrie Turner and Brumsic Brandon, Jr., into mainstream syndication in the sixties and seventies.

process."[2] Since then the term *yellow journalism*, popularly supposed to have derived from the Yellow Kid, has been applied to newspapers that feature sensational reporting and conspicuous display as a means of attracting readers.

In 1896 Hearst announced that the *Journal* would feature the first complete comic supplement — "eight pages of polychromatic effulgence that make the rainbow look like a lead pipe."[3] To Pulitzer's consternation, the jewel in the crown of Hearst's *Journal* comic supplement was *The Yellow Kid*, a new strip based on the former protagonist of *Hogan's Alley*. In retaliation Pulitzer commissioned artist George Luks, who would later achieve national notoriety as a member of the artistic circle known as the Ash Can School, to create a counter *Yellow Kid* for the *World*.

In 1897 Hearst commanded for the *Journal* the services of German immigrant Rudolph Dirks, who created *The Katzenjammer Kids*, a humorous child strip based on Wilhelm Busch's *Max und Moritz* (a book that enjoyed enormous popularity in the German-American community). Turning the tables, Pulitzer brought the disgruntled Dirks to the *World*, where his strip began to appear on June 4, 1914. The irate Hearst, taking legal action, won the rights to the name *Katzenjammer Kids*, thereafter drawn for the *Journal* by Harold Knerr. At the *World*, however, Dirks continued his creation under various titles, at first *Hans and Fritz*, then — in response to World War I anti-German sentiment — *The Captain and the Kids*, and, from 1918 to 1920, *The Shenanigan Kids*.

In 1912, Hearst formed International News Service, the first of the syndicates, greatly reducing the likelihood of multiple versions of the same strip. Three years later he created King Features Syndicate, an offshoot of International News. Other publishers were quick to follow. Soon the prolific King Features faced competition from the Chicago Tribune–New York News Syndicate and from United Feature Syndicate.

Such syndicates were able to perform tasks beyond the capabilities of the individual author or artist. Simultaneously supplying strips to newspapers throughout the world, they guaranteed the popular creator a large financial return, while controlling the rights to the feature and exacting a percentage of the fees paid for it.

To simplify their mission, the syndicates continued and streamlined the newspapers' practice of categorizing strips by subject. As Stephen Becker observed, "the years from 1907 to 1920 saw the first great crystallization in American comics, when the grand lines of the major categories became apparent: married couples; kids; adventure; girls; animals; slapstick."[4] Anticipating markets, syndicates also encouraged artists to create strips for new audiences. *Little Orphan Annie*, for example, was created in 1924 at the behest of Joseph Medill Patterson for the Chicago Tribune–New York News Syndicate.[5] *Buck Rogers*, was created in 1929 at the suggestion of John Flint Dille of the National Newspaper Service.[6] More recently, the syndicates have responded to both topicality and demands by special constituencies. In 1965 the Vietnam conflict inspired the short-lived *Tales of the Green Berets*, a saga whose time had not yet come. And in 1968 the civil rights movement stimulated *Dateline Danger*, the first integrated adventure strip; *Luther*, African-American artist Brumsic Brandon's ghetto-kid strip; *Friday Foster*, the tale of a black fashion model; and, in 1970, Ted Shearer's *Quincy*, a child strip set in the inner city.

Syndication, a tool of the marketplace, has always depended on popularity. With the sole exception of George Herriman's *Krazy Kat*, which never enjoyed a wide audience but which was beloved of William Randolph Hearst, strips that have not attracted mass readerships have been dropped. To gauge a strip's popularity, syndicates employ the reader survey. To ensure that strips do not alienate their audience, newspapers employ a plethora of personnel, including comic-strip editors.

Despite these constraints, the medium has attracted master artist-authors. Through their visions of civilization, its dreams and discontents, powerfully expressed in inventive line and language, such pioneers as Winsor McCay, Lyonel Feininger, George Herriman, George McManus, Harold Foster, Harold Gray, Chester Gould, Al Capp, Milton Caniff, Alex Raymond, Burne Hogarth, Walt Kelly, Will Eisner, Dale Messick, Jules Feiffer, and Nicole Hollander have been able to transcend the limitations of a commercial medium and to transform it into an enticing and entertaining means of communicating with all America.

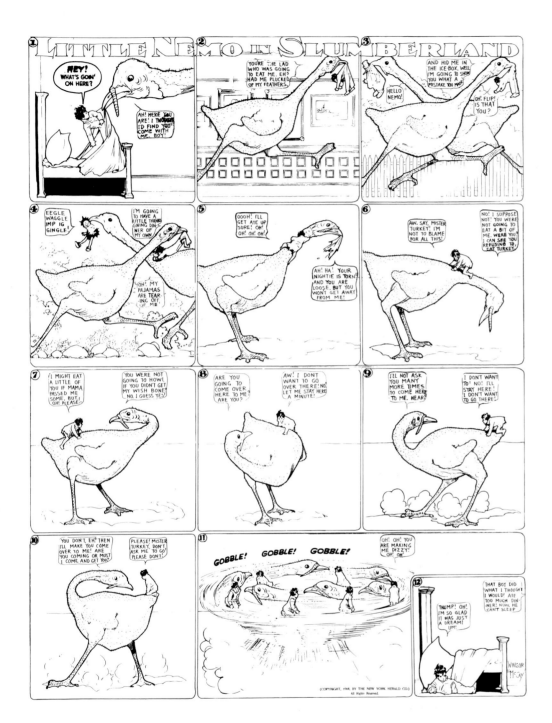

Winsor McCay, *Little Nemo in Slumberland*, November 22, 1908

Copyright *New York Herald*.
Original pen and ink drawing.
Swann Collection, Division of Prints and Photographs, the Library of Congress.

While *The Yellow Kid* celebrated an earthy urban paradise and *Buster Brown* created an ideal suburb for the upwardly mobile, Winsor McCay's *Little Nemo in Slumberland* explored the world of the subconscious. Each week the strip's hero, the slight, youthful Nemo, at once "no one" and Everyman, struggled with gigantic aggressors, including adults and animals, in the pursuit of Utopia, symbolized by the elusive Princess and by Slumber itself. Although drawn in the sinuous line of art nouveau, *Little Nemo* anticipated the explicit dreamscapes of the Surrealists, which also suspended and inverted the physical laws governing conscious existence. *Little Nemo* is the first sustained comic-strip narrative, its epic story unfolding over a five-year period. Between 1905 and 1910 — the golden age of *Little Nemo* — McCay's theme gradually evolved from a search for transcendence through fantasy to a head-on confrontation with current events, culminating in the didactic Shantytown (1908) and Mars (1910) sequences.

One of the most enduring and endearing of early comic creations was the innocent, be he or she kid, cat, or crazy. Among the first of the kid protagonists was Outcault's aforementioned Yellow Kid, a gritty urchin residing in the imaginary abode of Hogan's Alley, who made his first appearance on May 5, 1895, in the *New York World*. In this strip Outcault established the archetype of the idiot savant as social commentator. Enormously popular, the strip's urban setting, crowded frames, expressive style, and slapstick humor reflected a country in transition, a land of burgeoning cities and immigrant populations. To these new Americans, *Hogan's Alley* was comfortingly familiar, evoking the crowded tenements and ethnic neighborhoods of early-twentieth-century New York, a modern Tower of Babel, in which one communicated through gesture and pantomime.

Other seminal strips featuring child protagonists included *Buster Brown*. Begun by Outcault in 1902 and intended for an upper-class, suburban audience, *Buster* featured staid figures, arranged progressively in simplified settings; stilted dialogue, plenteous and didactic; and a concluding moralizing exemplum. Such was the strip's success that for decades *Buster Brown* served as a guide to children's haute couture.

While *The Yellow Kid* celebrated the vitality of immigrant urban experience and *Buster Brown* the pleasures of affluent country life, Winsor McCay's *Little Nemo in Slumberland* (1905) explored the world of the subconscious. Its publication coinciding with Sigmund Freud and Carl Jung's psychoanalytic research on dreams, *Little Nemo* was set in the realm of Morpheus, a palace of subconscious delights in which archetypal conflicts, including those between youth and age, action and reflection, male and female, were waged. Although drawn in the sinuous line of art nouveau, *Little Nemo* anticipated the explicit dreamscapes of the Surrealist painters, who also suspended and inverted the physical laws governing conscious existence. *Little Nemo* was the first extended comic narrative, its epic story unfolding over a five-year period.

Whether episodic or epic, however, many early comics pioneered as protagonist the visionary outsider. Mutes, madmen, children, and animals constitute the comics' early populations. Frederick Burr Opper's Happy Hooligan (1900), Milt Gross's Count Screwloose (1929), Carl An-

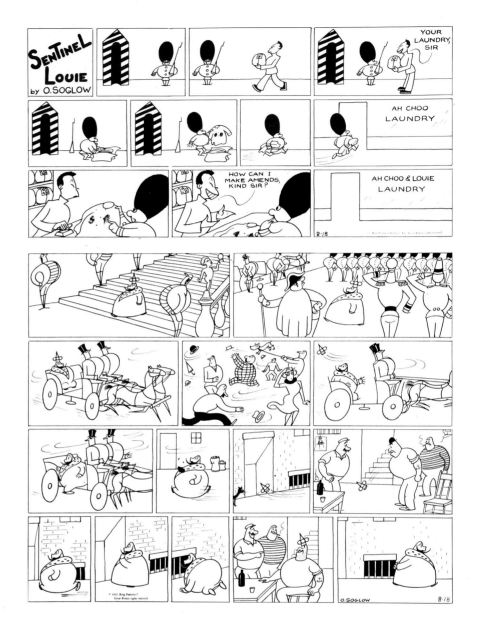

Otto Soglow, *Sentinel Louie* and *The Little King*, August 18, 1935

Among the most enduring of archetypes employed in the comic strip is that of the visionary outsider, be he or she child, madman, or mute. Frederick Burr Opper's Happy Hooligan (1900), Milt Gross's Count Screwloose (1929), Carl Anderson's Henry (1932), and Otto Soglow's Little King (1934) have all played the role of idiot savant, opening, through their ingenuity, a new window to an old world.

Harold Knerr,
The Katzenjammer Kids,
November 29, 1936

Copyright 1936 King Features Syndicate, Inc.
Original pen and ink drawing.
Swann Collection, Division of Prints and
Photographs, the Library of Congress.

Rollo, a hypocritical
goody-goody dandy inspired
by Outcault's *Buster Brown*,
was the nemesis of
the Katzenjammer Kids.
The Kids' madcap antics
were at one time the subject
of two rival strips —
The Captain and the Kids
by Rudolph Dirks and
The Katzenjammer Kids
by Harold Knerr.

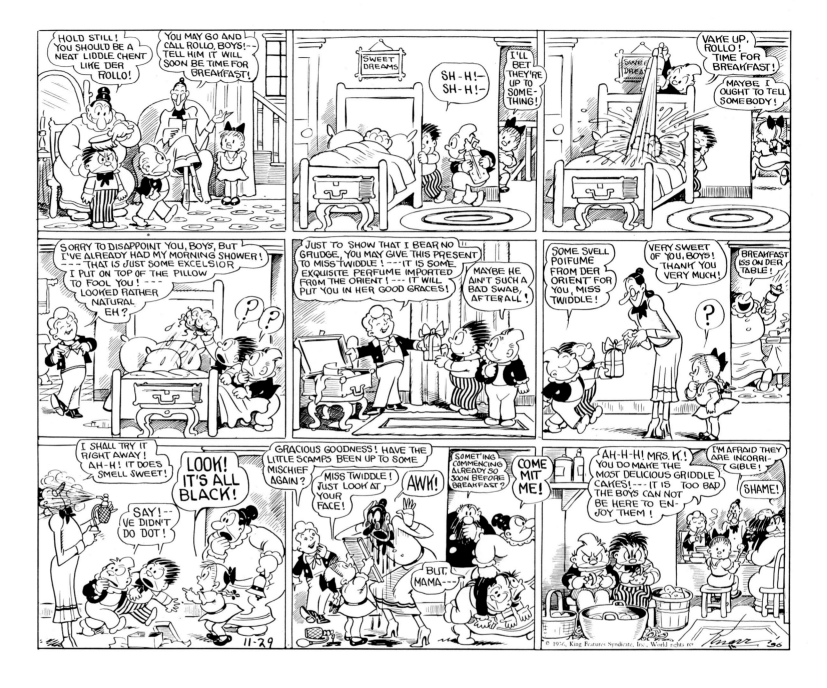

derson's Henry (1932), Otto Soglow's Little King (1934), and a rich variety of feline commentators beginning with George Herriman's Krazy Kat (1913) have played the role of wise fool, sagely interpreting our vanity fair.

Following the first comics' low-mimetic protagonists were the high-mimetic heroes of the Wagnerian adventure strips. Influenced by the developing technologies of photography and film, the artists orchestrating these epic adventures expanded their visual and verbal repertoires, depicting vast architectural vistas, developing complex formulas for depicting the body in motion and the face emoting, extending the story line, and introducing esoteric iconographies while utilizing such cinematic devices as multiple angles and chiaroscuro, the dramatic contrast of light and dark. While the first comics were most often picaresque and debunking, the adventure genre featured epics, the heroic plots of which unfolded over the years. Pioneered in 1906 by Charles W. Kahles's *Hairbreadth Harry* but brought to perfection in the twenties, the adventure strip was, on one hand, related to the venerable tradition of the illustrated book, and, on the other, to the development of the moving image. The comics genre most closely linked to the fine-arts tradition, it permitted in physical scope and thematic range the artist to treat major subjects in a grand style. Flourishing in the heyday of the gargantuan Sunday newspaper comics supplement, the adventure strip enabled its masters to earn such accolades as "the Rembrandt of the comics" (Milton Caniff) and "the Michelangelo of the comics" (Burne Hogarth). As the comics' size dramatically diminished in the fifties, the adventure strip declined, for the reductions did not permit the artist the space the heroic tales demanded. The graphic novels of the eighties have revived the genre, but their black contemporary vision, such as that of Frank Miller's *Batman: The Dark Knight Returns*, contrasts sharply with the glorious interpretation of human nature shared by the adventure comic's early masters.

Despite the fact that the majority of adventure comics were developed during the Great Depression and World War II, they sang a romantic paean to man's infinite potential. Among the most exciting examples of this genre were science-fiction strips such as *Buck Rogers* (1929) by writer Phil Nowlan and artist Dick Calkins, and *Flash Gordon* (1934) by Alex Raymond; primeval jungle sagas, including *Tarzan* (1929) by Hal Foster and Burne Hogarth, *Mandrake the Magician* (1934) by creator Lee Falk and artist Phil Davis, and *Sheena, Queen of the Jungle* (1937) by Will Eisner and Samuel M. Iger; medieval epics, among them Foster's *Prince Valiant* (1937); blood-and-guts military and flight tales, such as *Terry and the Pirates* (1934) by Milton Caniff; and the superheroes strips, including *Superman* (1938) by Jerry Siegel and Joe Shuster, and *Wonder Woman* (1941) by William Moulton Marston and H. G. Peter.

Individual contributions to this genre include those of Roy Crane and Milton Caniff, who adapted dramatic lighting to comic-strip purposes; Alex Raymond, who created a shorthand for distinguishing different character types; Hal Foster, who applied techniques from the classical landscape tradition; and Burne Hogarth, who mastered the portrayal of the figure in motion and created a rich iconography in which nature is the mirror of man's mental state.

While social commentary took the form of an oblique and optimistic call to arms in the romances created by these artists, the trauma of the Great Depression was explicit in the work of Harold Gray, Chester Gould, and Al Capp. Economic collapse, unemployment, labor unrest, and the gangster era — such are the subjects of *Little Orphan Annie* (1924), *Dick Tracy* (1931), and *Li'l Abner* (1934). This conservative triumvirate depicted a world in transition in a variety of styles, ranging from Gray's minimalism (the comics counterpart of Grant Wood's simplified regionalism), to Gould's distorted medieval ménage, to Capp's agitated expressionism. Utilizing diverse storytelling techniques, including editorial comment, moralizing exemplum, and tall tale, each expressed his outrage at the anarchistic thirties while yearning for a simpler place and time. This nostalgia was personified by the good country people of Gray's native Midwest, by Gould's quixotic Dick Tracy, and by Capp's natural man, Li'l Abner.

During most of the history of American cartooning, until the last ten or fifteen years, the newspaper comic-strip tradition thrived quite apart from the phenomenon of the comic book. The first comic books were no more than compilations of comic strips, such as the 1905 collec-

Frederick Burr Opper, *And Her Name Was Maud!* and
Happy Hooligan, August 9, 1931

Two of Opper's most beloved strips, both utilizing the outsider as commentator, were *And Her Name Was Maud!*,
an animal strip that featured a mule, and *Happy Hooligan*,
first published on March 26, 1900. In 1937 the *New York
Times* said of Happy Hooligan that "although his metamorphosis from a pudgy tramp to a lank outcast was marked,
he never lost his tin-can hat nor his healthy vulgarity."

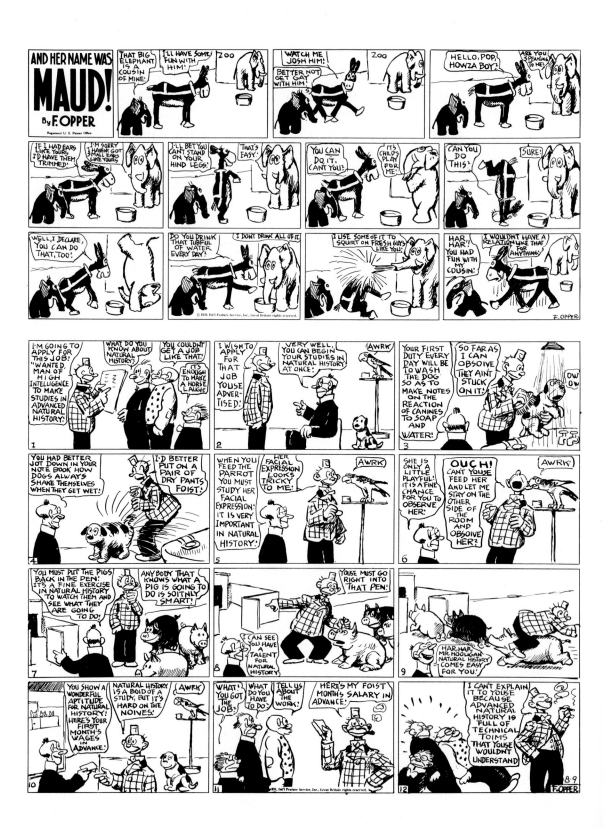

tion of McCay's *Dreams of the Rarebit Fiend* issued by F. A. Stokes. A distinct comic-book tradition did not evolve until the thirties and forties, at which time well-known heroes like Superman were born. Some of these heroes were later adapted into comic strips, but for the most part, comic-book heroes did not make the leap into the newspaper; instead they remained between paper book covers, sometimes enjoying unusually long lives there, like the still internationally popular Archie.

In the 1950s, both the comic-book creators and their colleagues, the comic-strip artists, became joined in adversity. As the pace of social change accelerated, the subjects of the comics expanded. In newspaper strips, topical representations ranged from the literal to the metaphoric. *Dick Tracy*, for instance, forcefully embodied the gangster era. *Prince Valiant*, on the other hand, poetically evoked American patriotism. As the comics became more topical, their critics became more vocal. On the left, supporters of President Franklin Delano Roosevelt called for the suppression of *Little Orphan Annie*. On the right, Senate subcommittees focused their attention on the proliferation of crime and horror comic books, widely blamed for juvenile delinquency.

Increasingly politically active, individual cartoonists fought back. Walt Kelly caricatured Senator Joseph McCarthy in the pages of *Pogo*, casting him as Simple J. Malarkey. Nevertheless, the industries engaging creators of comic strips and comic books sought to pacify such critics. The fifties witnessed, in the pages of the newspapers, the domestication of the adventure strip, as hero after hero took a wife. The comic-book industry created the Comics Magazine Code of America and adopted a code of self-censorship. Despite this measure, as *Forbes* editor Joe Queenan recently noted in the *New York Times Magazine*, "By the end of the Eisenhower years, the roster of some fifty [comic-book] publishers had dwindled to fifteen, mostly putting out cheerful but inane products."[7]

The decline in the number of comics produced and the restrictions on subject matter served to dissuade many young artists from seeking publication in the traditional comics pages. Instead an explosion of cartooning occurred in what have come to be known as underground comic books. It was the work of a few pioneering publishers, like William

Gaines of *Mad* magazine, that inspired this generation of artists to turn to books rather than strips as their medium. Among those so influenced were R. Crumb and Bill Griffith, who were to capture in their "comix" the zeitgeist of Vietnam-era America. Undertaking the sixties hegira to San Francisco, they there created through self-publication in underground organs a cartoon renaissance. No subject was sacred. Pushing to its limit the constitutional right to freedom of expression, aggressively seeking to shock the sensibilities of middle-aged, middle-class America, these artists violated all taboos.

As the years passed, however, these same artists expanded their repertoires to include the endearing as well as the alienating subject. Crumb, for example, turned from cynical satire of the traditional family, such as that of *Whiteman* and *Joe Blow*, to an affectionate analysis of the flawed and fragile nature of marital and parental relationships, depicted in *Aline 'n' Bob in Our Lovely Home*. Griffith's *Zippy*, much to the artist's amazement, was syndicated nationwide in aboveground newspapers by King Features.

By the end of the 1980s, a unique cross-fertilization between the underground comic-book industry and the comic strip had occurred. The work of former underground artists (Jim Davis's *Garfield* and Nicole Hollander's *Sylvia* join *Zippy* as prime examples) had broken into the mainstream, achieving national syndication and notoriety. Today, when one seeks the best art available in comic narrative, one needs to look not only to the newspaper strips but to comic books for innovation and graphic excellence. The latter is particularly evident in the autobiographical cartoons of the seventies and eighties, in which the focus is on personal experience. Foremost among these comic books are Harvey Pekar's touching *American Splendor*, Lynda Barry's poignant evocations of growing up poor in an ethnic Seattle neighborhood, and — of course — Art Spiegelman's masterful *Maus: A Survivor's Tale*. The personal focus is also characteristic today of the most popular of newspaper strips, among them *Cathy*, one of the first "working-girl" strips to be penned by a woman, and *For Better or for Worse*, one of the first family strips to be created by a wife and mother.

Now intimate in both subject and size, the comics have progressed

Walt Kelly, *Pogo*, May 5, 1953

Copyright © 1953 OGPI. Distributed by Los Angeles Times Syndicate.
Original pen and ink drawing.
Swann Collection, Division of Prints and Photographs, the Library of Congress.

As the pace of social change accelerated, the subjects treated by comics expanded, encompassing immigration, assimilation, economic collapse, urban blight, crime, and war. As the comics became more overtly topical, their critics became more vocal. On the left, New Deal supporters clamored for the suppression of *Little Orphan Annie*. To the right, the U.S. Senate subcommittees investigating juvenile delinquency excoriated comic books and their creators, holding hearings on April 21, 22, and June 4, 1954. Individual cartoonists fought back. Walt Kelly satirized Senate scourge Joseph McCarthy in the pages of *Pogo*, caricaturing him as "Simple J. Malarkey."

Charles Schulz, *Peanuts*, July 10, 1952

Copyright United Media. Reprinted by permission.
Original pen and ink drawing.
Swann Collection, Prints and Photographs Division, the Library of Congress.

The gentle whimsy of such early child strips as *Little Jimmy* was revived by Charles Schulz in *Peanuts*. While the majority of kid strips had featured all-male casts, however, Schulz modified the genre by stating as its leitmotiv the battle of the sexes, in which the self-confident Lucy continuously bests the self-doubting Charlie Brown. In this early episode, Lucy anticipates the self-assertion of the women's movement, while Charlie Brown is the first of the sensitive males.

from the large format and archetypal themes spectacularly character-istic of the first strips, through an explosion of cinematic adaptations embodied in the heroic adventure sagas, to small-scale abstractions bespeaking bewildered self-psychoanalysis. In the contemporary comic, solitary man has truly become the measure of all things. Undermined by history, the revived adventure strip, such as Frank Miller's *Batman: The Dark Knight Returns*, is anti-heroic, its setting dangerous, its pro-tagonist disenfranchised.

Like the businessmen who created Hollywood unaware that they had fathered an art form, the first creators of comics did not consider themselves artistic genies but journalists performing work for hire. Still today, in an era of universal educational opportunity, relatively few comics creators hold college degrees. Often self-taught, many come from blue-collar backgrounds and are first-generation artists.

No topic is too risky for today's comics creators. Exercising the American right to express freely one's opinion of the body politic and national temper, contemporary cartoonists have charted new thematic territory, from alcoholism to xenophobia. The Holocaust, the greatest tragedy in human history, is the subject of Art Spiegelman's remarka-ble *Maus: A Survivor's Tale*. Imaginatively combining animal, domes-tic, and adventure genres, Spiegelman from 1973 to 1986 developed the story of his parents, Anja and Vladek. Published in book form in 1986, *Maus* helped to establish the graphic novel as a genre, and lifted comics as autobiography to new heights of epic expression.

In re-creating this universal tragedy, Spiegelman utilizes age-old storytelling devices. For example, he accelerates the narrative's pace by shifting the story from past to present and by alternating the setting from Rego Park, New York, to numerous locations in Poland, including Auschwitz (Mauschwitz). True to comic conventions, he draws upon the animal fable, depicting the Jews as mice, the Nazis as cats. Within *Maus*, Spiegelman acknowledges comic-strip precedent. In one episode, for example, his father comments with uncustomary enthusiasm, "Someday you'll be FAMOUS like . . . what's his name? . . . You know, the big-shot cartoonist . . . YAH! WALT DISNEY!"

The setting itself emerges frequently as a character in contempo-rary comics, including Will Eisner's *A Contract with God* (1978), Harvey Pekar and Drew Friedman's *New York: City with a Heart* (1987), Mark Alan Stamaty's *Washingtoons*, and Kim Deitch's *Holly-woodland* (1987). The use of the city as character was, in fact, pioneered by Will Eisner in *The Spirit* (1940). Unlike Superman's Metropolis and Batman's Gotham, which are glamorous symbols of modern progress, *The Spirit*'s New York is blighted but possesses a cunning life of its own, the ultimate catalyst for the many misadventures enacted therein. Unlike the Spirit itself, the city is vigorously aggressive, asserting itself immediately in the strip's first frame, the famous Eisner "splash page," which introduces every adventure. The urban jungles of Charles Burns and the decaying neighborhoods of Kim Deitch contain many elements found in Eisner's work, including the theme of the persistence of the past. From the antiquated and dangerous New York subways to the dilapidated abandoned mansions of the stars of the silent screen, many younger artists recall the bittersweet moments of an earlier America. Visions of the nation's capital, on the other hand, range from Stamaty's frenzied *Washingtoons*, in which crudely drawn VIPs and meaningless blather fill the frames to overflowing, to Trudeau's streamlined *Doones-bury*, in which the White House and the Supreme Court are often de-picted from a worm's-eye view, which endows these edifices with a grandeur that may or may not be appropriate to the edicts issued therein.

While little influenced by fine-arts fads, comics have themselves ex-erted enormous influence on arts and letters, contributing stylistic, icon-ographic, and linguistic innovations. Among such legacies are McCay's proto-Surrealist investigation of the world of dreams; Feininger's many-faceted international boyhood narratives, which predate Cubist innova-tions; Milt Gross's imaginative coining of phrases; Herriman's lyrical adaptation of animal fable and ethnic idiom; Gray's totemic moralism; Gould's cruel expressionism; Caniff's chiaroscuro; and Hogarth's anthro-pomorphizing symbolism.

Progressing from representation through abstraction to revived verisimilitude, these styles have been utilized to express fantasies of un-limited human potential symbolized by flight, whether on a magic bed,

Burne Hogarth, *Tarzan: The Intruders*, August 20, 1944

Trained in the history of art at Northwestern University and at Columbia University, Burne Hogarth developed a technique of pictorial narration uniquely suited to the demands of the adventure strip. Combining sensitive physiognomic expression, dramatic juxtaposition of large areas of black and white in a simplified chiaroscuro, progressive emphasis on the portrayal of action, and classical composition, Hogarth perfected the adventure epic. Among the numerous cinematic techniques Hogarth adapted to comic-strip purpose was the representation of each frame from a different point of view. Hogarth also developed a complex iconography, in which nature and its creatures mirror Tarzan's inner conflicts.

Lee Falk and Phil Davis, *Mandrake the Magician*, October 20, 1940

The adventure strip featured exotic locales, a panoply of peoples, and heroes and heroines of titanic stature. In this episode of *Mandrake the Magician*, which began publication as a daily in 1934 and as a Sunday page in 1935, we meet the Queen of the Amazons, a female chauvinist, who decides the fate of her hostages based on their physical appearance.

William Ritt and Clarence Gray, *Brick Bradford in the Middle of the Earth*, July 10, 1937

As America prepared for war, comic-strip artists created heroic conflicts set in distant times and foreign lands, metaphoric calls to arms. Originated as a daily in 1933 and as a Sunday page in 1934, author William Ritt and artist Clarence Gray's eclectic adventure strip combined elements of the jungle epic with those of the science-fiction saga.

in a spaceship, or through one's own power, as in *Little Nemo, Flash Gordon,* and *Superman;* the ethnic American's affectionate enthusiasm for his new homeland, raucously manifested in Milt Gross's vaudevillian *Banana Oil!* and *Nize Baby,* in Harry Hershfield's *Abie the Agent,* and in Frederick Opper's vulgar *Happy Hooligan;* fastidious fascination with fashion, lovingly recorded in McManus's tongue-in-cheek *Bringing Up Father,* John Held, Jr.'s Jazz Age *Margy,* and Russell Patterson's sophisticated *Mamie* and *Film Flam;* the changing work force described in Russ Westover's *Tillie the Toiler,* Cliff Sterrett's *Polly and Her Pals,* and Martin Branner's *Winnie Winkle, the Breadwinner;* international catastrophies, such as the Great Depression and the gangster era, powerfully embodied in Gray's *Orphan Annie* and Gould's *Dick Tracy;* nuclear-age America, its fears and foibles, documented in the musings of *Feiffer, Doonesbury,* and *Sylvia;* the American underground, rebelliously given voice by R. Crumb's *Fritz the Cat* and Gilbert Shelton's *Fabulous Furry Freak Brothers;* inner journeys through the past and present, undertaken in Harvey Pekar's *American Splendor,* Lynda Barry's *Ernie Pook's Comeek,* and Aline Kominsky-Crumb's *Power Pack Comics.*

In the following pages, you are invited to meet those comic-strip and comic-book artists who have examined the American national conscience and expressed their findings in fine line and powerful prose. Through exquisite original pen-and-ink drawings from major public and private collections, one can trace the artists' first expressions of ideas that would change America. While considerations of size require a brief discussion of a limited number of comics creators, you are invited to meet many more masters and mistresses of graphic art in our "Who's Who in the Comics" supplement.

Milt Gross, *Banana Oil!*, May 28, 1924

The English language was forever enriched by the contributions of Milt Gross, who in his strips at once celebrated the joys of Yiddish while coining expressions of utter originality, many of which have since become common parlance. Like many early strips drawn by America's "unmeltable ethnics," Gross's *Banana Oil!*, which began in 1921, debunked conventionality and "polite" society.

Winsor McCay, *Dream of the Rarebit Fiend*, April 20, 1913

McCay's misgivings about his career in the movies are illustrated by this *Dream*, in which film is depicted as a short-lived fad.

Clifford Sterrett, *Sterrett's Idea of Winsor McCay*, 1906

From the *Wheeling* (W.Va.) *Register*.

Interviewed by the *Buffalo Enquirer* on July 16, 1912, cartoonist Winsor McCay proclaimed, "There will be a time when people will gaze at [paintings] and ask why the objects remain rigid and stiff. They will demand action. And to meet this demand the artists of that time will look to the motion picture people for help and the artist, working hand in hand with science, will evolve a new school of art that will revolutionize the entire field." McCay himself was to become one of the founding fathers of American animation. Often utilizing his comic strips as test grounds for experiments in the representation of motion, McCay created comic-strip epics of transcendent importance. In this portrait of the artist, Clifford Sterrett introduces numerous attributes associated with the personality of his sitter — the chafing dish, a reference to McCay's *Dream of the Rarebit Fiend*, a briefcase emblazoned "Dull Care," an emblem of McCay's strip *Pilgrim's Progress*, a cloud of smoke emanating from McCay's cigar, in which appears a Satanic muse, and, in a more literal vein, the artist's well-known diamond stickpin, hat, and drawing board.

2

Winsor McCay, American Master

The career and achievements of Winsor Z. McCay were distinctively American. Universally applauded for his proto-Surrealist dream comic-strip epic *Little Nemo in Slumberland,* McCay is also recognized by historians as one of the fathers of the American animated cartoon. But on the way to these achievements, he was also a sign painter, a scenic artist for a freak show in Cincinnati, a poster painter, and a traveling performer on the vaudeville stage. In addition to animation and comic strips, he drew editorial cartoons and designed sets for Victor Herbert's spectacular musical version of *Little Nemo.* His career, in other words, is almost a paradigm of the career of the American artist or writer, with early immersion in the real world taking precedence over formal academic preparation.

McCay was born in Spring Lake, Michigan, on September 26, 1871, the son of lumberman and real estate entrepreneur Robert McCay and his wife, Janet Murray McCay.[1] Following a brief period of instruction under artist John Goodison at Ypsilanti Normal School, McCay moved to Chicago, where he was employed by a poster firm that specialized in large, gaudily colored woodcuts depicting the attractions of melodramas and minor traveling circuses.[2] Among the marvels represented were "bearded women, sword swallowers, fire-eaters, and similar attractions."[3] This contact with the fantastic provided the artist with a fertile subject, to which he could apply the command of perspective and meticulous observation taught him by Goodison.

Sometime about 1889 McCay arrived in Cincinnati, possibly as a sign painter for a traveling carnival, and stayed on as a "scenic artist" and poster painter for Kohl and Middleton's Vine Street Dime Museum, a kind of permanent freak show.[4] In contrast to McCay's studio, "a dingy little room on the top floor of the museum," the facade of Kohl and Middleton's, decorated by McCay, was ablaze with color and alive with bizarre forms inspired by the "profitably deformed exhibits" within, "an edition deluxe of fat women, snakes, living skeletons, and ossified men."[5] An idea of the effect produced by the posters and decorations supplied by the artist can be gathered from the description of a contemporary viewer. "As a rule," asserted Montgomery Phister, drama critic of the *Cincinnati Commercial Tribune,* the garishly illustrated ornamental facade showed huge serpents crawling through the purple vistas of dark woodlands, the dogfaced boy with each of his hairs standing at end . . . Anna Mills, the girl with enormous feet . . . occupying a spacious place in the foreground . . . the "What Is It?" crunching a bone between its sawlike teeth, and the handless man darning socks with a needle and thread between his toes.[6]

Unfortunately for the museum, "interest was greater upon the outside than within the . . . emporium of wonders."[7] This decade of acquaintance with the grotesque left its mark on McCay's style, and his later work is replete with carnival motifs, including distortions based on trick mirrors, exotic animals, clowns, and dancers.

A second influence exerted on McCay's development during his fifteen years in Cincinnati was that of newspaper reporting, a direct outgrowth of his work for the dime museum. McCay's advertisements of its wonders created such a stir among Cincinnati's citizenry that the artist was asked to provide drawings of these attractions for the press, no "regularly employed newspaper artist [wishing] to devote their attention to these nightmares."[8] At the *Cincinnati Commercial Tribune* McCay was instructed in the technique of newspaper illustration by Joe Alexander, manager of the art room.[9] Among the illustrations provided by the artist for the *Tribune* in 1898 were black-and-white landscapes based on photographs, detailed architectural interiors, and a series of what might be termed proto–comic strips illustrating the satiric verses of Jack Appleton. McCay's work of this period is characterized by crowded frames, an abundance of black-and-white areas, complex cross-hatching, and variety of texture. Anticipations of his later stylistic simplicity can be seen in his calligraphic caricatures.

Perhaps the most important practice derived from McCay's experience as an artist-reporter was his system of "memory sketching," whereby he established certain formulas for representing bodies at rest and in motion.[10] In the germinal *Tales of the Jungle Imps by Felix Fiddle*, McCay used such sets not to depict actual objects but to enliven a fantastic world. Accompanying verses by George Randolph Chester, this sequence of forty-three illustrations ran in the *Cincinnati Enquirer*'s 1903 Sunday supplement from January 18 through November 18. The

epic demonstrated McCay's talent for imaginatively designing a newspaper page and introduced themes that were to recur in his New York work, including exploration of the exotic world of the jungle, the predator, and metamorphosis. Each of the *Tales* described the adaptations gentle and beautiful animals must make in order to survive. Thus we have "How the Mosquito Got His Bill," "How the Alligator Got His Big Mouth," and "How the Lion Got His Roar." In this series, McCay created two memorable types, which appeared in each adventure: Felix Fiddle, the author, a mute old man with long white beard, tall hat, and briefcase, who watches each transformation with great detachment, and the characters of the Jungle Imps, who later appeared in *Little Nemo in Slumberland*, McCay's greatest comic strip.

The success of *Tales of the Jungle Imps* was such that late in 1903 McCay was recruited by James Gordon Bennett, Jr., publisher of the *New York Herald* and *New York Evening Telegram*. For the *Herald* McCay created the comic strips *Hungry Henrietta* and *Little Sammy Sneeze*, which as early as 1905 provided a test ground for the artist's experiments in animation. For example, in an episode of *Hungry Henrietta* published on January 8, 1905, the baby protagonist is taken to the photographer. Frames two through five, identical in setting, are seen from the same fixed point of view, as if the artist's eye were the lens of a camera. Only the position of the figures changes from frame to frame, in keeping with the progress of the plot. The excitement provided by the strip is visual; as relatives and photographer perform absurd acrobatics to fix the baby's attention, Henrietta bursts out crying.

In contrast to the experiments in the representation of ordinary motion undertaken in *Hungry Henrietta* and *Little Sammy Sneeze*, McCay's first dream epic, *Dream of the Rarebit Fiend*, dealt with the psychic life of an adult dreamer. Each episode featured a different protagonist whose sleep would be disturbed by a nightmare cast, which included many of the exotic carnivores introduced in *Tales of the Jungle Imps*. These nightmares were not induced by drugs or alcohol but by eating Welsh rarebit. The intensity of the dream experience varied from mild embarrassment in going for a stroll without one's pants to horror at being pursued by one's own furnace. Visual distortions no doubt based

Winsor McCay, *Little Nemo in Slumberland*, October 15, 1905

Utilizing verisimilitude to create a fantastic universe, McCay in *Little Nemo* expressed unlimited human potential through flight, be it on a magic bed or on the back of the dream mount, Somnus. The first sustained comic-strip narrative, *Nemo*'s quest was to continue for six years, during which the artist became increasingly preoccupied with social problems and personal crises. Finally, McCay sought surcease from these demons in animation. His first film, *Little Nemo*, was released in 1911.

Winsor McCay, *A Tale of the Jungle Imps — How the Mosquito Got His Bill*, June 14, 1903

The mosquito, a recurring figure in McCay's oeuvre, first appeared in *A Tale of the Jungle Imps*. In this 1903 sequence the insect is originally large, female, and musical. Tormented by the Jungle Imps, the dusky embodiments of disorder, the mosquito consults the monkey, who outfits her with a horrible weapon. After quaffing the Imps' blood, the mosquito is utterly transformed. In the last frame, an apocalyptic mosquito squadron surges toward the reader. The misadventure is observed detachedly by the elderly commentator, Felix Fiddle. Sporting a long white beard, clad in a long overcoat and stovepipe hat, burdened with a briefcase, and armed with an umbrella, Felix Fiddle contrasts in every way with the Jungle Imps. He embodies reason, they chaos. He is elderly, they are young. He is clothed, they are naked. He is white, they are black. He is solitary, they are communal. The Imps, mosquito, and Felix were to appear in McCay's later work as Impy in *Little Nemo in Slumberland* (1905), Steve the Mosquito in the animated *Story of a Mosquito (How a Mosquito Operates)* (1912), and Mr. Bunion in *Pilgrim's Progress* (1905).

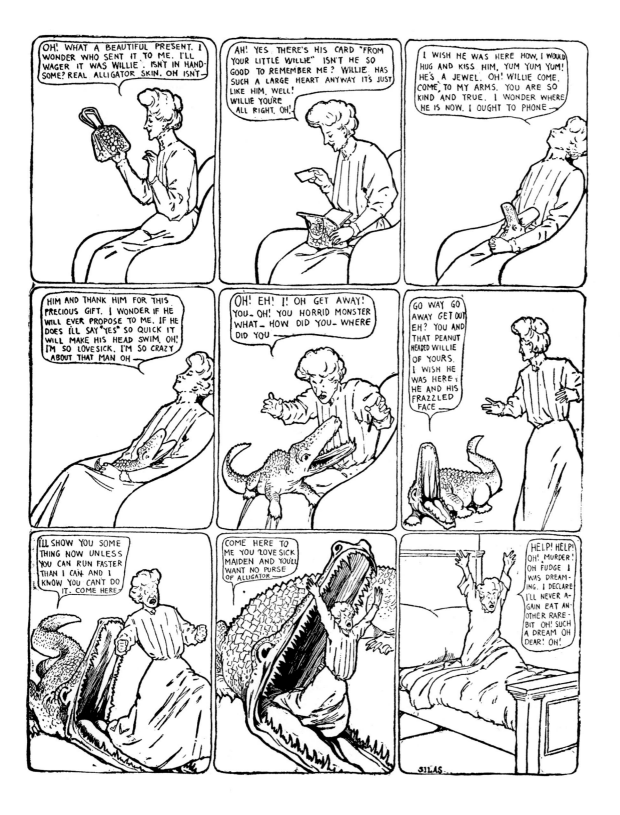

Winsor McCay, *Dream of the Rarebit Fiend*, 1905

James Gordon Bennett, Jr., publisher of the *New York Evening Telegram*, recruited McCay, who created for him the adult strip *Dream of the Rarebit Fiend*. In this episode, a frustrated spinster receives an alligator bag from a timid suitor. As she clasps it to her, the purse becomes larger and larger, finally devouring the maiden lady. For *Dream of the Rarebit Fiend* McCay adopted the pen name "Silas."

on carnival trick mirrors are utilized in one strip, providing an example of the dime museum's continuing influence on McCay. In the same vein, another strip reveals a circus elephant balancing itself on a tightrope suspended over the dreamer's bed, reminding the viewer of McCay's circus travels. In addition to imagery based on personal experiences, stock themes of nineteenth-century literature are embodied in the strip. Thus in one episode an unfortunate dreamer is buried alive, as in a story by Poe, and in another meets his double (or multiple), a common theme in both American and European literature. Also included among the dreams of the rarebit fiend is a 1905 episode that anticipates McCay's vaudeville act, which opened the following year. In it the dreamer, an elderly man married to a lovely young lady, takes "youth tablets." These are all too effective, and in frames one through seven he is taken from old age to infancy. McCay's vaudeville act consisted of a series of quick sketches entitled "The Seven Ages of Man," in which the artist depicted countenances "from the cradle to old age, never once altering the original outline of his subjects' faces."[11] In 1906 the well-known film adaptation of McCay's *Rarebit Fiend* was made by Edwin S. Porter.

A second comic strip McCay created for the *Evening Telegram* in 1905 was *Pilgrim's Progress*, which alternated with *Dream of the Rarebit Fiend*. A visual allegory, the strip's title was taken from that of John Bunyan's seventeenth-century masterpiece. The protagonist was a tall thin man dressed in a black suit and top hat, carrying a briefcase emblazoned "Dull Care." McCay explained his intention in creating the strip in a notation on a trial drawing that survives in the Gelman Collection of the Ohio State University Libraries. "In Mr. Bunion's progress," writes the artist,

> he tries all manner of schemes to get rid of his burden "Dull Care" but like the cat it comes back. I can get a lot of fun out of it and think it offers as good a field as the Rarebit. He will always be looking for "Glad Avenue" and will have an occasional visit to Easy Street but his burden will stick with him. I will have him try to burn it, bury it, throw it in the sea, blow it up, advertise it for sale or give away, get it run over by trains, hit by autos and hundreds of things he will try to do to get rid of it but can't — I hope you will see my scheme it's a good one.

In McCay's work of 1905 we can discern two possible directions. In the world of the rarebit fiend, the monotony of daily existence is replaced by an alternative universe governed by unpredictable rules. In *Pilgrim's Progress*, however, daily cares press upon the protagonist with exaggerated force. These two tendencies provide a constant tension in McCay's work. Elements of the day-to-day world continuously intrude in the world of fantasy, although for three years McCay was able to maintain this fantastic focus in *Little Nemo in Slumberland*.

The first episode of *Little Nemo in Slumberland* appeared in the *New York Herald* on October 15, 1905, immediately distinguishing itself from all of the artist's earlier work. Although *Little Nemo*, like *Rarebit Fiend*, is a dream strip, its protagonist is a child, not an adult. McCay's son, Robert Winsor, provided the model for Nemo, who is a youthful Everyman, as indicated by his Latinate name, which means "no one." In Slumberland, fantastic adventures, including travels in time and space, are undertaken in a world of grandiose architecture, perhaps inspired by Chicago's Columbian Exposition of 1893.

The definitive style in which these adventures are rendered was achieved during the apex of American interest in art nouveau. The enthusiasm of America for this sinuous line and flat patterning culminated in Alphonse Mucha's triumphant reception in New York in 1904, at which time he opened an American studio. McCay transformed the serpentine line and irrational color of art nouveau by an absolute command of perspective and an interest in motion. Through a successive imagery and the addition of verbal content in the balloons, he created a compelling visual narrative, an altogether personal version of the turn-of-the-century international style. Much of the imagery of *Little Nemo* is borrowed from the art nouveau vocabulary. Peacocks, lilies, swans, and water flora abound. Elements of the traditional fairy tale are also retained, exemplified by the old king with the beautiful young daughter (as in the tale of King Midas) and the contest in which the young man must test himself. Added to this vocabulary and content is personal imagery derived from McCay's association with carnivals and the dime museum: exotic animals, clowns, performers, and freaks. In several aspects, McCay's vision anticipates Surrealist explorations: appearances

Winsor McCay, *Gertie the Bashful Dinosaur*, released by Box Office Attractions on December 28, 1914

Winsor McCay, *Hungry Henrietta*, January 8, 1905

Continuing his investigations into the representation of motion, McCay in *Hungry Henrietta* depicted each frame from the same point of view in a comic-strip adaptation of time-lapse photography. Set in a photographer's studio, the strip explicitly refers to McCay's interest in technology, which was to culminate in his contributions to the development of the animated film.

are unstable, nature is hostile, objects come together in irrational conjunctions, mechanical devices are frequently threatening. In these fantasies, McCay creates an alternate world in which the unexpected is ordinary, and from which the mundane is excluded.

Gradually, however, an entirely unprecedented obsession with social problems intruded upon *Little Nemo*. In the March 22, 1908, sequence, Nemo is led by a pack of wolves (traditional symbols of hunger) to cliffs overlooking Shantytown, a ramshackle example of urban blight. As he enters the slum, Nemo is met by an angel, who confers upon him a wand. Nemo will use this wand to make the blind see and the lame walk. Having restored an amputee's leg, Nemo instructs the boy, "Throw away your crutches!" The crowd that has gathered gasps, "Look! He's cured cripp!" "Who is it?" On April 19, 1908, the Christ-like Nemo restores to life a dying child. After going to church, he declares, "Now I am ready to visit your sick sister. Where do you live? Where is she? We will go to her at once!" At the door of a tenement Nemo is met by the child's mother, who holds a ragged baby in her arms. Next to the doorway is an eviction notice. In the attic a dying girl sleeps on a pallet of crates. Nemo touches her pallet with his wand, and it becomes a golden sarcophagus, as she awakens in a field of Easter lilies (traditional symbols of rebirth). As he is awakened by his mother to search for eggs, Nemo expresses his displeasure at his inability to affect social change. "Yes, it's me who is dreaming. Just as I thought! Pshaw!"

Social problems again asserted themselves in the famous Mars sequence, which began on April 24, 1910, the last great adventure of *Little Nemo in Slumberland*. McCay's desire to convey a "message" is indicated by his increasing attention to dialogue. McCay is trying to say something that cannot be expressed by images alone but demands the printed word. As the airship nears the planet's surface, the Slumberland party notes that Mars is plastered with signs: Private Property, No Trespassing, Keep Off This Air. In frame three the praises of home ownership are sung by billboards that demand, "Why pay rent? Own a home in the sky!" (Perhaps in the spirit of the old union refrain: "You'll have pie in the sky when you die.") As Nemo's airship descends, the viewer is confronted by hundreds of identical homes, although there is no sign of human life or vegetation. Nemo now finds himself unable to breathe. As he collapses on deck, two fly-winged, duckfooted Martians approach and inform the party that, on Mars, even oxygen must be purchased from the capitalist tyrant, B. Gosh. This last adventure in Slumberland signaled the end of the strip as an imaginative stimulant for the artist. Thereafter, McCay's greatest achievements were to be in the field of cartoon animation.

Many of McCay's animations were inspired by his comic-strip creations. Released by Vitagraph on April 8, 1911, the cartoon *Little Nemo* features a cast drawn from its comic-strip predecessor: the antagonist, Flip, the mischievous Impy, Little Nemo himself, the Princess, and the Slumberland physician, Dr. Pill, appear in that order. Unlike the comic strip, however, the animation has no specific plot. Conventional dramatic development is replaced in the cartoon by an abstract animism. Every dot and line is possessed of a peculiar vitality and is metamorphosed into plant, animal, and abstract form. The distinction between the animate and inanimate is blurred, as a line can with equal ease become a human body or an ornamental design. As in the comic strip the marvelous, personified by Nemo and the Princess in their dragon chariot, is mixed with the mundane, represented by Flip and the automobile with which he is always associated. In adapting his comic-strip characters as animations, McCay was assisted by his youthful friend and neighbor John A. Fitzsimmons.

After completing *Little Nemo* in January of 1911, McCay began work on his second animation, *The Story of a Mosquito* (*How a Mosquito Operates*), completed in January of 1912. As was the case with *Little Nemo*, the second animation was based on a comic-strip source. Here the inspiration was an early *Rarebit Dream* episode in which a smug mosquito bursts, having gorged itself on an alcoholic's blood. The animation featured as its protagonist Steve, a debonair mosquito-about-town, dapperly dressed in the fashion of Felix Fiddle. After tipping his top hat to the audience, Steve sharpens his bill on a grindstone carried in his briefcase. Having gluttonously quaffed a dreamer's blood, Steve explodes. In all of McCay's cartoons there is a continuing interaction between comic strip and animation.

Winsor McCay, *Dream of the Rarebit Fiend*, March 16, 1913

The artist's awareness of the fragile and illusory nature of both creativity and love is the theme of this late *Dream*, a whimsical conclusion to McCay's comic-strip career.

While showing *The Story of a Mosquito* during a vaudeville tour in March of 1912, McCay announced plans for a third animation, intended as part of a prehistoric epic planned in conjunction with the American Historical Society. The end result, *Gertie*, copyrighted by the artist on September 15, 1914, sold to William Fox, and released through Box Office Attractions on December 28, 1914, is closely related to a *Rarebit Dream* episode published in the *Herald* on May 25, 1913, wherein a magnificent pink dinosaur emerges from a cave to devour rocks and consume tree trunks. Upon release *Gertie* was advertised in the December 26, 1914, *Moving Picture World* as "the greatest comedy film ever made! Gertie is a tango dancer. — She is as big as the Flatiron building and eats 'em alive — from whales to elephants!"

Gertie was the first of McCay's animated cartoons to include a complicated landscape as background. In composing these backgrounds, McCay was again assisted by John Fitzsimmons. Fitted with a cave for a shelter, an ocean for fountain, and a tree for nourishment, *Gertie* was shown as part of McCay's vaudeville act. For the performance the artist would dress as a circus-lion tamer, synchronizing his movements with those of the drawn dinosaur. On July 12, 1916, the *Detroit Tribune* reported McCay's plans to create his first and only animation based on an historic event, *The Sinking of the Lusitania*. The first of the artist's works on celluloid, the cartoon was copyrighted on July 19, 1918, and released by Universal-Jewel Productions the next day. McCay's other animations include *The Centaurs*, *Flip's Circus*, and *Gertie on Tour* (ca. 1913 to 1924), as well as a series of animated *Dreams of the Rarebit Fiend* advertised by *Moving Picture World* on October 29, 1921, as "Twelve 1000 Feet of Honest Laughs Per Month." Three in number, these "dreams" included *The Pet*, in which "an invented house pet . . . grew, after it had been poisoned with a dose of 'rough on rats,' into an all-devouring monster. . . . Taller than a ten-story building, the monster destroys everything in its path, until, as the film comes to an end, hundreds of army bombing planes place a quietus upon the mischievous doings of 'The Pet.'"[12] The two other animated "dreams" were *Bug Vaudeville* and the problematic *Flying House*, the result of the paired efforts of Winsor McCay and his son, Robert.

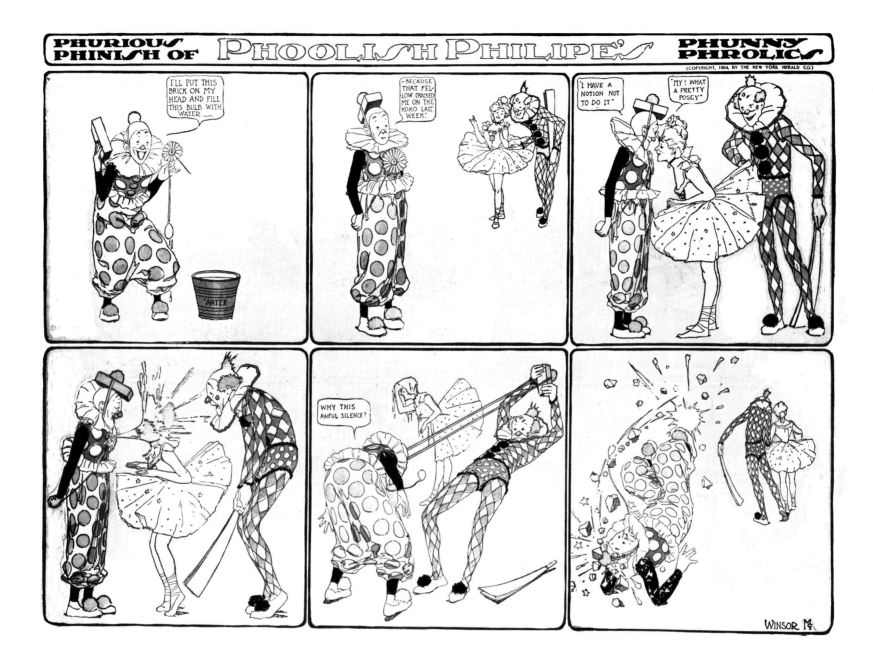

Winsor McCay, *Phoolish Philipe*, May 29, 1904

Many of McCay's experiments in the depiction of motion were conducted in the pages of his comic strips. Here, in a sequence inspired by his travels with the circus and his tenure at the dime museum, figures emerge from a blank background, a device McCay was to employ in his animated *Little Nemo* (1911).

In evaluating McCay's masterful animations, it is important to note that most of the animals featured are fantastic, as are the dragon of *Little Nemo* and the protagonists of *The Centaurs*; microscopic, as is the main character in *The Story of a Mosquito*; extinct, as are Gertie and her friends. These protagonists were intentionally chosen to avoid the charge that the motion created within the animation was based on transcription of photographs. In the case of *Gertie*, asserted Claude Bragdon, "McCay chose a dinosaur to prove to his critics and detractors that he worked independently of models and photographs. He used to get down on his hands and knees and go through certain bodily maneuvers, watching and timing every movement so that Gertie should have all the naturalness of life."[13] That McCay was an accomplished photographer is certain, the artist having on one occasion made a trip to Menlo Park, New Jersey, to discuss certain technical problems with Thomas Edison.[14] By inventing animals that never existed, or by approximating the motions of insects too small to study, McCay demonstrated his understanding of the principle behind all motion while at once displaying his vast imaginative ability.

Like many American artists born in the nineteenth century, McCay found himself obliged to enter the world of commercial illustration in order to survive, but his talent and personality were strong enough to enable him to adjust to the demands of the marketplace without sacrificing the quality of his work. His love of technology led to his pioneering efforts in the development of the film, although he himself never exploited the commercial possibilities of the medium. His oeuvre reflects the tensions originating in his paradoxical personality. An intensely private person, McCay became a vaudevillian but performed in absolute silence. An accomplished inventor who contributed to the development of the American motion picture, McCay maintained an ambivalent attitude toward technology, in the comic strip *Dream of the Rarebit Fiend* treating the mechanical as a threat and in real life refusing to drive an automobile. An artist of vast imaginative ability with an affinity for the fantastic, McCay suffered from a troubled social conscience, which manifested itself in the intrusion of reality into the world of the dream.

Winsor McCay, *Pilgrim's Progress*, 1906

In *Pilgrim's Progress* McCay depicted the monotonous world of the wage slave, symbolized by the briefcase, "Dull Care." The funereal protagonist, Mr. Bunion, in every episode attempts without success to rid himself of this prosaic burden. Created at the same time that McCay was developing his fantastic tour de force, *Little Nemo in Slumberland*, *Pilgrim's Progress* provides insight into the world from which the artist sought escape in Slumberland.

3

George Herriman and His Black Kat, Krazy

George Herriman, *Self-portrait*, 1940

Original pen and ink drawing.
From the collection of Mark J. Cohen, Realtor.

In the inscription to this sketch, Herriman proclaims to Louise Swinnerton, "Here's your Turk and this letter —now be a good girl and pull off [up?] your pajamas."

America's early comic-strip masters, Winsor McCay and George Herriman, were strikingly similar in personal style and social sympathy. Both were nomadic men of little formal education whose academic theater was the open road. Drawn to the itinerant life of commercial illustration, they journeyed on parallel highways from dime museum to newspaper to theater to film. They were recluses whose regional roots were shrouded in secrecy. Yet both were attracted to the bombastic hustle of the big city in the heyday of newspaper expansion. There they became key figures in the development of the American comic strip. Their allegiance to the audience of this most "mass" of media is readily apparent in their work. The proletarian affinities of both cartoonists are patent. Both are champions of the underdog. Topical allusions abound in their strips, from the didactic sequences of McCay's *Little Nemo in Slumberland* to the social satires enacted on the vast mesas of Herriman's enchanted Coconino County, the setting of *Krazy Kat*.

Specific social issues, such as women's suffrage, are often treated by both cartoonists. In his *Man from Montclair* McCay satirizes social climbing and snobbism, revealing their hypocritical core. In *Krazy Kat's* royalty sequence, and in a strip documenting the development of the cat-mouse romance, Herriman unmasks royal "pretenders."[1]

The work of both anticipated mainstream international art movements and styles, including Dada and Surrealism. McCay anticipated the iconography of the Surrealist movement with its belief in psychic autonomy. In *Little Nemo in Slumberland*, for example, he celebrated the subconscious made manifest in the dreamworld, explored the essential fluidity and instability of appearance, and brought objects together in irrational conjunction. Well before its popularization by Dali, Herriman also utilized as his mise-en-scène the vacant plain, the animated and constantly changing sky, and the protean form. Herriman's use of language is as inspired as is his mastery of line. The verbal content of his strips — combining African-American linguistic conventions such as alliterative hyperbole with Creole patois, Hispanic slang, and evocative Native American place names — was to inspire a generation of poets, including e. e. cummings.[2]

George Herriman's origin in New Orleans, however, could not have been a more radically different beginning from McCay's birth in Spring Lake, Michigan.

Into the cosmopolitan, polyglot society of New Orleans George Herriman was born on August 22, 1880. Patrick McDonnell, Karen O'Connell, and Georgia Riley de Havenon, in *Krazy Kat: The Comic Art of George Herriman* confirm what has long been suspected — Herriman's African-American ancestry.[3] On his birth certificate, Herriman's race is identified as "colored," a designation corroborated by the 1880 U.S. census, which describes his parents as "mulatto."[4] Allusions to an African-American heritage are ambiguous and oblique in Herriman's art. *Musical Mose*, one of his first strips, recounts the misadventures of a good-natured African American who attempts unsuccessfully to "pass" for white through various ethnic impersonations that nevertheless unmask him. "Isn't yo rather dark complected for a Scotchman?" asks his wife, and suggests, "Why dusn't yo impussanate a cannibal?" "Ah wish mah color would fade," Mose whimsically remarks.[5] Herriman's awareness of his own background is uncertain. Among his contemporaries he was known as "The Greek." As fellow cartoonist "Tad" Dorgan reminisced, recalling his first impression of Herriman, "He looked like a cross between Omar the tent maker and Nervy Nat when he eased into the art room of the *New York Journal* twenty years ago. We didn't know what he was, so I called him the Greek, and he still goes by that name."[6]

The most important legacy of Herriman's mutually enriching cultural patrimonies is Krazy Kat — a black cat of ambiguous sexual identity born into a strip of its own right on October 28, 1913, on the pages of newspaper magnate William Randolph Hearst's *New York Evening Journal*. Of surpassing sweetness of temperament, Krazy transforms the "slings and arrows of outrageous fortune" through his/her transcendent optimism, while describing the world through which he/she passes in a dialect of unparalleled richness. The masterpiece of Herriman's artistic maturity, the strip was to run for twenty-one years, garnering such admirers as critic Gilbert Seldes and artist Pablo Picasso, and surviving its transformation into an animated cartoon, a ballet, and — most recently — a novel.

The central themes of *Krazy Kat*, which ended with the artist's death in 1944, were identity, the nature of personal relationships, and the structure of society. These themes were explored through the venerable convention of the animal fable, set on the severe stage of a desert landscape and enlivened by Herriman's artistic and poetic genius. The dramatis personae of this ritual drama, in the words of George Herriman, "that you may know them," are Gooseberry Sprig, the Duck Duke; Joe Bark, Moon Hater and Bone Mangler, and B. Boswell Barque; Bum Bill Bee; Kolin Kelly, Dealer in Bricks; Joe Stork, Purveyor of Progeny to Prince and Proletarian, and Komplicator and Kompromisor; Walter Cephus Austridge, the Kalaharan Dickey-Bird; Officer B. Pupp, symbol of Law and Order; Don Kiyoti, Aesthete, Castillian Nobleman of a Most Soapy Nature, and Gentleman of Invisible Means and Subconscious Mind, and his Man or Amanuensis, Sancho Pansy; Mock Duck, Oriental and Launderer de Luxe; the Señora Anita Gata Blanca, Poor Widda; Barney Borracho, Proprietor of the Paloma Blanca Pulqueria; J. Turtill and Terry Turtle, Diamond Broker; Kristopher Katapillar, a Worm; Judge Jacques Rabbit; Mr. Damon Duvv of the Well Known Peace Family; and, most important, the protagonist, Krazy Kat, and his nemesis and amor, Ignatz Mouse.[7]

The obsession of Kat with Mouse is atavistic and archetypal, transcending barriers of class, sex, and species. In the May 4, 1919, episode, some years after the strip began, Herriman describes the prehistoric origins of the relationship, setting the episode in dynastic Egypt (1919 B.C.) and revealing that both Kat and Mouse had prior identities. "Reverse, Oh! Reel of Time!!" proclaims the first frame. " 'Kleopatra Kat,' Siren of the Nile . . . full of wile and wisdom tells her child 'Krazy' a thing, or two" — namely, "let no menial transgress." Despite this prohibition, Krazy succumbs to " 'Eros' — The Conqueror," in the person of Marcantonni Maus, who, having consulted "The Sage of Karnak," beams Krazy with a "message of love" indented "in everlasting brick" as Krazy reposes on her pylon. Not only is Krazy's love object unconventional — so is the role Krazy has chosen, according to which the rodent has become the hunter, the cat his prey.

Compounding this complication is the additional impediment of Ignatz's marriage, for Ignatz *is* a married mouse with numerous progeny.

George Herriman, *Krazy Kat*, November 6, 1932

A consummate artist, Herriman alternated lights and darks to emphasize certain areas of the page, creating contrapuntal rhythms to the left-to-right sequence of the individual frames. Herriman saw each of his strips as a unit, not merely a succession of boxes. Here, individual frames appear to float within the space of a large, single page.

Furthermore, Ignatz is a henpecked mouse, dwarfed by his wife, Magnolia. Out of compassion for Krazy, Magnolia determines to thwart Ignatz's assaults, oblivious to their erotic undertones. "Woman," warns the mouse, "don't you interfere with my happiness."[8]

Adding to the complexity of the cat-mouse relationship is the presence of a rival for Krazy's affection, Offissa Pupp. Ignatz and Pupp are a study in contrasts. The amoral Ignatz is egocentric, small, wiry, energetic, ectomorphic; the principled Pupp chivalric, large, heavy, phlegmatic, endomorphic. Ignatz ("possessor of obscure wealth") is unemployed and anarchistic; Pupp is that staunch defender of the status quo, a policeman.[9] Krazy is obsessed with Ignatz, oblivious to Pupp. Although given zest by Pupp, the primary relationship is that of Ignatz and Krazy, an affair of opposites. Krazy is resolutely optimistic, Ignatz steadfastly cynical; Krazy empathetic, Ignatz self-absorbed; Krazy generous, Ignatz exploitative; Krazy black, Ignatz white.

This raises the central question of the strip: who and what is Krazy Kat? Of Krazy's gender, Herriman stated that the cat was "androgynous, but willing to be either,"[10] surely the first such comic-strip hero/heroine. Other clues to the conundrum of Krazy's identity can be found in his/her unique dialect. Krazy is the only major character who does not speak standard English. Ignatz and Pupp express themselves in "the King's English." Krazy alone spouts a unique patois. The ambiguity of Krazy's gender corresponds to the complexity of his/her tongue. In all aspects of his/her being, Krazy embodies polarities and oppositions.

Co-worker cartoonist Tad Dorgan was intrigued by both Herriman's appearance and accent: "His first name is Garge, because that's the way he pronounces it himself . . . Garge has a peculiar way of drawling. He is never in a rush as he drawls his words. He calls garden 'gorden,' he calls harness 'horness,' he calls cigars 'cigors,' and so on."[11]

Like Herriman himself, Krazy is an inventive linguist. Reflecting on the function of speech, Krazy muses, "Lenguage is that we may misunda-stend each udda."[12] Krazy's initial use of language, given contrapuntal accompaniment by Herriman's explications, is whimsical, an expression of love for Ignatz. Contemplating the mouse's portrait, Krazy affectionately comments: "It's a pitcha of 'Ignatz,' a old-fashioned pitcha

George Herriman, *Krazy Kat*, December 15, 1935

The eternal triangle with a new twist informed *Krazy Kat*. As described by poet e. e. cummings, who was himself influenced by Herriman's linguistic invention, "Dog hates mouse and worships 'cat,' mouse despises 'cat' and hates dog, 'cat' hates no one and loves mouse."

George Herriman, *Krazy Kat*, March 13, 1931

The central theme of *Krazy Kat*, a strip beloved of William Randolph Hearst, is identity. Is Krazy male or female, black or white?

of him as a yoot."[13] Through language, Krazy transforms Ignatz's vices into virtues. Of the mouse's cowardice and braggadocio Krazy observes, "L'il Ainjil, how brave his mind is."[14] When Ignatz attempts to drown him, Krazy gushes, "L'il Lolly-pops, How he loves me."[15]

Finally, on June 24, 1936, his tongue loosened at long last by a mysterious concoction known as Tiger Tea, Krazy unburdens himself powerfully and combatively in a long African-American rap known as "the dozens."

> I'm a ten-toed tiger —
> I'm a polo bear in a skwoil kage
> Tunda in a tea-potz —
> Wah — wooooooo —
>
> Boom —
> Krazy Ket
> The Kannon Krecka —
> Wah — Wah
>
> Boom Boom
> I'm a poiminint
> Tidal wave in a
> Notion of dynamite
> Pow — WOW . . .[16]

Turning tables, reversing roles, Tiger Tea transforms the reticent Krazy into a formidably aggressive character, reversing his long-established role. The culmination of Herriman's progress as a poetic pilgrim, this extraordinary sequence was created at a time when his painterly talents were in decline, constrained by arthritis and the decreasing amount of space allotted strips in the Sunday paper. Herriman's mature style, achieved from 1913 to 1925, is characterized by vast vistas through which miniscule characters pass, and by low horizon lines, spatial plenitude, infinite recession, calligraphic pen strokes, and literary whimsicality. His later style, characteristic of the period from 1925 until his death in 1944, is marked by full frames of standard size, high horizon lines, limited spatial recession, formulaic and repetitious landscapes dominated by large figures seen close up. Compensating for the strip's diminished artistic interest, however, is its vigorously virile poetic power, incorporating African-American folk idiom.

Informing Herriman's artistic, philosophical, and poetic development were the circumstances of his birth. New Orleans in 1880 had become an inhospitable environment for individuals of mixed ancestry. A scant seventeen years after the Emancipation Proclamation, an even shorter fifteen years removed from Lee's surrender at Appomatox, two years after the end of Reconstruction, the South was a dangerous

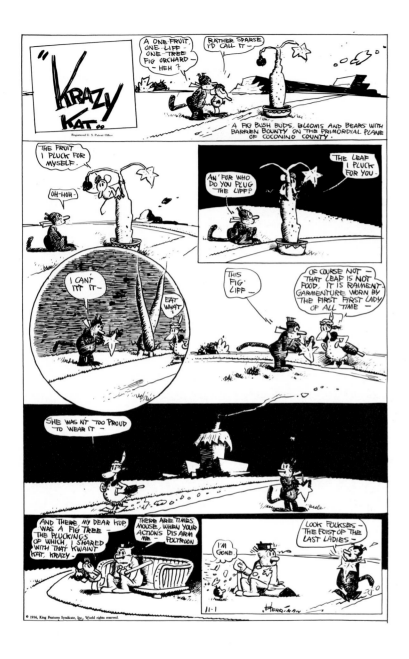

George Herriman, *Krazy Kat*, November 1, 1936

Described by Herriman as "androgynous, but willing to be either," Krazy Kat is here
represented as "the foist of the last ladies."

place for both former slaves and freemen of mixed blood. Of the latter,
African-American historian E. Franklin Frazier concluded that there
was strong identification with the dominant (majority) cultural tradition. Indeed, many freemén of mixed race avoided any contact with
slaves or former slaves and steadfastly pursued educational opportunity
abroad, most often in France and England.[17] The ambivalence of Herriman's parents and the ambiguities of assimilation perhaps account for
the rather late emergence of overtly African-American elements in the
artist's work.

Another factor that may have distanced the young artist from this
tradition was his parents' decision, following enactment of various Jim
Crow laws, to leave New Orleans for Los Angeles — there, perhaps, to
"pass" for white. This decision was probably reinforced in 1896 by the
U.S. Supreme Court, which in *Plessy v. Ferguson* gave legal sanction
to the concept of "separate but equal," and effectively forced families of
mixed heritage into radical choices. The course of economic expediency
was often chosen. Although often deplored during the proud cultural re-
surgence of the 1960s, a decision to "pass" in the 1880s was often made
on the basis of sheer economic pragmatism. This was sometimes the
only way to ensure "equal opportunity," all things being separate.

With the single exception of E. Simms Campbell's *Cuties* panel,
cartoons by African-American artists did not enjoy syndication in mainstream newspapers until 1965, although a separate comic-strip tradition
developed in the black press.[18] It is a matter of conjecture whether Herriman would have been hired as a cartoonist by a mainstream American
newspaper at the turn of the century had his African-American heritage
been known. Herriman's awareness of his roots is indicated by the in-
ternal evidence of his strips and by various statements attributed to the
artist. According to one report, "the always private Herriman, who
never publicly divulged any information about his personal life or
background, once told a close friend he was Creole, and because his hair
was 'kinky' thought he might have had some 'Negro blood.'"[19] Herriman
chose never to be seen or photographed or drawn without his Stetson
hat.[20] Tad Dorgan reported, "He always wears a hat. Like Chaplin and
his cane, Garge is never without his skimmer. [Harry] Hershfield says

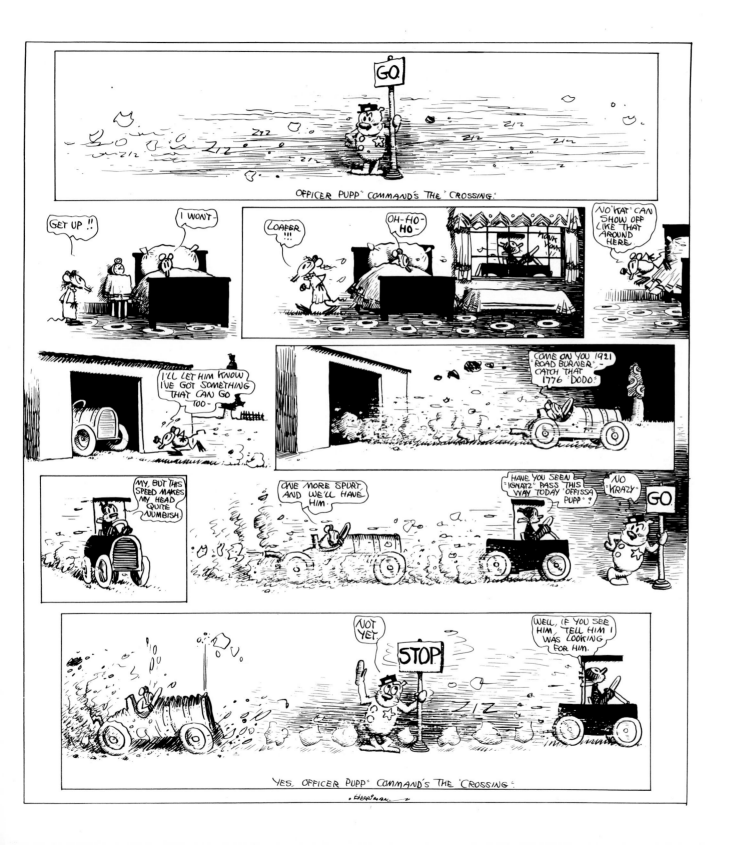

George Herriman, *Krazy Kat*, 1921

Krazy Kat's obsession with Ignatz mouse is beset with difficulties. Not only is Ignatz hostile to Krazy, he is of another species, quite possibly of the same sex, and already married. While Krazy inspires violence in Ignatz the anarchist, he arouses protectiveness in Officer Pupp, the embodiment of law and order.

Attributed to Pat Sullivan, *Felix the Cat*, December 18, 1932

Born as an animated film in 1917, *Felix the Cat* became a King Features comic strip in 1923. As active as Krazy was passive, Felix was the first of the feline cynics.

that he sleeps in it."[21] Whatever his awareness of his roots, Herriman chose to express in his strip his sympathies for the disenfranchised.

In 1920, for example, Herriman good-naturedly agitated within the strip on behalf of the Nineteenth Amendment to the U.S. Constitution. In the April 25 episode of *Krazy Kat* (now — fittingly — in the collection of Garry Trudeau) Ignatz espies from behind a wall a banner proclaiming "Women Suffrage." The mouse lustily announces, "Now that the dear girls are in 'politics' I'll have to perk up, and show some interest — yezza." To his consternation, Ignatz discovers that it is Krazy wielding the banner. Chagrined, Ignatz retorts, "I take it all back, I'm for no 'party' that has that 'Krazy Kat' in it," and lets fly a brick. The brick hits Offissa Pupp's suffrage sign. As Krazy watches Ignatz perform a compulsory suffrage cheer, he sighs, "L'il Dahlink he's in fava of woman's suffering, bless his soft blue eye."[22]

Similarly, in the May 24 episode, Krazy bemoans the fate of the Native American: "Oh the poor Injin, the poor, poor Injin." Herriman's lifelong interest in the Native American and his domain demonstrated itself in the setting of *Krazy Kat* — Arizona's Monument Valley; in the Navajo names with which the strip abounds; in references to magical hallucinogens, of which Tiger Tea is the most potent, and — most importantly — in Krazy's identification with the dispossessed.

The strip abounds with playful social statements. The March 21, 1920, episode introduces Damon Duvv, described by Krazy as "L'il pacifisk, l'il gentle bird, what a sweet etmispeer of love and iffection he creates among everthings." Soon the gentle emissary of peace is locked in pugilistic combat with Gooseberry Sprig, the Duck Duke, whom he easily bests, admonishing, "Peace unto you, brother — *and* let this be a lesson to you, y'bald face gazooni." Herriman himself, like Damon Duvv, was no mean boxer. As Tad Dorgan reported,

> Garge has three hobbies. They are Arizona Indians, chili con carne, and boxing gloves. He once knocked a guy cold on the elevated station at Forty-second Street, New York City, and has been living on the "rep" ever since. No one has ever found out what this knocked out gent did to Garge, but it must have been something awful, because he has never once lost his temper with us and he has been through some tough afternoons and evenings.[23]

Damon Duvv of the Well Known Peace Family, like his creator, is wild when riled.

Herriman, like so many American artists, was a man of the people. His origins and his art reflect the richly various cultures merged in the American "melting pot." The circumstances of his birth, the westward expansion of the epoch, the influence of technology, and the phenomenal growth of the newspaper — all contributed to set the stage on which one of the most universal of comic-strip dramas was to be enacted.

e. e. cummings has described the protagonist of *Krazy Kat* as "powerlessness personified."[24] Armed only with unbounded love and gentleness, this feline Everyman/Everywoman embodies the eternal optimism of a young nation in which all defeats are temporary and all wrongs rightable. The strip's stock resolution establishes it as a comedy. Each ritual ending — in which Ignatz clobbers Krazy with a brick — is happy. As the brick bashes the hero, Krazy proclaims himself/herself to be a "heppy heppy kitty." *Krazy Kat* is an allegory of assimilation and the search for acceptance and love. Undeterred by Ignatz's selfishness and brutality, Krazy chooses to interpret seeming rejection and cruelty as love. In so doing, he/she transcends and triumphs.

Gus Arriola, *Gordo*, August 13, 1945

Not until the civil rights movement of the sixties were minority artists to enjoy widespread syndication. An exception was *Gordo*, created in 1941 by Gustavo Montano Arriola, which featured a paunchy middle-aged Mexican bachelor, his orphaned nephew, Pepito, and plenteous dialect. In this postwar episode, Gordo, having tired of "keeling . . . Jop jorks," expresses his longing for peace and home.

Children's Voyages, Domestic Struggles:
The Kid and Family Strips

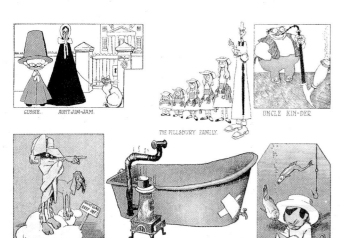

Lyonel Feininger, *The Kin-der-Kids — The Kin-der-Kids
Portrait Gallery*, April 29, 1906

In 1906, while midwesterner Winsor McCay and southerner George Herriman were among those establishing New York City as America's artistic and literary capital, the early comic strip's third master, New York–born Lyonel Feininger resided in Berlin. The son of German concert musicians, Feininger had left New York in 1887 to pursue his education abroad, first as a music student in Hamburg and later as an art student at the Royal Prussian Academy in Berlin and at the Colarossi Academy in Paris. Like McCay and Herriman in America, Feininger supported himself as a newspaper cartoonist, his work appearing in *Ulk* and *Lustige Blätter*. In 1906, the artist was persuaded by James Keeley of the *Chicago Sunday Tribune* to create two comic strips for that paper. These were *The Kin-der-Kids*, which was to run from April 29, 1906, to November 18, 1906, and *Wee Willie Winkie's World*, which appeared from August 19, 1906, to January 20, 1907. The transatlantic passage of the strips, which were mailed each week from Berlin to Chicago, is reflected in both their form and content. The strips also echo the artist's status as a world citizen, sojourner, and pilgrim — in communications historian Rosemary Gallick's words, "the American in Germany, the German in America."[1]

In *The Kin-der-Kids*, Feininger continued the development of the most popular genre of early-twentieth-century comics, the child or "kid" strip, while enlarging its scope and expanding its style. The kid strip, originated by cartoon pioneer Richard Felton Outcault, was continued in 1896 by German immigrant Rudolph Dirks, who drew upon its iconography for his *Katzenjammer Kids*. In this strip he depicted the adventures of adolescents Hans and Fritz, cartoon descendents of German artist Wilhelm Busch's *Max und Moritz*, popular in the United States since its translation into English in 1871. The Katzenjammer Kids are turn-of-the-century tricksters, represented in a vitally expressive style appropriate to the strip's hilarious subject matter.

Retaining the kid strip's traditional all-male prankster cast, Feininger transformed the genre by replacing slapstick comedy with symbolic content, and by depicting epic psychological struggles in a sophisticated international style. Like Winsor McCay's *Little Nemo in Slumberland*, Feininger's *Kin-der-Kids* is an odyssey. Whereas McCay's elusive quest was pursued in the dreamworld, or unconscious mind, Feininger's rollicking adventure took place on the high seas. Like McCay's Nemo, Feininger's kids were child protagonists. Whereas McCay's Everyman battles inner demons, exorcised only upon awakening into the conscious life, Feininger's children attempt to flee by water from the constraints and inhibitions of the adult world, forcefully personified in the children's gaunt, funereal Aunty Jim-Jam.

An international cast, the Kin-der-Kids were first introduced to *Chicago Sunday Tribune* readers on April 29, 1906, in an episode depicting "Feininger the Famous German Artist Exhibiting the Characters He Will Create." Suspended like marionettes from the artist's fingers, they included Strenuous Teddy, a pint-sized caricature of then-president Theodore Roosevelt; the gluttonous Piemouth; Japansky, an aquatic robot; and Sherlock Bones, the family dog — a reference to the high esteem accorded canines in Britain, the United States, and Germany. On May 6, 1906, the boys depart New York "Triumphant in the Family Bathtub."[2] Crying and waving good-bye, they take leave of the Statue of Liberty, setting sail on a universal sea, reminiscent of the adolescent artist's own departure for Hamburg in 1887.[3] The exuberant adolescent males are pursued by the stern Aunty Jim-Jam. As Rosemary Gallick has observed, Aunty's name "suggests a certain irony: 'jam' refers to an unpleasant predicament; 'jimmy' means to push or force open."[4] As the boys and their dog navigate the sea, so Jim-Jam and her cat command a skyborne "relief expedition," first by balloon, then by airplane.[5] In a reversal of conventional water symbolism, Aunty Jim-Jam (representing the female principle) is aerial. No course is charted by the youthful navigators. Instead, sail is spontaneously set, in contrast to the single-minded pursuit by Jim-Jam, who carries an ample supply of castor oil with which to douse her quarry upon capture. Concerning the castor oil's function, Feininger's son, Lux, speculated, "It will never be known now whether the medicine was finally to be swallowed or not. Neither can we find out whether the artist interpreted Aunty's obstinacy of intention to administer the hated purgation as essentially helpful (if benighted) or as purely vengeful. Perhaps the conflict contained in the adventure was insoluble."[6] The epic ended abruptly

50

on November 18, 1906, when Feininger ceased production of the strip because of a contract dispute with the publisher.[7]

His second strip, *Wee Willie Winkie's World*, began in August 1906, a scant four months after the inauguration of *The Kin-der-Kids*, and continued to appear in the *Chicago Sunday Tribune* until January 20, 1907. The strip, whose title was derived from an English nursery rhyme,[8] was within the fairy-tale tradition from whence sprang Winsor McCay's *Little Nemo in Slumberland*. Typical of Germanic fairy tales, *Wee Willie Winkie's World* is a universe in which the child is peculiarly isolated. Unlike the external conflict between impulse (the boys) and duty (Aunty Jim-Jam) waged in *The Kin-der-Kids*, Wee Willie Winkie's world is one of fearful insecurity, rendered, however, in the most exquisite of artistic styles. As if to emphasize the psychic drama of Wee Willie's inability to express or assert himself, Feininger eliminated balloons from the strip, replacing them with printed legends — told in the voice of the omniscient author-artist — that convey the protagonist's hopes and fears. A solitary traveler, Wee Willie has neither friend nor enemy. He is the sole actor in the strip's drama. Conflict is achieved by Willie's interaction with an anthropomorphized natural environment, its roots deep in Teutonic pantheism. This protean universe, constantly and threateningly transforming itself, accorded the artist an opportunity to experiment with subject and style free from the restraints of narrative conventions.

As in *The Kin-der-Kids*, the sky, in Feininger always associated with archetypal female forces, is a threatening element. Speculates Willie in an August 26, 1906, adventure, "Ha! It's a big, fat Aunty-Cloud wiz goggle-eyes, and she's growin' an' growin' and growin'! Ha! Now she is reaching out after Williewinks an' growin' an' growin' — bigger 'n' bigger —" Against this suffocating feminine threat, Willie attempts to assert his masculinity, using as his standard his grandfather's umbrella: "Ol' Aunty-Cloud, Williewinks is not afraid; got grandpa's big brown umbrelly — so — go away!"[9]

Feininger's status as a citizen of two continents found symbolic expression in his strips. The ocean bridging the artist's worlds provided the universal setting of *The Kin-der-Kids*. The tension between id and

George McManus, *Bringing Up Father*, December 6, 1953

McManus's precise rendering of his strips' settings anticipated the work of artists such as Charles Sheeler. In this episode, Jiggs scales walls, penetrates a boiler room, and emerges from a sewerlike tunnel. The flat pattern of pipes, girders, and other industrially produced structural elements looks forward to Precisionist innovations.

superego, youth and old age, male and female, and bourgeois duty and self-expression was symbolized by the insistent aerial intervention of Aunty Jim-Jam and the earthly appetites of the nautical Kin-der-Kids. The isolation of the individual, the eternal battle of the sexes, and the nature of creativity were given voice in *The Kin-der-Kids* and *Wee Willie Winkie's World*. These themes were conveyed in a simplified, innovative, geometric style indebted to Japanese woodcut tradition and anticipating Cubist innovation.

Although Feininger abandoned the comic strip in 1907, it nevertheless provided a potent source of inspiration for the artist until his death in 1956. One of several comic-strip creators also to achieve international fine-arts fame as a painter and graphic artist, Feininger exhibited with the Berlin Secession in 1910 and with the German painter Franz Marc and the Russian Vasili Kandinski in the 1913 *Blau Reiter* show. Although an American citizen and therefore an enemy alien, Feininger elected to remain in Berlin during World War I. In 1919 he joined the fledgling faculty of the Weimar Bauhaus. After a fifty-one-year exile, Feininger returned to the United States in 1937, his Cubist masterpieces having been denounced as "degenerate" by the Nazis.[10] In 1953, he re-created as wooden toys the characters and settings of *The Kin-der-Kids*.[11] Photos of this collection form part of the famous Feininger Archive in Harvard University's renowned Busch-Reisinger Museum of Germanic Culture.

Of his early achievements as a cartoonist, Feininger observed, "I am continually experiencing the gratification of knowing myself to be gradually becoming a popular artist, who is sure of finding appreciation and gratitude for his endeavors! And it is after all a sweet sensation to know that one is in touch with so great a portion of humanity."[12]

Although Feininger's elevation of the child strip to epic level was accomplished in a few short months, fellow cartoonists further refined this most popular of genres. Having conceived that lovable urban urchin, the Yellow Kid, for example, R. F. Outcault created a second child strip, the long-lived *Buster Brown*, in 1902. A fashion model for children's clothes, the foppish Buster was a thinly veiled reference to Little Lord Fauntleroy, designed to appeal to a higher class of reader than did

The Yellow Kid. Residing at "Brownhurst on Creek," Buster frequented fashionable resorts, including Palm Beach, usually in the company of his sweetheart, Mary Jane, and his faithful dog, Tige. The strip's plot rarely varied. In every episode Buster plays a boyish prank for which he is justly punished. The final frame makes explicit the moral to be derived from this cautionary comic-strip tale. For example, Buster, sent to public school as a punishment for tormenting his governess, philosophizes, "Resolved! That now I am happy — I am going to the Public School. — Private schools may be all right for dudes & idiots but I want to know my fellow man. Emerson said 'send your boy to school and the other boys will educate him.'" Faithfully following this formula, Outcault continued the strip until his retirement on August 15, 1920.[13]

Other artists to contribute significantly to the development of the kid strip include Gene Byrnes and Percy Crosby, whose respective creations, *Reg'lar Fellars* and *Skippy* were comic-strip counterparts of the protagonists of Mark Twain's novels of boyhood; Harold Gray, whose fiercely political *Little Orphan Annie* was the bane of the New Deal; and James Swinnerton, whose whimsical *Little Jimmy* established the gentle tradition of the child savant continued in 1950 by Charles Schulz in *Li'l Folks*, subsequently syndicated as *Peanuts*.

Reviving the child strip after a period of dormancy in the forties, Schulz introduced complex and contrasting psychological types, including Charlie Brown, the personification of gullibility and self-doubt, who anticipated the "sensitive male" of the sixties; Lucy, the smug embodiment of female superiority, predating the acerbic "feminists" of the seventies; and Snoopy, the super-realist and perennially detached observer. Schulz's whimsy soon won the hearts of all America. The effective use of the child as surrogate for the reader was again demonstrated.

In November 1985 another kid strip captured the imagination of America. This was *Calvin and Hobbes*, the brainchild of Bill Watterson. Writer Philip Herrera analyzed the strip's magic in the June 1987 *Connoisseur*:

Calvin is a six-year-old boy. Hobbes is his stuffed tiger, who is also, given the alchemy of Calvin's imagination, alive. . . . Calvin is an up-to-date Walter Mitty. . . . He deals with authority by turning teachers into monsters, parents into gorillas. . . . It is all done so gracefully that the reader gladly accepts the fantasy — until the final panel. Then, as Max Jacobs would say, the doubt between reality and imagination lifts. Unless it falls.[14]

The development of the family strip parallels that of the child strip. While Feininger and his creations were circumnavigating the globe, a young cartoonist named George McManus was discovering American marital mores in his ground-breaking comic strips. During this voyage of domestic discovery, McManus was to explore American class structure, the immigrant experience, the relationship of the sexes, the world of high fashion, and the limits of artistic expression.

Born on January 23, 1884, in St. Louis, Missouri, McManus was the son of Irish immigrants from Limerick and Westmeath. Critical to the artist's development was his father's profession — that of theater manager for the St. Louis Opera House.[15] Through this association, reported author Martin Sheridan, "young George, thrown into close contact with the carefully groomed notables of the stage in the Naughty Nineties, early set up an ideal for dress which . . . won for him the title of the 'best-dressed cartoonist.' "[16] A second influence exerted by the world of theater was that of the actual dramas he witnessed. In 1896, McManus was moved by *The Rising Generation*, a drama featuring Irish actor Bill Barry.[17] According to Sheridan, McManus "felt that a knockout strip could be created by using the idea behind 'The Rising Generation.' . . . In this popular drama, the experiences of a laborer's family suddenly becoming wealthy were presented. Why not a comic strip based on the resistance of the head of the house to his family's social ambitions, he reasoned."[18]

In 1913, having sounded the theme of ersatz domestic crisis in *The Newlyweds* (1904), McManus created his master strip, *Bringing Up Father*. Like *The Rising Generation*, the strip documented the dilemmas of an Irish working-class couple upon whom wealth has suddenly been thrust. The strip's dramatis personae included Jiggs, a former hod carrier; Maggie, his wife, a former washerwoman; Nora, his beautiful

George McManus, *Bringing Up Father*, 1916

In this early episode Jiggs attempts to dispose of a pet given Maggie by an effete cosmopolitan friend.

Bringing Up Father by George McManus

George McManus, *Bringing Up Father*, March 17, 1935

The battle of the sexes inspired McManus's masterful *Bringing Up Father*. First published as a daily in 1913, the strip depicted the conflict between Jiggs, an easygoing, nouveau riche Irish immigrant, and Maggie, his socially ambitious, Anglophile wife, in an abstract, geometricized style later termed art deco. Like a musical score, the strip's composition was given brio by the imaginative use of Jiggs's ebony tuxedo. Symbolically, the tuxedo represented the confinement of Jiggs's upper-crust life-style, which he constantly sought to escape.

daughter; and Junior, his ne'er-do-well son. As historian Coulton Waugh has observed,

> the theme . . . is that money has flooded a simple Irish workman's life in amounts large enough to satisfy any dream — and while this brings out all the Maggie in Maggie, it also brings out all the Jiggs in Jiggs — this Jiggishness being the really attractive feature of the strip, ameliorating, to some degree, the fights and brawls, the unpleasant picture of marriage which it portrays. As Maggie scrambles furiously for the top rung on the ladder, Jiggs looks wistfully at the bottom and makes pathetic attempts to return to it.[19]

McManus depicted the trials and tribulations of those who realize the American dream in a uniquely personal style. He formulated this unmistakable artistic signature as a turn-of-the-century fashion artist for the *St. Louis Republic*.[20] Drawing upon such international sources as the Secessionist juxtaposition of fabric and pattern, McManus created a distinctive blend of geometric simplification, interior decoration, architectural embellishment, and textural contrast. Developing simultaneously in the applied and decorative arts, such elements were in the thirties termed art deco.

Appearing for the first time on January 2, 1913, in William Randolph Hearst's *New York American*, *Bringing Up Father* was set in New York during the apex of Irish immigration. The portrait painted by McManus of these new arrivals is endearing and optimistic. Recalling his humble origins, the sentimental Jiggs variously reminisces,

> Do you remember, Maggie, when . . . the rich McHaffey kids wuz sick — they had a real doctor call at their house. . . . An' the day I got me first raise workin' in Finnigan's brick yard. . . . Maggie — I remember . . . How we envied the brick-top Dugan kids because their brother wuz a lamp-post lighter. . . . Your uncle "Lem" who never wore a collar an' never used glasses — he preferred drinkin' out of a bottle. . . . An those good old Sunday dinners when the family would git together an' fight —[21]

The strip's setting alternated between Jiggs and Maggie's swank uptown apartment, which served as an austere setting in which to display conspicuously Maggie's splendid apparel and many purchases, and the richly vivacious, crowded Brooklyn tenements constituting Jiggs and Maggie's "old neighborhood." Penetrating Jiggs's digs are pretentious

Chic Young, *Blondie*, November 12, 1931

The marriage of Blondie and Dagwood was by no means foreordained. In the strip's first episodes, Blondie was sought after by many suitors and scorned by Dagwood's patrician family.

parasites, including society snobs and bogus British aristocrats. The tenement tenants, on the other hand, are aggressively authentic and riotously vulgar.

McManus's affection for his Irish origins compelled the artist to return Jiggs again and again to his humble haunts. In 1923 and in 1938, McManus used the device of a convenient bankruptcy to achieve this return ("So we're broke now, all on account of your going into the movie business. It's terrible!" scolds Maggie).[22] These reversals enabled Jiggs to escape the effete unreality of Park Avenue and to enjoy once again the vigorous physical pleasures of Brooklyn — abundant and simple food, cards, cronies, and drink. The artist knew whereof he drew. During the Depression McManus himself lost a fortune.[23]

Animating the strip are oppositions of sex, class, and country of origin. Masculine vulgarity in contrast to feminine pretentiousness; working-class enthusiasm to snobbish ennui; Irish gusto to British dilettantism. An emissary between these worlds, Jiggs is a man without a country. On one hand, he is forbidden by his wife to entertain his friends at home;[24] on the other, to return to his former haunts. Jiggs's attire — top hat and tuxedo — symbolizes his dilemma. Worn on all occasions, it constitutes a confining uniform and serves as a reminder — in the words of author Thomas Wolfe — that "you can't go home again." The somber ebony of Jiggs's tuxedo, which serves as a compositional anchor in the strip, is relieved by the intriguing patterns of Maggie and Nora's stylish clothing. Klimtian in complexity and juxtaposition of fabric, their garb served as an index to American haute couture for half a century.

McManus's fondness for high fashion was matched by his love of interior decoration and architectural ornament, a penchant he indulged in a grand comic-strip tour of America conducted in 1939 and 1940. Expressive of the artist's love of country, the strip included stops at Boulder Dam, Chicago (twice), the Grand Canyon, Broadway, Brooklyn, Erie, Niagara Falls, Detroit, Pittsburgh, Philadelphia, Lake Placid, Washington, Boston, Trenton, Cleveland, and Atlantic City — all portrayed in loving detail according to the artist's uniquely personal vi-

Gene Byrnes, *Reg'lar Fellers*, April 1, 1936

The comic-strip equivalent of Mark Twain's "a boy comes of age" novels, *Reg'lar Fellers* went so far as to borrow names, such as Puddinhead, from its literary antecedents.

Walter Berndt, *Smitty*, October 17, 1936

Smitty, whose main character was a bald, lisping savant, was among the first kid strips to have an adult theme — that of the child as worker. Such strips were worlds apart from the fantastic universes envisioned by pioneer cartoonists McCay and Feininger.

sion.[25] Interviewed by *Collier's* in 1952, McManus recalled the "great pains" that the meticulous stylization of such sites required.

> I once spent two weeks on a picture. . . . This was a New Year's Day in the late thirties and I had Jiggs looking north in New York's Times Square, with the square faithfully pictured in every detail. . . . Again, when I took Jiggs and Maggie and Nora around the world and on their tour of the United States, the backgrounds had to be accurate and the work was prodigious.[26]

The visual excitement generated by *Bringing Up Father* included not only that of the panoramic vista but that of the intimate detail as well. Among the whimsical devices McManus introduced to the comic strip was the drama within the drama — characters come to life in the pictures hanging on the walls. They comment on the regular characters in the strip; they drop ashes from their cigars onto Maggie's carpet; they even emerge from their frames. They originated, according to McManus, when there were a couple of figures he wanted to get into a picture frame on the wall, "but for balance and design the frame couldn't be large enough to accommodate them," so he drew them outside the frame.[27] Recalled McManus in 1952, "I've been doing that sort of thing ever since and it's become a sort of trade mark of the strip. In my drawings, figures emerge at will from picture frames and from lamp shades; they even toss things from one picture to another."[28]

America was as generous to the artist as was McManus to his comic-strip creatures. As author William Kennedy has noted, in his prime Jiggs had eighty million readers in forty-six countries and sixteen languages. McManus bragged that he was as rich as Jiggs, having earned some $12 million over the forty years he drew the strip.[29] Furthermore, McManus reaped the proceeds of *Bringing Up Father*'s translation into stage plays, radio programs, and motion pictures by Christie Brothers, Metro-Goldwyn-Mayer, Vitagraph, and Monogram, including four films in which the artist himself played Jiggs.[30] In recognition of the artist's depiction of America as a land of unrivaled economic opportunity, McManus was honored on the occasion of the strip's twenty-fifth anniversary by a congressional dinner in the Capitol and by testimonials from such prominent national figures as U.S. Supreme Court judiciary.[31] In this master strip McManus created at once a uni-versal parable of unlimited economic opportunity and a morality tale of domestic oppression, told in a style of supreme artistic inventiveness.

Variations on the theme of domestic relations have been sounded over the years by countless other comic-strip artists, including Chic Young, creator of *Blondie*. Where McManus documented the dilemmas of the nouveau riche, however, Young treated the tribulations of the bourgeoisie. Ironically, given its domestic denouement, *Blondie* began in 1930 as the chronicle of a liberated working girl and her numerous suitors. Soon Blondie succumbed to the blandishments of Dagwood, and the formula that was to be maintained for fifty years was established — that is, the saga of the efficient wife and the well-meaning but bungling husband.[32] Paralleling shifts in the American economy from plenty to want, and in political ideology from left to right, the strip's focus changed from Blondie's alluring independence and sexuality to Dagwood's troubles at the office (often punctuated by the exclamation of his autocratic boss, Mr. Dithers, "Bumstead, you're fired!").

Overtones of social insecurity pervade *Blondie*. Young established a new triangle, similar to that of Arthur Miller's 1949 Pulitzer Prize–winning play, *Death of a Salesman:* the capricious boss, the wage-slave husband, and the family whose financial demands forever yoke husband to boss. McManus's vision of America as a land of unlimited opportunity, typical to this day of immigrants and their sons and daughters, is superseded in Young's work by a sense of diminished possibility born of the Depression. Nevertheless, *Blondie* remains among the most popular of all comics, syndicated to over two thousand newspapers, the subject of forty motion pictures, a radio series, and a television series.[33]

The popularity of the domestic strip, of which *Blondie* is the premier example, is deeply rooted in its appeal to traditional family values. However, the domestic strip was originally intended to attract as its audience the increasing numbers of young women entering the work force. In fact, the first domestic cartoons were termed "girl" strips. Among the many such cartoons conceived for this new constituency were *Polly and Her Pals*, originated in 1912 by Cliff Sterrett; *Somebody's Stenog*, started in 1918 by A. E. Hayward; *Winnie Winkle, the Breadwinner*, begun in 1920 by Martin Branner; and *Tillie the Toiler*, created in 1921 by Russ Westover. As time passed, their fashion-plate protagonists became flappers, matured, and married, following the same life cycles as did their readers — with significant exceptions. As described by Branner, this domestication originated in the encroaching self-censorship practiced by the papers, and included, as late as 1942, prohibitions against the depiction of birth or death.[34] Indeed, the *Baltimore Sun* dropped *Winnie Winkle* when its married protagonist became pregnant.[35]

In the forties, the "girl" strip declined in popularity. The exception to this rule was *Brenda Starr*, originated in 1940 by Dale Messick, one of the first girl strips to be penned by a woman. Chronicling the exploits of a daring female reporter, *Brenda Starr* transcended the restrictions of the domestic strip by incorporating elements of the adventure strip, then at the height of its popularity. The formula followed by the original girl strip, however, survives today in *Apartment 3-G*, created in 1961 by psychiatrist and author Nicholas Dallis and drawn by artist Alex Kotzky. Unlike the evolutionary *Tillie the Toiler, Polly and Her Pals, Winnie Winkle*, and *Brenda Starr*, however, the residents of *Apartment 3-G* exist in a time warp, their ages and personalities forever fixed, their only stable relationship with a male that which exists with the aging, asexual Professor who will always live downstairs.

Not so the protagonists of the phenomenally popular seventies strips *Cathy* and *For Better or for Worse*, two of the few domestic strips to be drawn *by* women. Begun in 1976 by advertising executive Cathy Guisewite, *Cathy* documents the professional and personal problems of a single working woman. While utilizing the time-tested conventions of the girl strip, including the protagonist's evolution in age, appearance, and attitude, and reflecting changing fashions in apparel and interests, *Cathy* is a post-Freudian creation, characterized by obsessive self-analysis and constant variations on the themes of loneliness and isolation.

Given the strip's predictable psychoanalytic focus, some readers were outraged when Guisewite attacked the record of Ronald Reagan during the 1988 presidential campaign. Among the complainants was Judy Hughes, president of the National Federation of Republican Women, who, in a letter to the *Washington Post* printed on November 5,

1988, wrote: "The comic pages are designed for mindless amusement, not mindless distortion. They are not meant to be a forum for political endorsements, which is why most newspapers have the good sense to place political cartoons on the editorial pages. Until Guisewite changes the tone of her comic, I suggest you move 'Cathy' to a more suitable section."

While *Cathy* concerns the predicament of the upwardly mobile, single wage earner, *For Better or for Worse* examines the world of the middle-class nuclear family. Created in 1975 by Canadian Lynn Franks Johnston, the loosely autobiographical cartoon documents the day-to-day dilemmas of a "dentist's wife," the epithet by which Johnston herself is known in her native Corbeil, Ontario.[36] Drawing upon the conventions of the domestic strip, *For Better or for Worse* features a family in flux — children are born, circumstances change, characters adapt. While maintaining its mainstream appeal, the strip occasionally tackles tricky albeit universal problems. In July 1986, for example, *For Better or for Worse* dealt with birth defects. The cartoon consistently tops reader-opinion polls.

The ability of the domestic strip to reflect the changing interests of its audience is a powerful source of its popular appeal. Rituals of courtship, marriage, childbirth, and child-rearing are compelling universal concerns and ensure the success of the strip that communicates these preoccupations. No less an artist than underground innovator R. Crumb has turned his attention to these themes. With his artist wife, the talented Aline Kominsky-Crumb, Crumb created for *Weirdo* 23 (Summer 1988) *Aline 'n' Bob in Our Lovely Home*, a gentle reflection on the Crumbs' domestic life in rural California.

While the adventure strip appeals to our romantic idealism, domestic strips provide reassurance that the trivial tasks comprising day-to-day existence have cumulative meaning and that the milestone events of courtship and marriage, as experienced by comic-strip characters who are the reader's beloved familiars, are meaningful experiences reflecting the purposeful nature of the universe.

CHAPTER **5**

Law and Disorder: *Little Orphan Annie, Dick Tracy,* and *Li'l Abner*

arold Gray, *Little Orphan Annie*, 1931

printed by permission: Tribune Media Services.

e first of the adventure strips to feature a girl protagonist, *Little Orphan Annie* was created in 1924 at the ecific request of publisher Joseph Medill Patterson. Soon *Annie* evolved from a picaresque tale featuring a ucky orphan into a passionate examination of social phenomena including the Great Depression. Whatever e trial, Annie and her protector, munitions magnate Daddy Warbucks, suffered it with stoicism and confidence the capitalist future.

While social commentary had been indirect during the optimistic early years of the comic strip, the trauma of the Great Depression was reflected in major strips that came of age in the thirties. International economic collapse, unemployment, Prohibition, the breakdown of law and order, the gangster era — such were the subjects of Harold Gray's *Little Orphan Annie*, Chester Gould's *Dick Tracy*, and Al Capp's *Li'l Abner*, all three of which portrayed an America in transition.

This they did in various artistic styles ranging from Gray's minimalism — the comic-strip counterpart of Grant Wood's simplified regionalism — to Gould's distorted medieval ménage to Capp's agitated expressionism. Utilizing diverse storytelling techniques, including editorial comment, moralizing exemplum, and tall tale, each expressed his outrage at the anarchistic present while yearning for a simpler place and time. This nostalgia is personified by the good country people of Gray's native Midwest, by Gould's romantic idealist, Dick Tracy, and by Capp's natural man, Li'l Abner.

Gray continued the kid strip, albeit with a twist to the right, in *Little Orphan Annie*, created in 1924 in response to Chicago Tribune–New York News Syndicate chief Joseph Medill Patterson's demand for a child strip featuring a girl.[1]

Born in Kankakee, Illinois, on January 20, 1894, Gray, who spent the first twenty-three years of his life on a farm, embodied many of those attitudes associated with the agrarian Midwest: rugged individualism, a frontier mentality, the Protestant ethic of redemptive hard work, an interest in economics informed by social Darwinism, and a benevolently paternalistic view of labor relations.[2] These beliefs were to be severely tested in the crucible of historic reality forged in 1929 by the Great Depression, which radically transformed the artist and his creation, *Little Orphan Annie*.

As originally conceived, the strip chronicled the trials and tribulations of a plucky foundling in an orphanage directed by her nemesis, Miss Asthma — a formula derived from the English novelist Charles Dickens, whom Gray much admired. In 1925, Mrs. Oliver Warbucks, a nouveau riche socialite, hoping to dazzle high society with her charitable works, adopts Annie. Annie immediately proves an unsatisfactory acqui-

1966

Harold Gray, *Little Orphan Annie*, January 9, 1966

Reprinted by permission: Tribune Media Services.
Original pen and ink drawing.
Bea and Murray A. Harris Collection.
Photo by Joe Goulait, Courtesy Smithsonian Institution Traveling Exhibition Service (SITES).

sition: her blunt grit irritates Mrs. Warbucks's refined sensibilities, and Mrs. Warbucks repeatedly returns Annie to Miss Asthma's "home." Annie, however, has captured the heart of "Daddy" Oliver Warbucks, a former rolling-mill foreman who has become a successful defense contractor.

On a trip to England, Mrs. Warbucks acquires a more satisfactory companion — "dear little Selby Adlebert Piffleberry of the Herring Piffleberrys." But, unbeknownst to the fawning Mrs. Warbucks, Piffleberry is really the willing cat's-paw of that veteran confidence man, the Count de Tour. Together, Piffleberry and de Tour attempt to divest Warbucks of his fortune, only to be foiled by Annie's shrewd intervention. (The postwar nationalism of this episode is shared by other comic strips of the period: in *Bringing Up Father*, Maggie is infatuated by Sir Von Platter, and Li'l Abner must contend with such suspicious foreigners as Baron Slinkovitch.)

In 1929 such picaresque adventures were subsumed in a grand elemental theme — that of survival. Whereas the Depression had provided George McManus with a welcome opportunity to return Jiggs to his beloved humble haunts, it afforded Gray the chance to more precisely define his characters and their ideology through their fall from economic grace. Familiar to generations as stars of strip, stage, and screen, they include the unsinkable adolescent entrepreneur, Orphan Annie; her faithful canine companion, Sandy; munitions magnate "Daddy" Warbucks; gruff but gold-hearted boarding-house proprietress "Maw" Green; that benevolent Oriental assassin, the Asp; and the genial genie Punjab.

While the causes of Jiggs's frequent financial reversals were only obliquely mentioned,[3] Warbucks's sudden entrepreneurial demise is graphically dissected in a series of strips that ran from January through December 1931.[4] As the year begins, we find Annie ensconced in Warbucks's mansion, hard at work learning to spell "yacht."[5] This academic idyll, however, is doomed to be short-lived. Warbucks's mighty adversaries, including competitor J. J. Shark and false friend Bullion the Banker, have manipulated the stock market to effect his downfall. Soon repossessive wolves are at the door, and Warbucks is attempting sto-

ically, but in vain, to keep the news from his ward. Not content with having ruined Warbucks, Shark sets the magnate's manse afire. Warbucks fears that he himself might be suspected of arson, and he plunges penniless into the night, Annie and Sandy in tow.

The trio is soon afflicted by a sequence of coincidental disasters. The four horsemen of the ensuing economic apocalypse are age, want, illness, and isolation. Against the ruthless grinding of powerful financial forces is pitted the disinterested, defiant charity of individuals — kindly "Maw" Green, who lodges the weary travelers; Jake, the Yiddish greengrocer, who offers Annie a job; and Flop House Bill, a dwarf, who eventually helps Warbucks to reestablish and revenge himself. But first, Warbucks must suffer all possible indignities. After a long and discouraging search for employment, Warbucks finally secures a job as a truck driver, only to be caught in a terrible accident (he swerves to avoid hitting a street urchin) that leaves him blind. Unable to accept Annie's charity, Warbucks becomes a knight of the road, determined not to make himself known to her until once again he can become her protector. In his absence, Annie is befriended by another "Daddy" — Dr. Lens, an ophthalmologist who eventually will restore Warbucks's sight.

These adventures are depicted in a Spartan style that sharply contrasts with the balloons' plenteous dialogue. The extreme simplification characteristic of Gray's style even extends to his creatures' features — Annie's eyes have no pupils! Writer Coulton Waugh insightfully analyzed the reason for this omission in his seminal *The Comics*:

> Annie is surrounded by a peculiarly sinister but fascinating world, the threatening tone of which is sustained by a unique technical device. . . . This trick consists of drawing the eyes of all the characters as ovals. . . . Result: the reader, taking his cue from the plot, the character's gesture, or the expression of the mouth, supplies the eye-meaning for himself, and this meaning is clearer and more forceful than if the eye details were completely drawn. . . . Restraint, suggestion: these are the particular tools of the comic cartoonist, the essence of whose job is to do much with little.[6]

While McManus's millionaire Jiggs, also always attired in evening wear, surrounds himself with luxury, a chic flat, and a wife and daughter dressed in the height of fashion, Gray's magnate, Warbucks, lives a

Darrell McClure, *Little Annie Rooney*, July 15, 1951

Copyright 1951 King Features Syndicate, Inc.
Original pen and ink drawing.
Swann Collection, Division of Prints and Photographs, the Library of Congress.

Little Orphan Annie inspired other "girl" strips, most derivatively *Little Annie Rooney*. Among the features common to both strips were an orphan girl and her dog. The totemic abstraction of *Little Orphan Annie*, however, contrasted with the energetic realism of *Little Annie Rooney*.

life of austere ostentation. His surroundings and treasures are only described, rarely depicted. "It all *feels* fine — thick carpet, big easy chairs — panelled walls," observes blind "Daddy," as he and Flop House Bill equip the office from which Warbucks will direct his financial counterstrike.[7] This visual reserve perhaps suggests the artist's distrust of sensuous excess.

Both in form and content, the strip achieves its success by way of contrast, a variation on the Manichaean struggle between good and evil, light and darkness. The altruism of individuals contrasts with the selfishness of the mob (or "pee-pul," as Gray satirically termed the masses).[8] Reversing McManus's gender equation, Gray contrasts Warbucks's masculine desire to excel and his eager embrace of the material rewards of success with Annie's good-natured acceptance of adversity and relative indifference to worldly possessions. In combatting his enemies, be they gangsters, foreign powers, or labor leaders, Warbucks is a towering titan, a solitary superman who alone determines the destiny of millions while remaining a bedrock of strength for his few devoted followers. Opposing him are ruthless but often ultimately incompetent gangs of exploiters, whose perfidious leaders are as feckless as are their followers. These forces of anarchy must be subdued by the triumph of Warbucks's superior will. "Daddy" stands outside and above the law. Would-be assassins enter his home and are never seen again.[9] In eliminating them, "Daddy" commands the services of the Asp, his lethal Oriental henchman, for organized "law and order" is at best powerless, at worst corrupt.[10]

The strip's didacticism is famous: "Sure," reflects Warbucks, "I believe in short hours of work, lots of holidays with pay, all that stuff — it would be great if we could *all* afford to knock off any old time — but as I see it, a *few* men *have* to work hard and take heavy chances and battle heavy odds and worry nights, so that millions may have that 'fuller life' you mention, instead of *every day* off *without pay*."[11] Occasionally it was relieved by eschewing domestic settings and sailing o'er the seas to exotic ports of call. In such locations physical rules were often suspended. Witness Mr. Am, a magus older than Methuselah, who transforms Warbucks's Russian enemies into carefree simians by means of a vapor escaping from a box worthy of Pandora.[12]

More often, the artist, who exhorted aspirant cartoonists to "Keep your characters in hot water all the time, but don't have it hot enough to scald their courage," employed formulaic plots, according to which business demands required "Daddy" abroad.[13] In his absence, Annie is often abducted. Escaping her captors, she sets out again for the heartland. In rural retreats she is given shelter by a series of poor but hardworking recluses whose ward she becomes. In return for their charity, she penetrates and resolves the mystery surrounding their isolation, and vanquishes the stealthy adversaries who stalk them. Like Warbucks, Annie's newfound friends are individualistic outsiders, frugal, taciturn, and unbending. They neither need nor want the society of others, and shun social intercourse with all but their few intimates.

The strip's implicit xenophobia was made explicit during an interview with Gray by fellow cartoonist and conservative Al Capp. Reminisced Capp,

> I met Harold Gray for the first — and only — time over 30 years ago. He was, even then, a legend. I was but a rumor that had just gotten started. He said: "I know your stuff, Capp. You're going to be around a long time. Take my advice and buy a house in the country. Build a wall around it. And get ready to protect yourself. The way things are going, people who earn their living someday are going to have to fight off the bums!"[14]

Gray's disillusionment is understandable in light of the changing times. Traumatic changes in the body politic, the world economy, and weapons technology — with grave implications for international security, economic survival, and personal safety — took place between 1911 and 1941, a thirty-year period coinciding with Gray's adolescence, manhood, and maturity. Unlike the verdant optimism of an earlier generation of cartoonists, Gray's vision of America was profoundly pessimistic, tempered by the harsh realities of his own time and place. Whereas Winsor McCay, Lyonel Feininger, George Herriman, and George McManus believed in the essential goodness of man and the perfectibility of the democratic process, Gray distrusted most men and all social systems.

Gray's artistry has been endlessly analyzed. Some have seen him as a great "naive" artist, the Grandma Moses of the comic strip. His totemic male figures suggest in grandeur and immobility the icons of Easter Island. "Annie lives, as a rule, in a world of men, a clever device focusing attention on her femininity. The enormous height of these friends or foes is another device. It makes Annie petite; it means that however capable she may have become, the world is against her physically."[15]

While the strip's male figures are gigantic and immobile, Annie and her faithful dog, Sandy, are alive with energy, hair and fur bristling with electricity. The somber attire of the male figures also contrasts with Annie's fiery mane and red dress. Through scale, shape, and color Gray emphasizes Annie's role as dramatic catalyst, pictorially reinforcing the strip's story line. Loud with loneliness, Gray's minimalist interiors and surreally empty landscapes suggest the same threatening isolation as do the paintings of his contemporary, Edward Hopper.

Reacting to the same stimuli (postwar disillusionment, economic collapse, breakdown of world order, and incipient anarchy) that had elevated Gray's kid strip from picaresque narrative to political analysis, his fellow midwesterner, Chester Gould, on October 4, 1931, introduced the hard-boiled, anticrime masterpiece *Dick Tracy*.[16] Silent, square-jawed, vaguely aristocratic, Tracy, the comic-strip counterpart of such fictional archetypes as Dashiell Hammett's Sam Spade and Raymond Chandler's Philip Marlowe, is the tough guy the times demanded. While Warbucks wields the weapon of money, Tracy packs a pistol. Unlike Warbucks, who begins his occupational rise as foreman in a rolling mill, Tracy (according to some sources, the model for Bob Kane's 1938 Batman) is to the manor born and has no need to elevate his social standing. Indeed, his ostensible boss, Chief Brandon, is often depicted as a good-natured but bumbling bureaucrat. Like his counterparts in contemporary detective fiction, Tracy is content to remain a man of the people. Like the ultimately unattached Warbucks (whose two wives disappear completely early in the strip), Tracy is single and unencumbered by domestic obligations. Although engaged on and off to Tess Trueheart, Tracy is immune to seduction, distrustful of ties to either individuals or organizations, a subscriber to a canon of lonely individualism. The celebration

of the celibate as hero bespeaks the time-honored taboo circumscribing the expression of sexuality in American art and literature.

Against Tracy are arrayed the forces of evil, a medieval rogues' gallery of increasingly deformed and sadistic villains. Contemporary cartoonist Art Spiegelman recently provided an explanation of Gould's fantastic physiognomy: "For Gould, a true disciple of [Swiss artist Rudolphe] Töppfer [1799–1846], a face was almost literally a 'map,' a map of hell, indicated by the most peculiar configuration of lines he could manage, and, in one memorable instance, by no face at all, a Blank."[17] Gould himself, while acknowledging the influence of the grotesques created by American writer Edgar Allan Poe, provided his own explanation of his caricatures in *The Celebrated Cases of Dick Tracy:* "I wanted my villains to stand out definitively so that there would be no mistake who the villain was. . . . I never looked at them as being ugly, but I'll tell you this. I think the ugliest thing in the world is the face of a man who has killed seven nurses — or who has kidnapped a child."[18]

Such villains are cunningly presented in a December 28, 1941, episode wherein Gould's detective is presented with a special New Year's gift, "The Book of Dick Tracy," an album of adversaries. "This," narrates the donor,

> is Little Face, head of a stick-up gang, who *almost* froze to death, and lost both ears. This is Deafy, head of the Bicycle Ring, who was sent to prison December 17, 1940. This is "Mamma" and the Midget who went out West to escape the law. As I remember it, the Midget was scalded to death in a shower bath. This is Karpse, the Villain, who perfected a method of making poison gas out of molasses. He met death by his own hands, December 23, 1938, in a hotel room. This one is Edward Nuremoh, who staged a fake marriage to Tess Trueheart just to meet the terms of his grandmother's will, then walked over a cliff to his death, August 29, 1939. And this is Redrum, the "Man-Without-a-Face," a murderer whom you caught and put behind bars, January 3, 1938.[19]

The style in which Gould renders the outrages of these fiends is highly abstract and extremely simplified. As Spiegelman observed,

> Gould understood better than anyone that comic-strip drawing isn't really drawing at all, but rather a kind of diagramming. The stunningly composed black-and-white panels, which progressed more and more toward abstraction

Leonard Starr, *Annie*, February 27, 1989

Continued today by Leonard Starr, the strip continues to feature abundant dialogue. Warbucks's right-wing philosophy, however, has been modified, and Gray's emblematic naïveté replaced by technical sophistication.

over the years, are a kind of blueprint Expressionism. The strip is festooned with labels and arrows; diagrams of fingers point at diagrams of arms; backgrounds shift as dizzyingly as Herriman's (though less obtrusively); the scale of objects to people changes from image to image, obeying no natural laws, only the laws that govern storytelling.[20]

The exploits of Gould's master criminals are set in the heyday of the gangster era, reflecting contemporary realities. Gould's hellish vision of the modern city as nightmare netherworld — an observation first made by Winsor McCay in the 1908 Shantytown and 1910 Mars sequences of *Little Nemo in Slumberland* — reflected the national crime wave cresting in thirties America. Mystery writer Ellery Queen (pseudonym of novelists Frederic Dannay and Manfred Lee) recited a litany of actual crimes occurring in urban America the week that *Dick Tracy* first appeared: "In New York, in a daring daylight raid, three armed men invaded the home of Deputy Police Commissioner Barron Collier . . . a bomb exploded in a Bronx garage as dry men seized Dutch Schultz's beer. . . . In Chicago, on October 3, a football crowd jeered Scarface Al Capone. . . ."[21]

Whereas McCay attributed urban violence to powerful financial interests, Gould sought its sources in the depravity of the criminal underclass and in man's flawed nature. In *Dick Tracy* he elevated the conflict between reason and instinct, spiritual aspiration and bestial nature, superego and id, to the level of epic struggle. Eschewing grays and halftones, Gould presents a world pictorially reflecting the struggle between good and evil. As Coulton Waugh emphasized, Gould

takes each form as it comes before him, reduces it to an effective essential, and draws it with a hard, wooden outline. The process does not sound attractive; actually, however, it is extraordinarily effective; it allows Gould to dwell with a kind of passionate insistence on the procession of criminals who knife their way through the strip, and on the minute details connected with their crimes.[22]

The "passionate insistence" of Gould's artistic technique is reinforced by his wordplay, the names of his villains, like their facial features, providing clues to their characters. The villain Redrum's name, for example, is the word *murder* in reverse.

Cartoonist Al Capp also repudiated contemporary urban life in his

Chester Gould, *Dick Tracy*, August 13, 1936

Reprinted by permission: Tribune Media Services.
Original pen and ink drawing.
Bea and Murray A. Harris Collection.
Photo by Joe Goulait, Courtesy Smithsonian Institution Traveling Exhibition
Service (SITES).

1934 masterpiece, *Li'l Abner*, which romanticized the natural man of Appalachia and depicted Depression-era Kentucky as an earthly paradise. Harkening back to the proletarian slapstick of such early strips as Opper's *Happy Hooligan* (1900), *Li'l Abner* was at once domestic comedy, adventure epic, and social satire. The plot detailed the ordeals of the Yokum family of Dogpatch, Kentucky — Pansy Yokum, its omnipotent matriarch; Lucifer Yokum, the ineffective paterfamilias; and Abner, the good-hearted but slow-witted bumpkin son. Other stock characters included the Scraggs, low-life, blood-feuding rivals of the Yokums, and Daisy Mae Scraggs, Abner's romantic interest. As the years passed by, a bizarre succession of animal scapegoats appeared in the strip — Salomey, the Yokums' pet pig; and Capp's fantastic masochistic animals, the schmoo and the kigmy.

Unifying the strip were the elemental conflicts presented therein. "Death, love, and power," proclaimed the artist, "are the three great interests of man. They are the sources of all the stories in *Li'l Abner*, mainly because there are no others."[23]

Born in New Haven, Connecticut, on September 28, 1909, Alfred Gerald Caplin was disabled by a streetcar accident on August 21, 1919. As Capp recalled the trauma, "I hopped off the ice cart in front of the barber academy — and directly in the path of a huge old-fashioned trolley car. I was caught under the wheels and before the car could be stopped my left leg was severed at the thigh."[24]

In later life, Capp was to rail at historians who disregarded the impact of his disability on his iconography. In *Li'l Abner*, Capp compensates visually, depicting Abner's visage as his own self-portrait, rendering his hero supremely athletic, infinitely mobile, and physically perfect. Unlike his creator, however, Abner is dull-witted. Blonde Daisy Mae, the first in a succession of sensuous women, is the voluptuous embodiment of stereotypical self-sacrifice and dependency; dusky Moonbeam McSwine, that of sensual languor. Li'l Abner and Daisy Mae are an Appalachian Adam and Eve, their idealized relationship the reverse of that of Mammy and Pappy Yokum, of whom the artist wrote, "Pappy could do nothing, which was what his family expected of him, and Mammy could do anything, and that was all she was expected to do."[25]

Dick Locher and Max Collins, *Dick Tracy*, March 1, 1989

Reprinted by permission: Tribune Media Services.

Today, *Tracy* continues, tackling such space-age problems as that of mutant-human and computer viruses while retaining the geometric compositions, the stark contrasts of black and white, and the weird villains that were Gould's trademarks.

Al Capp, *Li'l Abner*, April 30, 1939

Launched in 1934 during the Great Depression, *Li'l Abner* sung the praises of agrarian existence among the noble savages of Appalachian Kentucky. Troubles quickly emerged in this American Eden — the corrupting influence of the big city, nefarious government intervention, and foreign governments. Culminating in Sadie Hawkins Day, a celebration of role reversal during which women pursue men, the strip depicted sexuality as a power struggle. Uniformly, women are depicted as coolly competent, men as ineffective; women as voraciously libidinous, men as passive. Here, in a sequence that anticipates Capp's attacks on feminism, the leader of an Amazonian Kentucky island coven kidnaps "Mammy," who has donned male attire. Full of innuendo, the strip examines the "nacheral" relationship of women to men.

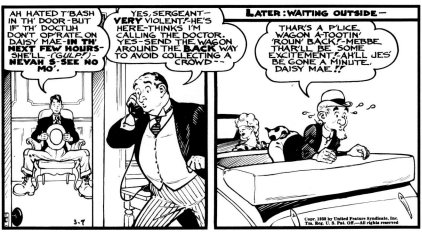

Al Capp, *Li'l Abner*, March 7, 1938

The perhaps apocryphal origin of *Li'l Abner*, according to Capp, was an expedition to Appalachia made when the artist was fifteen.[26] Capp's wife, Catherine, remembered that the inspiration provided by the expedition was reinforced by a vaudeville act. "One night while Al was working for [Ham] Fisher, we went to a vaudeville theater in Columbus Circle. One of the performances was a hillbilly act. . . . They stood in a very wooden way with expressionless deadpan faces. We thought they were just hilarious. We walked back to the apartment that evening, becoming more and more excited with the idea of a hillbilly comic strip."[27]

Whatever muse originally inspired the strip, between 1934 and 1977 *Li'l Abner* was to evolve from a good-natured critique of a nation of confidence men and social-climbers to a blistering attack on ideas, institutions, and individuals found by Capp to be "liberal." Among Abner's splendid early adventures were encounters with Pansy Yokum's well-to-do sister, the self-styled "Beatrixe, Duchess of Bopshire," who lures her nephew to "New Yawk," there to improve him; Mimi van Pett, a Park Avenue socialite; Baron Slinkovitch of Skurvia, and Scarloff, his minion;

the incorrigible Marryin' Sam; the murderous boxer, Slugger Bashmug (a reference to Capp's days as Ham Fisher's assistant on *Joe Palooka*); Mrs. Dolores Eppingham, the arbitrator of etiquette; Mary Ann Astorbux, an eight-year-old heiress who is the subject of a scandalous custody battle; Madame Mercedes Scorpio, a gold-digging psychic; Hip Tong, head of the outlaw "House of the Dragon"; Mrs. Sneerworthy; desperado Gat Garson, Abner's nefarious double; the sinister Doctor Lopez and his weird assistant, Sanchez; Hattie Haggle, the richest woman in New York; and Sassy Sandra, a nubile nymphet. While many of these early episodes referred to headline-news events such as the Vanderbilt custody case, all were contrived to dramatize the essential goodness of the Yokum family; in later adventures, the strip's emphasis was to shift from Capp's fictional family to historic realities that engulf the Yokums — the Cold War, the protest movement of the sixties, and feminism.

As the strip's subject evolved, Capp's style changed. Early episodes featured lightly drawn, calligraphic characters who are statically situated; later adventures revealed clearly defined, vigorously alive protagonists whose figures were circumscribed by thick black lines and whose gestures were extravagantly exaggerated. Increasingly, Capp's characters were depicted in motion or dramatically silhouetted against the sky. Camera angles were adopted, chiaroscuro utilized. Originally straightforward, the dialogue also became more complex, punctuated by dramatic asides, sly innuendo, excited exclamations, and self-revelatory thoughts.

The female figures for which Capp is justly famous underwent similar metamorphoses. Mammy became shorter, compact, energized; Daisy Mae, taller, fulsome; Moonbeam McSwine, sinuous. As Daisy Mae's charms wax, Abner's interest wanes. Generalizing from the particulars of Abner and Daisy Mae's relationship, Capp created what was to become an American folk event, Sadie Hawkins Day, a celebration of sexual-role reversal in which the hunter becomes the hunted. In an October 16, 1939, proclamation the Mayor of Dogpatch declared: "Whereas there be inside our town a passel of gals what ain't married but craves something awful to be . . . we hereby proclaims and decrees . . . Saturday, November 4th, *Sadie Hawkins Day*, whereon a foot race will be held, the unmarried gals to chase the unmarried men and if they ketch them, the men by law must marry the gals and no two ways about it." The Dogpatch bachelors, like Warbucks and Tracy, lack interest in the opposite sex. In Dogpatch, every day is Sadie Hawkins Day. The battle of the sexes, a theme of *Li'l Abner* since the strip's inauguration in 1934, culminated in an attack on the women's movement in 1974. Initially depicted as voluptuous and seductive, Capp's later women are portrayed as masculine and emasculating. Folksinger Joan Baez, espousing both protest politics and feminism — two of Capp's bêtes noires — became a personal target of the artist's poisoned pen.

Discussing his political development, Capp in 1970 reflected,

It has taken me thirty years to realize what a superior understanding of our even-then developing ruling class, the bums, [Harold] Gray had. They aren't the unemployed or the rejected, as we liberal young snots thought. Read your front page this morning. It will be full of crimes they committed last night. Crimes which required health, strength, and energy. Then turn to the back pages and read about the jobs they scorn, under "Help Wanted. No Experience Necessary."[28]

"My politics didn't change," protested the artist. "I had always been for those who were despised, disgraced, and denounced. That was what changed. Suddenly it was the poor hardworking bastard who was being denounced."[29] Capp died in 1979, on the eve of the neoconservative triumph of the eighties. The strip's shift to the far right can be measured from its original apotheosis of Appalachia and celebration of the natural man to its consideration of the pressures brought by Daisy Mae and Mammy Yokum on Abner to conform socially (i.e., marry), through responses to social change in the sixties, to blatant personal attacks (such as that made on Baez) and outright editorializing in the seventies.

The strip's evolution from rustic fantasy to strident propaganda was, however, occasionally relieved by the insertion of a strip within the strip, "Fearless Fosdick by Lester Gooch," a parody of Chester Gould's *Dick Tracy*. Variations on *Li'l Abner*'s major themes of natural man's physical and psychic freedom, civilization and its discontents, and the insatiable sexual appetite of the female were all sounded in "Fearless Fosdick," whose hero possesses and exaggerates many of the traits of Gould's Tracy — insouciance in the face of danger; nonchalance; intractability; and a studied indifference to his voracious sweetheart, Prudence Pimpleton. Capp also satirized the heavy-handedness of Gould's interpretation of his villains' physical imperfections as the visible manifestation of evil incarnate. For example, in a 1943 Fosdick episode the gun-toting arch-villain Bomb Face boasts:

You and I, Fearless Fosdick, we'll go TOGETHER. Fortunately, I was born with a bomb for a head! Naturally, I have led a life of crime. And, naturally, you have tracked me down and cornered me, curse you!! But I, "Bomb Face," will have had the last laugh!! When this cigarette burns down to my highly incendiary lips — my head will explode — and you and I, Fosdick — we'll both meet our maker together!! Ha!! Ha!! Ha!!

Undaunted, Fosdick tackles the felon, aims him at his gang, and destroys both boss and minions. "G-Golly!" reflects Li'l Abner,

Fo' a minute ah reckoned thet mah ideel, "Fearless Fosdick," were a g-goner!! Tsk! He ought to know better than t' chum around wif sech onusual gennulmen. Fust thar was Banana-Face, then Spinach Face — then Hamburger-Face — and this last one, Bomb-Face! My — he were hot-haided!! Wonder what

Al Capp, *Li'l Abner — Fearless Fosdick by Lester Gooch*,
May 13, 1943

In this strip-within-a-strip admirer Al Capp satirized *Dick Tracy*, introducing the "highly incendiary" villain Bomb Face, whom Fosdick humorlessly dispatches. Drawn in wartime, the strip also contained a satire of the famous Gould "crimestoppers" frame. In "Advice fo' Chillun" Capp exhorted young Americans to save "thar fats an' scraps" to beat the "Japs."

kinda peekoolyar gennulman he'll git mixed up wif next?

Meanwhile, in his studio, cartoonist "Lester Gooch" proclaims, "And now I've created for my public the last word in hideous, howling horror — Stone Face!"[30]

Gray, Gould, and Capp, a triumvirate of conservative cartoon geniuses, created in their masterworks a dark vision of America. In the urban hells and rural retreats of their strips were reflected the broken dreams of a generation. The demise of the small businessman, the loss of the family farm, and the triumph of the international financier were recurrent themes in *Little Orphan Annie*, as were the breakdown of law and order and the many aspects of class and gender warfare the themes of *Dick Tracy* and *Li'l Abner*. That these strips, originating in the roaring twenties and Depression thirties, effectively gave voice to the concerns and captured the imagination of the nation is supported by their staying power: *Annie* ran for forty-four years (1924–1968); *Dick Tracy* was penned by Gould from 1931 until his death in 1985, a fifty-four-year record; and *Li'l Abner* from 1934 through 1977, a saga of forty-three years' duration.

These strips remain fertile sources of inspiration for younger cartoonists. *Annie*, for example, inspired underground creator Gilbert Shelton's satire, *Little Orphan Amphetamine*, and *Dick Tracy* Shelton's spoof *Tricky Prickears*, the saga of a bumbling blind detective. Relatives of the bizarre villains created in *Dick Tracy* can be found in *Hard Boiled Defective Stories* by Charles Burns, whose cynical hero El Borbah is himself a grotesque.[31] And Capp's influence, filtered through the achievement of Basil Wolverton, winner of Capp's 1946 "Ugly Woman" contest, can be discerned in the powerful work of R. Crumb. Furthermore, these artists' concepts have been renewed by a second generation of mainstream cartoonists, including Leonard Starr, who revived *Little Orphan Annie*, and Max Collins, who draws *Dick Tracy*.

Gilbert Shelton, *Tricky Prickears, the Fabulous Furry Freak Brothers' Favorite Law Enforcement Officer*, 1970

Underground artist Gilbert Shelton also satirized Gould's *Dick Tracy* in *Tricky Prickears*, the saga of a detective who, although both blind and deaf, always gets his man through misadventure. Shelton also poked fun at Gould's "crimestoppers" panel, including in the second frame a "crimestompers meinkampf." In this episode, Prickears unwittingly foils an anarchist plot to bomb the Statue of Liberty.

Chester Gould, *Dick Tracy*, January 19, 1949

Reprinted by permission: Tribune Media Services.
Original pen and ink drawing.
Swann Collection, Division of Prints and Photographs, the Library of Congress.

Replete with diagrams and visual directives, *Dick Tracy* was created in 1931 as a comic-strip response to the gangster era. Its cast included the square-jawed Tracy, his partner Sam, and a rogues' gallery of disdainful and eccentric villains whose deformities were keys to their particular perversions.

Al Capp, *Li'l Abner*, November 4, 1949

Reprinted with permission of Capp Enterprises, Inc.,
c/o Broude & Hochberg, 75 Federal Street, Boston, MA 02110. All rights reserved.
Original pen and ink drawing.
Swann Collection, Division of Prints and Photographs, the Library of Congress.

Capp increasingly peopled *Li'l Abner* with scapegoats and masochists — the pig, Salomey, the Shmoo, and, here, the kigmy, who enjoys being booted by Abner almost as much as Krazy Kat loved being beaned by Ignatz mouse.

Al Capp, *Self-portrait*, 1973

Original pen and ink drawing.
From the collection of Mark J. Cohen, Realtor.

Hal Foster, *Prince Valiant*, March 19, 1938

Copyright 1938 King Features Syndicate, Inc.
Original pen and ink drawing.
Milton Caniff Collection, The Ohio State University Cartoon, Graphic, and
Photographic Arts Research Library.

First published on February 13, 1937, *Prince Valiant* introduced the chivalric code to the comic-strip reader on the eve of World War II. Although Foster chose the medieval period for the imaginative scope it permitted, he was soon to lace the strip with topical allusions, including war with the "Huns."

CHAPTER **6**

High Adventure: From Tarzan to Terry

Detail from Zack Mosley, *Smilin' Jack*, June 28, 1941

Contrasting with the dark drama of Depression America depicted in *Little Orphan Annie, Dick Tracy,* and *Li'l Abner* were the Wagnerian epics unfolding in the adventure strips. The adventure strip encompassed many subgenres, among the most exciting examples of which were science-fiction strips such as *Buck Rogers* (1929) by writer Phil Nowlan and artist Dick Calkins, and *Flash Gordon* (1934) by Alex Raymond; primeval jungle sagas on the order of *Tarzan* (1929) by Harold Foster, Burne Hogarth et al., and *Tarzan*'s counterpart, *Sheena, Queen of the Jungle,* by Will Eisner and Samuel M. Iger; medieval epics, including *Dickie Dare* (1933) by Milton Caniff, R. B. Fuller's *Oakey Doakes* (1935), and Foster's *Prince Valiant in the Days of King Arthur* (1937); blood-and-guts military and flight tales such as Zack Mosley's *Smilin' Jack* (1933) and Caniff's *Terry and the Pirates* (1934); and cowboy yarns, which included *Red Ryder* (1938) by Fred Harmon. Finally, this period saw the birth of the superheroes such as Jerry Siegel and Joe Shuster's Superman (1938) and his feminist shadow, Wonder Woman (1941), the creation of psychologist and inventor William Moulton Marston and artist H. G. Peter.

Harkening back to the enthusiastic belief in the perfectability of man and the progress of society espoused by first- and second-generation American master cartoonists, these self-assured strips were populated by virile, sociable, all-American heroes and cunning, sociopathic, exotic adversaries. As the adventure strip evolved, its villains, whether historic anachronisms or extraterrestrials, came to reflect increasingly menacing international threats. Thus, Flash Gordon confronts "the yellow peril" in the person of Ming the Merciless on the planet Mongo; Prince Valiant wages war against the Hun; Tarzan battles the Nazis; and Terry and the Pirates participate in the Chinese repulsion of the Japanese invaders.

Richly imaginative in style and story, these adventure strips featured unfamiliar locales; a panoply of peoples; heroes and heroines, villains and villainesses of titanic stature. Whereas the expressionist work of Gray, Gould, and Capp was characterized by a horror of vacuum, crowded frames, gross caricature, and burgeoning balloons, the adventure strip was conceived as a visual tour de force, complete with vast

Alex Raymond, *Secret Agent X-9*, April 26, 1934

The creator of *Flash Gordon*, cartoonist Alex Raymond collaborated with writer Dashiell Hammett on *Secret Agent X-9*, which first appeared on January 22, 1934. Set in a world of elegant urban corruption, *Secret Agent X-9* was the comic-strip counterpart of the hard-boiled detective fiction of the thirties.

Joe Shuster and Jerry Siegel, *Superman*, 1943

landscapes rendered from multiple viewpoints lit by dramatic contrasts of light and dark, the balloon often an extraneous element. The didactic strips of the expressionist conservatives were essentially literary, those of the adventure artists unabashedly visual, reflecting the influence of the motion-picture epic. Among the adventure strip's master exponents, Roy Crane and Milton Caniff adapted dramatic lighting effects to comic-strip purpose; Alex Raymond created a physiognomic shorthand for distinguishing different character types; Hal Foster applied techniques derived from the classical landscape tradition; and Burne Hogarth mastered the portrayal of the figure in action and created a rich iconography in which nature is the mirror of man's mental state.

As the nation plunged into the Great Depression, the adventure strip soared into outer space and penetrated the heart of darkness. On January 7, 1929, Calkins and Nowlan created *Buck Rogers*, the first science-fiction epic, for the John F. Dille Syndicate. That same day Foster first published the comic strip *Tarzan* for United Feature Syndicate. The exotic adventures of astronaut and jungle lord soon captured the imaginations of a world-weary country. These pivotal strips were to undergo multiple metamorphoses and to inspire numerous imitators. The most imaginative of their successors were the masterful *Flash Gordon* and the well-plotted *Jungle Jim*, both begun in 1934 by Alex Raymond.

As aerial as Dick Tracy was earthbound, Flash Gordon nevertheless subscribed to similar conventions. Both protagonists were well-born. For example, in the strip's first episode, that of January 7, 1934, we learn that Flash is "a Yale graduate and world-renowned polo player." Flash accidentally becomes embroiled in an outer-space brouhaha when the plane on which he and the lovely Dale Arden are passengers crashes near the observatory of mad scientist Dr. Zarkov. Forced by Zarkov to participate in a kamikaze flight into outer space, Flash and Dale seize control of the rocket and land on the planet Mongo, where they become the prisoners of Ming the Merciless and his lustful daughter, Aura. To escape their clutches, Flash must survive a series of gladiatorial ordeals in which he is challenged by mutants and monsters. Such hybrids — inspired by H. G. Wells's 1933 novel, *The Island of Doc-*

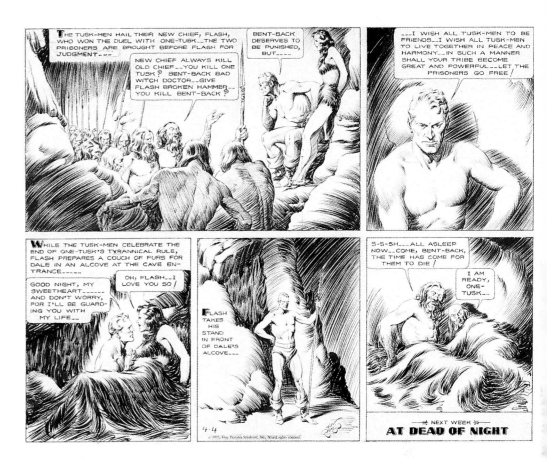

Alex Raymond, *Flash Gordon*, April 4, 1937

As the country plunged into the Great Depression, comic-strip America soared into outer space. Created in 1934, *Flash Gordon* featured exotic locales, high-mimetic heroes, and interplanetary populations. During World War II, Flash's adventures and adversaries were obliquely topical.

tor Moreau — include hawk, lion, and monkey men, as well as "snarling Tygrons," "armor-plated Wolvrons," and "Tsak, the Two-Headed Guardian of the Tunnel of Terror," a futuristic Cerberus. Flash and Dale must also fend off the ominous amorous overtures of Ming and Aura. This, essentially, is the plot of *Flash Gordon*. Hero and villain, heroine and villainess — both are equal in status, intelligence, and physical perfection. What differentiates them is a matter of morality. Ming and Aura are intelligent sensualists who see no reason to restrain primal passions and physical desires. Flash and Dale, however, are undeniably conventional middle-class Americans, whose values include self-restraint and "fair play." Ming describes the differences: "We on this planet have progressed far beyond you earthlings. The reason for our success is that we possess none of the human traits of kindness, mercy, or pity! We are coldly scientific and ruthless."[1] Articulated in 1934, Ming's Nietzschean philosophy echoed the bombastic tirades of Adolf Hitler, who became the German führer that same year.

Matching the epic conflict of *Flash Gordon* is the grand style in which it is depicted. Originally of rigid format, with frames of standard size, tightly drawn figures, and plenteous balloons, from 1934 through 1944 *Flash Gordon* became increasingly painterly, atmospheric, calligraphic, cinematic. Eventually, the artist completely dispensed with balloons, confining the script to narrative legends.

In 1944, with America at war with an adversary more merciless than Ming, Raymond abandoned the strip to join the marine corps, serving as a combat artist in the South Pacific aboard the aircraft carrier USS *Gilbert Islands;* he was never to return to *Flash Gordon.*[2] "Perhaps," mused the late great comic-strip collector Woody Gelman, "it was the grim reality of war that made Raymond forsake his fantasy hero."[3] In any event, Raymond in *Flash Gordon* had met and vanquished the evil empire to which he had obliquely alluded. After the war, Raymond created his third successful strip, *Rip Kirby*. Avoiding the fantastic elements that had enlivened *Flash Gordon*, Raymond chose as his protagonist a bespectacled, pipe-smoking, mild-mannered detective, whom he involved in earthly confrontations with petty criminals. Although beautifully drawn, the strip featured none of the literal or figura-

tive flights of fancy for which *Flash Gordon* was justly famous. In 1956, at the young age of forty-seven, Raymond died in an automobile accident.

While Flash Gordon battled Ming the Merciless, Tarzan combatted jungle adversaries and Prince Valiant waged war against medieval opponents. Both strips, the creations of Canadian-born Harold Foster, contained elements common to *Flash Gordon:* a tall, handsome, aristocratic hero (Tarzan, in reality an English lord; Prince Valiant, son of the King of Thule); an equally well-born, strong-willed, and attractive heroine (Jane, and Aleta, Queen of the Misty Isles); cunning and cruel foes with grossly physical desires; glorious battles, including hand-to-hand combat and epic clashes; exotic, panoramic landscapes; people from many nations and races; and magic, superstition, and fantasy. Inspiring the action was a high code of personal honor; belief in a just war; courtesy toward women and children; family values; wanderlust; and a desire to embrace the unknown.

Foster explained why he chose the Middle Ages as the historic backdrop for *Prince Valiant in the Days of King Arthur:* "The medieval period gave me scope, that's why I picked it. At first I thought of the Crusades but the theme was too limited. With Prince Valiant I have a leeway of almost three centuries due to lack of written records."[4] Created in 1937 — the year of Hitler's repudiation of the Treaty of Versailles and of the Japanese invasion of China — the strip, under the guise of medieval epic, sounded a clarion call for patriotic self-sacrifice and increased military might, and warned of the dangers of appeasement. The reasons for Prince Valiant's violent response to danger are described in early episodes. For example, in the February 13, 1937, inaugural episode Val's father, the King of Thule, is depicted "pursued by his merciless enemies" from his homeland to the chalk cliffs of Britain, a veiled reference to the European diaspora. Met by the savage indigenous inhabitants, the king is forced to retreat further to the fens, the Druidic haunts of prehistoric monsters and uncanny witches. In this primitive environment, the young prince soon learns that the best defense is a good offense. Bloodily dispatching monster, ogre, and villain, Val completes his rites of passage.

Our Story: WHEN THE MISTS OF DAWN LIFT, A SHIP DRAWS INTO THE STRONG-HOLD OF GUNNAR FREYSSON, AND ARMED WARRIORS DISEMBARK.

AND PRINCE VALIANT ORDERS THAT THE WOMEN AND CHILDREN BE HERDED DOWN THE BEACH OUT OF HARM'S WAY.

THEN THEY WAIT BEHIND THE PALISADE FOR THE RETURN OF THE RAIDERS.

WEARIED BEYOND ENDURANCE BY THEIR LONG STRUGGLE ACROSS THE SNOWY MOUNTAINS, THEY SUBMIT WITH HARDLY A WOUND. ALL EXCEPT GUNNAR FREYSSON AND HIS SON, HELGI !

KNOWING THE CRUEL FATE THEIR RAID HAS EARNED THEM, THEY PREFER TO DIE FIGHTING. BOTH DRAW THEIR WEAPONS AND SPRING AT VAL !

WITH MERCIFUL SWIFTNESS VAL CUTS DOWN HIS TWO EXHAUSTED ATTACKERS. "BETTER TO BE A BUTCHER THAN WITNESS HEIR DEEDS HAVE MERITED," HE MUTTERS.

BUT THE SIGHT OF BLOOD INFLAMES HIS MEN AND HE IS HARD PUT TO PREVENT THEM FROM PUTTING THE PRISONERS TO THE SWORD. "HOLD !" HE CRIES. "THESE ARE THE MEN WHO ARE TO REBUILD WHAT THEY HAVE DESTROYED !" NEXT WEEK:- A Debt Paid.

Hal Foster, *Prince Valiant*, May 13, 1956

While abandoning the balloon in favor of the narrative legend, Hal Foster, who created both the Arthurian *Prince Valiant* and the comic-strip adaptation of *Tarzan*, introduced classical compositional devices to the cartoon genre. These include pyramidal arrangements of forms and tunnel-like penetrations into background.

Burne Hogarth, *Tarzan*, April 4, 1948

Hogarth's expressive iconography elevated the comic strip
as art form. Achieved by means of opposition, it included
contrasts of race, gender, and texture, combined in agitated action. Here Hogarth's characters, vigorously alive,
engage in combat, Tarzan in the first frame hurling a figure through space, his feat emphasized by the artist's en-
closure of the action in a narrow vertical space.

All the while, however, contemporary events cast dark shadows in the strip's fantastic world. Foster described this subliminal intrusion: "I wanted a strip that would permit me to do fantasy. I wanted to show magicians, ogres, and dragons beside knights. However, the characters in the strip became too real. . . ."[5] The implicit allusion to Hitler's mad march through Europe was made explicit in the January 21, 1940, episode, wherein Prince Valiant attempts to stem an earlier barbaric invasion. "Three long weeks have passed," the legend tells us, "since Val last saw his little 'Legion of Hun-Hunters.' In the meantime he has learned one great fact: the once-invincible Hun can be beaten. . . . A terrible responsibility for so young a lad — should he fail all Europe will be overrun by the Hun." At the time of the episode's publication, Hitler had triumphantly entered Austria (1938), occupied Czechoslovakia (1939), and invaded Poland (1939). Yet to come were the Nazi invasions of the Netherlands, Belgium, Luxembourg, and France (1940).

The international turbulence of Val's military life contrasts with the domestic tranquility of his personal life. Devoted to king and country, Val is also the embodiment of filial piety and domestic virtue. As the war ends, Val marries the fair Aleta, and soon becomes the father of many children. As the decades pass, his progeny involve Val in some very twentieth-century complications, including the emerging problem of drug abuse. In the November 12, 1967, episode, for example, his contrite son confesses, "Oh mother, I feel terrible. The drug that drives men to madness has been given me and I don't know what awful things I've done under its spell."[6] While acknowledging the changing times, Foster continued to espouse chivalric values in *Prince Valiant* until his retirement in 1971.

The qualities of moral courage, heroic valor, and physical strength characteristic of *Prince Valiant* were also found in *Tarzan*, a strip created in 1929 by Foster but brought to perfection by Burne Hogarth, who did the Sunday page from 1937 to 1950. In Hogarth's *Tarzan* the military metaphors of Foster's *Prince Valiant* were discarded and twentieth-century villains introduced into a primitive world. From August 6, 1944, through March 11, 1945, for example, the Lord of the Jungle engaged in actual battle with real Nazis. So taken was Hogarth

Burne Hogarth, *Tarzan*, May 6, 1945

Burne Hogarth brought to perfection *Tarzan*, endowing the strip with expressive and iconographic significance while technically transforming it. Utilizing frames whose height or length reinforce the power of the image within, Hogarth created classical triangular and fanlike compositions, dramatically lit and seen from multiple angles. This episode, for example, features scenes seen from above and below, cropped compositions, and Tarzan depicted both as he flees into the background and as he rushes toward the reader.

Burne Hogarth, *Tarzan*, February 29, 1948

Copyright © 1948 Edgar Rice Burroughs, Inc.
Original pen and ink drawing.
Swann Collection, Division of Prints and Photographs,
the Library of Congress.

A link between man's primitive past and contemporary civilization, Tarzan mediates between the savagery of the jungle and the corruption of the urban world. Here, Tarzan, loyal to the black Wakambas, rejects the temptations proffered by the villainous white hunter, Marlow.

with this epic struggle that in November 1945 he created a second strip, *Drago*, which depicted the nefarious doings of an unrepentant arch-Nazi, the evil Baron Zodiac. It was in *Tarzan*, however, that Hogarth achieved his celebrated style.

Combining the facial formulas developed by Alex Raymond, the use of large, simplified areas of black and white pioneered by Roy Crane and later perfected by Milton Caniff, and numerous cinematic devices, including the utilization of multiple viewpoints for battle scenes, a technique originated by D. W. Griffith, Hogarth transformed the comic strip from an illustrative vehicle into an intensely personal medium for self-expression.[7]

Based on Renaissance concepts of anatomy and composition, Hogarth's narrative technique was ideally suited to the demands of the adventure strip. His mastery of expressive anatomy, demonstrated in depictions of heavily muscled males in action, earned for him the epithet, "the Michelangelo of the comic strip." His classical compositions — generally featuring a fanlike frieze of figures with Tarzan at its apex — were varied by encasing them in frames of unusual height, length, or width; by suggesting infinite spatial recession by the dramatic play of light and dark areas; and by employing multiple viewpoints, including bird's and worm's-eye angles.

Hogarth's technical proficiency is matched by the imaginative diversity of Tarzan's adventures. While Hal Foster closely followed Edgar Rice Burroughs's original story line, Hogarth ignored the unities of place and time, moving Tarzan from prehistory to the present. Between 1937 and 1950, Tarzan's adventures became increasingly fantastic. In a May 6, 1945, episode, for example, the Lord of the Jungle is transported to the age of the dinosaurs, and menaced by a tyrannosaurus, whose overwhelming size is emphasized by the verticality of the frame in which he is contained. In an April 17, 1949, episode, Norse warriors battle an African tribe. And in a particularly disturbing adventure, Tarzan — bent double — pursues through long, narrow corridors an altogether fantastic race of hybrids whose gigantic, swollen heads rest on spider-like appendages.

During its thirteen years as a Sunday strip, *Tarzan* evolved from adventure epic to psychic drama. In this interior journey, nature becomes an increasingly important vehicle for the expression of Tarzan's emotional states and inner conflicts. On the occasion of the publication of Hogarth's *Jungle Tales of Tarzan*, Walter James Miller, Professor of Contemporary Literature at New York University, provided insight into Tarzan as archetype: "The essential truth of the Tarzan myth is that *man can and must become his own ancestor and descendent. . . .* Tarzan's parents are marooned on a jungle coast. To survive, they must be able to *regress in time* to a primitive outlook, to a primitive reality. . . . Later Tarzan must fight his way *forward into time.*"[8]

Symbolically, Tarzan's journey of self-discovery is mirrored by nature. "When Tarzan feels stultified," emphasizes Professor Miller, "— as by jealousy — the foliage seems to close over his path. When he is sharply aware of his loneliness, his nakedness is surrounded by thorny tendrils. . . . But when he feels free and assertive, the jungle opens into wide pathways. Tarzan's feelings are always externalized."[9] From confrontation with external enemies — such as jungle predators, human foes, and fantastic adversaries, *Tarzan* evolved into an exploration of man's dual and warring nature.

In *Terry and the Pirates* the battle cry sounded in *Flash Gordon*, *Prince Valiant*, and *Tarzan* reached a crescendo. Begun on October 14, 1934, *Terry and the Pirates* encompassed the War in the Pacific, including the Japanese invasion of China, describing these unfolding events in a style suited to the extreme conflicts depicted, a dramatic chiaroscuro that earned its creator, Milton Caniff, the accolade "the Rembrandt of the comics." Like its sister adventure strips, *Terry and the Pirates* featured handsome and well-bred heroes and heroines, coldly ruthless villains and villainesses, exotic locales, culture clash, and supreme self-sacrifice — inspired in content and form by cinematic innovations. Describing the influence of the motion picture, Caniff said:

Orient. Adventure. Pirates. That's it, pirates! Piracy is practiced along the China Coast today just as it was a thousand years ago. The play is cast. The sets are up. Sounds like a movie. Why not? The movies have learned to appeal to the greatest number of people. Use motion picture technic [sic] in the execution. First panel: Long shot with the speaking characters in the middle fore-

Milton Caniff, *Terry and the Pirates*, May 14, 1939

The chivalric code was given a contemporary interpretation
in *Terry and the Pirates*, drawn by Milton Caniff from October 22, 1934, to December 26, 1946. Like the space, jungle, and medieval sagas, this war strip, set in China,
starred all-American heroes who preferred action to reflection. While Caniff employed the same cinematic devices as
did Foster and Hogarth — action rendered from multiple
angles, characters in silhouette, and classical compositions,
he defined action through dramatic contrasts of light and
dark, for which he was designated "the Rembrandt of the
comic strip."

Milton Caniff, *Terry and the Pirates*, January 7, 1945

Reprinted by permission: Tribune Media Services.
Original pen and ink drawing.
Milton Caniff Collection, The Ohio State University Cartoon, Graphic, and
Photographic Arts Research Library.

Terry fondly recalls the Dragon Lady in this wartime episode. Although it was set in contemporary times, Caniff's strip espoused all the chivalric values of a medieval epic.

Milton Caniff, *Dickie Dare*, August 19, 1933

Although best known for his inspiring tales of World War II, Milton Caniff began his cartoon career as a creator of medieval epics. Begun in July 1933, *Dickie Dare* already contained artistic innovations including the use of multiple viewpoints pioneered in film and the use of dramatic contrasts of dark and light areas.

George Wunder, *Terry and the Pirates*, April 26, 19[

Among the many members of the School of Caniff was George Wunder, who succeeded Caniff in December 1946 as the cartoonist for *Terry*.

ground. Second panel: Medium shot with dialogue to move the plot along. Third panel: Semi-closeup to set reader for significant last speech. Fourth panel: Full closeup of speaking character with socko line.[10]

The counterpart of such cinematic calls to arms as the 1943 film *Casablanca*, *Terry and the Pirates* inspired and unified the American public by providing familiar meat-and-potatoes heroes and elevating their adventures into a shared national experience.

Caniff's cinematic contributions to the development of the adventure strip were continued by his assistant, Alfred Andriola. After serving a three-year apprenticeship on *Terry and the Pirates*, Andriola in 1938 began his lyrical comic-strip adaptation of Earl Derr Biggers's detective drama, *Charlie Chan*. In 1943 he created *Kerry Drake*. Stated Andriola, "I write dialogue like a movie continuity, plotting it weeks in advance of the actual drawing."[11]

Ironically, cinematic influence, while vastly enlarging the possible range of artistic expression, was short-lived. The national penchant for technological innovation that transformed the comic strip also led to its demise as an essentially visual medium. Gradually, electronic media, such as radio and television, supplanted the print genres, including the newspaper and magazine, as a means of communication. The need for an expanded gallery of advertisers by a dramatically decreasing number of newspapers led to restrictions on the number and size of comic strips. These reductions in scope and scale, coupled with the code of comic-book self-censorship adopted as a result of the controversy generated by Frederic Wertham's May 29, 1948, *Saturday Review* article, "Comics, Very Funny!" and 1954 book, *Seduction of the Innocent*, provide a backdrop against which was to be enacted the ideological drama of the fifties social satirists.

Milton Caniff, *Terry and the Pirates*, May 31, 1942

Reprinted by permission: Tribune Media Services.
Original pen and ink drawing.
Milton Caniff Collection, The Ohio State University Cartoon, Graphic, and Photographic Arts Research Library.

While contemporary events were alluded to in the conflicts and characters of *Flash Gordon*, a world at war was explicitly envisioned in Milton Caniff's contemporary epic *Terry and the Pirates*. The Japanese invasion of the Pacific is depicted in this nighttime episode.

Dick Calkins and Rick Yager, *Buck Rogers*, 1946

First published on January 7, 1929, *Buck Rogers* embodied man's loftiest ambitions during the depths of the Great Depression. By representing worlds beyond our universe, the creators of *Buck Rogers* celebrated infinite human potential during an era of diminished possibility. While such scenes as that depicted in this 1946 episode are familiar to today's television-era viewer, their dramatic impact at the time of publication was considerable.

Zack Mosley, *Smilin' Jack*, June 28, 1941

While *Terry and the Pirates* described naval encounters in the Pacific, *Smilin' Jack* featured aerial adventures. Begun on October 1, 1933, as *On the Wing*, Smilin' Jack flew his last mission in 1973.

Wayne Boring, *Superman*, n.d.

Created by Siegel and Shuster in 1938, *Superman* embodied unlimited human potential during the dark days of the Holocaust. Unbound by dimensions of time and space, the man of steel commanded as the theater for his heroic exploits all of human history.

Allen Saunders and Elmer Woggon, *Steve Roper*, August 30, 1950

After the War, the dramatic chiaroscuro and action-packed plot of the military epic were adapted to the requirements of the detective story.

Alfred Andriola, *Kerry Drake*, April 28, n.d.

A one-time assistant to Milton Caniff, Alfred Andriola created two strips that bespeak Caniff's influence: *Charlie Chan* and *Kerry Drake*, both detective stories.

V. T. Hamlin, *Alley Oop*, September 24, 1948

Alley Oop appeared on September 9, 1933, one of a series of jungle strips best exemplified by *Tarzan*. Like *Tarzan*, *Alley Oop* featured a jungle setting, a noble savage, and prehistoric beasts. Unlike *Tarzan*, the strip was satiric in nature, harkening back to the slapstick tradition of early cartoons.

Austin Briggs, *Flash Gordon*, June 25, 1944

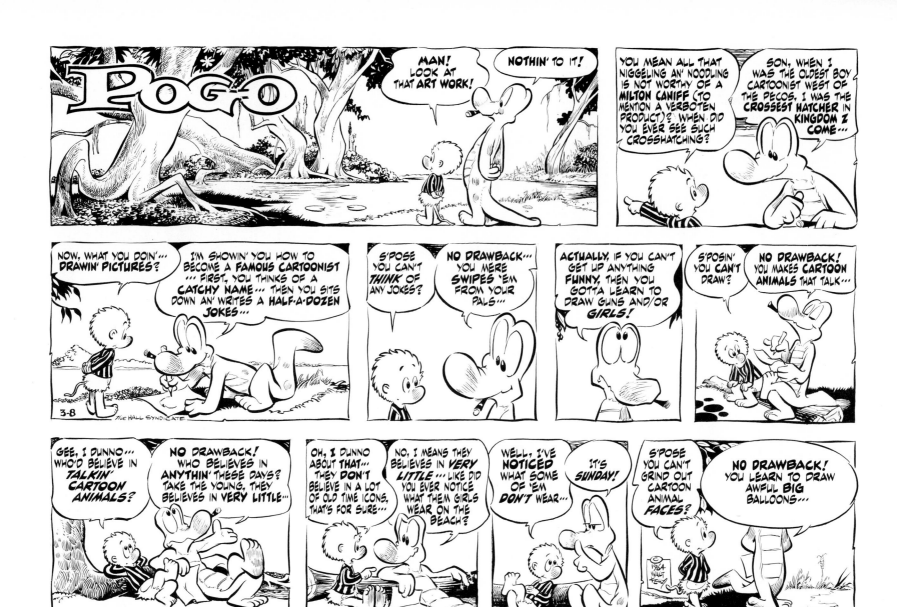

Walt Kelly, *Pogo*, March 8, 1964

CHAPTER **7**

The Anti-hero: Alienation and Social Commentary in the Worlds of *Pogo*, *The Spirit*, *Feiffer*, *Doonesbury*, and *Bloom County*

Detail from Jules Feiffer, *Feiffer*, n.d.

Superman, Flash Gordon, Tarzan, Prince Valiant — heroic titans whose moral might no adversary could withstand — were superseded in the fifties by a new generation of anti-heroes, foremost among whose socially conscious creators was Walt Kelly. Said Kelly in 1959, describing his powerful *Pogo*, "We actually have no heroes as such . . . because I don't believe in heroes."[1] Elsewhere Kelly concluded, "Good cartoonists are subversive. They are against things."[2]

By 1954 there was no surfeit of targets for the cartoonist's potent pen. The most visible of which was Dr. Frederic Wertham, who that year had published *Seduction of the Innocent*, a controversial attack on comic books and their creators, which laid responsibility for all the ills of the modern age, including murder, rape, and juvenile delinquency, on the shoulders of America's comic-book cartoonists. Reacting to this and similar criticism, the Comics Magazine Association of America in 1954 adopted an official code of comic-book self-censorship, formalizing a practice that for years had been followed by syndicates and newspapers.

This official code of self-censorship was later revised in 1971 "to meet contemporary standards of conduct and morality." Today its provisions include mandated swift and sure retribution for sin ("in every instance good shall triumph over evil and the criminal be punished for his misdeeds"); the apotheosis of authority ("Policemen, judges, government officials, and respected institutions shall not be presented in such a way as to create disrespect for established authority"); the glorification of marriage and the family ("All situations dealing with the family should have as their ultimate goal the protection of the children and family life"); an attempt to stop drug traffic ("Narcotics or drug addiction shall not be presented except as a vicious habit"); and the prohibition of obscenity ("Profanity, obscenity, smut, vulgarity, or words or symbols which have acquired undesirable meanings . . . are forbidden").[3] Whether motivated by pragmatic business considerations (parents, the audience of Wertham's cautionary tale, controlled the purse strings of progeny), or by an attempt to reestablish values undermined by time, technology, and greed, the code — as historical hindsight confirms — did not reflect what was happening in the "real" world: government corruption continued, divorce rates skyrocketed, and drugs became the big-

G. B. Trudeau, *Doonesbury*, June 26, 1974

Berke Breathed, *Bloom County*, 1985

The worst fears of his characters are made manifest in this dream sequence. In contrast to the symbolic conflicts enacted in Winsor McCay's *Little Nemo in Slumberland*, the nightmares of Bloom County residents reflect everyday concerns, including fear of legal reprisal by rival syndicates.

gest of businesses and a source of international concern. What the code accomplished, however, was a restriction on comic-book content paralleling the contemporaneous diminution of newspaper-strip form. Comic commentators reacted to such institutionalized restriction by asserting their constitutional right of free expression. The first to do so was Kelly, whose call to artistic arms came in an animal allegory.

From April 22 to June 17, 1954, Senator Joseph McCarthy conducted television hearings aimed at exposing communist influence in the U.S. Army. The hearings were the culmination of a chain of events set in motion shortly after World War II. Following the euphoria of international military victory, the government set its sights on domestic enemies: gangsters, the subject of Senator Estes Kefauver's 1951 investigation of organized crime; communists, the target of Senator McCarthy's hearings, given impetus by the March 29, 1951, conviction of Julius and Ethel Rosenberg for wartime espionage, and dramatized by their execution on June 19, 1953; and finally, cartoonists. As Milton Caniff recalled,

> Senator Kefauver and a well-meaning committee of Congressmen were holding hearings relating to the evils of the comic books of the day. This was not directed toward newspaper cartoons, but the publicity was touching us and rubbing off. Besides, the comic-book cartoonists were brothers. Kelly organized a counter-move against the negative press all cartoons were getting. In the U.S. Court House on Foley Square in New York a group of cartoonists and illustrators came early and occupied the front seats. As the hearings went on, the Congressmen became aware that we were drawing their portraits. It is hard not to "pose" when that is going on. Before it ended, the jury was hardly listening to the unhappy book artists. After the session we went from one legislator to another delivering the art. Each Congressman flew home with a half dozen drawings of himself — and a dim recall of the testimony. The Elf of the Okefenokee had cast another spell![4]

In *Pogo*, begun on October 4, 1948, in the *New York Star*, Kelly was to take on his most formidable adversary, Senator Joseph McCarthy. The stage of his self-proclaimed "subversive" strip was set in the Okefenokee swamp, a wildlife refuge. *Pogo*'s dramatis personae included Pogo the Possum, an incurable optimist and distant spiritual relative of Krazy Kat; Albert, the crotchety alligator; Dr. Howland Owl, an inventor; Porkypine, a misanthrope; and Captain Churchy La Femme, a turtle. "I chose animals," said Kelly, "largely because you can do more with animals. They don't hurt as easily, and it is possible to make them more believable in an exaggerated pose than it is the human."[5] Kelly described his Okefenokee as "a last frontier, a proper setting for American fairytales. . . . The only thing that inspired me toward an involvement with the Southern swampland was my conviction that people are universally frail. It struck me that perhaps Southerners as a much maligned people would not mind being a little more downtrodden."[6] Of the strip's scope the artist reflected,

> Normalcy in POGO has included Simple J. Malarkey, whom many took to be a mid-west Senator in the mid-fifties; an owl who spoke in the stammering rhythms of a President of the United States; a speakeasy school for all children in Virginia who were barred from attendance because the State felt it should close *all* schools to stave off the perils of segregation [sic]; and recently the rightist Jack Acid Society which was an outright attack on all Vigilante Committees. . . . It should be made clear that to leave out treatment of political themes would be to ignore a mine of comic material so vast that it has at this point merely had its surface sounded with a Geiger counter.[7]

Influences on Kelly's artistic development include the work of George Herriman ("He had an underlying philosophy," observed Kelly, "which was that the gentle will survive"[8]); the Walt Disney Studio, where Kelly worked as an animator from 1935 to 1941, assisting in the productions of *Snow White*, *Fantasia*, *Dumbo*, *Pinocchio*, *The Reluctant Dragon*, and *Baby Weems*;[9] and the *Uncle Remus* stories of Joel Chandler Harris, whose inspiration Kelly acknowledged in 1953 with *Uncle Pogo's So So Stories*.[10]

For his attack on McCarthy, Kelly drew on yet another inspirational source, Lewis Carroll's *Alice in Wonderland*, a classic repopularized by Disney's 1951 animation. Carroll's depiction of the trial of the Knave of Hearts by the Red Queen, asserted Kelly, "is one of the greatest pieces of satirical writing. Whether he intended it that way or not, I don't know, but it certainly fit our whole McCarthy period."[11] In *The Pogo Stepmother Goose* (1954), the artist excoriated the senator, casting him in the mad role of the Red Queen ("Off with their heads!"). The U.S.

Will Eisner, *The Spirit*, splash page, December 1, 1940

The playful nature of Eisner's reluctant superhero, the Spirit, is revealed in this delightful pen and ink drawing, wherein the Spirit chastises an amorous admirer. The aggressive female and bashful male recurred in many adventure strips, from Al Capp's *Li'l Abner* to Jerome Siegel and Jerry Shuster's *Superman*. In Eisner and Iger's *Sheena, Queen of the Jungle*, the artists again employed this formula, creating a dominant superheroine who saved both ignorant savages and her innocent fiancé from multiple misadventures.

Senate followed suit, censuring McCarthy on December 2, 1954.

Kelly's depiction of McCarthy as the Red Queen was his second satirization of the senator, who appeared as Simple J. Malarkey in *Pogo* from May 1, 1953, through October 16, 1954.[12] In later life, Kelly expressed skepticism regarding the impact of his impassioned denunciation of this twentieth-century witch-hunter and McCarthy's fall from political grace: "McCarthy, in our country, finally got in trouble with his own private court, the Senate."[13]

Space, jungle, and Arthurian England, the exotic areas explored by other comic-strip adventurers, were abandoned in favor of interior journeys in the work of Will Eisner, another great social satirist of the fifties. Drawing upon the traditions of Yiddish theater, including self-deprecating monologue, Eisner on June 2, 1940, created the most unique of superheroes, the self-doubting and befuddled Spirit.

In a speech delivered at the Philadelphia Comic Expo on July 9, 1983, and transcribed in the March 1984 *Comics Journal*, Eisner described his protagonist's reluctant status as a superhero and ongoing identity crisis:

> As far as the *Spirit* is concerned, the only reason the Spirit had a mask and wore gloves is because it was purely a spineless concession on my part to the syndicate. When we started, they said what are you going to do, and I said I'd like to do a series of short stories, and they said, do a costumed character. . . . The Spirit was as confused about his role in Society as I was.[14]

Eisner quickly involved his reluctant superhero in a series of ill-fated adventures, each of which would end accidentally and ambiguously. The Spirit's adversary and amour was simultaneously New York City, the scene of the artist's birth and boyhood. Unlike Superman's Metropolis and Batman's Gotham, which are glamourous symbols of modern progress, The Spirit's city is a sad stage of urban blight, possessing a cunning life of its own, the ultimate catalyst for the many misadventures that unfold therein. Unlike the tentative nature of The Spirit himself, the city is vigorously aggressive, asserting itself immediately in the strip's first frame, the famous Eisner "splash page" that introduces each adventure.

The Spirit's limited distribution does not account for Eisner's enor-

Will Eisner, *The Spirit*, splash page, April 3, 1949

The fanciful, tongue-in-cheek adventures of Eisner's *Spirit* include those involving time travel, myth, and magic. Often the artist used the strip's title as an integral part of the episode's first page, referred to as the "splash page."

Jules Feiffer, *Feiffer*, n.d.

Two memorable figures recur in *Feiffer*: Bernard Mergendeiler, the embodiment of self-doubt, and, shown here, the female dancer, a symbol of optimism and human endurance.

mous influence. Instead, this can be attributed to his personal generosity in hiring numerous fledgling cartoonists, chief among them Jules Feiffer. From Eisner, Feiffer was to borrow urban setting, interior monologue, and a sense of benighted wonder at the absurdity of the universe. Excising the trappings of the adventure strip, Feiffer was to explore explicitly the obsessions only implicit to Eisner's universe.

Born in the Bronx on January 26, 1929, Feiffer attended Pratt Institute from 1947 to 1951 while working as Eisner's assistant. Drafted in 1951, Feiffer served in the U.S. Signal Corps, where he created animated cartoons and originated *Munro*, a comic strip chronicling the adventures of a four-year-old who is conscripted by mistake. More important to Feiffer's artistic development than academic training or professional preparation, however, were the impact of his urban environment and the influence of contemporary Jewish comedians such as Mort Sahl, Mike Nichols, and Elaine May, sources similar to those that had inspired Eisner.[15] Indeed, Feiffer's protagonists, most often depicted isolated center stage against a blank background, can be interpreted as stand-up comics spouting humorous monologues.

Begun in October 1956 as *Sick, Sick, Sick*, Feiffer's strip first and fittingly appeared in the *Village Voice*, the house organ of the fifties counterculture. ("After failing to sell cartoons to more conventional markets," the artist recounted, "I began giving them free to the *Village Voice*."[16]) *Sick, Sick, Sick* soon found an avid intellectual audience. Like the humorous expressions of pioneer cartoonist Milt Gross, creator of *Banana Oil* (1921) and *Count Screwloose of Tooloose* (1929), Feiffer's *Sick, Sick, Sick* immediately entered the Beat lexicon. Like Harry Hershfield, the first comic-strip artist to celebrate his Jewish heritage, Feiffer affirmed his ethnicity, transforming the slapstick vaudevillian humor of his cartoon progenitors into tongue-in-cheek contemporary psychoanalytic soul-searching.

Feiffer's protagonists personify the ying and yang of human potential. The battle of the sexes, a staple of comic humor from George McManus to S. Clay Wilson, in Feiffer's work suggests a Jungian interpretation. The creative force, or anima, is personified by the female Dancer, an embodiment of optimistic artistic transcendence; self-doubt and hopelessness, by the character of Bernard Mergendeiler.[17]

Biographical self-reference, heavily disguised by early comic creators such as McCay and Herriman, and thickly veiled by creators of adventure strips such as Foster and Hogarth, entered the cartoon's thematic arsenal in *Sick, Sick, Sick*. At the same time, Feiffer abandoned conventional narrative elements, including intricate plot, sequential storytelling, and unifying backgrounds, in favor of discrete episodes plumbing specific personal or social issues. Feiffer's protagonists are heroes in miniature, valiant only in their futile attempts to conserve their environment and to control themselves.

Continuity in the strip (in 1959 retitled *Feiffer*) was maintained through its reference to current events and its depiction of successive presidencies.[18] In depicting Eisenhower, Feiffer drew on the grand cartoon tradition. "Too lazy in those years to work from photographs, I cast him from the image in my mind: Daddy Warbucks."[19] As the years and the presidencies rolled by, Feiffer again made reference to the grand tradition in his portraits of Gerald Ford. "I put an empty tin can on his head and drew him as Happy Hooligan, Frederick Opper's foolish hero in the Sunday comics just past the turn of the century. Hooligan couldn't get anything right either, and we loved him for it. I could just as easily have drawn him as Joe Palooka."[20]

The personal and political are united in *Feiffer* by the power principle. "Powerlessness," declared the artist, "is my meat, home base, what I like best to draw about."[21] Among the unresolved struggles enacted in the strip are the battle of the sexes (in which both combatants are unarmed), male rivalry, race relations, power politics, and the threat of a nuclear holocaust. "The Bomb," mused Feiffer, "seemed to symbolize our post-war helplessness. We were the biggest, richest, most powerful country in the world and we felt surrounded. . . . Everyone felt powerless. Blacks felt powerless, as did all minorities; middle-class whites felt powerless, corporations felt powerless, environmentalists felt powerless, homosexuals felt powerless and thugs who preyed on homosexuals felt powerless, and the police felt powerless."[22] Later, the themes of gender antagonism, spiritual impotence, and nuclear annihilation first sounded in *Feiffer* were to resound with nihilistic variation in *Raw* magazine.

More immediately related to *Feiffer*, however, is *Doonesbury*, the

WHO LOST VIET NAM?

"NOT I," SAID IKE. "I JUST SENT MONEY."

"NOT I," SAID JACK. "I JUST SENT ADVISORS."

"NOT I," SAID LYNDON. "I JUST FOLLOWED JACK."

"NOT I," SAID DICK. "I JUST HONORED JACK AND LYNDON'S COMMITMENTS."

"NOT I," SAID JERRY. "WHAT WAS THE QUESTION?"

"YOU LOST VIETNAM," SAID HENRY, "BECAUSE YOU DIDN'T TRUST YOUR LEADERS."

Jules Feiffer, *Feiffer*, n.d.

Counterpointing the self-obsessing of many episodes are editorializing indictments of the political process. Here Feiffer poses the question "Who lost Viet Nam?" to a succession of presidents, depicting Gerald Ford as comic-strip character Happy Hooligan, complete with tin-can hat.

G. B. Trudeau, *Doonesbury*, March 8, 1988

Like *Feiffer*, *Doonesbury* tackles controversial issues and names public figures, as in this post–Supreme Court decision episode.

Berke Breathed, *Bloom County*, 1988

Breathed satirizes xenophobia and self-promotion in this delightful episode.

1970 creation of Garry Trudeau. Initially a saga of sixties student life, *Doonesbury* developed into an increasingly complex critique of specific social policies. Continuing Feiffer's tradition of economy of stylistic means, including calligraphic caricature and vestigial background, Trudeau boldly stated current concerns, pushing to the limit the permissible in newspaper strips. Feiffer had earlier described the phenomenon of newspaper self-censorship: "In 1960 I was courted by the Hale Syndicate for national syndication. I told them that I was worried about selling out. I was afraid of losing my status as a cult cartoonist. . . . After a year of syndication I began to see censorship not as a problem but as a form of quality control. If they didn't run me, it meant I was doing something right."[23] Like Feiffer, Trudeau numbered among his targets politics and poverty, ambition and its discontents, intellectual and artistic posturing, and the office of the presidency. Trudeau's cast of characters, like Feiffer's, matures with the passage of time. From their beginnings as Walden communards, his gentle, well-bred, upwardly mobile protagonists have become admen, congressional aides, artists, earls, and film stars, all the while endlessly obsessing.

Trudeau's minimalist artistic style is eloquently exemplified in the artist's recent satirization of Vice President Dan Quayle, whom he represented by a single, drifting, white feather.

Censorship itself has often been the self-satiric subject of *Doonesbury*. In a July 8, 1988, Sunday strip, for example, Dr. Whoopee (a.k.a. Sal Doonesbury) lectures on AIDS awareness. In response to a question from the audience about public-service announcements ("How about in the comics?"), "Dr. Whoopee" proclaims, "No, no, it's too serious a subject." In the March 7, 1988, daily, Trudeau celebrates the judgment in *Flynt v. Falwell*, in which the Supreme Court unanimously rejected the Reverend Jerry Falwell's claim of intentional infliction of emotional distress occasioned by the publication of an advertisement parody. Quoting from the Court's decision upholding the right of artists to satirize public figures, the strip reads:

In Washington, D.C., a landmark decision is handed down. "One of the prerogatives of American citizenship is the right to criticize public men. . . ." "Were we to hold otherwise, there can be little doubt that political cartoonists would be subjected to damage awards without showing that their work falsely defamed its subject. The judgement of the Court of Appeals is accordingly reversed." Whew.

Paradoxically, Trudeau's adaptation of Feiffer's lean, clean line and cold eye led Feiffer to experiment himself. In August 1988 Feiffer described this impetus to Gary Groth of the *Comics Journal:* "I was simply boxed in and defeated by my own logic. . . . The other thing that helped me get out of it was Trudeau and other people who came along and were doing the same thing, and finally I realized that I was being forced out of my own position, because everybody was beginning to look too much alike."[24]

Among those whose style is also indebted to Feiffer's pioneering simplifications is Berke Breathed. Whereas Garry Trudeau can be seen as the artistic heir of Jules Feiffer, however, Berke Breathed may be seen as that of Walt Kelly. In *Bloom County*, Breathed created an agrarian world akin to Kelly's rural swamp, in which a mélange of outsiders and animals comment on the foibles of contemporary life. Unlike Trudeau's kindly upper-middle-class cast, which only occasionally includes the absolutely disenfranchised, Breathed's dramatis personae are drawn from historically powerless groups — poor whites, blacks, people with disabilities — and assembled in a boarding house. Unlike the conscience-stricken yuppies of *Doonesbury*, the *Bloom County* boarders neither come from nor aspire to traditional nuclear families or professional castes. Strip lawyer Steve Dallas is a self-centered schlemiel. Ambitions are cast in whimsical, poetic allegories of flight — such as the aspiration to become an astronaut. Unlike the tight thematic unity of *Doonesbury*'s plots, those of *Bloom County* are impressionistic, staccato, and disparate, creating by accretion a bizarre and wacky universe. In this weird world a personal computer worships a television, which it assumes to be God, and animal protagonists embody the best and worst of the human psyche. Bill the Cat is all id, Opus the Penguin extreme superego.

In October 1988 Breathed described the evolution of his terminally nasty feline to Mark Jannot of the *Comics Journal:* "That was about 1982 when I'd just started cartooning. I'd probably just created Bill the

Cat as a response to Garfield, which had exploded I think about a year or two before. . . . I had watched Garfield go from an underground comic strip with a mean and snarly cat to being strictly a creation to sell merchandise."[25]

While Bill the Cat is a countercultural assertion, Opus is Everyman. Continued Breathed, "He is what things happen to, he is the person who is the recipient of much of the action."[26]

Synthesizing his influences, Breathed stated:

> If you were to break me down as a cartoonist, as to what my influences have been, it would be Jules Feiffer and Walt Disney. And I think that's what Bloom County is a combination of. . . . We're commenting, we're letting people know how we feel about things, we're picking out the ironies, we're refining them, and we're revealing the hypocrisy where we see it. But I have no presumption that I'm going to change anybody's attitudes.[27]

The slick sweetness of the Disney Studios' animated animals and the introspective musings of Feiffer's self-conscious intellectuals are synthesized in biting, blue-collar *Bloom County* satire and in Breathed's 1989 surrealist strip, *Outland.*

Kelly, Eisner, Feiffer, Trudeau, Breathed, social satirists all, these artists have each reacted to the same stimulus — man's war against himself. The fragile impermanence of human relationships in a world of instantaneous change, the specter of nuclear annihilation, our bumbling body politic, the mad military, domestic surveillance — such are the subjects that inspire these gentle strips, all penned in the spirit of George Herriman, all expressing whimsically the vague hope that the meek will somehow inherit or at least remain on the earth. Perhaps Feiffer best described the collective consciousness of such cartoonists: "The more outraged I am as a citizen, the more fun I find as a cartoonist. In the long and short run I may not affect much but the state of my own sanity. The cartoon keeps it in bounds, it continues the illusion of hope, it raises for me the distant possibility of actual solutions to some of our problems. That possibility is my muse."[28]

8

Notes from the Underground

R. Crumb, *Self-portrait*, 1987

Original pen and ink drawing.
From the collection of Mark J. Cohen, Realtor.

There is an important chapter of comic art in America that existed outside the mainstream, coming into its own during the turbulent era of the 1960s. As the sixties dawned, the national psyche experienced both frightening social insecurity and heady idealism. Whereas the assassination of President Lincoln in 1865 was the final act in the Civil War drama, the murder of President Kennedy in 1963 was the prologue to ten years of domestic division. While anticipation of global conflict in the forties inspired the creation of immortal and omnipotent supermen, the zeitgeist of Vietnam spawned a short-lived generation of self-centered and socially irresponsible anti-heroes created by an underground circle of artists. These artists were primarily West Coast–based; prominent among them were Gilbert Shelton, S. Clay Wilson, Trina Robbins, and Robert Crumb. Of this group Robert Crumb, creator of the irrepressible Fritz the Cat, was the leading voice.

Described by writer Robert Hughes as "a kind of American Hogarth, a moralist with a blown mind,"[1] Crumb was born in Philadelphia on August 30, 1943, one of five children of career marine Charles Crumb and his wife, Beatrice Hall. The itinerant life of an army brat, which included sojourns in Albert Lea, Minnesota; Ames, Iowa; Oceanside, California; Upper Darby, Pennsylvania, and — later — Milford and Dover, Delaware, is reflected in the wanderings of the powerful characters Crumb was later to create. Among these were "the gnomic sage, Mr. Natural, the Priapus of the Midwest"; "that morsel of 13-year-old jailbait, Honeybunch Kaminsky," and — of course — that feline road warrior, Fritz the Cat.[2]

Completely self-taught, Crumb, like the first fathers of American illustration, achieved his technical proficiency as a journeyman illustrator, first for the Latex Corporation, then at the American Greetings Corporation in Cleveland. The broad themes stated by Crumb, including the quest for spiritual meaning, the search for personal identity, and the conflict between man's higher and lower natures, were first explored in a series of juvenile comic strips that he created with his brother Charles. Combining adventure, animal, domestic, and fantasy genres, these were contained in *Foo* (1958), a self-published magazine that Crumb peddled door-to-door, and in *The Yum-Yum Book* (1963–64), published by Scrim-

R. Crumb, *Fritz Bugs Out*, 1965

From R. Crumb's *Fritz the Cat: Three Big Stories!*, 1969

Fritz the Cat tunes in, turns on, and drops out of the college scene, following advice offered by a crow reminiscent of Paul Terry's 1946 animation, *Heckle 'n' Jeckle.*

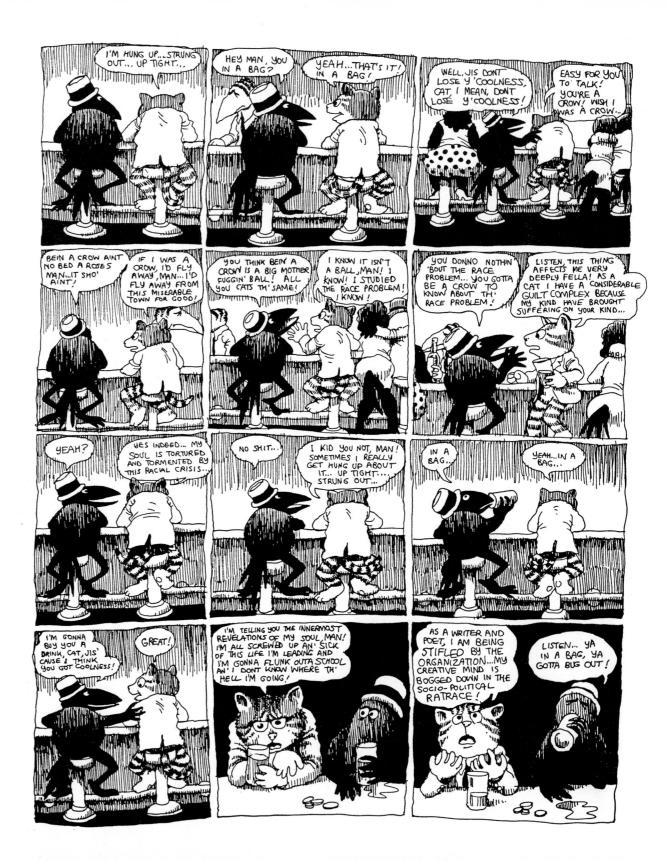

shaw Press in 1975. Although juvenalia, this work was endowed with a power beyond its progenitor's youth. In it, sure pencil and brushstrokes spin action-packed yarns of picaresque heroes restrained by time and taboo.

Although self-taught, Crumb absorbed the influences of a host of artists, among them — according to Crumb — the great medieval artist Hieronymus Bosch; the northern Renaissance painter of peasants Pieter Breughel; the English satirist William Hogarth; American political cartoonist Thomas Nast; and contemporary comic artists Carl Barks, John Stanley, Harvey Kurtzman, and Basil Wolverton. But Crumb's talent as both artist and author link him most closely with master satirist Al Capp. Exciting plots, explosive dialogue, and vigorously expressive line are characteristic of both, as are their identification with the outsider, dislike of pretension, distrust of government, and preoccupation with the powerful and the powerless. Sadists and masochists, powerful females and impotent males populate both their worlds, which are vigorously composed. Corrupting urban odysseys, naive anti-heroes, such are the elements common to these chroniclers of the political right and left.

The raunchy feline protagonist that was to become Fritz appears in many of Crumb's early stories. The artist recalled the cat's genesis: "My brother Charles and I did a lot of 'two-man' comics all through our teen years. . . . Fred became one of the characters in our 'Pogo'esque animal two-mans. Charles' characters began calling Fred 'Fritz.' So then his name became 'Fritz.' His personality gradually developed. I started doing long solo stories with Fritz as the star character."[3]

Despite the fantastic nature of Fred/Fritz's early adventures, the strips contained fledgling autobiographical references. Such autobiography — eschewed by the comic strip's first creators — was to characterize comics created by the baby-boom generation.

For example, in *Cat Life* (1959–60) Fred is manhandled by the artist's sister Sandra and rescued by Crumb himself. Observes Fred, "that human with the glasses named Robert sure is kind."[4] Furthermore, the feline Fred's father is "macho," as was Crumb's marine father, later satirized as "Whiteman." "You wouldn't want me to think that my own son was a chicken . . . now would ya, . . . SON?" chides Papa cat.[5] Soon

Fred became Fritz, stood upright and tomcatted. Like the family pet that had inspired Crumb, Fred/Fritz was now "your typical big old nasty dirty tomcat."[6] Among his first female victims is Fred, the Teen-Age Girl Pigeon, a groupie enamored of Fritz, who has become a rock star. Fred pursues Fritz, who gallantly escorts her to his bed, wherein he devours her.[7]

Inspired by Beat-generation novelist Jack Kerouac, in 1965 Crumb sounded the seductive, picaresque theme of the open urban road in the extended narrative "Fritz Bugs Out." In so doing, Crumb captured the imagination of student America, which answered his comic clarion call to tune in, turn on, and drop out. "As a writer and poet," proclaims Fritz, now a college student, "it is my duty to get out there and dig the world . . . to swing with the whole friggun' scene while there's still time!!!"[8] Emboldened by a vision of unlimited spiritual freedom, Fritz sets his books, shackles of his student life, ablaze. Free from collegiate fetters, Fritz — like Little Orphan Annie before him — embarks on a cross-country odyssey. In his wanderings, however, Fritz encounters not the "good country people" of Harold Gray's white America, but ghetto hustlers, including jive-talking crows (a nod to cartoon prototypes Heckle 'n' Jeckle), who advise him, "Ya in a bag, ya gotta bug out!"[9] Momentarily inspired by the plight of the masses, a strident Fritz preaches revolution to the ghetto residents in the cadences of an inner-city preacher: "You have carried heavy burdens for the bosses! You have sweat your lives away for the bosses! The bosses, they ride around in limousines! The bosses, they're eating strawberries and cream! Come the revolution there gonna be no more limousines! Come the revolution there gonna be no more strawberries and cream!"[10]

Another early incarnation of Fritz was that of secret agent. Exploiting the then-current popularity of Ian Fleming's *James Bond*, Crumb in 1965 cast the cat as "Special Agent for the C.I.A."[11] As the saga unfolds, the feline secret agent, wearing shades and piloting a speeding automobile, is stopped while en route to "headquarters" by an ursine traffic cop. While the officer is issuing the ticket, Fritz speeds away. At headquarters, like Bond before him, Fritz is besieged by Miss Oglemouse and a bevy of beautiful mammal secretaries. Ushered into the presence of "the Chief," Fritz is given a dangerous assignment — subversion of the "Chinese ultimate weapon," a "sinister mysterious weapon that doesn't even use nuclear energy!"[12] In a heavy-handed satire of Cold War paranoia, the Chief describes the dangers of the assignment:

> If there's one thing I hate worse than a Communist, it's a Chinese Communist, and that's what our big threat is today! They're utterly ruthless . . . vicious . . . heartless . . . unmercifully cruel . . . they've devised torture methods far worse than anything the Nazis could think of! That's why I'm putting you on this assignment, Fritz . . . you've got nerves of steel . . . guts of iron! . . . The survival of Western civilization may depend on your success![13]

Arriving in Peking, Fritz is immediately captured and taken to Captain Stin Ki Chin Ki, "Head of Secret Police Force! Most feared man in are [sic] of China!" who consigns him to the U.S.A. Torture Room.[14] There Fritz is seduced by counterspy Su Su, "Chinese sex bomb and beautiful temptress," who begs him to take her with him to "Amerika."[15] Her plea is overheard by Captain Chin Ki, who consigns the pair to a bottomless pit, where they are swallowed by a monster but escape by threading the labyrinth of his intestine. Boarding a mining cart, the pair penetrate the secret laboratory of "Tung Nchiki, number one scientist of the People's Republic of China," who reveals the secret of the dread Chinese weapon — its capacity to carry 400 million Chinese, who will soon be dropped on the United States.[16] As the Chinese prepare to execute him, Fritz describes the many attractions of America: "It's the land of the free and the home of the brave . . . where everybody can think and say what they damn well please, without havin' to worry about a firing squad."[17] The scientist, however, is more interested in sports cars than ideology. Tung launches the rocket and, with Fritz and Su Su, parachutes into Detroit. Tung lands a job with General Motors and Su Su goes to modeling school, the contemporary version of living happily ever after.[18]

Such strips were to see publication neither in the papers nor in traditional comic books. Excluded by virtue of subject, they were intentionally conceived in violation of the Code of the Comics Magazine Association of America. Whereas the comics code forbade "distrust of

106

Gilbert Shelton and Dave Sheridan, *Fat Freddy's Cat — I Led Nine Lives!*, n.d.

Among the many cynical feline protagonists beloved of the underground movement was Fat Freddy's Cat, an offshoot of Shelton's *Fabulous Furry Freak Brothers*.

the forces of law," Crumb fostered such distrust. While the code decried "scenes of excessive violence," Crumb gloried in graphic, Gouldesque depictions of it. Whereas the code explicitly prohibited the representation of "nudity," "rape," "seduction," and "sex perversion" in the name of "protection of family life," Crumb attacked that institution itself, portraying it as the pedophile's purview.

Instrumental in introducing Crumb's work to America at large were traditional book publishers. In 1968, Viking issued — albeit with two abridged pages — *R. Crumb's Head Comix*, a comprehensive sampler of such favorites as Fritz, Mr. Natural, and The Old Pooperoo. In 1969, Ballantine published *R. Crumb's Fritz the Cat: Three Big Stories!* Such compendiums served to nationalize Crumb's audience. Previously, his work had appeared in the underground press, including the *East Village Other*, where his contributions date from October 1967; *Yarrowstalks*, a Philadelphia tabloid, in which Mr. Natural first appeared in May 1967; and the notorious *Zap Comix*, published in San Francisco by Apex Novelties, the contents of which resulted in numerous obscenity trials.

Reflecting their creator's youthful exuberance, the first Fritz episodes are characterized by joie de vivre, economy of means, delicacy of touch. Later work, recalling the riotous vulgarity of style and subject in such comic-strip antecedents as Frederick Opper's *Happy Hooligan*, Gus Edson's *Gumps*, and Al Capp's *Li'l Abner*, is agitated in style and dark in vision. For example, "Fritz the Cat Doubts His Masculinity" documents the protagonist's depression, and "Fritz the No-Good" the world of the welfare recipient.[19] The exuberant self-confidence of the single Fritz of 1965 is eroded by the mean-spirited self-loathing of the drug-crazed, unemployed, married father of 1968. Rejected by his long-suffering wife, a stoned and shiftless Fritz mutters, "Now . . . now I'm free to get rid of all my repressions an' live out my fantasies."[20] Instead of exploring the limits of personal freedom, however, Fritz seeks solace from Winston, his former girlfriend, and falls in with a gang of sadistic sexist revolutionaries. While attempting to blow up a bridge, Fritz is foiled by the police and incarcerated. That sixties staple, "a legal-defense fund," is created to spring him from the slammer.[21]

R. Crumb, *Mr. Natural Meets God*, n.d.

Copyright R. Crumb. From *R. Crumb's Head Comix*, 1988.

Created in 1967, Mr. Natural was a laid-back philosopher who shared many physical attributes with God the Father.

Gus Edson, *The Gumps*, June 6, 1937

The vitality of such early domestic satires as *The Gumps*,
which ran from February 12, 1917, through 1949, continues
in the autobiographical family sagas now penned by former
underground cartoonists.

R. Crumb and Aline Kominsky-Crumb, *Aline 'n' Bob in Our Lovely Home*, page from *Weirdo*, no. 23, 1988

A collaboration between husband and wife, this late domestic strip in the tradition of such family sagas as *The Gumps* and *Gasoline Alley* is full of wry observation on the human comedy.

H. C. Fisher, *Mutt and Jeff*, 1919

Billy De Beck, *Barney Google*, March 16, 1932

The underground artists of the sixties sought inspiration in the sight gags and slapstick humor of the comic strip's early masters, among them Bud Fisher and Billy De Beck.

Shortly thereafter, Fritz "Becomes a Drug Addict."[22] And, finally, in 1972, flush from the success of his animated cartoon, Fritz becomes an obnoxious "Superstar" and is murdered by one of the many women he has wronged.[23] Describing Fritz's demise, Crumb commented, "And so, finally, he had to be 'offed.' In 1972 I felt compelled to have him killed. It was the only way I could resolve in my own mind what had become of him. He's definitely better off dead. Another casualty of the 'sixties."[24]

Fritz's transformation from plucky optimist to self-indulgent cynic reflects changes both in Crumb's personal life and in the national character. Between 1959 and 1972, Fritz's thirteen-year lifespan, President John F. Kennedy had been assassinated, the Reverend Martin Luther King, Jr., and Senator Robert F. Kennedy murdered, and the United States mired in the quicksand of Vietnam. The beginning of the seventies was marked by the drug-induced death of countercultural icon after icon: Jimi Hendrix, Janice Joplin, Jim Morrison. During the same period, Crumb met and married Dana Morgan (1964), worked intermittently at American Greetings Corporation in Cleveland (1962–65), began experimenting with LSD (1965), "escaped" to San Francisco when he "met two guys in a bar who said they were driving west,"[25] fathered a son, Jesse (1968), suffered, to his horror, the reincarnation of his beloved comic cat as a Ralph Bakshi animation (1970), experienced a nervous breakdown (1971), and met the woman who would become his second wife, Aline Kominsky.[26] The early idealism of the sixties gave way to the sad cynicism of the seventies. The altered consciousness of youth gave way to the depression of early middle age.

The most traditional of Crumb's comic prototypes, Fritz was to spawn a line of cynical feline successors. Like George Herriman's Krazy Kat and Pat Sullivan's lonely outsider, Felix the Cat, Fritz was a bewildered wanderer in a hostile world. He was followed by a legion of wise-guy comic cats including Gilbert Shelton's Fat Freddie's Cat; Kim Deitch's Waldo the Cat; Jim Davis's Garfield; and Berke Breathed's Bill the Cat. Of all these, however, Fritz was the most anthropomorphized. Physically partaking of near-human attributes, Fritz also shared an angst-ridden, guilt-driven psyche. It is impossible to imagine Krazy, Felix, Fat Freddie's Cat, Garfield, or Bill the Cat beset by domestic woes, obsessed with relationships, or fixated on mortality. The vulnerability of Fritz is made clear by such comparisons, as is the scope of Crumb's artistic landscape.

Fritz was not Crumb's only creation during this turbulent period. In 1967, he began two of his most successful strips: *Mr. Natural*, which in May first appeared in *Yarrowstalks*, no. 1, and *Mr. Snoid*.[27] While Fritz was a street fighter alternately overwhelmed by responsibilities and corrupted by success, Mr. Natural and the Snoid personified psychic dualisms: light and dark, superego and id. Sporting a long white beard and robe, Mr. Natural is a modern Moses, his message: "[It] don't mean sheeit."[28]

Drawn from the "fine" arts and filmic traditions, the guru closely resembles representations of God the Father, such as that created in Michelangelo's Sistine Chapel frescoes. Indeed, Crumb directly alludes to religious representation in "Mr. Natural Meets God," first published in 1968 in the *East Village Other*.[29] In this — the ultimate adventure strip — Mr. Natural is run over by a speeding car and wakes up in Heaven. There he is enthusiastically greeted by a blowhard God the Father (a larger and more hirsute version of himself, who chortles with self-satisfaction, "How do you like it?"). Indifferent to the beatific vision and celestial choir, Mr. Natural honestly responds, "Well, it's a little corny if you ask me! . . . I mean, the whole concept is a little outdated, don't you think?" Seething with anger, the indignant Supreme Being orders his angel to cast Mr. Natural into the outer darkness.

While Fritz changed with the passage of time, Mr. Natural remains the same, a man for all seasons, conspicuously out of place in the consumer culture of the seventies. In 1977, Flakey Foont, his formerly devoted disciple, subdues the sage, dresses him in a pair of madras Bermuda shorts, and commits him to a state-run mental institution.[30] "Poor ol' guy," muses Flakey to his sidekick, Ruth Schwartz, "he used to be so sharp an' clear-headed back in the sixties . . . the man was brilliant . . . what went wrong?" "Maybe he couldn't cope with the seventies," Schwartz speculates, "his mind snapped under the stress of th' changing times. . . ." "He wuz a popular cultural hero ten years ago . . . he was loved by millions!" Foont reminisces. Summarizes Schwartz, "An'

R. Crumb, page from *R. Crumb's Snoid Comics*, 1980

Also created in 1967 was the Snoid, Crumb's favorite cartoon character, a principle of naked aggression.

now all he's got left is us . . . his only friends . . . it's a real tragedy."

No such fate awaited the infantile Snoid, whose credo, "I Do What I Want!" contrasts with Mr. Natural's exhortation to live according to "the forgotten 'Secret of Life' . . . HANG LOOSE!"[31] The Snoid, like Rumpelstiltskin, springs from the fecund fairy-tale tradition of the irascible misogynist dwarf. "Now here's a dude with absolute self-confidence!" observes Crumb of his creation.

> Never had a self-doubt in his life! And NO QUALMS of conscience have ever stood in his way! The result: this ugly little creep has more cute girls chasing after him than a 747 jet-plane can haul! There's no law to prevent the landscape from being littered with the women this nasty little fellow has used up and thrown away! . . . The ultimate reactionary, Mr. Snoid. . . . The Snoid is a kind of rotten guy. He was my favorite character. He had absolutely no redeeming qualities.[32]

Mr. Snoid manifests the artist's desire to outrage. One would think this would be a difficult accomplishment in the United States, where one out of every six feature-length films released in the sixties was a sex-exploitation movie,[33] but the print media has always held a special spot in the would-be censor's heart. And the legacy of Frederic Wertham's *Seduction of the Innocent*, with its premise that comic books provide American youth with an occasion to sin, continued. In "The Snoid Goes Bohemian," the protagonist becomes a pretentious "action" painter who humiliates his college co-ed girlfriend, Beverly Baumstein, one of many meaty "earth mothers" to populate Crumb's work.

The tension between the artist and his creation is dramatically drawn in the prologue to *R. Crumb's Snoid Comics*, wherein the Snoid emerges from the drawing pad (as Inky had earlier emerged from animator Max Fleischer's *Inkwell*), pushes Crumb aside with a "One side, sucker! I'm taking over here. . . . You shut up!," kicks the artist in the teeth, and announces, "you won't have to put up with anymore of his tiresome ruminations. . . ."[34] Among the "tiresome ruminations" to which the Snoid refers are those strips in which Crumb analyzes his "female problems." For example, in "My Troubles with Women, Another 'True Confession' by Your Favorite Neurotic Cartoonist," the artist reconstructs the history of his relationship with the opposite sex.[35]

Describing his high-school years, Crumb complains,

> Another thing that used to get my goat was the way girls would moon over the most obnoxious strutting banty-rooster rock stars, movie stars, etc. I'm telling you, I was acquiring a low opinion of women. . . . The next thing I knew I was married. . . . It's hard to say who was more neurotic, me or her. . . . Then something amazing happened in my bleak life . . . in the late sixties I did some LSD-inspired "comix" which made me an "underground" cult hero . . . beautiful young "hippie chicks" began making themselves available. . . . My contempt for women was only increased with the bitter knowledge that these former cheerleaders and surfbunnies were the same ilk that had snubbed me in high school. . . . It was about this time that FEMINISM was coming up strong. . . . "Sisterhood" added a new perspective to the game. . . . But I will say this to all you feminist gals . . . the truth is, you gotta be a cocky guy in this world if you wanna get laid . . . especially if you're ugly like me! You gotta be some kinda hot shot or other, or you just do not get laid![36]

From this perspective, Crumb fired numerous shots in the battle of the sexes, attacking domestic issues with a ferocity reserved by earlier artists and writers for international conflicts. Among his targets was the nuclear family, the myth of which he debunked in the infamous "Joe Blow" sequence, published in July 1969 in *Zap Comix*, no. 4. This strip, which dealt openly with incest, became the subject of coast-to-coast obscenity charges. In 1970, *Zap Comix*, no. 4, was put on trial in New York when the manager and two employees of an East Side bookstore were prosecuted for selling it to police officers. In *People v. Kirkpatrick*, the court held that *Zap*, no. 4, was legally obscene.[37] The judge described the issue as "shock-obscenity" and rejected the argument that its creators were recognized artists. In the judge's opinion "A Michelangelo could find no solace from legal restraint if his art be obscene."[38]

At the very same time that *Zap*, no. 4, was on trial in New York, the underground strip was also being prosecuted in Maryland. There the owner of a small shop called the Joint Possession was prosecuted for the sale of the *Washington Free Press* to an undercover officer. The trial judge refused to accept expert testimony, such as that offered by *Washington Post* art critic Paul Richard and Corcoran Gallery of Art Acting Director Walter W. Hopps. The store owner was convicted. On appeal, the chief issue was whether a two-page comic by R. Crumb, reprinted from *Jive Comix*, was obscene. The appellate court reversed the conviction, stating that "Good taste, whatever that elusive concept may be, will no doubt frequently be offended by much that in a democratic system is permitted freely to be published and to be disseminated. This is a small price to pay for the preservation of cherished and indispensable First Amendment freedoms."[39] Like many artists determined to shock the middle class, Crumb had succeeded beyond his wildest expectations. Reflecting on the results, Crumb concluded "I was just being a punk."[40]

Crumb's uncompromising depiction of male rage and sexual hostility, as well as his prominence among underground artists, were to make him the target of feminist ire. Recalled Trina Robbins, queen of the underground and one of the founders of *Wimmen's Comix*, in a *Blab* festschrift honoring Crumb: "I recall the first of those newly styled misogynist strips of his that I saw; Crumb had just drawn it, and I eagerly expected it to be another one of his typically sweet comics. But by the time I got to the end, I was horrified! . . . Now, I hadn't even heard of the term 'women's liberation' yet . . . but I knew anti-woman hostility when I saw it."[41]

Drawing upon separate iconographic traditions, Crumb created three memorable archetypes — Fritz the Cat, Mr. Natural, and the Snoid. Crumb's acute awareness of the dark side of the human psyche, the chthonic depths of the human heart, expressed in the Snoid, prevents his work from becoming clichéd or propagandistic. Like its aging leader, Mr. Natural, and its first citizen, Fritz the Cat, the Snoid is a card-carrying member of the sixties countercultural community. While Fritz is its corrupt Everyman, Mr. Natural embodies its gentle aspiration, the Snoid its angry rebelliousness. The compulsive sexuality that springs from Crumb's pen is an attempt to transcend the limits of a possibly meaningless existence through grossly physical experience, artistic expression and sexual impulse being perhaps the only avenues through which to affirm life.

9

Detail from Dale Messick, *Brenda Starr, Reporter*, December 9, 1945

While Capp and Crumb were creating wantons and earth mothers, female artists were asserting their right to be comics creators. For eighty years, few had been able to penetrate this male domain. Like the fine-arts market, cartooning remained for decades the exclusive territory of white males. Not until the sixties civil rights movement would women and minority artists be sought to satisfy the demands of increasingly vocal markets.

In the strip's infancy, isolated women cartoonists had occasionally carved a newspaper niche for themselves. The strips drawn by these women were usually domestic in nature, depicting, with various degrees of sentimentality, idealized children and animals. Chief among these early creators were Rose O'Neill, who is best remembered for her 1909 *Kewpies* ("little Cupids"); Grace Gebbie Drayton, who depicted *The Terrible Tales of Kaptain Kiddo* (1909), and who lives on in the American imagination as the mother of the ever-popular *Campbell Kids* (1905); and Frances Edwina Dumm, the first female editorial cartoonist, famous for her dog strip, *Cap Stubbs and Tippie* (1917). The styles of O'Neill and Drayton, like those of certain nineteenth-century book illustrators, featured a fussily rendered pen line that circumscribed chubby children with huge heads, large, appealing eyes, and snub noses. Dumm's agitated, sketchy line, on the other hand, was employed to tell the Twainesque tale of a boy and his dog.

The first woman to expand the repertoire of the female cartoonist beyond the kid strip was Martha Orr, creator of *Apple Mary*, which today survives as *Mary Worth*. Author Allan Saunders, who took over the strip in 1940, recalled its earthy origin:

> Until the '30s, serious continuity strips had concerned themselves pretty generally with war, space-exploration, and crime. But a strip called *Apple Mary*, started in 1934, quietly won a substantial following by depicting the rigors of life during the Great Depression.
>
> Inspired, perhaps, by a hit movie, *Lady for a Day* featuring May Robeson, it starred a dumpy, pugnacious matron named Mary Worth who pushed an apple-cart on city streets and coped valiantly with the mortgage-foreclosure and bullies who tried to take advantage of her crippled grandson.[1]

Over the past fifty-six years Mary has changed from stout blue-

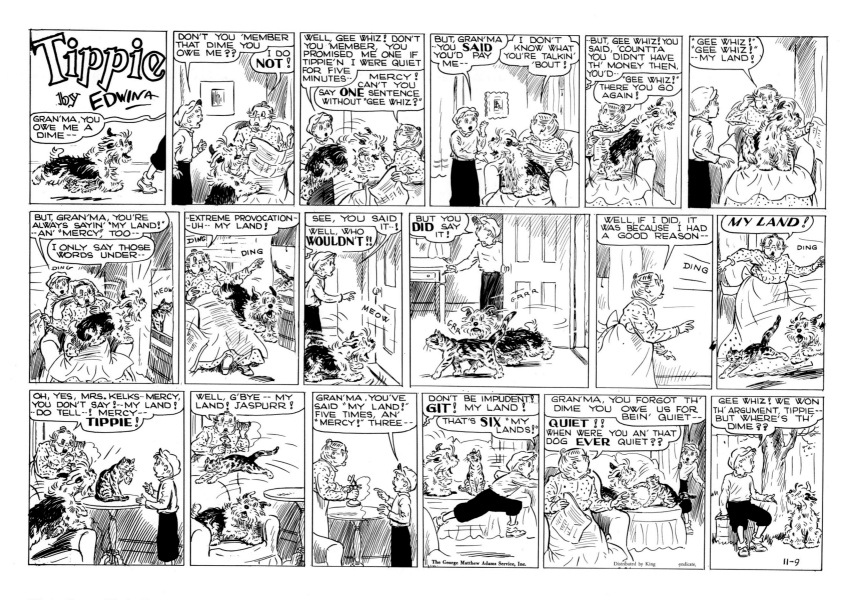

Edwina Dumm, *Tippie*, November 9, 1947

Unlike the handful of early female cartoonists who chose to work within the tradition of the illustrated children's book, Dumm spun Twainesque yarns of a boy and his dog.

Russ Westover, *Tillie the Toiler*, April 17, 1934

Copyright 1934 King Features Syndicate, Inc.
Original pen and ink drawing.
Swann Collection, Division of Prints and Photographs,
the Library of Congress.

Like the other "girl" strips penned by male cartoonists, *Tillie the Toiler* depicted clothes and suitors as women's only interests.

Attributed to Max Fleischer, *Betty Boop*, November 14, 1934

Copyright 1934 King Features Syndicate/Fleischer Studios, Inc.
Original pen and ink drawing.
Swann Collection, Division of Prints and Photographs,
the Library of Congress.

In *Betty Boop*, first an animation and then a strip, Fleischer created the most popular of comic-strip bimbos.

Paul Robinson, *Etta Kett*, July 16, 1938

Etta Kett (i.e., etiquette) was a cartoon guide to "excruciatingly correct" behavior for young, upwardly mobile adults in the thirties.

Lynn Johnston, *For Better or for Worse*, January 31, 1983

While *Cathy* appealed to the single, working woman, *For Better or for Worse* claimed as its audience those married with children. *For Better or for Worse* is one of the first domestic strips created by a woman.

collar activist to svelte bourgeoise busybody. Whereas *Apple Mary* was an elderly working woman struggling to live on the fringe of industrial America, *Mary Worth* is a self-certified lay analyst in a sunny suburban-California condominium. Mary's progression reflects the population migration from Rustbelt to Sunbelt and the upward social mobility of two generations. Alice, the homeless bag lady of *Doonesbury*, is *Apple Mary*'s contemporary soul sister.

Although the vast majority of "girl" strips created in the teens and twenties were drawn by men, they often provided exciting "role models." Such strips, designed to appeal to young ladies entering the work force, include *Polly and Her Pals*, begun in 1912 by Clifford Sterrett; *Winnie Winkle, the Breadwinner*, created in 1920 by Martin Branner; *Tillie the Toiler*, originated in 1921 by Russ Westover; and, of course, the indefatigable *Little Orphan Annie*, the 1924 brainchild of Harold Gray.

Whereas Polly, Winnie, and Tillie were all "working girls," restrained by both office routine and family ties, Little Orphan Annie was a self-reliant adventuress. While Polly, Winnie, and Tillie were also fashion plates, utilized by their creators to display haute couture, Annie scorned such show, wearing like a shield her sterling character. Paradoxically, her independence made Annie the target of sixties underground cartoonists, whose work often carries as a subtext the subjugation of women. For example, in 1969 Gilbert Shelton satirized Harold Gray's epic in "Little Orphan Amphetamine, The Freak Brothers' Favorite 14-Year-Old Runaway."[2] In this spoof, the spoiled orphan is raped by a middle-aged man with whom she hitches a cross-country ride, and violated in San Francisco by a commune of "speed fiends" with whom she has sought shelter. Unable to cope with these outrages, Annie, sucking her thumb, phones "Daddy." " 'Daddy,' " begs Annie, " 'Gruntcakes [Shelton's satiric equivalent of Gray's Sandy] and I need $400 so we can fly home and see my doctor and my shrink.' " In this ten-frame strip, Annie is reliant on five men: "Daddy," her "ride," the speed fiends with whom she crashes, her physician, and her psychiatrist. Nothing could be further from the modus operandi of Harold Gray's plucky heroine, on whom Warbucks often depends. Ironically, "Little Orphan

Rose O'Neill, *The Kewpies*, March 28, 1936

Cliff Sterrett, *Polly and Her Pals*, January 4, 1919

Created in 1912, *Positive Polly*, the antecedent of *Polly and Her Pals*, was designed to appeal to women entering the work force. As *Polly and Her Pals*, the strip featured the lastest in fashions. Like *Bringing Up Father*, it examined the relationship between the sexes. In this episode, for example, Polly and her mother attempt unsuccessfully to stifle her father's desire to smoke.

HOW TO DRAW CARTOONS

BY THE FAMOUS ARTIST TEACHER MRS. LYNDA

"I can teach you to draw so that anyone will want to be your partner." -L.B.

ITS FUN! ✓
ITS EASY! ✓
ALL YOU NEED TO BEGIN IS:
A pencil →
A pen →
Paper →
And a HUMAN BRAIN!

WHEN DO WE START!
THIS PARTS EASY!

WADA WE WAITIN FOR!

SO: **LET'S GO!!!!!**

The first thing you'll want to think about is what you'll say in the INTERVIEW with TIME MAGAZINE after they select YOU as CARTOONIST of the YEAR!!! Its sure to happen, so write down some of your PROFOUND THOUGHTS on the subject in the space provided: _ _ _ _ _ _ _ _ _ _ _ _ _ _

LEARN FROM OTHERS! LETS TAKE A LOOK AT HOW OTHERS DO IT!

SHAPE OF THE HEAD →

"SPIDER MAN"   "PEANUTS"
"L'il ORPHAN ANNIE"   "NANCY"   "LYNDA BARRY"

NOW YOU TRY

| 1 | 2 | 5 | 6 | 9 | 10 |
| 3 | 4 | 7 | 8 | 11 | 12 |

Be SURE to use ALL OF THE SPACE PROVIDED! YOU HAVE ROOM FOR 12 DIFFERENT SHAPES SO LET YOUR IMAGINATION "GO-GO" WILD! YOU'RE PROBABLY GOING TO HAVE TO DRAW PRETTY SMALL!! BUT CARTOONISTS MUST DRAW SMALL SO IT WILL ALL FIT IN THAT COMIC STRIP! ON SUNDAYS YOU CAN DRAW BIGGER!

FACIAL FEATURES eyes, NOSE and MOUTH

	"SPIDERMAN"	"PEANUTS"	"ANNIE"	"NANCY"	"LYNDA BARRY"
EYES: "DOORWAY to the SOUL"	◣◢	• •	0 0	◠ ◠	
Nose: "GIVES CHARACTER"	NONE	C	\	—	◉
MOUTH: SHOWS FEELING	NONE	◡	◿	—	🍌

NOW! MIX 'N' MATCH!

CREATE YOUR OWN CHARACTER! TRY TO FLOW W/ IT!

YOU GIVE IT A TRY! HAVE FUN WITH IT!

use this space for your drawing →

| | 1 | 2 | 3 | 4 |
| 5 | 6 | 7 | 8 | |

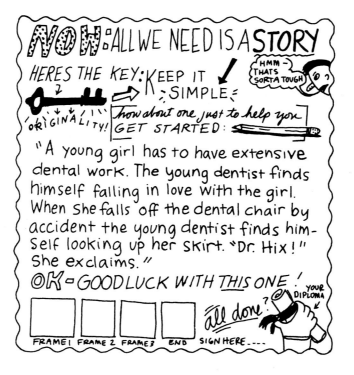

NOW: ALL WE NEED IS A STORY

HERES THE KEY: KEEP IT SIMPLE

HMM - THATS SORTA TOUGH

"ORIGINALITY!"

how about one just to help you GET STARTED:

"A young girl has to have extensive dental work. The young dentist finds himself falling in love with the girl. When she falls off the dental chair by accident the young dentist finds himself looking up her skirt. "Dr. Hix!" She exclaims."

OK - GOOD LUCK WITH THIS ONE!

| FRAME 1 | FRAME 2 | FRAME 3 | END |

SIGN HERE ----

all done?   YOUR DIPLOMA

Lynda Barry, *How to Draw Cartoons*, 1981

First printed in *Girls and Boys*, Real Comet Press, Seattle, © 1981 Lynda Barry.

In this delightful instructional sequence, Barry satirizes the very principle of comic-strip creation, mixing and matching the features of cartoon icons.

121

Ernie Bushmiller, *Fritzi Ritz*, November 16, 1941

Amphetamine" begins with a quote from Mao Tse-tung: "Genuine equality between the sexes can only be realized in the process of the socialist transformation as a whole." Certainly Gray's world, the capitalist sine qua non, is a more hospitable environment for women with wanderlust than that of counterculture cartoonist Shelton.

Annie's love of the open road and lust for high adventure, savagely satirized by Shelton, were also hallmarks of *Brenda Starr*, the brainchild of Dale (née Delia) Messick, which appeared for the first time on June 30, 1940. The first adventure strip penned by a woman, the cartoon documented the exploits of a beautiful reporter whose assignments often took her around the world. Messick's first concept was even more revolutionary — Brenda was to have been a lady bandit, an anti-heroine operating totally outside the system.[3] Among the conventions Messick inverted in *Brenda Starr* was that whereby a helpless heroine, menaced by villains and rogues, is rescued by an omnipotent hero. In *Brenda Starr* the helpless heroine is replaced by the hapless hero. Basil St. John, Brenda's "mystery man," is threatened by an adversary more relentless than the most ghoulish of Chester Gould's villains — a fatal degenerative tropical disease. Perversely exotic, this malady responds only to a mysterious serum distilled from the elusive black orchid, the grail that Basil and Brenda pursue o'er land and sea. The sinister notion of an impersonal, uncontrollable, and unconquerable evil was new to the strip. Its dark shadow, while sometimes dissipated by Brenda's stunning appearance and sterling professionalism, unified the strip, subordinating other adventures to the status of subplot.

Another dark specter, that of racism, was attacked by African-American cartoonist Jackie Ormes, who in 1937 created *Torchy Brown from Dixie to Harlem*, a topical strip of the realist school, which ran only in minority newspapers. Observed former comic-strip editor Richard Marschall, "A comic strip about a Black heroine raised in the South, facing all sorts of ills from racial prejudice to rape attempts; travelling north ultimately to appear at Harlem's Cotton Club; involved in assorted adventures, including battling environmental pollution . . . it sounds tailor-made, and the product of the hip 1980s."[4]

The wide range of issues treated in the little-known *Torchy Brown*

is also a trademark of *Sylvia*, the controversial creation first published in 1979 by Chicago artist Nicole Hollander. Hollander has described the dearth of role models offered the aspiring woman cartoonist: "It didn't occur to me to be a cartoonist. [In cartoons by men] women as characters make up a lesser proportion of images than men do. . . . It's just one more instance where little girls don't get to see themselves. I think it's damaging. I think it reinforces being invisible, and it reinforces being powerless."[5]

Hollander's observations are confirmed by an analysis of the strips of comic-strip masters. The work of these first fathers, while replete with celebrations of male potential, is remarkable for its exclusion of representatives of the opposite sex. In this exclusion, the comic strip reflects American literary precedents, such as those established by Herman Melville and Mark Twain. For example, the Princess is the lone continuing female character to appear in Winsor McCay's *Little Nemo in Slumberland*, her role that of the whimsical romantic object of Nemo's quest. Other characterizations of women in *Little Nemo* include that of Little Mary, the dying slum child whom Nemo restores to life in the famous Shantytown sequence. While women in *Little Nemo* are either ethereal muses or tragic victims, female representation in Feininger's *Kin-der-Kids* is limited to that of the sinister spectral spinster, Aunty Jim-Jam, against whom the boys join forces. In George McManus's *Bringing Up Father*, women are social climbers and spendthrifts; in Capp and Crumb, voluptuous wantons and earth mothers. In the work of these cartoonists, the few women represented are depicted as different from men in nature and aspiration; the same observation is often true of representations of minorities.

The adventure strip, however, is the one area of exception. *Prince Valiant* features the capable Queen Aleta (Foster's famous representation of Val spanking Aleta notwithstanding). *Flash Gordon* contains such memorable women as the evil Princess Aura. And *Terry and the Pirates* boasts the unscrupulous Dragon Lady, as well as a host of heiresses. Furthermore, Sheena, Queen of the Jungle, and Wonder Woman starred in their own strips, wherein, although scantily clad in tiger skin and strapless halters, they vanquished countless adversaries.

Martin Branner, *Winnie Winkle, the Breadwinner*, April 11, 1926

Although conceived as a working-girl strip, the Sunday episodes of *Winnie Winkle* were devoted to the exploits of Winnie's brother Perry.

Ernie Bushmiller, *Nancy*, March 9, 1941

The delightfully feisty Nancy and the self-reliant entrepreneur Little Orphan Annie were two of the few pre–feminist-era cartoon representations of the assertive female.

Ken Ernst, *Mary Worth*, July 1, 1947

Copyright 1947 Publishers Syndicate/Courtesy King Features.

The forties saw the style of the adventure strip adapted to the needs of the domestic saga. Here, the dramatic play of dark and light used to enliven the wartime dramas of Milton Caniff is applied to pedestrian tribulation.

Martha Orr, *Apple Mary*, May 6, 1936

Copyright 1936 Publishers Syndicate/Courtesy King Features.
Original pen and ink drawing.
Bea and Murray A. Harris Collection.
Photo by Joe Goulait, Courtesy Smithsonian Institution Traveling Exhibition Service (SITES).

As envisioned by her creator, Martha Orr, Apple Mary was a pugnacious blue-collar Depression-era activist. After Orr's retirement from the strip, Mary became an officious domestic intermeddler.

Dale Messick, *Brenda Starr, Reporter*, December 9, 1945

Basil St. John, the elusive mystery man of reporter
Brenda Starr, first appeared in the December 9, 1945, episode. One of the few adventure strips to feature a female
protagonist, *Brenda Starr* combined fantasy, mystery, and
domestic intrigue.

The superhero tradition continues with a modern message in Hollander's *Sylvia*. Among Hollander's self-proclaimed "insulting and irritating" superheroes are Wondermom ("flying all over creation to see if she can make your life more pleasant"), Superwoman ("travel agent/therapist: 'You're depressed, you feel old, which is nonsense, but anyway I made reservations. You'll take the Concorde to Paris on Tuesday.' "), Love Cop ("rushing around hither and yon trying to prevent incompatible people from becoming involved"), interfering Super Cops ("policing the country making sure you're doing what everyone else is doing . . . and as often"), Credit Card Cop ("criss-crossing the country bullying people into living within their means"), Smoke Stomper ("tirelessly criss-crossing the country being abusive to women smokers to get them to quit"), and Super Lawyer, an absolutely necessary hero for the litigious eighties.[6] These dei ex machinae, custom-created to suit the pseudo-crises of contemporary life, are officious intermeddlers.

Among the most beloved of *Sylvia*'s stock characters is Gernif, the compulsively curious Venusian, to whom Sylvia often explains the American scene, and whose sayings embody interplanetary modern folk wisdom. "Luxst und shahme fourevr frayshe," asserts the Venusian. Sylvia translates, "It's easier to remember humiliation than your mother's phone number."[7] Other members of the comic cast include the Devil, who adroitly comments on human foibles and combines in his surrealist Hell the best and worst of modern America. "This week in Hell: You see a neon sign that reads: Cajun Food/Live Music/Free Drinks! You push open the door and you're in a dentist's office."[8] There is also Sylvia herself, a middle-aged, cigarette-smoking, beer-drinking, self-assured sage; Sid, her barkeep; Ramon, the local stud; and her cat. Other strip regulars include Susan, a mad housewife, who flaunts her multiple identities/split personality: "housewife/ethical relativist/gourmet," "housewife/snakehandler/educator," "housewife/plastic surgeon/Charles Bronson lookalike," "housewife/periodontist/parapsychologist."[9]

Stylistically, this innovative strip continues the minimalist tradition established by Feiffer — vestigial background, calligraphic caricature, great punch line. Ideologically, in the words of *Village Voice* writer Jan Hoffman, "*Sylvia* sits three bar stools to the left of Garry Trudeau and Jules Feiffer."[10]

While *Sylvia* good-naturedly tackles such topics as Iran-Contra, abortion, equal pay, and affirmative action, the talented cartoonist Lynda Barry explores race relations, class consciousness, and the battle of the sexes in the blue-collar Seattle neighborhood of her childhood. Drawn in an intentionally naive style, Barry, best known as the creator of *Ernie Pook's Comeek*, depicts, from a child's viewpoint, the joys and sorrows of a richly imaginative life bounded only by income and opportunity.

In *The Fun House* (1987) Barry, utilizing expressive, asymmetrical frames jammed with black-lettered narrative, celebrates the power of the imagination. Subdivided into chapters on school, play, home and family, and friends, *The Fun House* depicts everyday occurrences in a working-class 1960s neighborhood, all transformed by the vision of the prepubescent narrator. The crowded frames and plenteous dialogue — which is directly addressed to the reader — create the illusion of breathless immediacy and affectionate intimacy characteristic of childhood communication.

What is communicated?

In "The Substitute," recounts Barry, "our usual teacher had actually quit because of us . . . we heard she had to move to North Dakota where children have better respect."[11] To replace her, the school commands the services of Miss Bevens, substitute teacher, whose outstanding characteristics include "a big pointy bosum and fake teeth that flipped around." The class is at once fascinated and repulsed as Miss Bevens shamelessly munches on a chicken leg. On Miss Bevens's last day, the class intones her "favorite song of 'John Brown's Body Lies a Moldering in the Ground' " and the narrator demands to know, "If we hated her so much how come a lot of us started crying?"

The mysterious ways of teachers are also the subject of "Science," wherein adolescent Ernie Barta, as his science project, displays "the talented Bruce Lee, Jr." (a grasshopper whom he has trained to smoke a miniature cigar) to his teacher, Mrs. Brogan. Unimpressed, Mrs. Brogan forces Ernie to release Bruce Lee, Jr., as she sings "Born Free." The two strips illustrate the trials suffered by pupils at the mercy of the

Nicole Hollander, *The 1978 Feminist Funnies Appointment Calendar: Witches, Pigs and Fairy Godmothers.*

Nicole Hollander's trenchant observer, Sylvia, first appeared as Ms. September in *The 1978 Feminist Funnies Appointment Calendar.* Soon Sylvia commanded her own strip, in which she wryly interprets the American comedy.

cathy®   by Cathy Guisewite

Cathy Guisewite, *Cathy*, June 18, 1984

One of the first "girl" strips to be penned by a woman, *Cathy* was immediately successful, expressing the preoccupations of contemporary careerists.

Aline Kominsky-Crumb, *Moo Goo Gaipan*, page from *Weirdo*, no. 20, 1987

Autobiographical elements abound in the work of *Weirdo* editor Aline Kominsky-Crumb.

benign but balmy.

Childhood stoicism is also the theme of "Baton" and "Bikes," stories in which girls and boys undergo their respective rites of passage. Although their heads swell with enormous lumps caused by the batons they are incapable of catching, the girls refuse to complain. ("This one hardly even hurts. Does yours hurt?" "Heck no! Why should it hurt?" "No reason.") Similarly, Barry remembers of boys' bicycle accidents, "no matter how much it hurt you had to yell 'Rupture!' first, which would make you start laughing at the same time you were crying because you're bleeding and man look how wrecked-up your bike is."[12]

Parental desertion and death are also stoically accepted. In "Train I Ride" a six-year-old walks the railroad tracks in search of the mother who has abandoned him. "All he knows," recounts his older brother, "is that she rode the train and that if he can get on the train he'll find her. Stupid kid thinks there's only one train in the whole wide world."[13] "Tom's Mom" recounts the graveside vigil of a bereaved child, who, accompanied by his best friend, visits the cemetery. "We drove on our bikes past about a million graves till we came to his mom's. We got off our bikes and couldn't even say nothing. Finally Tom starts saying the pledge of allegiance and I say it with him. By the end of it we are crying."[14] The inadequacy of words to express such loss, and the necessity of solemn ceremony are movingly captured by Barry.

In reading the strip, the viewer becomes a child again. Barry effects this transformation in two ways: all is seen from the point of view of a nine-year-old child — the heads of adults are rarely depicted for they are out of the range of vision; and the reader is directly addressed, child-to-child, by the strip's narrator. In this way Barry reverses the hands of time, enabling the reader to become again a child.

As re-created by Barry, childhood is a time of vulnerability and pain transcended only by laughter and imagination. Like the adults they will become, children can be both kind and cruel. Cruelty, however, is a class prerogative. In "How Things Turn Out" Barry explains this concept.

In school, of course, there were the Queen Girls and then there were the rest and at the bottom of the rest were the ones, whatever you want to call them, the

Lynda Barry, *Girls and Boys*, 1980

First printed in *Girls and Boys*, Real Comet Press, Seattle, © 1981 Lynda Barry.

The mysteries of male bonding are explored in this hilarious sequence, in which two crude characters speak a dialogue of phallic obsession.

ones you would be ashamed to have to touch.

If you were really rich you could never be at the very bottom because too many kids would still want to play with your stuff. If you were really poor you could never be on top because it was just too embarrassing.[15]

Like that of children, the world of pets includes both the vicious and the virtuous. "Good Dog" is the saga of the narrator's abortive attempt to befriend Timmy, "a wild tied-up kind of dog who sometimes got loose and would rip giant holes in your pants and also try to dance with you." Irritated by the protagonist's friendly overtures, which include renditions of "The Hills Are Alive" and "Rice-A-Roni the San Francisco Treat," Timmy attempts to bite her.[16]

The gentle Pixie, on the other hand, is destined to be killed with kindness by her misguided owner, Mrs. Santos. Mrs. Santos dresses Pixie in clothing, feeds her cake and ice cream, and adorns her doghouse with a statue of the Virgin Mary, a field of plastic flowers, and pictures of movie stars, including Robert Mitchum. Despite — or perhaps because of — this coddling, Pixie is destined for an early grave, for, as the crosses marking the final resting places of her predecessors Trixie and Dixie attest, she is "Mrs. Santos's third dog this year."[17]

The universality of the experiences recounted by Barry, and the consummate artistry with which she renders them, have made her one of America's most popular self-syndicated artists.

Also enjoying enormous popularity is syndicated cartoonist Cathy Guisewite, who continues the "working-girl" strip tradition pioneered in *Winnie Winkle, the Breadwinner, Polly and Her Pals,* and *Tillie the Toiler,* for the first time from the perspective of a woman cartoonist. Among *Cathy*'s subjects are sexual mores, courtship customs, and romance rituals; parent-child relationships; personal appearance; and office politics. Gently self-satiric, the strip is the 1976 creation of a former midwestern advertising executive. As do such perennial favorites as *Gasoline Alley* and *Blondie, Cathy* evolves with the reader. In the tradition of "girl" strips such as *Fritzi Ritz* and *Polly and Her Pals,* the protagonist's physical attributes change with the times, and her attire provides an index to the absurdities of fashion. Unlike its venerable comic-strip antecedents, however, *Cathy* explores the heroine's inner

Trina Robbins, *The Garden Party*, 1982

Copyright Trina Robbins, from *Wimmen's Comix.*

Trina Robbins is one of the founders of the alternative publication *Wimmen's Comix.*

conflicts and expresses her social philosophy. Typical of strips created by cartoonists born after World War II, among them Lynda Barry and Art Spiegelman, *Cathy* abounds in biographical self-reference.

While *Cathy* explores the lonely world of the young, single, upwardly mobile professional, *For Better or for Worse*, a family strip drawn by Canadian Lynn Johnston, documents that of the nuclear family. As the title *For Better or for Worse* implies, Johnston's strip — unlike that of male creators of domestic strips — explores both the light and dark sides of family life. In Johnston's world, love sometimes does not endure, and bad things do happen to good people. Nevertheless, the strip celebrates the enduring triumphs of the resilient human spirit.

The richly various work of female underground cartoonists includes the tragic search for emotional fulfillment conducted in *Lonely Nights Comics*, a painful autobiographical work by Dori Seda.[18] In this compilation Seda depicts the desperate struggle of an alcoholic to attain professional recognition and personal commitment.[19] Seda's saga is the dark side of the working woman's world created in *Cathy*. Described by R. Crumb as "her own best cartoon,"[20] Seda is the sad star of her own tragic odyssey. The epilogue of *Lonely Nights Comics*, for example, provides an epitaph for Seda's untimely death.

> (It's not a good idea to kill your main character, especially when it's yourself!) In the previous story Dori was brutally strangled to death by a maniac. She was buried a couple of days later in Park Hill cemetery. Foul play was suspected. At the coroner's request, Dori's grave was unearthed for an autopsy. Upon opening the casket, all that could be found inside was a large spider![21]

Autobiographical reference also abounds in the engaging work of *Weirdo* editor Aline Kominsky-Crumb. In *Power Pack Comics* Kominsky-Crumb re-creates her childhood on Long Island with mother "Blabette" and father "Arnie," her adolescence, and her adult life.[22] Kominsky-Crumb's matter-of-fact portrayal of her own insecurities makes this a comic contemporary *Story of O*. While Lynda Barry's childhood memories are poeticized and wistful, Aline Kominsky-Crumb's are unflinchingly personal and painful.

Since its inception, *Wimmen's Comix* has provided an alternate outlet for the best in underground cartooning. Among the artists pop-

Nicole Hollander, *Sylvia*, March 15, 1987

One of the few feminist cartoonists to work within the superhero tradition, Hollander creates figures uniquely suited to the contemporary scene.

Stan Drake, *The Heart of Juliet Jones*, December 18, 1958

The domestic-strip tradition of the officious female intermeddler was continued in *The Heart of Juliet Jones*, a cartoon soap opera penned by the realist master Stan Drake.

ularized through its pages have been the prolific Trina Robbins, as well as such important talents as Alison Bechdel, Angela Bocage, Cynthia Martin, and Carol Tyler. Between the covers of *Wimmen's Comix* are topical tales of child abuse, alcoholism, infidelity, and isolation — the dark side of the hopeful, romantic illusions of the first female protagonists created by such male cartoonists as Westover, Branner, and Sterrett.

From mainstream to underground, comics by women artists have provided a history of heady aspiration and bleak despair. Not surprisingly, those cartoons that have enjoyed the greatest commercial success have celebrated hope or have provided humorous transcendence.

Reflecting the limited opportunities women have enjoyed, few female cartoonists have themselves created fantastic superheroines. Sheena, Queen of the Jungle, was the brainchild of Will Eisner and Samuel Iger; Wonder Woman, that of William Moulton Marston. Sylvia's Superheroes, despite their super powers, limit their interventions to domestic affairs. The themes of subjugation and domination explicit in *Sheena, Queen of the Jungle*, and *Wonder Woman* are noticeably absent in equally successful strips by women cartoonists. Although they have seldom created such omnipotent personages, women artists have been powerfully influenced by such strips. During an interview for the *Journal of Popular Culture* conducted by historian Ronald Levitt Lanyi in the spring of 1979, underground cartoonist Trina Robbins, the undisputed leader among women underground-comics creators, enumerated such influences as *Sheena, Queen of the Jungle* ("Right on!"), *Señorita Ria, Nyoka, Jann of the Jungle,* and *Torchy Todd,* all of which featured powerful protagonists.

From *Apple Mary* to *Wimmen's Comix,* powers brought to bear by female cartoonists have been used to explore urgent social issues or to document domestic trials and tribulations. When they have been employed to create alternative universes, as in Trina Robbins's futuristic *Speed Queen versus the Freudians,* these new worlds have been symbolic embodiments of contemporary struggles. Perhaps the adventure strip, embodying as it does aspiration and unlimited potential, is still a foreign genre for the woman cartoonist.

Grace Gebbie Drayton, *Dimples*, 1915

Among the first female comic-strip creators, Drayton combined in her cartoons nursery-rhyme elements and moralizing exempla.

CHAPTER 10

New Directions — Mouse to *Maus*

Detail from Charles Burns, *Living in the Ice Age*, 1984

The social upheaval caused by the war in Vietnam stimulated both the revival of old and the creation of new forms of artistic expression. In music, this phenomenon is exemplified on one hand by the revival of folk and protest songs and on the other by the innovations of British "invaders," including the Beatles and the Rolling Stones. In the fine arts a renewed interest in representational expression such as that of magic realism and pop art was manifested, as was a curiosity about the most experimental and abstract of art forms, including conceptual art and multimedia "happenings." In the comics, mainstream traditions were continued by cartoonists such as Garry Trudeau, while avant-garde experimentation was undertaken by new-wave masters like R. Crumb, whose strips ventured into forbidden subject areas while re-animating the gritty urban expressionism of early prototypes, among them *Hogan's Alley*. The titles of these underground "comix" capture the revolutionary spirit of troubled times — *Zap*, *Insect Fear*, *Uneeda Comix*, *Snatch Comics*, *Jiz Comics*, *Big Ass Comics*, *Bijou Funnies*, *Motor City Comics*, *Home Grown Funnies*, *San Francisco Comic Book*, *Wimmen's Comix*, and *Bogeyman Comix*. After the evacuation of American troops from Vietnam on April 30, 1975, the United States returned to domestic normalcy, the end of this divisive military combat coinciding with the conclusion of a highly experimental period in American art. As contemporary cartoonist Art Spiegelman remembered,

> The flaming promise of Underground Comix — *Zap*, *Young Lust*, and others — had fizzled into cold, glowing embers. Underground comics had offered something new: comics by adults, for adults; comics that weren't under any obligation to be funny, or escapist pulp; comics unselfconsciously redefining what comics could be, by smashing formal and stylistic, as well as cultural and political, taboos. . . . Then, somehow, what had seemed like a revolution simply deflated into a lifestyle. Underground comics were stereotyped as dealing only with Sex, Dope, and Cheap Thrills. They got stuffed back into the closet, along with bong pipes and love beads, as Things Started To Get Uglier.[1]

In 1975, attempting to "provide a lifeboat for the best of the San Francisco–based cartoonists," Art Spiegelman and Bill Griffith established the quarterly magazine *Arcade*. "But," recalls Spiegelman, "the pressures were too great. Griffith seemed to be developing an ulcer.

I doubled my nicotine habit and ran back to New York. The lifeboat sank. . . .”[2] Between 1975 and 1980, consumer enthusiasm for alternate forms of artistic expression waned. At the same time, a handful of publishers, among them Last Gasp, Kitchen Sink, Rip Off Press, and Fantagraphics, continued to publish the best of underground, now middle-aged, cartoonists. Refreshed by a return to his roots and a sojourn in Europe, in 1980 Art Spiegelman established *Raw*. Variously subtitled *The Magazine of Postponed Suicides*, *The Graphix Magazine for Damned Intellectuals*, *The Graphix Magazine That Lost Its Faith in Nihilism*, *The Graphix Magazine for Your Bomb Shelter's Coffee Table*, *The Graphix Magazine of Abstract Depressionism*, *The Graphix Magazine That Overestimates the Taste of the American Public*, *The Torn-Again Graphix Magazine*, and *The Graphic Aspirin for War Fever*, *Raw* was issued as a large-format book and featured both European and American "underground-comix cronies."[3] It also included a variety of inserts, one of which was to forever transform the nature of the comics.

This was *Maus: A Survivor's Tale*, the story of the artist's parents, Vladek and Anja Spiegelman. Published in book form in 1986, *Maus* helped to establish the "graphic novel" as a genre and lifted comics as autobiography to new heights of epic expression. Parts of *Maus* had first appeared in 1973 in *Short Order Comix*, no. 1. Among the stories told in this painfully personal memoir are those of the courtship of Spiegelman's parents in prewar Poland; their marriage and the birth in 1937 of their first child, Richieu; Vladek's conscription into the Polish Army; the personal devastation and loss of life wrought by the Holocaust, including the deaths of Spiegelman's grandparents, aunts and uncles, cousins, and brother; his own mental breakdown; his mother's suicide; and the artist's relationship with his exasperating elderly father.

The underground artist's ambivalence toward commercially successful cartoon classicists was succinctly stated by R. Crumb in 1978: "I'd abandoned my childhood dreams of becoming a big-time professional cartoonist because by the time I was a senior in High School I clearly discerned that the medium had become constricted, formulized, locked into a strict set of stifling commercial standards. I considered myself

Art Spiegelman, from *Maus: A Survivor's Tale*, 1973–1986

The setting of *Maus* alternates between present-day Rego Park and war-torn Poland. As a subtext, the strip examines the conflict between the artist and his survivor father.

Art Spiegelman, from *Maus: A Survivor's Tale*, 1973–1986

Art Spiegelman, from *Maus: A Survivor's Tale*, 1973–1986

Here Spiegelman, Senior, predicts that his son will someday be as famous as the creator of Mickey Mouse.

hopelessly inadequate to meet these standards."[4]

In fact, Spiegelman's work does reflect cartoon prototypes. Early anthropomorphic cartoon mice include Herriman's irascible Ignatz Maus/Mouse, Disney's 1928 Steamboat Willie, Ubbe Iwerks's 1930 Mickey Mouse, and the animated Mighty Mouse, whose omnipotence contrasts with the impotence of Spiegelman's mice.

Writer Adam Gopnik provides brilliant insight into *Maus*'s adaptation of this limited anthropomorphism: "Spiegelman's animal heads are, purposefully, much more uniform and mask-like than those of any other modern cartoonist. His mice, while they have distinct human expressions, all have essentially the same face. As a consequence, they suggest not just the condition of human beings forced to behave like animals, but also our sense that this story is too horrible to be presented unmasked."[5]

Spiegelman's world, as represented in *Maus*, is one of poignant paradox and unbearable irony. Unable to stem the tide of history, which has cost him everything, his father is obsessed with mastering the most trivial of pursuits — counting his innumerable pills, talismen against the final disaster; compulsively repairing his house in Rego Park, his Polish home utterly destroyed; collecting the discarded debris of a dying civilization, perhaps to be of some use during a future holocaust. The strip's power derives in part from its refusal to stereotype characters or to offer simple solutions. "Good," "love," and "friendship" are outmoded concepts in the world of Vladek Spiegelman, who instructs the ten-year-old Artie, "Friend? Your friends? . . . If you lock them together in a room with no food for a week . . . THEN you could see what it is, friends!"[6]

Although a victim, Vladek is unlikable, insensitive to the feelings of his long-suffering second wife, Mala, whom he decries in her presence, and to the needs of his son, Artie, which are subservient to his compulsions. Self-congratulatory about his cunning and instinct for self-preservation, he is a frail old man, maddeningly human.

Spiegelman's self-portrait is complex. Torn between filial piety and guilt over his mother's suicide, haunted by the past, and skeptical about the future, Spiegelman is the artist as Everyman. Spiegelman's style reinforces the tensions of his plot and the contradictions of his charac-

Art Spiegelman, *Self-portrait*, 1986

In this self-portrait Spiegelman, the son of Holocaust survivors, depicts himself as a mouse, a cartoon convention adopted to tell the story of the greatest tragedy in human history.

art spiegelman

Bill Griffith, *Daily Strip*, from *Weirdo*, no. 24, 1988

Former underground cartoonist Bill Griffith expresses his amazement that he has been nationally syndicated in this delightful self-portrait.

ters. With the exception of the rendering of the cast's heads as those of animals, the strip is drawn realistically. There are no fantastic elements: no superheroes promising deliverance, no unexplained coincidences to heighten the drama, no poetic license to lyricize the plot or ennoble the characters. No fantasy is necessary; the Holocaust is intrinsically surrealistic, an unthinkable mass perversion, beyond belief in its intergenerational impact, requiring no artistic enhancement to cast its lurid spell. The use of the small and helpless mouse to represent man caught in the mousetrap of history is sufficiently symbolic. The use of mice by other cartoonists to express joy in creation's harmony (Steamboat Willie), wily acumen (Ignatz), or compensatory power (Mighty Mouse's clarion call: "Here I come to save the day!") contrasts with Spiegelman's insightful ability to embody in the same symbol the prosaic and hopeless struggle against evil.

While expanding the strip's scope, Spiegelman also assisted at the birth of a new genre, that of the "graphic novel." This publishing phenomenon would result in 140 new titles in the first half of 1988 alone.[7] Other extraordinary ventures in this category include *Batman: The Dark Knight Returns*, *Saga of the Swamp Thing*, and *The Shadow: Blood and Judgement*.[8] Unlike Spiegelman's bravura sole performance, however, these riveting stories, sumptuously produced and aimed at the mainstream literary market, are the products of a team effort akin to that of a medieval workshop or modern movie, complete with a cast of authors, artists, and special-effects assistants. Writer Beth Levine has attempted to define the genre: "They're not traditional novels, and they're not traditional comic books. They go by the catch-all phrase of 'graphic novels' because not even the people who write and/or publish them can agree on just what they are."[9]

Within the genre of graphic novel, *Maus* is an intimate autobiography, *Batman: The Dark Knight Returns*, an existential treatise on alienation. A modern morality tale told by a cynic, *Batman* is visualized in a richly cinematic style in the tradition of Burne Hogarth, Milton Caniff, and Will Eisner. Written ("story and pencils") by Frank Miller, inked by Klaus Janson and Miller, with "colors and visual effects" by Lynn Varley and "letters" by John Constanza, *The Dark Knight* gives us Bob Kane's

Batman in the winter of his discontent. Batman's confidence in his own mission has eroded, his ward, Robin, dead, his faith in the future shattered. Replacing his former certainty of being an instrument of divine retribution is a newfound cynicism, part and parcel of the deterioration of his American dream. As the story unfolds, the aging hero is locked in the past. When it concludes, he has been buried alive and exhumed. Now Batman lives in a chamber in the bowels of the earth with a band of punk followers, there preparing for Armageddon. "We have years," he reflects, "as many as we need . . . years — to train and study and plan. . . . Here, in the endless cave, past the burnt remains of a crimefighter whose time has passed. . . . It begins here — an army — to bring sense to a world plagued by worse than thieves and murderers. This will be a good life. . . . Good enough."[10] Its color as brilliant as its vision is black, *The Dark Knight* combines a combustive blend of abstract color, rich blacks, full-page frames, dramatic aerial and worm's-eye perspectives, onomatopoeic sound effects, exciting formulas for depicting the figure in motion, and marvelous and mythological borrowings. All recall the fecund experiments conducted by the first comicstrip masters, whose work was unencumbered by precedent. *The Dark Knight*, like the work of Winsor McCay, Lyonel Feininger, and George Herriman, features interpenetrating frames of various shapes, juxtaposed complementary colors abstractly applied, and a fascination with myth and magic.

The iconography of these founding fathers is also part of the artistic vocabulary of *Raw* contributors Bill Griffith and Kim Deitch. In *Zippy the Pinhead*, Griffith drew from the same carnival and freak-show imagery that had so inspired Winsor McCay, presenting the pinhead clown as idiot savant. Griffith combines circus iconography with protean setting, time travel, altered states, and social commentary — all devices pioneered by Winsor McCay. *Yow*, no. 1, contains an adventure entitled "A Dope in High Places." Beginning at the Pussy Kat Ranch fifty miles outside of Las Vegas, this action-packed saga of corrupt U.S. Senator Morton Lufkind of Rhode Island moves to Washington, D.C., where Lufkind attends a "prayer breakfast . . . [a] meeting with the Cub Scouts, and [a] C.I.A. front money drop," then telescopes to Mardi Gras

Kim Deitch, opening page from *Hollywoodland*, 1987

In *Hollywoodland* Deitch depicted fantastic occurrences in the decaying film capital.

Bill Griffith, *Zippy: "Framed and Hung,"* 1986

New Orleans, jumps to the senator's Haitian hideaway, cuts to Lufkin's home in the suburbs of Providence, and segues to his victory party in a Manhattan hotel. The cast of characters is as varied as are the strip's panoramic settings. Juxtaposing bureaucratic blowhards, Long Island mobsters, "feds and fags," magazine moguls, prostitutes, and pinheads, "A Dope in High Places" is the anthem of our national absurdities.[11]

In a second episode from *Yow*, no. 1, "Time Out of Mind," Zippy, through the kaleidoscopic medium of the New York City Museum of Natural History, becomes a mental traveler, visiting ancient Egypt; Rome in 53 B.C.; turn-of-the-century Hester Street in New York; the African jungle; "the tribal village of Levittown," site of the artist's boyhood; nineteenth-century Japan; and the California gold rush of 1849. Unifying these adventures is Zippy's unique perspective — that of a baby boomer in a throwaway society. Captured in the evocative past, Zippy can only think of the pedestrian present.

In ancient Rome, for example, Zippy muses, "I wonder when 'My Favorite Martian' goes on around here," and announces to the citizens milling in the Forum, "If you're waiting for Elizabeth Taylor — I already saw 'Cleopatra' and she looked puffy!!"[12] Indeed, Zippy's consciousness, his entire frame of reference, is shaped by television and film. In fact, the power of electronic media to evoke Buddhistic contemplation is the theme of "Back to Pinhead: The Punks and the Monks," an episode that appeared in *Yow*, no. 2, in which Zippy blissfully contemplates a bevy of washing machines housed in a downtown Des Moines Laundromat. As he does so, he captures the imagination of a cult of Buddhist monks and a gang of punk rockers. His cryptic utterances lead the monks to believe him a messianic outer-space "meta-king" versed in the "methods of omniversal awareness," and the devotees proclaim him their leader. At Zippy's direction, the monastery's "meditation room" is soon equipped with "Whirlomatics" and television sets, and the holy ones find themselves, "through this sudsy orifice awash in the eye of being," participants in Zippy's divine madness.[13]

Carnival imagery, altered consciousness, the presence of the past, and the mysteries of the invisible world also characterize the work of Kim Deitch. Best known as the creator of *Hollywoodland*, the artist was born in Los Angeles in 1944, the son of animator Gene Deitch. Educated at Pratt Institute, Kim Deitch — like others before him — was drawn by the lure of the open road. After a stint with the Norwegian Merchant Marine, Deitch took a series of odd jobs, including that of psychiatric aide at New York Hospital, an experience which was to shape his viewpoint and to cast thematic and iconographic shadows over his oeuvre. Interviewed by Monte Beauchamp for the *Comics Journal* in July 1988, Deitch recalled: "Walking through the halls, it was as if you could have been in 1930 with the pictures on the walls and the style of furniture."[14] The deeply felt presence of the past, experienced for the first time in New York Hospital, was to characterize all of Deitch's work, as was the theme of divine madness. Deitch's first comic book, *Corn-Fed Comics*, no. 1 (Portland, Oreg., 1972), begins with the introduction of Madam Fatal, a sleuth who is in reality the elderly Richard Stanton. Called upon to solve the mystery of the kidnapping of the cryonically preserved corpse of his college chum Hugo Cartwright, the sage proves remarkably resourceful, dismissing gangsters with cane blows and well-aimed kicks. Disguised as Madam Fatal, Stanton persuades brain surgeon Philip Mayberry to place Cartwright's brain in the virile body of a gorilla.

The second *Corn-Fed* adventure, "Venusian Madness," stars Miles Microft, the renowned psychic detective. Microft is summoned to the Melford Rehabilitation Center, an asylum, at the request of Ian Farnsworth, former loan officer at the Union City National Bank. Restrained by a straitjacket, Farnsworth recounts the saga of mad scientist Riddel von Eckmeister, who has coerced the banker by force of poltergeist to embezzle $300,000. During his investigation, Microft falls in love with von Eckmeister's daughter, Blanche, whom he later unmasks as the "poltergeist." When von Eckmeister attempts to murder Microft, Blanche blasts her father. Learning that Blanche is not an eight-year-old child but an eighteen-year-old midget, Microft makes her his wife. The banker is vindicated, and the couple depart for a honeymoon aboard a train, unaware that they have unknowingly left their hometown in the grip of beings from another planet.

In the last *Corn-Fed* episode, "Cult of the Clown," Deitch draws upon the circus imagery so beloved of McCay and Griffith to spin a tale of an international clown conspiracy unmasked by a suburban father.

The themes of the wisdom of age, the vanity of earthly ambition, and the power of the unconscious, first sounded in *Corn-Fed Comics*, no. 1, were restated in *Hollywoodland*, a strip carried in the *Los Angeles Reader* in 1984.

Set in the decaying Los Angeles neighborhoods that were once home to titans of the film industry, the strip stars has-been actor Larry Farrel; former movie producer Isaac Bauman, a "wizened old man . . . [who] . . . has been running a unique, one patient at a time, sanitarium out of his Fairfax Avenue apartment for decades"; elderly psychic detective Miles Microft, now an alcoholic; African American Alonzo Jones, proprieter of a tiny convenience store; Alonzo's lacky, Sammy, whose "ghetto blaster" is really a secret communications center; Arlene Kartzmar, a failed television reporter; and the entertainment industry itself, including a nineteenth-century opera company, the silent movies of the teens and the twenties, Bauman's "Hollywoodland," a carnival shrine to the movies of the past, the La Brea Tar Pit Museum on Wilshire Boulevard, and "T. V. City," Arlene's employer.

Among the strip's influences, according to Deitch, was the silent movie, specifically the fifteen-chapter, 1917 Pathé serial, *The Mystery of the Double Cross*. This film, states Deitch in the afterword to *Hollywoodland*, was an important influence on the mood and tone of the strip.[15] Succinctly stated, *Hollywoodland* traces the convergence of several "losers" whose consciousnesses have been altered in common pursuit of the solution to a mystery. The sleuths: alcoholic psychic detective Microft; cocaine-snorting TV reporter Arlene; somnambulistic retired bit actor Farrel; and Beverly Fairfax, Mrs. Isaac Bauman, a legendary movie star of the silent screen who sleeps forever beautiful in a deathlike trance. The overriding presence of the past is embodied in the prehistoric exhibitions at the La Brea Tar Pit Museum; in the "Hollywoodland" carnival; in the ruined architecture of Los Angeles; and in the poignant memories of old-timers Bauman, Farrel, and Microft, all of whom have seen "better times." In the disposable society, *Hollywoodland* reminds us, human beings are at once the most expendable and most valued of

resources.

Deitch again returned to the world of entertainment for his third major work, the Ledicker saga, re-created in the superb *Weirdo* sequence beginning with "Murder on a Midway."[16] In this humorous epic a makeshift museum on a Texas highway houses "Kewpie's Hi-Way Wonders," the remnants of a nineteenth-century carnival. The detritus exhibited includes the remains of Little Widget, an untalented ukelele player; a film documenting the electrocution of George Washington Jones by the Ku Klux Klan on August 13, 1925; Wagandi, a pygmy; and the Mystery Shrine, the home of creatures from another planet. Presiding over the premises is Kewpie, the midget museum director and former wife of the late A. J. Ledicker, Jr. The whimsical notion that the wonders of the invisible world can be made manifest in a humble Texas truckstop recalls the optimism of the early twentieth century, when Winsor McCay celebrated man's unlimited imaginative potential as expressed in the dreamworld. In Deitch's strip, fantastic elements are juxtaposed with the flotsam and jetsam of modern America: 7-Eleven Big Gulp containers, video games, Hulk Hogan T-shirts. Within the cartoon coexist three time frames — the not-so-distant nineteenth century, when Colonel Ledicker created his emporium of wonders; the early twentieth century, when son A.J. gathered together the bizarre cast of characters that would so intrigue visitors from distant stars; the present, in which the narrator, Kewpie, interprets the past to the comic-strip reader; and the future, into which an airborne Coors beer truck is rushing. The style in which these lyrical adventures are recounted recalls modes of artistic expression in Depression America. Reminiscent of Harold Gray, Deitch's pen creates solid figures of awkward simplicity; dramatic chiaroscuro; and large balloons containing fast-paced dialogue.

A third *Raw* contributor, Charles Burns, envisioned an entirely different type of strip, as earthbound as Deitch's Ledicker cycle is fantastic. The most arresting of Burns's characters is El Borbah, the beerguzzling, pot-bellied, bullet-headed, taco-munching, cynical superhero detective whose adventures comprise *Hard-Boiled Defective Stories*. The style in which his amazing exploits are depicted has been described

Harvey Pekar and Gerry Shamray, *Late Night with David Letterman*, from *American Splendor*, no. 12, 1987

Autobiography is lifted to epic level in Harvey Pekar's soap opera of despair, *American Splendor*. Here Pekar suspiciously fields Letterman's interrogation.

by Lynda Barry:

> The most striking thing about [Burns's work] is the drawing. You can't believe a person could do it with regular human hands. It's the kind of drawing that would have scared the pants off you in grade school, not only because the images are so eerie, but because they are too perfectly done, and not good or evil enough for you to tell what you are supposed to think about them.[17]

Among the modern mysteries solved by this contemporary Phillip Marlowe are cases involving bionic people ("Robot Love"), fast food ("Dead Meat"), cryogenics and transplants ("Living in the Ice Age"), cults, such as the Brotherhood of the Bone ("Bone Voyage"), and infertility and artificial insemination ("Love in Vein").

A world more limited than the surreal contemporary landscape inhabited by El Borbah is that of Harvey Pekar, whose transcendent soap opera of life among the working poor, *American Splendor*, carries autobiography to new heights, while continuing a tradition of social realism evoking the nineteenth-century Russian novel. Whereas the comic strip's early creators had painstakingly preserved their anonymity, today's cartoonists, Pekar chief among them, celebrate their own experience, whether universal or esoteric.

While coming full circle in the revival of fantastic themes and full-page formats, new-wave cartoonists obdurately refuse to translate their comic creations into the media of electronic technology. While early masters such as Winsor McCay experimented with film and animation as a way of extending artistic vision, successful cartoonists such as R. Crumb and Art Spiegelman resolutely decry adaptations of their characters. Rejecting technological adaptations for fear of commercialization, contemporary cartoonists deny the comic strip's historical function — to increase newspaper circulation — and insist on the medium's intrinsic aesthetic and political integrity. Whereas the personal visions of the comic strip's first masters were expressed metaphorically, those of the avant-garde cartoonist are explicitly stated.

Thematically, however, the preoccupations of contemporary creators remain closely related to the work of the strip's first masters. Created in large urban centers, the comics have always utilized the city as setting and symbol. Full of original bright promise, Winsor McCay's turn-of-the-century urban vision became increasingly bleak, culminating in the grim 1908 Shantytown excoriation and in the strident 1910 Mars sequence. During the twenties and thirties Harold Gray depicted the city as the sanctuary of foreign agents, corrupt labor leaders, and gangsters, periodically returning Annie to his beloved rustic heartland, the Midwest. Chester Gould heightened the urban tensions understated in Gray's strip, depicting in *Dick Tracy* the final confrontation between the forces of good and evil, order and anarchy, a drama enacted on an urban stage. Similarly, the superheroes made their appearances only in the city — Superman, to leap the tallest buildings of Metropolis; Batman, to right the wrongs of Gotham City. In the world of Will Eisner's *Spirit* the city affectionately wears a human face, fulfilling its function as a refuge for "huddled masses yearning to breathe free." The urban centers later depicted by R. Crumb, however, are at once anonymous and alarming — "bad scenes" from which to "bug out." In the world of graphic novelist Frank Miller, the city is an inferno, dangerous to both mind and body. Interviewed by Kim Thompson for the *Comics Journal*, Miller explained that "the normal human response to the crime and unending hostility of the city would be to become as ungentlemanly and uncivilized as the city's customs demand. One Bernard Goetz is enough, though I'm amazed there aren't more people doing what he did."[18] In *The Dark Knight*, Miller depicts Batman as a victim of urban crime, brutalized and embittered. The Rego Park of Spiegelman's *Maus*, on the other hand, is a homey refuge from the horrors of sophisticated Europe, a contrast that bespeaks Spiegelman's international frame of reference.

But, whether dealing with the gritty realities of urban crime or exploring the rich interior landscape of the psyche, the American comic has since its infancy been remarkable for its fascination with the fantastic. The comics' penchant to express the inexpressible is unique in the history of the American visual arts. Since the colonial period American "fine" artists have always been most successful when limiting their repertoire to the depiction of people, places, and things. The portraits of John Singleton Copley, Gilbert Stuart, John Singer Sargent, Thomas Eakins; the landscapes of Frederic Church and Albert Bierstadt; the still lifes of the Peale family; the cityscapes of the Ash Can School and Edward Hopper — all are examples of the peak achievements of American artists. Until the diaspora of European artists to America in the thirties and forties, painters and sculptors who sought to explore alternative universes were few and — while on occasion attaining expressive heights, as did Thomas Cole and Albert Pinkham Ryder — commonly regarded as important eccentrics outside the mainstream of American art.

Despite their commercial function, the comics have always attracted those whose vision extended beyond the here and now. The reasons for this are many. The social class and ethnic origins of comic artists have been more varied than that of fine-arts creators. The period of time in which the comics creator began to function coincided with that in which photography and film came into their own, supplanting and surpassing painting and printmaking in their ability to represent reality and to capture actual moments in time.

The nature of the alternative universes created by comic artists has varied from the surrealist dreamworld of McCay's *Little Nemo*, with its key images of mushrooms, cacti, and other substances associated with altered subconsciousness, to the medieval epics of Harold Foster, the jungle odysseys of Burne Hogarth, the futuristic sagas of Dick Calkins and Alex Raymond, and the animal allegories of Walt Kelly, R. Crumb, Berke Breathed, and Art Spiegelman.

While some American comic artists have explored fantastic worlds, others have chosen to express themselves in pungent social commentary. Consequently, the distinction between the editorial cartoon and the comic strip has become blurred. The Pulitzer Prize for editorial cartooning, in fact, has recently become the purview of the comic-strip artists, awarded to both Trudeau and Breathed. Other notable social commentators include Jules Feiffer and Nicole Hollander. These editorializing cartoons are related in both form and content. Adhering to a formula pioneered by Feiffer to meet the diminished dimensions of contemporary cartoons, they feature sketchily rendered figures, often seen frontally or in profile, standardized settings, and copious dialogue. Within this format, the opinions rendered are as various as are the artists holding them. Feiffer and Trudeau are obsessive analysts; Hollander, the trenchant, dispassionate observer; Breathed, purveyor of bittersweet whimsy.

Satire itself sometimes takes fantastic form. *Pogo*'s animal protagonists sound the alarm that "we have met the enemy and he is us" during a period of intense national paranoia. *Sylvia*'s outer-space intimate, Gernif, observes with wry relish the human comedy. Whether articulating our dreams, celebrating our values, excoriating our hypocrisies, or expressing our fears, the comics have since their inception reflected our society, through word and image presenting the American panorama.

Charles Burns, *Living in the Ice Age*, 1984

Copyright 1984 Charles Burns. From *Hard-Boiled Defective Stories*, 1988.

Bearing a suspicious resemblance to Al Capp's Bomb Face, El Borbah, a tattooed, cynical muscle man, is the ideal detective for the urban eighties.

R. F. Outcault, *"The Yellow Dugan Kid,"*
September 7, 1896

Describing his brainchild to the Librarian of Congress, Outcault wrote: "His costume . . . is always yellow, his ears are large, he has but two teeth and a bald head and is distinctly different from anything else." Soon *The Yellow Kid* was to be the subject of a bitter court case between rival publishers William Randolph Hearst and Joseph Pulitzer, resulting in the appearance of two Kids — Outcault's in Hearst's *New York Morning Journal* and George Luks's in Pulitzer's *New York World*. In the character of the Yellow Kid, Outcault created a memorable prototype, that of the idiot savant as social commentator. Enormously popular, the strip's urban setting, crowded frames, expressive style, and slapstick humor reflected the familiar ethnic neighborhoods of turn-of-the-century New York, where one communicated through gesture and pantomime.

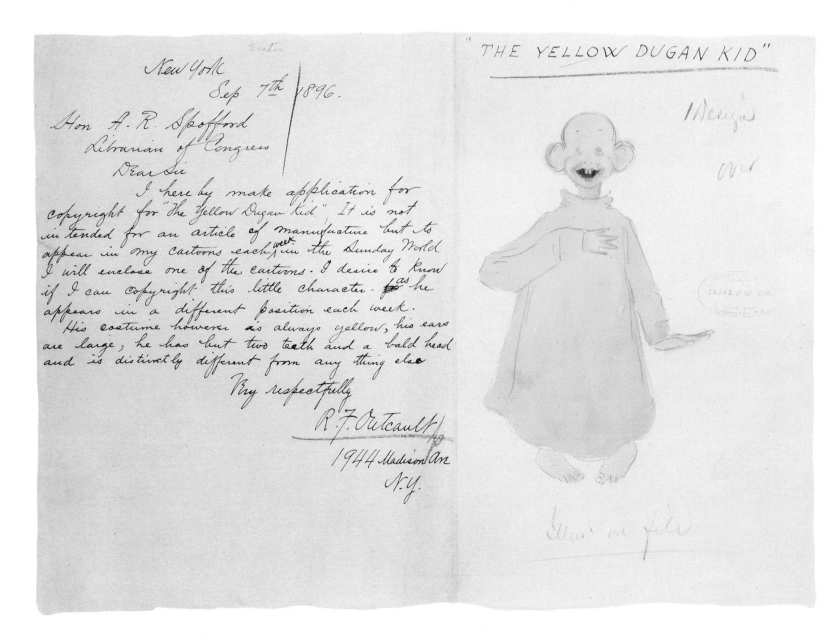

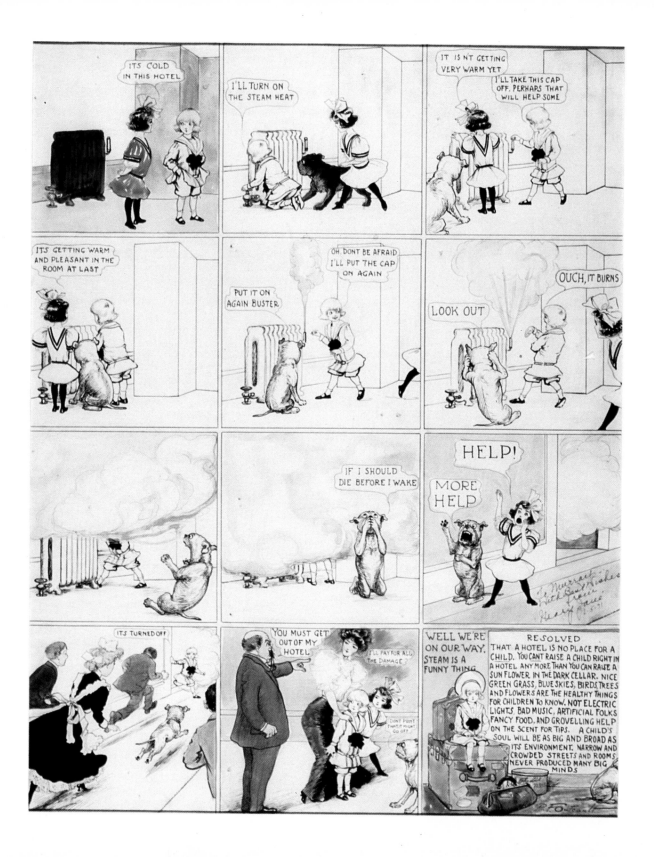

R. F. Outcault, *Buster Brown*, 1902

Lyonel Feininger, *Wee Willie Winkie's World*,
November 25, 1906

Lyonel Feininger, *The Kin-der-Kids — The Kin-der-Kids (abroad)*, May 20, 1906

Copyright 1906 *Chicago Tribune*.
Division of Prints and Photographs, the Library of Congress.

Utilizing abstract color and simplified form, Feininger states the teutonic theme of man against the elements. At home on the sea, the Kids are pursued by Aunty Jim-Jam, who pursues them in an airborn balloon.

Lyonel Feininger, *The Kin-der-Kids — The Kin-der-Kids'*
Narrow Escape from Aunty Jim Jam, September 2, 1906

Cubist master Lyonel Feininger created landscapes of faceted abstraction in which was depicted the battle of the sexes. Here funereal spinster Aunty Jim-Jam and her cat pursue the Kin-der-Kids and their dog. Contrasts enlivening the drama included those of age, sex, and element. Elderly Aunty Jim-Jam has launched an airborn expedition to capture the kids — a group of boys who have escaped by bathtub across the Atlantic Ocean.

Lyonel Feininger, *Wee Willie Winkie's World*,
September 30, 1906

Its title derived from the nursery rhyme of the same
name, *Wee Willie Winkie's World* is in the best German
fairy-tale tradition. Its isolated protagonist, Wee Willie,
wanders fearfully through an anthropomorphized natural
world. To emphasize the strip's visual qualities, Feininger
eschewed the balloons he had utilized in *The Kin-der-Kids*.

Winsor McCay, *Little Nemo in Slumberland,*
March 29, 1908

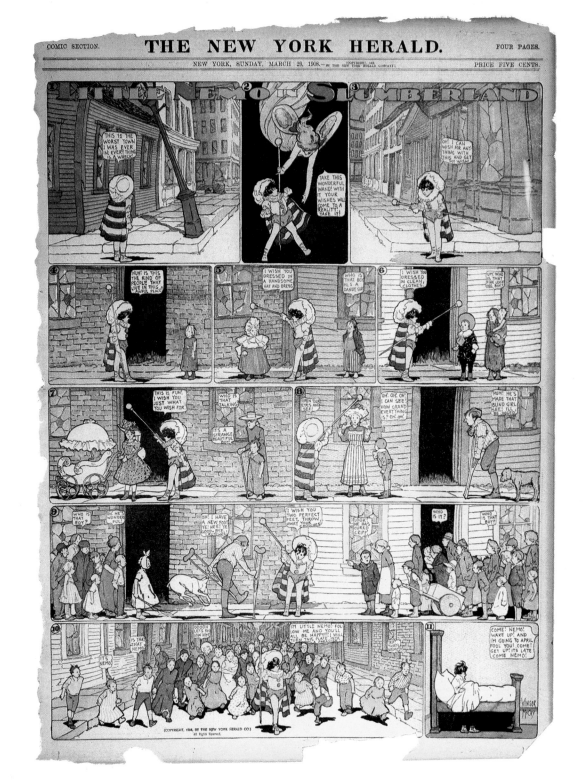

James Swinnerton, *Little Jimmy*, November 28, 1915

The sweetly innocent world of *Little Jimmy* contrasted sharply with the chaotic universe wrought by *The Katzenjammer Kids*. The strip's stock characters included Pinky and his bulldog Buck, an obvious adaptation of *Buster Brown*'s Tige.

George Herriman, *Krazy Kat*, November 17, 1918

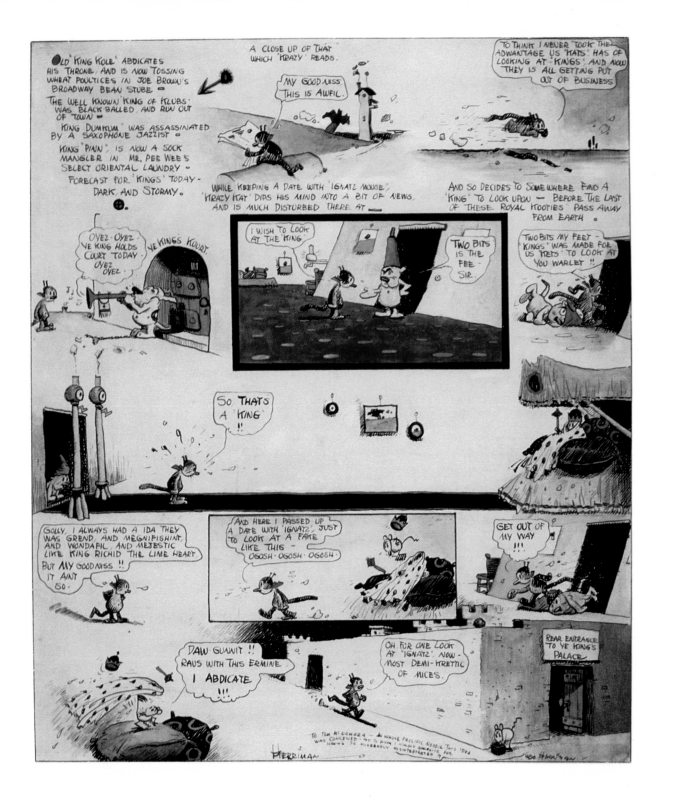

George McManus, *Snookums*, n.d.

Dating from the first decade of the century, this strip illustrates McManus's fondness for high fashion and carries as a subtext male lechery and female frivolity — the themes of his masterpiece, *Bringing Up Father*.

George McManus, *Bringing Up Father*, July 24, 1921

In 1913, as America prepared to march to war, artist George McManus sounded the comic-strip clarion call to battle between the sexes. Inspired by a turn-of-the-century play entitled *The Rising Generation*, McManus's *Bringing Up Father* chronicled the rags-to-riches conflict between Jiggs, an unpretentious Irish immigrant, and Maggie, his social-climbing wife. Depicted in the mannered style befitting a former fashion editor and featuring juxtapositions of lovingly rendered architectural ornament, drapery, dress, and upholstery, *Bringing Up Father* exploited Maggie's love of finery and conspicuous consumer display as the pretext for a tour de force of McManus's technical facility. Obscured by this virtuosity is the drama's dark domestic vision. Only happy in humble haunts, Jiggs is forced by Maggie and doomed by financial good fortune to be the unwilling intimate of poseurs and sycophants. The strip's manifold contrasts include clashes of class, culture, gender, and ethnicity.

Martin Branner, *Winnie Winkle, the Breadwinner*,
January 25, 1925

Cartoonist Martin Branner satirized Outcault's foppish
Buster Brown in *Winnie Winkle*, in 1922 introducing
Winnie's popinjay "adopted brother," Perry.

Bud Grace, *Ernie,* April 15, 1990

Bud Grace unites the disparate traditions of the cat strip and the fantastic invention in this episode of *Ernie*. Here, Ernie utilizes an "automatic catwasher," a Goldbergesque device combining a bowl of anchovies, an immobilizing machine, and a crank to clean Bobo, a fractious feline.

R. Crumb, *Keep on Truckin'*, 1967

Berke Breathed, *Bloom County*, 1988

The self-satiric *Bloom County* pokes fun at the artificiality of the comic-strip medium while providing a glossary of terms.

Frank Miller, Klaus Janson, Lynn Marley, and John Constanza, *Batman: The Dark Knight Returns*, 1986.

WHO'S WHO IN THE COMICS

Bibliographic references that appear at the end of the biographies are given in chronological order. Where they exist, works written by the artist, followed by works written by other authors but illustrated by the artist, precede the general references to his or her work.

All direct quotations by the artists included in these biographies are drawn from interviews with the author or questionnaires solicited by the author, unless a published source is cited. Where no bibliographical references are provided, the information included was, as above, culled from interviews with and questionnaires supplied by the artists.

The following abbreviations are used for frequently cited works:

AAA	*American Art Annual.* 36 vols., 1898–1945.	
Amory	Amory, Cleveland. *International Celebrity Index.* New York: Harper & Row, 1963.	
CB	*Current Biography,* 1945–	
Couperie and Horn	Couperie, Pierre, and Horn, Maurice, eds. *A History of the Comic Strip.* Trans. Eileen B. Hennessy. New York: Crown, 1968.	
Fielding	Fielding, Mantle. *Dictionary of American Painters, Sculptors, and Engravers.* Rev. ed. New York: James F. Carr, 1965.	
Horn	Horn, Maurice, ed. *The World Encyclopedia of Comics.* New York: Chelsea House, 1976.	
Mallett	Mallett, Daniel Trowbridge. *Index of Artists.* 2 vols. New York: Peter Smith, 1948.	
Nye	Nye, Russel. *The Unembarrassed Muse: The Popular Arts in America.* New York: Dial Press, 1970.	
Sheridan	Sheridan, Martin. *Comics and Their Creators.* Boston: Robert T. Hale & Co., 1942.	
Who's Who	*Who's Who in America*	
Who Was Who	*Who Was Who in America.* 9 vols. 1945–1968	

Nicholas Afonsky   1891(2)–1943

Born in Russia, Afonsky was one of five artists to draw *Little Annie Rooney;* others included Ed Verdier, Ben Batsford, and Darrell McClure (q.v.). Afonsky is also credited with work on *Ming Foo, Minute Movies,* and *Secret Agent X-9* (April–November 1938).

REFERENCES: Obituary, *New York Times,* June 17, 1943. Horn, pp. 454, 468, 494, 495, 605, 697.

F. O. Alexander   1897–

Franklin O. Alexander ("Alex"), best known for his editorial cartoons and for his continuation of C. W. Kahles's *Hairbreadth Harry,* was born, raised, and educated in Chicago. During World War I Alexander served in the camouflage corps of the U.S. Army in Europe. After his discharge, he worked as a commercial artist before turning to the comic strip. In 1931 Kahles died and Alexander moved to the *Philadelphia Ledger,* where he drew *Hairbreadth Harry* until 1939. After the strip was discontinued, Alexander served as the *Philadelphia Evening and Sunday Bulletin*'s editorial cartoonist, a position from which he retired in 1971. From June 18 to July 12, 1985, the Federal Reserve Board of Philadelphia hosted a retrospective of Alexander's work. His original comic-strip drawings are in the collections of the Museum of Cartoon Art in Rye Brook, New York, and of his daughter, Carolyn Alexander Russek. Alexander lives in retirement in Wyndmoor, Pennsylvania.

REFERENCE: James Tanis and Bill Aldrich, *Alexander Recycled* (Radnor, Pa., 1985). Bill Aldrich et al., *Battle for Belinda* (Philadelphia, 1987).

Brad Anderson   1924–

Winner of the 1976 National Cartoonists Society award for Best Panel, Brad Anderson is the creator of *Marmaduke.* Raised in Jamestown, New York, Anderson served in the U.S. Navy during World War II, later attending Syracuse University's School of Fine Arts. In 1954, inspired by his parents' boxer, Anderson began his single-panel cartoon detailing the misadventures of a Great Dane. *Marmaduke,* distributed by United Feature Syndicate, has appeared in twenty anthologies, which have sold more than ten million copies worldwide. The artist and his wife, Barbara, the parents of four grown children, live in Escondido, California.

REFERENCES: United Feature Syndicate, *Brad Anderson: Marmaduke,* n.d.

Carl Thomas Anderson   1865–1948

Carl Thomas Anderson was born in Madison, Wisconsin, on February 14, 1865, of Norwegian-immigrant parents Andrew and Mary Eid Anderson. He attended public schools in Janesville, Wisconsin, and Beatrice, Nebraska. From 1892 to 1893 he studied at the School of Industrial Art in Philadelphia. During the years 1894 to 1906 he worked as a cartoonist, in turn, at the *Philadelphia Times,* the *Pittsburgh Comet,* the *New York World,* and the *New York Journal.* While at Joseph Pulitzer's *World,* he created the Sunday strip *The Filipino and the Chick.* Later, at William Randolph Hearst's *Journal* he began *Raffles and Bunny.* For the McClure Syndicate Anderson created *Herr Spiegelberger* in 1903. He was fired from the *Journal* in 1906, only to be rediscovered by Hearst himself in 1934. In the meantime he supported himself as a freelance cartoonist, occasionally contributing to *Life, Puck, Judge,* and *Collier's.* It was at age sixty-four, while teaching a night class in cartooning, that Anderson created *Henry.* The strip appeared from 1932 to 1934 in the *Saturday Evening Post* and was taken over by Hearst's King Features Syndicate in 1934. In 1942 illness forced Anderson's retirement, and he bequeathed *Henry* to his assistants, Don Trachte (q.v.) and John Liney (q.v.). Anderson died a bachelor in Madison, Wisconsin, on November 4, 1948. The success of *Henry* may be due, in large part, to the appeal the mute naïf has always had for large audiences. Other comic-strip mutes include Otto Soglow's *Little King,* Max, the shoeshine boy of *Joe Palooka,* and, more recently, Ira Phillips's *Mister Mum.* In *Henry* the simplicity of the protagonist's personality finds its counterpart both in the minimal amount of action and dialogue and in the simple design of each frame.

REFERENCES: Sheridan, p. 20. Obituary, *New York Times*, November 5, 1948, p. 11. Mallett, p. 9. *Who Was Who* 2 (1943–50): 25. Dorothy McGreal, "Silence Is Golden," *World of Comic Art* 1 (Winter 1966–67): 10–17. Couperie and Horn, p. 72. Nye, p. 221. Horn, pp. 78–79.

Alfred Andriola 1912–1983

Alfred Andriola was born in New York City in 1912. In 1929 he dropped out of Columbia University's School of Journalism and, following a fruitless search for work, decided to combine his literary and artistic abilities as a comic-strip artist. In 1935 he began work in the studio of Milton Caniff (q.v.). After an apprenticeship of three years Andriola began his own strip, *Charlie Chan*, based on Earl Derr Biggers's hero of mystery stories and films. The strip, begun in 1938, was distributed by the McNaught Syndicate. Charles Raab assisted Andriola in its production. In 1943 Andriola began *Kerry Drake*. As Martin Sheridan has pointed out, Andriola wrote dialogue "like a movie continuity, plotting it weeks in advance of the actual drawing," then transcribing it to the strips, with his assistant doing the lettering. After that, he filled in the remaining space with pictures. Characteristic of Andriola's style is liberal use of large contrasting areas of black and white, which recalls his time with Caniff.

REFERENCES: Alfred Andriola, *Kerry Drake*, nos. 1, 2 (El Cajon, Calif., 1986). Alfred Andriola, ed., *Ever Since Adam and Eve* (New York, 1955). Sheridan, pp. 19, 23, 118–120, 288. *Who's Who* 40 (1978–79). Couperie and Horn, author index. Nye, p. 229. Horn, p. 82.

Robert "Bobbo" Armstrong 1950–

Robert "Bobbo" Armstrong, the creator of *Mickey Rat* and the inventor of the Couch Potatoes, was born in Pasadena, California, on February 21, 1950, the son of Alexander and Margaret Armstrong. After attending two years of junior college and Chounaird's Art School in Los Angeles, Armstrong began his career as a freelance illustrator, working for Harcourt, Brace, Jovanovich; Avon; Warner; and the *National Lampoon*. Armstrong is the originator of the underground *Mickey Rat*, nos. 1–4 (1972, 1973, 1980, and 1982). Since 1973 his work has regularly appeared in compilations of underground comics, including *Arcade*, *Weirdo*, *El Perfecto*, *Mondo Snarfo*, and *Comix Book*. Armstrong's other publications include *The Official Couch Potato Handbook* (Capra, 1983), *The Couch Potato Guide to Life* (Avon, 1985), and *The Couch Potato Cookbook* (Warner, 1988). States Armstrong, "I'm constantly striving to create funnier, better-drawn stories that mirror the quirky nature of real life with a few of the absurdities and ridiculous situations that I encounter daily." Armstrong lives in Dixon, California.

Thomas Armstrong 1950–

Tom Armstrong, creator of North America Syndicate's *Marvin* and *John Darling*, is a graduate of the University of Evansville, Indiana, where he majored in fine arts. In 1979, with *Funky Winkerbean* creator Tom Batiuk (q.v.), Armstrong began *John Darling*, the comic-strip saga of a talk-show host, which he drew until 1985. In August 1982 Armstrong began *Marvin*, a kid strip featuring a red-headed baby. An immediate success, *Marvin* was designated "Best Comic Strip of 1982" by the Northern California Cartoon and Humor Association. Seven Armstrong anthologies have appeared: *Marvin: A Star Is Born*; *Marvin: Explains the Facts of Life*; *Marvin: Born to Be Wild*; *Marvin: Spoil Me*; *Marvin: Shapes Up*; and *John Darling Takes One*. Marvin made his animated debut in a March 1989 CBS-TV special. Armstrong lives in Florida with his wife, Glenda, and children, Jonathan and Jennifer.

REFERENCE: North America Syndicate, *Marvin by Tom Armstrong* (New York, 1988).

Gus Arriola 1917–

Gustavo Montano Arriola was born in Florence, Arizona, the son of a Mexican father and a mother of Mexican and Spanish background. He was the youngest of seven brothers and two sisters. When he was six months old his mother died; later the family moved to Los Angeles. In high school Arriola became aware of his talent for caricature, and after graduation he became an animator for MGM studios, where he worked on *Tom and Jerry*. In 1941, according to H. Keen, Arriola conceived the idea of doing a strip consciously dealing with an ethnic group. The result was *Gordo*, whose subject was the love life of a paunchy, middle-aged Mexican, the guardian of his parentless nephew, Pepito. *Gordo*, which began in November 1941 in the *New York World Telegram*, was distributed by George Carlin of United Feature Syndicate. Its publication, however, was interrupted in October 1942 when Arriola enlisted in the armed forces, but was revived on June 24, 1946, five months after Arriola's discharge. In addition to the various conflicts that arose between the anti-establishment Gordo and his achievement-oriented nephew, the strip was notable for its animal chorus — a dog, pig, and rooster, who comment on the action. The last *Gordo* strip is that of March 2, 1985.

REFERENCES: Gus Arriola, *Gordo* (New York, 1950); *Gordo's Cat* (San Diego, 1981). "Gordo con Carne," *Newsweek* 32 (August 3, 1948): 55. H. Keen, "Lazy, But Full of Beans — That's Gordo, Señor," *Editor and Publisher* 81 (September 18, 1948): 46. R. C. Harvey, "The Comics Library," *Comics Journal* 101 (August 1985): 49–50. *Who's Who* 40 (1978–79). Horn, pp. 88, 287.

Tony Auth 1942–

Winner of a 1976 Pulitzer Prize for his *Philadelphia Inquirer* editorial cartoons, artist Tony Auth, with author and radio commentator Daniel Pinkwater (q.v.), is the creator of King Features Syndicate's *Norb* (1989), the comic-strip saga of an eccentric genius. Born in Akron, Ohio, on May 7, 1942, Auth is the son of William Anthony and June Kathleen Donnally Auth. Auth received his B.A. from the University of California at Los Angeles in 1965. From 1964 to 1970 he was the chief medical illustrator for Rancho Los Amigos Hospital in Downey, California. In 1971 he joined the *Inquirer*'s staff as an editorial cartoonist. Anthologies of Auth's work include *Behind the Lines* (1978) and *Lost in Space — The Reagan Years* (1988). Auth resides in Wynnewood, Pennsylvania.

REFERENCE: *Who's Who in the East* (1989–90). King Features Syndicate, *The Fantastical Tales of Norb* (New York, 1989).

Carl Barks 1901–

Carl Barks, a major influence on artists of the sixties counterculture, was born on March 27, 1901, in Marril, Oregon, the son of William Barks and Arminta Johnson Barks. In the thirties he joined the staff of the Walt Disney organization, performing in a variety of positions, including those of assistant animator and story-department artist. In 1942 the first of Barks's *Donald Duck* comic books appeared; this was *Donald Duck Finds Pirate Gold*, a production of Dell Publishing Company. This was followed in 1943 by *Donald Duck and the Mummy's Ring*. In December 1947 Barks introduced his signature character: Scrooge McDuck. In 1952 Uncle Scrooge was given his own comic book, the first of which was *Only a Poor Old Duck*. Barks lives in retirement in Grants Pass, Oregon, his achievement venerated by a new generation of comics creators.

REFERENCES: Carl Barks, *Walt Disney's Uncle Scrooge McDuck* (Millbrae, Calif., 1981); *Uncle Scrooge McDuck* (Berkeley, Calif., 1987). Michael J. Barrier, *Carl Barks and the Art of the Comic Book* (New York, 1981). Floyd Gottfredson, *Walt Disney's Mickey Mouse in Color* (New York, 1988). Horn, p. 97.

Dan Barry 1923–

Artist Dan Barry was born in Long Branch, New Jersey, on July 11, 1923. He attended Textile High School in New York, and studied under Raphel Soyer and Yasuo Kuniyoshi at the American Artists' School. In September 1941 he met cartoonist George Mandel, who suggested the idea of a career in comics. In August 1943 Barry joined the army, where he did a comic strip, *Bombrack*, for *Air Force* magazine. After his discharge in January 1946 he worked on comicbook features including *Captain Midnight, Crime Does Not Pay, Big Town, Gang Busters*, and *Airboy*. His first newspaper strip was the daily *Tarzan*, begun in 1947. In 1951 he was recruited by King Features Syndicate to do the daily *Flash Gordon*. From 1957 to 1963 Barry lived in Europe but continued his strips for King Features. On February 18, 1968, Barry published his first *Flash Gordon* Sunday page.

REFERENCES: Couperie and Horn, p. 131. King Features Syndicate, *Dan Barry*, Biographical Series, no. 146 (New York, n.d.); *Dan Barry: Flash Gordon* (New York, n.d.). Horn, pp. 100, 120, 185, 196, 254, 310.

Lynda Barry 1956–

Comic-strip artist, painter, author, and radio commentator Lynda Barry was born and raised in Seattle, Washington, where she attended Evergreen State College. The daughter of a Filipino mother, Barry grew up in a neighborhood "in transition." Her richly ethnic childhood was to evoke a series of fictionalized comic-strip memoirs, *Ernie Pook's Comeek*, of which the *Washington Post Book World* wrote: "To call Barry a cartoonist is to diminish her work . . . [which is] almost literature, literature that culminates in an unbearable poignant insight." Her comic strips now appear in over forty national news weeklies and in *Esquire* and the *Village Voice*. Her paintings have been exhibited at the Linda Farris Gallery in Seattle and at the Nine Gallery in Portland, Oregon. Barry now lives in Chicago.

REFERENCES: Lynda Barry, *Girls and Boys* (Seattle, 1981); *Big Ideas* (Seattle, 1983); *Naked Ladies, Naked Ladies, Naked Ladies* (Seattle, 1984); *Everything in the World* (New York, 1986); *The Fun House* (New York, 1987); *The Good Times Are Killing Me* (Seattle, 1988); *Down the Street* (New York, 1988). R. Fiore, "Funnybook Roulette," *Comics Journal* 92 (August 1984): 40–41. R. Fiore, "Funnybook Roulette," *Comics Journal* 101 (August 1985): 39.

Seymour Barry 1928–

Seymour Barry, brother of Dan Barry (q.v.) of *Flash Gordon* fame, was born in Manhattan on March 12, 1928. In 1943 he entered New York City's School of Art and Design. After graduation he assisted his artist-brother in drawing for comic books and attended classes at the Art Students League and the Brooklyn Museum. In 1949 Barry began inking the backgrounds and figures for *Flash Gordon*. When artist Wilson McCoy died in 1961 Barry was recruited by King Features to do the artwork for *The Phantom*.

REFERENCES: King Features Syndicate, *Seymour Barry*, Biographical Series, no. 223 (New York, n.d.). Horn, pp. 100, 551.

Tom Batiuk 1947–

Born in Akron, Ohio, on March 14, 1947, cartoonist Tom Batiuk graduated from Kent State University, from which he received a B.F.A. and a certificate in education. Upon graduation, Batiuk became a teacher of arts and crafts at Eastern Heights Junior High School in Elyria, Ohio. In 1970 he created a cartoon for the Elyria *Chronicle-Telegram* from which was to derive his master strip, *Funky Winkerbean* (1972). A second strip, *John Darling* (1979), was the result of a collaboration with cartoonist Tom Armstrong (q.v.). Batiuk's latest work, in collaboration with Chuck Ayers, is *Crankshaft* (1987), distributed by Creator's Syndicate. Batiuk lives in Elyria, Ohio, with his wife, Cathy, and son, Brian.

REFERENCE: North America Syndicate, *Funky Winkerbean* (New York, 1988).

Alison Bechdel 1960–

Bechdel grew up in rural Pennsylvania and attended Oberlin College in Ohio, from which she graduated in 1979, moving to New York City, where the first *Dykes to Watch Out For* cartoon was published in the 1983 Lesbian Pride issue of *Womanews*. Since then Bechdel has published two best-selling collections of her work and a calendar with Firebrand Books, and she has selfsyndicated her comic strip. *Dykes to Watch Out For* now runs in more than twenty-five gay/lesbian and feminist publications in the United States, Canada, and Scotland. Bechdel also draws the comic strip *Servants to the Cause* for the *Advocate*, the national gay news magazine. She has contributed work to *Gay Comix, Wimmen's Comix, Strip AIDS USA*, and illustrated two stories for Harvey Pekar's (q.v.) comic book *American Splendor*. She lives in Minneapolis, where she works part-time as production coordinator at the gay/lesbian newspaper *Equal Time*.

REFERENCE: Alison Bechdel, *Biography* (Minneapolis, 1989).

Walter Berndt 1899–1986

Smitty's creator, Walter Berndt, began his career as an office boy when, in 1916, having completed only six months of high school, he applied for a job at the *New York Journal*. There he met one of the masters of the comic strip, Tad Dorgan (q.v.). Dorgan developed a liking for Berndt and began to teach him cartooning. Thereafter, Berndt would substitute weekly for Dorgan, who on Mondays would do an eight-column sports cartoon. Berndt also drew a twocolumn gag panel, *Then the Fun Began*. In 1921 Berndt left the *New York Journal* and went to the Bell Syndicate, where he attempted a cartoon, *That's Different*, which — according to author Martin Sheridan — Berndt said he "couldn't draw . . . and the syndicate couldn't sell." He then joined the *New York World* to draw a strip called *Bill the Office Boy*, but asked to leave after only two weeks. From the *World*, Berndt took *Bill the Office Boy* to the *New York Daily News*. The publisher, Joseph Medill Patterson, liked the strip but wanted a different name for it; his eyes closed, Berndt picked up a telephone book and opened the pages to "Smith." In *Smitty*, the bureaucracy that stimulated Kafka's nightmare vision is viewed positively. The stratification of *Smitty*'s office world provides the security of an environment in which change is impossible and relationships fixed.

REFERENCES: Walter Berndt, *Smitty* (New York, 1922); *Smitty* (New York, 1928); *Smitty at the Ball Game* (New York, 1929); *Smitty, the Flying Office Boy* (New York, 1930); *Smitty, the Jockey* (New York, 1931); *Smitty in the North Woods* (New York, 1932); *Smitty in the Back Woods* (New York, 1932). Sheridan, pp. 219–220. Couperie and Horn, p. 45. Nye, p. 221. Horn, pp. 108–109, 505, 626.

Jack Berrill 1923–

Jack Berrill, the creator of Tribune Media Services' *Gil Thorp*, was born in Brooklyn in 1923. Following graduation from Brooklyn Technical High School in 1941, Berrill turned down a scholarship to Pratt Institute, preferring to pursue immediately his vocation as a cartoonist. His first position was that of copy boy in the art department of the *New York Daily News*, where he came to the attention of the legendary Martin Branner (q.v.). For seventeen years he worked as Martin Branner's assistant on *Winnie Winkle, the Breadwinner*. In 1958 he began *Gil Thorp*, a teen strip starring a high-school coach. The protagonist's name was an amalgam of two sources: Jim Thorp and a next-door neighbor. The father of six children, Berrill is married to an English teacher.

REFERENCES: Tribune Media Services, *Jack Berrill Biography*, n.d. Craig Neff, "Comic Strip Coach Gil Thorp: Going Strong After Twenty-five Years," *Sports Illustrated* 60 (March 12, 1984): 82. Robert Creamer, "Big News from Milford: Coach Thorp Weds," *Sports Illustrated* 62 (July 8, 1985): 14.

Gordon Bess 1929–1989

Born in Richfield, Utah, in 1929, Gordon Bess, creator of *Redeye*, served as an artist in the U.S. Marine Corps in San Diego and as staff cartoonist and comics editor for the corps' *Leatherneck* magazine in Washington, D.C. After his discharge as a staff sergeant in 1956, Bess worked in Philadelphia as a commercial artist, then as art director for a greeting-card company in Cincinnati. In 1967 he created his Native American strip, *Redeye*, for King Features Syndicate. That same year the strip was awarded the prestigious Alfred Prize for best foreign humor strip by France's Salon Internationale de la Bande Dessinée. In May 1988, upon Bess's final illness, King Features assigned Bill Yates (q.v.) and Mel Casson (q.v.) to write and to draw the strip.

REFERENCE: King Features Syndicate, *Gordon Bess* (New York, n.d.).

Mark Beyer 1950–

Born in Bethlehem, Pennsylvania, in 1950, artist Mark Beyer has frequently published in the pages of *Raw*. Like many other younger artists, Beyer often self-publishes. His best-known works include *Disturbing Evening and Other Stories* (1979) and *Dead Stories* (1982), as well as *Agony* (1987).

REFERENCES: "Raw Data," in Art Spiegelman and Françoise Mouly, *Read Yourself Raw: The Graphix Anthology for Damned Intellectuals* (New York, 1987). Peter S. Prescott, "Agony," *Newsweek* 111 (January 18, 1988): 70–72. Thomas M. Disch, "Agony," *Playboy* 35 (February 1988): 30–31.

Ray Billingsley 1957–

Ray Billingsley, one of the few African-American artists to enjoy national syndication in mainstream papers, is the creator of the child strip *Curtis*. Distributed by King Features Syndicate since 1988, the racially integrated kid strip features the feisty Curtis, baby brother Barry, the aloof Michelle, and Chutney, who adores Curtis unrequitedly. Billingsley was born on July 25, 1957, in Wake Forest, North Carolina, the son of Henry and Laura Billingsley. The artist attended the New York School of the Visual Arts, from which he received his B.F.A. in 1979. Billingsley's first strip, *Lookin' Fine*, was distributed from 1980 to 1982 by United Feature Syndicate. Billingsley states, "What I want to stress in *Curtis* is relationships. Family, friends — I like to delve into the aspects of what makes a person who he or she is. I want to show that we Blacks like to laugh at ourselves, just like everyone else." The artist resides in New York City.

REFERENCE: King Features Syndicate, *Introducing Curtis* (New York, 1988).

Bud Blake 1918–

Julian W. (Bud) Blake, creator of King Features Syndicate's *Tiger*, was born February 13, 1918, in Nutley, New Jersey, where he attended grammar and high school. After graduation, Blake studied art at the National Academy of Design. Eventually, he became executive art director of the Kudner Advertising Agency. He resigned in 1954 and began a career as a freelance cartoonist. In this capacity he created for King Features the daily panel *Ever Happen to You?*, which ran from 1955 to 1966. In May 1965 King Features began syndication of Blake's kid strip, *Tiger*, twice voted Best Humor Strip by the National Cartoonists Society. Blake lives in Damariscotta, Maine.

REFERENCE: King Features Syndicate, *Bud Blake* (New York, n.d.).

Angela Bocage 1959–

Angela Bocage, best known for her *Wimmen's Comix* strips, was born in Fayetteville, Arkansas, on April 27, 1959, the daughter of Patricia Thach Walton. She received her B.A. from the University of California at Santa Cruz, where she majored in fine art and minored in art history. Her work has been published in *Wimmen's Comix*, nos. 11–16; *Strip AIDS USA* (Last Gasp, 1988); *Taboo*, no. 4; *Weird Smut*, no. 3; *Cherry*, no. 9; *Street Music*, nos. 5, 6; *Gay Comix*, no. 11; *Renegade Romance*, no. 1; and in a variety of cause-related compilations. To support herself, Bocage is also a letterer of mainstream comics. A single parent, Bocage reflects:

"I wish I had more time to work on my real life's work, which is my baby and my comics; I've studied all my life to be an artist and in comics' marriage of words and pictures is my obsession. However, I want to be a good mother and keep a roof above us and clothes on us and food in us, so I do other freelance jobs. . . . I consider myself an *underground* cartoonist — 'cause no one controls what I do!" Among the serious subjects Bocage attacks in her underground strips is that of child abuse. In "The Joys of Childhood," for example, Bocage depicts a toddler who, terrorized by her mother, seeks protection from an imaginary monster. "It helps me not fight back or scream," explains the child. "It never wants to hurt my mother. It's unselfish. All it does is protect us." Bocage lives in San Francisco.

REFERENCE: Angela Bocage, "Bocage on Bocage," *(kar-ton') new comic arts journal* 1 (1988): 23–25.

Mark Bode 1963–

Mark Bode, best known as the creator of the underground *Miami Mice* and for his work on *Teenage Mutant Ninja Turtles*, was born on February 18, 1963, in Utica, New York, the son of legendary cartoonist Vaughn Bode and Barbara Bode. Bode attended The Art School in Oakland, California, The School of Visual Arts in New York City, and San Francisco State University. His publications include *Miami Mice*, nos. 1–4 (Rip Off Press, 1986–87); *Gyro Comics*, nos. 1–3 (Rip Off Press, 1988); and *Teenage Mutant Ninja Turtles*, no. 18 (Mirage, 1989). His work has also appeared in *Heavy Metal* (1981–82) and *Penthouse* (1987–89). Lesser-known comics include *The Cartoon Book* (1978), produced while Bode was a student at The Art School in Oakland, *The Best of the Cosmic Circus* (1978), *Severely Limited*, no. 3 (1986), *Grunts*, no. 1 (1987), and covers for *The Complete Cheech Wizard*, nos. 1–4 (1987), as well as features in *Rip Off Press Comics*, nos. 16 and 21 (1988). States Bode of his prolific family: "Bode comics have been in print for thirty years now. It seems only a flash in the big scheme of things. I owe a lot to comics. . . . I am one of the few second-generation cartoonists in the field. . . . This fact is due to being the born son of Cheech Wizard. My six-year-old daughter, Zara, draws too and without taking the Bode popularity too serious I look at it this way — I have one hell of a third legacy!!!" Bode lives in Berkeley, California.

Bruce H. Bolinger 1943–

Bruce H. Bolinger, best known as the creator of the underground comic *Stranger in a Strange Land*, was born in Johnstown, Pennsylvania, on April 12, 1943, the son of Himes and Betty Bolinger. In 1961 he graduated from Littleton (Mass.) High School and completed the Famous Artists cartoonists course. In 1968 he received his B.A. from The Art Center College of Design in Los Angeles. From 1968 to 1976 Bolinger worked as a staff artist, then as assistant art director of Brady Publishing Company in Bowie, Maryland. In 1976 Bolinger began his career as a freelance illustrator under the name of "Freehold Studio." His cartoons and technical and medical illustrations have appeared in diverse publications, including works published by Simon & Schuster; Prentice-Hall; Southwestern Publishing; Harcourt, Brace, Jovanovich; Mosby; Allyn & Bacon; the Instrument Society of America; and Scott-Foresman. In 1987 Bolinger's underground comics were first published by Rip Off Press. In June 1989 Rip Off Press issued *Stranger in a Strange Land*, a compilation of Bolinger's comic adventures. Bolinger began a collaboration with Don Martin of *Mad* fame in spring 1989. States the artist, "Although commercial artwork has kept me occupied for twenty years the cartooning I've done has provided the most satisfaction. With the publication of my first stand-alone comic a second career is rapidly unfolding. Creating comic entertainment is not exactly brain surgery but it'll do until I find honest work. But . . . in a way . . . it is brain surgery." Bolinger lives in Nicktown, Pennsylvania.

Roger Bollen 1941–

Cartoonist Roger Bollen, a native of Ohio, first worked, after his graduation from Kent State University, as an illustrator and designer for a Cleveland firm. At the same time, he was an art teacher at a local private school. In 1967 Bollen conceived *Animal Crackers*, which was released in mid-1968. A renowned illustrator as well as comic-strip artist, Bollen has illustrated Marilyn Sadler's *Alistair's Elephant* (1983), *It's Not Easy Being a Bunny* (1983), *The Very Bad Bunny* (1984), *Alistair in Outer Space* (1984), *P.J., the Spoiled Bunny* (1986), and *Alistair's Time Machine* (1986).

REFERENCES: *Who's Who* (1976–86). National Newspaper Syndicate, *Biographical Sketch of Roger Bollen, Creator of "Animal Crackers"* (Chicago, n.d.).

Joyce Brabner 1952–

Cleveland cartoonist Joyce Brabner, best known for her controversial Iran-Contra "graphic docudrama" *Brought to Light*, is the creator of Eclipse Comics' *Real War Stories*. Her work has appeared in numerous publications, including *Tits and Clits*, no. 7 (1988), and *Strip AIDS USA* (Last Gasp, 1988). In 1983, after what Brabner describes as "a bickering correspondence," she married cartoonist Harvey Pekar (q.v.). Their courtship is depicted in *American Splendor*, no. 10. Says Brabner of her work: "I'm principally an editor and organizer. Most of what I do in comics is nonfiction — comics-as-journalism or comic-book documentaries, usually produced in partnership with activist organizations. These are people who do good and brave deeds every day, or raise questions that don't always get heard or answered. Most comic-book artists and writers get tired of month-to-month mythmaking. When I introduce them to real heroes, their jobs become much harder, but more interesting. We generally work on behalf of groups that don't have — nor would ever spend — big bucks on self-promotion. Comics are still affordable, and can look like a million dollars." Brabner and Pekar live in Cleveland Heights, Ohio.

REFERENCES: Joyce Brabner, *Brought to Light* (Forrestville, Calif., 1988); *Sound Bites* (Forrestville, Calif., 1990). Kathleen Kisner, "War and Peace: The Comic-Book Version," *Cleveland Plain Dealer Sunday Magazine*, October 18, 1987. "Interview," *Booklist*, September 15, 1989.

Pat Brady 1948–

Pat Brady, a graduate of Wisconsin State University, in Whitewater, is the creator of *Rose Is Rose*, the domestic saga of a defiantly proud homemaker. Inspired by the appearance of militant housewives on the *Donahue* television show, the strip premiered on April 15, 1984, and is now syndicated by United Feature to over 270 newspapers. The strip's cast includes the Gumbo family — mother Rose, handyman father Jimbo, and toddler son Pasquale. Brady's first strip, an office epic entitled *Graves, Inc.*, appeared from 1980 to 1983. Brady lives in Chicago with his wife, Barbara, and daughter, Chloe.

REFERENCES: David Astor, "Pat Brady on the Rise of 'Rose Is Rose,' " *Editor and Publisher* 27 (July 19, 1986). Nick Reiher, " 'Rose' Captures the Heart," *Joliet* (Ill.) *Herald-News*, May 10, 1987. Rebecca Coudret, " 'Rose' Strip Grows Out of Life," *Evansville* (Ind.) *Sunday Courier*, May 22, 1988. Gene Koprowski, " 'Rose' Blooming for Sycamore's Pat Brady," *Dekalb/Sycamore* (Ill.) *Daily Chronicle*, December 4, 1988.

Brumsic Brandon, Jr. 1927–

Born on April 10, 1927, in Washington, D.C., African-American comics creator Brumsic Brandon is the son of Brumsic and Pearl Brooks Brandon. Brandon attended New York University. His best-known work is *Luther*, an inner-city strip, which has been published in book form by Paul S. Eriksson: *Luther From Inner City* (1969); *Luther Tells It As It Is* (1970); *Right On, Luther* (1970); *Luther Raps* (1971); *Outta Sight, Luther* (1971); and *Luther's Got Class* (1976). The recipient of numerous awards from such organizations as the National Conference of Christians and Jews, the White House Conference on Children, the Nassau County Black History Museum, and the Negro Business and Professional Women's Association, Brandon lives in Mt. Pocono, Pennsylvania.

REFERENCES: Brumsic Brandon, Jr., "No Kidding," *Ethical Society* 3 (Winter 1980–81).

Who's Who in the East (1989).

Martin Branner 1888–1970

Martin Michael Branner was born in New York City on December 28, 1888. He was educated in New York's public schools. While still a high-school student he tried unsuccessfully to get a job in the art department of the *New York World*. On August 21, 1907, he eloped with fifteen-year-old Edith Fabbrini. To support themselves the Branners created a vaudeville routine, and Branner supplemented his income by drawing ads for *Variety* and creating stage props for Fred Allen. During World War I, Branner served with the army in the chemical warfare division. After returning home in 1919 he sold a strip, *Looie the Lawyer*, to Bell Syndicate. He then began a Sunday feature, *Pete and Pinto*, for the *New York Sun* and the *New York Herald*. His work eventually came to the attention of Chicago Tribune–New York News Syndicate general manager Arthur Crawford. In the spring of 1920 Branner signed a contract to do *Winnie Winkle, the Breadwinner*. The strip made its first appearance that September and was published as a daily and Sunday feature. During the thirties it was published in book form in Paris to popular acclaim as *Les Exploits de Bicot*. As Branner continued to draw *Winnie Winkle*, his conception of the strip changed; at first he conceived *Winnie Winkle* as a gag strip, but in a short while he began to stress the development of characters over a duration of time. Following his retirement in 1962 the strip was continued by Max van Bibber, Branner's assistant since 1938. Branner died on May 19, 1970, in New London, Connecticut, survived by his two sons, Bernard and Robert.

REFERENCES: Martin Branner, *Winnie Winkle, the Breadwinner*, 3 vols. (New York, 1930–32); *Les Exploits de Bicot* (Paris, 1931); *Bicot pêche à la ligne* (Paris, 1932); *Bicot, magicien* (Paris, 1933); *Bicot, capitaine de pompiers* (Paris, 1934); *Bicot achète une auto* (Paris, 1940). Sheridan, pp. 20, 186–190. Helen Berke, *Winnie Winkle and the Diamond Necklace* (Racine, Wis., 1946). *Who's Who* 34 (1966–67): 245. Couperie and Horn, pp. 45, 49, 180. Nye, p. 222. Obituary, *New York Times*, May 21, 1970. Horn, pp. 128–129, 554, 703.

Berke Breathed 1957–

The second comic-strip artist to receive the Pulitzer Prize for Editorial Cartooning (1987), Berke Breathed was born in Los Angeles. Breathed began his creative career at the University of Texas, where, as an undergraduate photojournalism major, he successfully submitted a cartoon to the *Daily Texan*. Soon the cartoon expanded to a college comic strip, *The Academic Waltz*. Retitled *Bloom County*, the strip was syndicated in 1980 by the Washington Post Writers Group to thirty-five newspaper clients, and was immediately successful. By 1988 *Bloom County* was appearing in over a thousand publications. In an October 1988 *Comics Journal* interview with Chicago journalist Mark Jannot, Breathed described the influence of such disparate stylistic sources as Jules Feiffer and Walt Disney: "I think that's what *Bloom County* is a combination of. I love drawing animals. . . . The kind of things you can get away with an animal, or with — dare I say it — a cute character is more than you can get away with in other instances." In 1989 the artist retired *Bloom County* and began *Outland*. The artist resides in Evergreen, Colorado, with his wife, photographer Jody Boyman.

REFERENCES: Berke Breathed, *Loose Tails* (Boston, 1983); *'Toons for Our Times* (Boston, 1984); *Penguin Dreams and Stranger Things* (Boston, 1985); *Bloom County Babylon* (Boston, 1986); "Return to Magnum Opus," *Washington Post*, March 31, 1986, pp. B1–2. *Billy and the Boingers Bootleg* (Boston, 1987); *Tales Too Ticklish to Tell* (Boston, 1988); *The Night of the Mary Kay Commandos* (Boston, 1989); *Happy Trails* (Boston, 1990). *Washington Post Book World*, April 24, 1983. *Washington Journalism Review* (May 1983). *Los Angeles Book Review*, May 15, 1983. G. Buchalter, "Cartoonist Berke Breathed Feathers His Nest," *People* 22 (August 6, 1984): 93–94. Mark Jannot, "The Pariah Speaks," *Comics Journal* 124 (August 1988): 104–107; "Can Berke Breathed Be Taken Seriously?" *Comics Journal* 125 (October 1988): 74–106.

Morrie Brickman 1917–

Born in Chicago on July 24, 1917, *small society* creator Morrie Brickman attended Lowell Grammar School and Marshall High School. While working during the day as a shoe salesman, Brickman at night attended the Art Institute of Chicago. He then served as an unpaid apprentice to John Groth, art editor of *Esquire*. During World War II Brickman was a staff sergeant in the U.S. Army Corps of Engineers. After his discharge in 1945, he returned to Chicago, where he opened his own studio, the clients of which included advertising agencies. In May 1966 Brickman began *the small society*, which is distributed by King Features Syndicate. Bill Yates (q.v.) began collaborating with Brickman on *small society* in 1985 and, after Brickman's retirement, took over writing the strip with Mel Casson (q.v.) as artist in 1989.

REFERENCE: King Features Syndicate, *Morrie Brickman* (New York, n.d.).

Austin Briggs 1908–1973

Austin Eugene Briggs was born on September 8, 1908, in Humboldt, Minnesota, the son of Harry and Ethel Davison Briggs. From 1924 to 1926 he studied at the Wicker Art School in Detroit. He attended the Art Students League of New York from 1927 to 1928, supporting himself by illustrating Henry Ford's *Dearborn Independent* and contributing to national magazines. On May 12, 1927, Briggs married Ellen Jeanette Weber. From November 7, 1938, to May 4, 1940, Briggs drew Alex Raymond's (q.v.) *Secret Agent X-9*. Couperie and Horn note Briggs's use of the comic strip as a mirror for current events. *Secret Agent X-9*, for example, anticipated the entry of the United States into World War II. From May 27, 1944, to July 25, 1948, he drew the Sunday *Flash Gordon* page, having drawn the dailies from May 27, 1940, to May 29, 1944. When Briggs tired of that strip, it passed into the hands of Mac Raboy (q.v.), who did the Sunday feature, and Dan Barry (q.v.), who did the daily continuity. In 1950 Briggs helped found the Famous Artists School in Westport, Connecticut.

REFERENCES: Austin Briggs, *How I Make a Picture* (Westport, Conn., 1952). *Who's Who* 34 (1966–67): 254. Couperie and Horn, author index. Horn, pp. 131, 254, 347, 574, 605.

R. M. Brinkerhoff 1880–1958

The creator of *Little Mary Mixup*, Robert Moore Brinkerhoff was born on May 4, 1880, in Toledo, Ohio. His father, R. A. Brinkerhoff, together with Henry Chapin, had founded the *Toledo Post*, which later merged to form the *Toledo News-Bee*. After study at the Art Students League of New York and in France, Brinkerhoff returned to Toledo, where he became the *Toledo Blade*'s political cartoonist. He later worked on the *Cleveland Leader* and the *Cincinnati Post*. In 1913 Brinkerhoff moved to New York, where he joined the staff of the *New York Evening World*. The *World*'s staff artist, Will B. Johnstone, encouraged Brinkerhoff to attempt a comic strip. Around 1918 Brinkerhoff began *Little Mary Mixup*. According to Sheridan the strip was considered innovational when it appeared, due to its use of a girl as main character. Brinkerhoff died in Minneapolis on February 17, 1958.

REFERENCES: Sheridan, pp. 177–190. Mallett, p. 53. Obituary, *New York Times*, February 18, 1958, p. 28. *Who Was Who* 3 (1951–60): 104. Fielding, p. 42. Couperie and Horn, p. 119. Nye, p. 221. Horn, pp. 132–133.

Christopher Browne 1952–

Cartoonist Chris Browne was born on May 16, 1952, in South Orange, New Jersey, the son of comic-strip creator Dik Browne (q.v.). Raised in Connecticut, Browne briefly attended the Philadelphia College of Art. In 1974 he became associate editor of *The Funny Papers*, a tabloid that published reprints of master comics as well as the work of underground creators. In 1976 Browne's own work first appeared in the *National Lampoon*; in 1978, in *Playboy*, for which he created *Benny Juice*, *Born Toulouse*, *Tom Morrow*, *The Kinky Report*, and *Cruiser*. His cartoons also have appeared in *Heavy Metal*; *Epic*; *Esquire*; *Nuts*, nos. 1, 2; and *The Secret Life of Cats*. Following his father's death on June 4, 1989, Browne became the artist and writer of

King Features Syndicate's *Hagar the Horrible*, with which he had long been associated. He lives in Sarasota, Florida, with his wife, the former Carroll Smith.

REFERENCE: King Features Syndicate, *Christopher Browne* (New York: August 1989).

Dik Browne 1917–1989

Best known as the creator of *Hagar the Horrible*, Richard Arthur Allan Browne was born in Manhattan on August 11, 1917. In 1933 Browne joined the art department of the *New York Journal*; there he covered the trial of gangster Lucky Luciano. Browne next worked for *Newsweek*. From 1942 to 1946 he served in the U.S. Army, where he created the WAC cartoon *Ginny Jeep*. After the war, Browne became an advertising executive, creator of the Chiquita Banana and the Birds Eye Bird. He also redesigned Grace Gebbie Drayton's (q.v.) *Campbell Kids*. He later became the illustrator for New York bishop Fulton J. Sheen's popular television program. In 1954 he collaborated with cartoonist Mort Walker (q.v.) on the comic strip *Hi and Lois*. In 1973 he began *Hagar the Horrible*, featuring a comic-strip character based on Norse legend. Both strips were recipients of the coveted Reuben Award of the National Cartoonists Society. Browne died on June 4, 1989. His cartoon legacy is continued by his sons, Chris (q.v.) and Robert (q.v.).

REFERENCE: King Features Syndicate, *Hagar the Horrible* (New York, 1988). "Dik Browne: The Best of Hagar the Horrible," *School Library Journal* 32 (August 1986): 115.

Robert Browne 1948–

Robert Browne was born on June 17, 1948, the eldest son of cartoonist Dik Browne (q.v.). He attended the New York School of the Visual Arts and Yale University. In 1981, Browne began drawing *Hi and Lois*, a strip created in 1954 by cartoonist Mort Walker (q.v.). Bob Browne is an accomplished musician as well as artist: from 1967 to 1980 he served as both art director and studio musician for Philo Records in Vermont. Browne resides in Nokomis, Florida, and in Wilton, Connecticut, with his wife, Debra, and daughters, Rachel and Robin.

REFERENCE: King Features Syndicate, *Robert Browne* (New York, 1989).

Robert Burden 1952–

Robert Burden, creator of the cult classic *Flaming Carrot Comics*, was born on July 19, 1952, in Buffalo, New York, the son of W. E. Burden and Ella Haar Burden. After studying journalism at Marquette University in Milwaukee and the University of Georgia in Athens, Burden began his career as a freelance cartoonist, working for *Aardvark Vanaheim*, *Renegade Comics*, *Dark Horse*, and *Comico*. Burden describes the genesis of *Flaming Carrot*: "Flaming Carrot, America's foremost surrealist, blue collar super-hero, began as a lark in 1979 in *Visions*, no. 1. Over the years it has become one of the ten best-selling direct-market black and white super-hero comics and one of the highest-priced for back issues in the collectors' market." Burden's comic creations have appeared in *Visions*, nos. 1–4 (1979–82), *Flaming Carrot Comics One Shot*, no. 1 (1981), *MOO*, no. 1 (1981), *Flaming Carrot Comics*, nos. 1–22 (1984–89), and *GUMBY Summer Fun Special* (1987), of which Burden was the writer. The artist resides in Atlanta, Georgia.

Charles Burns 1955–

Born in Washington, D.C., in 1955, underground artist Charles Burns has published both comic strips and illustrations in widely respected periodicals at home and abroad. These include *Raw*, the *Village Voice*, *National Lampoon*, *Heavy Metal*, *Vanity* (Italy), *El Vibora* (Spain), and *Metal Hurlant* (France). Works in progress include *Teen Plague*, described by *Raw* as "an epic horror story."

REFERENCES: Charles Burns, *El Borbah* (Paris, 1985); *Big Baby* (New York, 1986); *Hard-Boiled Defective Stories* (New York, 1988). "Raw Data," in Art Spiegelman and Françoise

Mouly, *Read Yourself Raw: The Graphix Anthology for Damned Intellectuals* (New York, 1987).

Ernie Bushmiller 1905–1982

Ernest Paul Bushmiller, the son of Ernest George and Elizabeth Hall Bushmiller, was born in the Bronx on August 23, 1905. At the age of fourteen he became a copy boy at the *New York World*. He spent much of his time talking to the art staff, which included H. T. Webster, Milt Gross (q.v.), Herb Roth, and Rudolph Dirks (q.v.). At night he secretly attended classes at the National Academy of Design. In 1921 he became a cub artist at the *World*. Beginning in 1925 Bushmiller drew *Fritzi Ritz*, for which his fiancée, Abby Bohnet, served as model. On July 9, 1930, Bushmiller married the original Fritzi and the same year went to Hollywood at the request of Harold Lloyd as a writer for the film *Movie Crazy*. Nancy, originally a minor character in *Fritzi Ritz*, was given her own strip in 1938. Bushmiller composed his strip backwards, starting with the last frame, containing the punch line or "gag," which results in a peculiar, jolting conclusion.

REFERENCES: Ernie Bushmiller, "Nancy and Me," *Collier's* 122 (September 18, 1948): 23. "Comics and Their Creators," *Literary Digest* 118 (September 29, 1934): 11. Sheridan, pp. 172–174. "Nancy, Sluggo, and Ernie," *Newsweek* 31 (June 29, 1948): 60–61. *Who's Who* 34 (1966–67): 310. Couperie and Horn, p. 45. Joan C. Siegfried, *The Spirit of the Comics* (Philadelphia, 1969). *Who's Who in American Art* (1973, 1976, 1978). Nye, p. 223. Horn, pp. 144–145, 511. Obituary, *Chicago Times*, August 17, 1982. Obituary, *New York Times*, August 17, 1982. Obituary, *Newsweek*, August 30, 1982. Obituary, *Time*, August 30, 1982. Brian Walker, *The Best of Ernie Bushmiller's Nancy* (New York, 1988).

Gene Byrnes 1893–1974

Gene Byrnes was born in New York City in 1889. He was twenty-two years old when his art career began, the indirect result of a broken leg suffered in a wrestling match. While waiting for the leg to heal, Byrnes spent his time copying Tad Dorgan's (q.v.) cartoons. His first cartoon was a two-column panel entitled *Things That Never Happen*, published in California in 1915. Byrnes later became a sports cartoonist at the *New York Telegram*, where he also began the strip *"It's a Great Life If You Don't Weaken."* The strip's title became the slogan of the American Expeditionary Force during World War I. As an adjunct to *It's a Great Life* Byrnes began a two-column comic, *Reg'lar Fellers*. An immediate success, the child strip appeared daily and Sundays in the *New York Herald Tribune*. During the summer of 1941 a radio version of *Reg'lar Fellers* competed with *The Jack Benny Show*. The first of a series of motion pictures based on the strip was released on August 15, 1941. *Reg'lar Fellers* appeared in book form as early as 1921. The plot centered on the antics of such typically American figures as Jimmy Dugan, Pudd'n Head, Aggie, Bump, Flynn the Cop, Heinbockle the Baker, and Bull's Eye the Dog, and provided a cartoon equivalent of the local-color fiction so popular in the United States during the late nineteenth and early twentieth centuries. Byrnes died on July 26, 1974.

REFERENCES: Gene Byrnes, *Jimmy Dugan and the Reg'lar Fellers* (New York, 1921); *Reg'lar Fellers*, 2 vols. (New York, 1921); "Comics and Their Creators," *Literary Digest* 116 (December 30, 1933): 13; *Reg'lar Fellers in the Navy* (New York, 1943); *Dogs* (New York, 1946); *A Complete Guide to Drawing, Illustration, Cartooning and Painting* (New York, 1948); *A Complete Guide to Professional Cartooning* (Drexel Hill, Pa., 1950). Sheridan, pp. 84–85. Couperie and Horn, p. 45. Nye, p. 221. *New York Times Biographical Edition* (1974). Horn, pp. 146–147.

John Caldwell 1946–

Best known for his iconoclastic panels, cartoonist John Caldwell has since 1970 published regularly in *National Lampoon*, *Esquire*, *Omni*, *Penthouse*, *Writer's Digest*, *American Health*, and the *Saturday Review*. Compilations of his work include *Running A Muck*, *Mug Shots*, *The Book of Ultimates*, and — for children — *Excuses, Excuses*. From February 24, 1986, to October 21, 1989, *Caldwell* was distributed by King Features. Caldwell resides with his wife and

daughter in Cohoes, New York.

REFERENCE: King Features Syndicate, *Different* (New York, 1985).

Dick Calkins 1895–1962

Richard W. Calkins, the creator of *Buck Rogers*, was born in Grand Rapids, Michigan. His interest in science fiction began in grade school. After attending the Art Institute of Chicago, Calkins became a cartoonist for the *Detroit Free Press*. During World War I he was a flight instructor, and afterward continued to sign his name "Lt. Dick Calkins." After his discharge Calkins worked as a comic-strip artist for the *Chicago Examiner*. He later joined the John Dille Syndicate and originated a flight strip, *Sky Roads*, and another feature, *Amateur Etiquette*. On January 7, 1929, Buck Rogers crawled from a gas-sealed mine on the outskirts of Pittsburgh into the twenty-fifth century. The first of the science-fiction strips, *Buck Rogers* was soon followed by Alex Raymond's *Flash Gordon*, which began in 1933. *Buck Rogers* was the result of the collaboration of three men, the late John Flint Dille, president of the National Newspaper Service of Chicago, writer Phil Nowlan, and artist Calkins; later a scientist became part of the team producing *Buck Rogers*. The strip eventually became a radio program and part of a massive advertising campaign to sell cereal. Assisting Calkins with the artwork was Rick Yager (q.v.), who in 1932 became Calkins's apprentice. Calkins died on May 13, 1962, in Tucson, Arizona. *Buck Rogers* was discontinued in 1967.

REFERENCES: R. W. Calkins and Phil Nowlan, *Buck Rogers in the Dangerous Mission* (New York, 1934); *Buck Rogers in the Twenty-fifth Century* (Chicago, 1935); *The Collected Works of Buck Rogers in the Twenty-fifth Century*, introd. by Ray Bradbury (New York, 1969). Robert C. Dille, ed., *The Collected Works of Buck Rogers in the Twenty-fifth Century* (New York, 1977). Sheridan, pp. 225, 230. Obituary, *New York Times*, May 14, 1962, p. 29. Couperie and Horn, pp. 61, 69, 163. "Where Are They Now? Creators of *Buck Rogers* and *Flash Gordon*," *Newsweek* 74 (August 4, 1969): 8. Nye, p. 225. Horn, pp. 21, 79, 149, 422, 578, 623.

Jack Callahan 1889–1954

In 1940 Jack Callahan retired from the *New York American*, leaving behind him many creations including *Hon and Deary*, *Dizzy's Eating House*, and *Calamity Jane*. Callahan in 1926 had married Helen Carr, described by the *New York Times* as best known for her "sensational dive from the roof of the New York Hippodrome in *Happy Days* and *Cheer Up*." Callahan's strip *Freddy the Sheik* was part of the craze that began in 1921 with the publication of Edith M. Hull's best-selling novel *The Sheik*. Made into a movie starring Rudolph Valentino, the novel encouraged thousands of young men to adopt the exotic, masterful Latin look. Callahan's strip satirized the silliness implicit in the assumption of a sheiklike identity in twentieth-century America.

REFERENCES: Obituary, *New York Times*, August 26, 1954, p. 27. Nye, pp. 44, 328, 375, 377.

Milton Caniff 1907–1988

"The Rembrandt of the comic strip," Milton Caniff, was born in Hillsboro, Ohio, on February 28, 1907, the son of John William Caniff, a printer, and Elizabeth Burton Caniff. He graduated from Stivers High School in Dayton, Ohio, and earned a degree from Ohio State University in 1930. While still a high-school student, Caniff worked on the *Dayton Journal*, and in the summer before graduation, on the *Miami* (Ohio) *Daily News*. While an Ohio State undergraduate Caniff worked for the *Ohio Dispatch*. He was recruited by the Associated Press in 1932 and moved to New York, where he drew *Dickie Dare* and *The Gay Thirties*. In 1934 he was introduced by John McCutcheon to Joseph Medill Patterson. Patterson, according to *Current Biography*, told Caniff that he wanted a strip "based on a blood-and-thunder formula, carrying a juvenile angle, and packed with plenty of suspense." The locale, he insisted, must be the Orient — the last outpost for adventure. Accordingly, *Terry and the Pirates* made its first appearance on October 19, 1934. The strip became a radio show, written by Al Barker, on September

25, 1938. The Julien Levy Gallery, New York, presented a show of Caniff's work in December 1940, and his work was also exhibited at the Metropolitan Museum of Art in New York. During World War II Caniff drew *Male Call*, a strip specifically designed to meet the needs of the soldier. In 1947 Caniff began *Steve Canyon*, and *Terry* was passed on to George Wunder (q.v.). Caniff died on April 3, 1988. The last *Steve Canyon*, a memorial strip drawn by Bill Maudlin, appeared on June 4, 1988. Caniff's legacy is embodied in the monumental archive of original artwork and documents housed in the Ohio State University Library for Communication and Graphic Arts, Columbus, Ohio. Summarizing Caniff's achievement cartoonist Jules Feiffer (q.v.) declared, "When he drew men and women in action, their poses became definitive. The ultimate sock in the jaw, the ultimate leap into space, the ultimate tumbling body, the ultimate kiss, the ultimate raised eyebrow, the ultimate lonely walk off into the distance."

REFERENCES: Milton Caniff, *Male Call* (New York, 1945, 1959); *Terry and the Pirates* (New York, 1946); *April Kane and the Dragon Lady* (Racine, Wis., 1947); "Steve Canyon and Me," *Collier's* 122 (November 20, 1948): 36; "Don't Laugh at the Comics," *Cosmopolitan* 145 (November 1958): 43–47; *Milton Caniff's Steve Canyon* (New York, 1959); *Steve Canyon: Operation Convoy* (New York, 1959); *Steve Canyon: Operation Eel Island* (New York, 1959); *Steve Canyon: Operation Foo Ling* (New York, 1959); *Steve Canyon: Operation Sunflower* (New York, 1959); *Enter the Dragon Lady* (New York, 1975); *Meet Burma* (New York, 1975); *Let's See If Any One Salutes* (New York, 1976); *Terry and the Pirates* (New York, 1976); *Terry and the Pirates, China Journey* (New York, 1977); *Terry and the Pirates, The Normandy Affair* (New York, 1977); *Terry and the Pirates, Meet Burma* (New York, 1977); *Terry and the Pirates, Enter the Dragon Lady* (New York, 1977); *Terry and the Pirates*, vols. 1, 7–10 (New York, 1984–86). "Terry and the Pirates Storm Art Gallery in New Adventure," *Newsweek* 16 (December 16, 1940): 48. "Terry and the Pirates Invade New York Art Gallery," *Life* 10 (January 6, 1941): 34. Sheridan, pp. 119, 121, 136, 155, 253. John Bainbridge, "Significant Sig and the Funnies," *The New Yorker* 19 (January 18, 1944): 25–30. CB, 1944, pp. 83–85. Alexander Samalman, ed., *Milton Caniff: The Rembrandt of the Comic Strip* (Philadelphia, 1946). Collie Small, "Strip Tease in Black and White," *Saturday Evening Post* 219 (August 10, 1946): 22–23. "Not for Kids," *Time* 48 (December 2, 1946): 61–62. "Escape Artist," *Time* 49 (January 13, 1947): 58–65. "Caniff, Canyon, and Calhoun," *Newsweek* 29 (January 20, 1947): 64. Mac Cullen, "Cartoonist at Work," *Scholastic* 50 (February 10, 1947): 29. "Such Language: London *Daily Express* Trial Run of Steve Canyon," *Time* 50 (August 25, 1947): 54. E. H. McTighe, "Milton Caniff's Modern Home," *Better Homes and Gardens* 27 (December 1948): 58. "Syndicated Cartoon Feature," *Design* 54 (June 1953): 212–13. "Cartoon Feature," *Design* 59 (May 1958): 100–101. "Steve Canyon, New TV Star," *Flying* 63 (September 1958): 46. Amory, p. 98. *Who's Who* 34 (1966–67): 332. Dorothy McGreal, "Milton Caniff: More Irons in the Fire Than a Blacksmith," *World of Comic Art* 1 (Winter 1966–67): 44–45. Couperie and Horn, author index. Nye, pp. 225–228, 236. Lawrence E. Mintz, "Fantasy, Formula, Realism, and Propaganda in Milton Caniff's Comic Strips," *Journal of Popular Culture* 12 (Spring 1979): 653–680. John Paul Adams, *Milton Caniff, Rembrandt of the Comic Strip* (Endicott, N.Y., 1981). Arn Saba, "I'm Just a Troubadour Singing for My Supper," *Comics Journal* 108 (May 1986): 60–102.

Al Capp 1909–1979

Alfred Gerald Caplin was born in New Haven, Connecticut, on September 28, 1909, the son of Otto Philip and Matilda Davidson Caplin. Later the family moved to Bridgeport, where Capp attended public schools. After high school, he studied at the Chicago Academy of Fine Arts, the Designers' Art School, the Philadelphia Museum, and, following his family's move to Boston in 1928, the Boston Museum of Fine Arts. On September 12, 1932, — as A. G. Caplin — he took over the already existing *Mr. Gilfeather*, a panel distributed by Associated Press. Eventually, he became assistant to Ham Fisher (q.v.), creator of *Joe Palooka*. In one episode, Capp persuaded Fisher to include a number of hillbilly characters, which later became Capp's Yokum family. In August 1934 *Li'l Abner* made its first appearance, distributed by United Feature Syndicate. E. J. Kahn credits Capp with originating *Abbie 'n' Slats*, later drawn by Raeburn Van Buren. A motion-picture version of *Li'l Abner* appeared in 1940, produced by RKO Studios and written by Capp himself. The strip became a successful musical in the early six-

ties. In 1946 John Steinbeck, suggesting a redefinition of the terms *art* and *literature*, proposed that Capp be awarded the Nobel Prize. "I think Capp may very possibly be the best writer in the world today," he wrote. "I am sure that he is the best satirist since Laurence Stern. . . ." A collection of 3,095 daily and Sunday *Li'l Abner*s and 688 daily and Sunday *Fearless Fosdick*s is housed in Boston University's Mugar Library.

REFERENCES: Al Capp, "Case for the Comics," *Saturday Review* 31 (March 20, 1948): 32–33; *The Life and Times of the Shmoo* (New York, 1948); "Silent Upon a Park in Dogpatch," *Theatre Arts* 33 (March 1949): 24–25; "There Is a Real Shmoo," *New Republic* 120 (March 21, 1949): 14–15; "It's Hideously True: Little Abner," *Life* 32 (March 31, 1952): 100–102; *Discussion* 32 (April 21, 1952): 11; "New Comic Strip," *Saturday Review* 36 (April 11, 1953): 27; Al Capp, *The World of Little Abner*, introd. by John Steinbeck, fwd. by Charles Chaplin (New York, 1953); *Bald Iggle* (New York, 1956); *The Return of the Shmoo* (New York, 1959); *From Dogpatch to Slobbovia*, with commentary by David Manning White (Boston, 1964); "My Life as an Immortal Myth: Experiences at the First International Exhibition of the Comics," *Life* 58 (April 30, 1965): 97–100; "Interview," *Playboy* 12 (December 1965): 89–110; *The Hardhat's Bedtime Book* (New York, 1971); *The Best of Li'l Abner* (New York, 1978); *Li'l Abner, Vol. 1, 1934–1935* (Princeton, Wis., 1988); *Li'l Abner, Vol. 2, 1936* (Princeton, Wis., 1988). Sheridan, pp. 134–135. Russell Maloney, "Li'l Abner's Capp," *Life* 20 (June 24, 1946): 58–64. CB, 1947, pp. 92–94. "Li'l Abner's Mad Capp," *Newsweek* 30 (November 24, 1947): 60. E. J. Kahn, "Ooff!! (sob!) Eep!! (gulp!) Zowie!!!," *The New Yorker* 23 (November 29, 1947): 45–50; 23 (December 6, 1947): 46–50. "Leviticus vs. Yokums," *Newsweek* 32 (November 29, 1948): 58. "Miracle of Dogpatch," *Time* 52 (December 27, 1948): 48–49. "Shmoos," *The New Yorker* 24 (January 1, 1949): 14–15. "Sacking of the Shmoos: *London Sunday Pictorial*," *Time* 54 (May 24, 1949): 63. "Taming of the Shmoo," *Newsweek* 34 (September 5, 1949): 22. "Unthinkable: Li'l Abner's Marriage," *Time* 59 (March 31, 1952): 53. "Capp's New Girl, Long Sam," *Newsweek* 43 (June 14, 1954): 92. "Rap for Capp," *Time* 70 (September 9, 1957): 29. "Mary Worm and Mr. Rapp," *New Republic* 137 (September 23, 1957): 8. "Li'l Abner," *Newsweek* 58 (July 17, 1961): 54. "Shmoo's Return," *The New Yorker* 39 (October 26, 1963): 39–40. Max Rafferty, "Al Capp: An Authentic Homegrown Genius Type," *World of Comic Art* 1 (June 1966): 2. Who's Who 34 (1966–67): 335. Couperie and Horn, author index. Nye, pp. 227–228, 234. Arthur Asa Berger, *Li'l Abner; a Study in American Satire* (New York, 1970). "Missionary to the Campus," *Newsweek* 75 (June 22, 1970): 79. William F. Buckley, Jr., "Al Capp at Bay," *National Review* 22 (October 20, 1970): 1124. R. Handley, "Capital Punishment," *Esquire* 74 (November 1970): 160–161. Al Capp, "TV Address, March 30, 1971," *Vital Speeches* 37 (May 15, 1971): 477–478. "Dogpatch Is Ready for Freddy," *Time* 110 (October 17, 1977): 78. Obituary, *New York Times*, November 6, 1979. "Mr. Dogpatch," *Time* 114 (November 19, 1979): 116. "Al Capp, RIP," *National Review* 31 (November 23, 1979): 1479. Horn, p. 154.

Gene Carr 1881–1959

Artist Gene Carr, creator of *Lady Bountiful*, was born on New York's East Side on January 7, 1881, and at the age of nine became a messenger for the *New York Recorder*. In 1898 he was discovered by William Randolph Hearst, who had seen a sports cartoon by Carr. Among Carr's many employers were the *New York Herald*, the *Philadelphia Times*, the *New York Evening Journal*, the *World*, the McClure Syndicate, and King Features Syndicate. Some of Carr's numerous comic strips were *Lady Bountiful*, *Phyllis*, *Romeo*, *All the Comforts of Home*, *The Prodigal Son*, *The Bad Dream That Made Bill a Better Boy*, *Father*, *Willie Wise*, *Stepbrothers*, *Bill*, *The Jones Boys*, *Flirting Flora*, *Reddy and Caruso*, and *Metropolitan Movies*. In 1922 *Metropolitan Movies*, a feature on the back page of the *New York Morning World*, was published in book form under the title *Kid Kartoons*. Carr died of a heart attack on December 9, 1959, at his home in Walpole, New Hampshire.

REFERENCES: Gene Carr, *Kid Kartoons* (New York, 1922). *Who's Who* 9 (1916–17): 405. Mallett, p. 69. Sheridan, p. 17. Obituary, *New York Times*, December 10, 1959, p. 29. *Who Was Who* 3 (1951–60): 139. Fielding, p. 28. Horn, pp. 160–161.

A. D. Carter 1895–1957

Couperie and Horn's *History of the Comic Strip* credits Augustus Daniel Carter with initiating the sentimental child strip. Carter's strip, *Just Kids*, was the product of his study at the Art Students League of New York and his newspaper experience at the *Brooklyn Times* and *Eagle*. Its antecedents include Tom McNamara's *On Our Block* and Carter's own 1916 *Our Friend Mush*, which ran in the *Philadelphia Inquirer*. Encouraged by cartoonist Clare Briggs, Carter took the strip to King Features Syndicate, which began distributing *Just Kids* on July 23, 1923. Nye places the strip within the tradition of "sentimentalized boyhood" as exemplified by Gene Byrnes's (q.v.) *Reg'lar Fellers*, *Peck's Bad Boy*, and *Tom Sawyer*. Carter died of a heart attack on June 25, 1957, at his home in Mamaroneck, New York.

REFERENCES: Obituary, *New York Times*, June 26, 1957, p. 31. Couperie and Horn, p. 45, 163. Nye, p. 221. Horn, p. 161, 349.

Mel Casson

Best known as the illustrator of King Features Syndicate's *Redeye*, Mel Casson also wrote and drew United Feature Syndicate's *Boomer* until 1982. Casson has served on the Board of Governors of the Newspaper Comics Council and of the National Cartoonists Society.

REFERENCE: King Features Syndicate, *Mel Casson* (New York, n.d.).

John Celardo 1918–

Born on December 27, 1918, in Staten Island, New York, John Celardo graduated from Port Richmond High School in 1936. After graduation, he attended the New York School of Industrial Arts. In 1938 he worked in the arts program of the WPA. Celardo was hired in 1939 by the legendary Will Eisner (q.v.) as a comic-book illustrator. In 1940 he became assistant art director at Fiction House, a publisher of comic books. Celardo was drafted by the U.S. Army in 1941. He attended officer candidate school in 1943, and was subsequently stationed in Europe as an infantry company commander. Discharged with the rank of captain in 1946, Celardo returned to Fiction House. In 1948 he began a career as a freelance artist. From 1958 to 1968 he drew *Tarzan* for United Feature Syndicate. Since 1973 he has been associate comics editor at King Features Syndicate, for which he drew *Buz Sawyer* from 1982 to 1989.

REFERENCE: King Features Syndicate, *John Celardo* (New York, 1989).

Max Collins 1948–

Max Allan Collins, who scripts the Tribune Media Services–revived *Dick Tracy*, began his stint with America's most famous detective in 1977. Born in Muscatine, Iowa, Collins holds a B.A. and an M.F.A. from the University of Iowa, renowned for its writers workshop. In addition to scripting *Dick Tracy*, Collins has published numerous works of fiction, including a series of novels featuring Chicago detective Nathan Heller. He has also written the *Batman* comic book for DC Comics, and is the author of a critical study of writer Mickey Spillane that was acclaimed by the Mystery Writers of America. Other awards include the Shamus Award of the Private Eye Writers of America for the best novel of 1984. Collins lives in Muscatine with his wife, Barbara, and son, Nathan.

REFERENCE: Tribune Media Services, *Max Allan Collins Biography* (Chicago, 1988).

Guy Colwell 1945–

Guy Colwell, best known for the magic realism of such canvases as *Race Street* (1970) and *Divisidero* (1972) and for the comics *Inner City Romance* and *Doll*, was born on March 28, 1945, in Oakland, California, the son of artist Esther Jensen Colwell and Claude Colwell. After graduating from Berkeley High School in 1963, Colwell attended the California College of Arts and Crafts in Oakland. From 1966 to 1967 he worked for Mattel Toy as a sculptor. Refusing to be inducted into the military, Colwell was incarcerated for a year and a half at McNeil Island Prison Camp, an experience that profoundly influenced his art. Interviewed by *City Arts Monthly* reporter James Phoenix, Colwell explained its impact. "Prison opened my eyes to reality. In that sort of environment you had to be real wide-eyed, real attentive to what was going on around you. To be aware, to be safe, you had to pay a lot of attention to reality rather than living in fantasy, and that did very much carry over into what I was doing. After I got out of prison, I started developing this style that captured that clear, sharply focused reality." After his release, Colwell worked as a court artist for both *Good Times* and the *San Francisco Examiner*, covering such pivotal political events as the trial of the Soledad Brothers. His comics creations include *Inner City Romance*, nos. 1–5 (Last Gasp, 1972–77); *Young Lust*, no. 5 (1975); and *Doll*, nos. 1–3 (Rip Off Press, 1989). Colwell lives in Auburn, California.

REFERENCES: Thomas Albright, "Unsettling Visions With Force," *San Francisco Chronicle*, September 17, 1975. James Phoenix, "Guy Colwell, Humanist Realist," *City Arts Monthly* (June 1982). Kady Bourn-Stevenson, "Portraits: Human Figure Common Element in Artist's Work," *Auburn Journal*, n.d.

Robert L. Crabb 1951–

Underground creator Robert L. Crabb, best known for *Tales of the Jackalope* and *Rockers*, was born on January 3, 1951, in Grass Valley, California, the son of Marvin and Jessie Crabb. From 1980 to 1983 Crabb was editorial cartoonist for the *Nevada County Democrat*. In 1984, with cartoonists R. Crumb (q.v.), Dan O'Neill, Gary Hallgren, and others Crabb created a special Democratic-convention cartoon section for the *San Francisco Chronicle*. His comics include *Junior Jackalope*, nos. 1–2 (1982–83), *Tales of the Jackalope* (1985–86), *Rockers* (1988–89), and features in *Weirdo*, *Rip Off Comics*, *Snarf*, and the *Co-evolution Quarterly*. Says Crabb, "I try to portray real-life situations with my comics. The point is not just to look at the scabs, but also what's beneath them!" Crabb and his wife, Kate, live in Nevada City, California.

Roy Crane 1901–1977

Royston Campbell Crane was born in Abilene, Texas, on November 22, 1901. He attended Hardin-Simmons University during 1918–1919, the Chicago Academy of Fine Arts in 1920, and the University of Texas until 1922. In 1919 he worked in the art department of the *Fort Worth Record* and, from 1921 to 1922, was a reporter for the *Austin American*. In 1924, while on the staff of the *New York World*, Crane began the strip *Wash Tubbs*, syndicated by NEA. *Captain Easy* was begun in 1929; the first Sunday page appeared on July 30, 1933. In order to obtain material for the strips, Crane journeyed to Cuba and Mexico. Couperie and Horn credit Crane with establishing one of the major categories of the comic strip, the adventure comic, and with introducing political propaganda into the medium. In 1943 Roy Crane abandoned *Captain Easy* and created *Buz Sawyer*, the saga of a pilot in the naval air force, who did for the navy what *Terry and the Pirates* had done for the army. The strip was syndicated by King Features. After Crane's departure, *Captain Easy* was taken over by Leslie Turner. Today *Captain Easy* is continued by the team of cartoonist Bill Crooks and writer Mick Casale. Most recently drawn by John Celardo (q.v.), *Buz Sawyer* ceased publication on October 7, 1989.

REFERENCES: Roy Crane, *Wash Tubbs* (New York, 1974); *The Complete Wash Tubbs and Captain Easy*, vol. 1, Introd. Bill Blackbeard (New York, 1987). "Comics and Their Creators," *Literary Digest* 118 (August 18, 1934): 10. *Who's Who* 34 (1966–67): 465. Couperie and Horn, author index. Nye, p. 225. Horn, pp. 183–184, 636, 674, 691.

Percy Crosby 1891–1964

Percy Leo Crosby, artist and political propagandist, and the creator of *Skippy*, was born on December 8, 1891. A native of Brooklyn, Crosby studied at the Art Students League of New York and at Pratt Institute. Among Crosby's early positions were jobs at the *New York Call* and *Globe*. For the latter he did a feature entitled "Politicians and Other Comic Subjects." The strip, syndicated by King Features beginning on October 18, 1926, was made into a motion picture starring Jackie Cooper in 1931. The syndicated *Skippy*'s antecedents include *The Clancy Kids*, created in 1915 for the McClure Syndicate, and a *Life* magazine *Skippy*. Crosby was politically active in the thirties, agitating for the repeal of Prohibition and, later, against Franklin D. Roosevelt, labor unions, and Communism. In 1942 Crosby retired and *Skippy*, begun in 1923, was discontinued. Crosby died in New York on his seventy-third birthday, December 8, 1964.

REFERENCES: Percy Crosby, *That Rookie from the Thirteenth Squad* (New York, 1918); *Between Shots* (New York, 1919); *Skippy from Life* (New York, 1924); *Skippy* (New York, 1925); *Always Belittlin'* (New York, 1927); *Dear Spooky* (New York, 1927); *Skippy* (New York, 1929); *Skippy and Other Humor* (New York, 1929); *A Cartoonist's Philosophy* (McLean, Va., 1931); *Patriotism: a Dialogue* (McLean, Va., 1932); *Skippy Rambles* (New York, 1932); *Vets and Wets, Let's Go* (Washington, D.C., 1932); *Sport Drawings* (McLean, Va., 1933); *The Story of Skippy* (Racine, Wis., 1934); *Three Cheers for the Red, Red, and Red* (McLean, Va., 1936); *Essay on Roosevelt's Second Inaugural Address* (McLean, Va., 1937); *Would Communism Work Out in America?* (McLean, Va., 1938); *Skippy* (Westport, Conn., 1977). "Comics and Their Creators," *Literary Digest*, 118 (September 8, 1934): 12. Jerry Robinson, *Skippy and Percy Crosby* (New York, 1978). Sheridan, pp. 11, 288. Mallett, p. 96. Obituary, *New York Times*, December 14, 1964, p. 35. Couperie and Horn, pp. 45, 170. Nye, p. 221. Horn, pp. 186, 506, 622. Joan Crosby Tibbetts, "Percy Crosby and Skippy," *Doll News* (1989): 6–11.

R. Crumb   1943–

Arguably the most influential comic artist of the late twentieth century, Robert Crumb was born on August 30, 1943, in Philadelphia. One of five children born to career marine Charles V. Crumb and Beatrice Hall Crumb, Crumb was raised as a Roman Catholic and briefly attended Catholic schools. Itinerant like many other military families, the Crumbs resided at various times in Albert Lea, Minnesota; Philadelphia; Ames, Iowa; Oceanside, California; Milford and Dover, Delaware. After graduating from high school, the despondent Crumb moved to Cleveland, where he obtained work as a color separator for the American Greetings Corporation. There he created an office strip, *Roberta Smith, Office Girl*. In 1964 he met and married his first wife, Dana Morgan, of Cleveland Heights. In 1965 he published his first comic strip in Harvey Kurtzman's *Help!* Encouraged by this success, Crumb moved to New York, where he met the legendary comic-strip collector Woody Gelman, who hired him at Topps Chewing Gum. Later that year Crumb went to Chicago, there to create the comic characters that would make him famous — Mr. Natural, the Snoid, and Angelfood McSpade. Like thousands of other members of his generation, Crumb in 1967 moved to San Francisco. That same year saw publication of *Mr. Natural* in *Yarrowstalks*, no. 1, one of hundreds of underground, underfinanced journals that sprang up across America. In 1968 the first adventures of *Fritz the Cat* appeared in *Cavalier*, another alternative publication. The lure of the open road, deriving from the odysseys of his youth, became a central theme of the *Fritz the Cat* saga. Soon Crumb had become the patron saint of the underground "comix" movement. His status was assured when, in 1969, *Zap*, no. 4, became the subject of coast-to-coast obscenity prosecutions. Crumb met artist Aline Kominsky (q.v.) in 1971; they married in 1978 and live in seclusion in Winters, California. Crumb's prolific pen has created countless characters that have become part of American underground mythology. These include the irrepressible Fritz the Cat; earth mother Angelfood McSpade; self-pitying Flakey Foont and Shuman the Human; middle-class, middle-American Whiteman; the laid-back guru Mr. Natural; and the obnoxious Snoid. Recently, Crumb has extended his mastery of comic-strip genres, previously exemplified by his transformation of the animal, adventure, and slapstick genres, to the domestic strip, in which he lovingly depicts the trials and tribulations of Bob, Aline, and daughter Sophie in their rural retreat. A comprehensive bibliography containing 544 entries is included in Donald Fiene's *R. Crumb Checklist*.

REFERENCES: R. Crumb, *Fritz the Cat* (New York, 1968); *Head Comix* (New York, 1968);

Crumbland et autres pecadilles (Yverdon, 1975); *R. Crumb's Yum Yum Book* (San Francisco, 1975); *R. Crumb's Carload o' Comics* (New York, 1976); *The Complete Fritz the Cat* (New York, 1978); *R. Crumb Sketchbook* (Frankfurt am Main, 1978); *Sketchbook 1966–'67* (Frankfurt am Main, 1981); *The Complete Crumb: Volume One: The Early Years of Bitter Struggle* (Westlake Village, Calif., 1987); *The Complete Crumb: Volume Two: Some More Early Years of Bitter Struggle* (Westlake Village, Calif., 1988); *R. Crumb's Head Comix* (New York, 1988). Harvey Pekar, "Rapping About Cartoonists, Particularly R. Crumb," *Journal of Popular Culture* 3 (Spring 1970): 687–688. Jacob Brackman, "The International Comix Conspiracy," *Playboy* 17 (December 1970): 9. Marjorie Alessandrini, *Robert Crumb* (Paris, 1974). Horn, pp. 33, 187, 189, 498. Tex Filippo, "Crooning Cartoonist Scores with Hula Medley," *Rolling Stone* 212 (May 6, 1976): 102. Donald Fiene, *The R. Crumb Checklist of Work and Criticism* (Cambridge, Mass., 1981). G. Hackett, "R. Crumb Keeps On Drawing," *Newsweek* 102 (July 25, 1983): 9. Charles Bukowski, *There's No Business* (Santa Barbara, 1984). R. Crumb, "The Straight Dope From R. Crumb," *Comics Journal* 121 (April 1988): 48–138. "Comments on Crumb," *Blab!* 3 (Fall 1988): 74–128.

Nicholas P. Dallis   1911–

Nicholas P. Dallis, M.D., creator and author of North America Syndicate's *Rex Morgan, M.D.*, *Judge Parker*, and *Apartment 3-G*, is a graduate of Temple University School of Medicine and a diplomate of the American Board of Psychiatry and Neurology. Dallis has served as Director of the Mental Hygiene Center in Toledo, Ohio, and as consulting psychiatrist to the Toledo Juvenile Court. In 1948 as "Dal Curtis" he created *Rex Morgan, M.D.*; in 1952, as "Paul Nichols," *Judge Parker*; in 1970, *Apartment 3-G*. All three strips feature benevolent, celibate professional men — a physician, a judge, and a professor. Dr. Dallis, one of the most prolific and influential of comics authors, lives with his wife, Sally, in Scottsdale, Arizona.

REFERENCE: North America Syndicate, *Nicholas P. Dallis, M.D.* (New York, 1989).

Jim Davis   1945–

Born on July 28, 1945, *Garfield* creator Jim Davis was raised on a small farm in Marion, Indiana. After graduation from Ball State University, where he claims to have had "the lowest cumulative grade-point ratio in the history of the university," Davis worked for an advertising agency. In 1969, he became cartoon assistant to Tom Ryan (q.v.), creator of *Tumbleweeds*. He later created *Gnorm Gnat*, a strip about an insect, which ran for five years in an Indiana newspaper. *Garfield* was introduced to forty papers by United Feature Syndicate on June 19, 1978. By May 1981 the strip was appearing in five hundred papers; by August 1987, in two thousand. Davis describes *Garfield* as "strictly an entertainment comic strip built around the strong personality of a fat, lazy, cynical cat. 'Garfield' obviously avoids any social or political comment." The strip received "Best Humor Strip" awards from the National Cartoonists Society in 1982 and 1986. Davis and his wife, Carolyn, an elementary-school teacher, have one son, Alex.

REFERENCES: Jim Davis, *Garfield at Large* (New York, 1980); *Garfield Bigger Than Life* (New York, 1981); *Garfield Gains Weight* (New York, 1981); *The Garfield Mix or Match Storybook* (New York, 1982); *Garfield Takes the Cake* (New York, 1982); *Garfield, the Knight in Shining Armor* (New York, 1982); *Garfield, the Pirate* (New York, 1982); *Garfield Eats His Heart Out* (New York, 1983); *Garfield Goes on a Picnic* (New York, 1983); *Garfield on the Town* (New York, 1983); *Garfield A to Z Zoo* (New York, 1984); *Garfield Book of the Seasons* (New York, 1984); *Garfield Counts to Ten* (New York, 1983); *Garfield Sits Around the House* (New York, 1983); *The Second Garfield Treasury* (New York, 1983); *Garfield, His Nine Lives* (New York, 1984); *Garfield Loses His Feet* (New York, 1984); *Garfield in Disguise* (New York, 1985); *Garfield Makes It Big* (New York, 1985); *Garfield Rolls On* (New York, 1985); *Garfield* (New York, 1986); *Garfield Out to Lunch* (New York, 1986); *The Garfield Trivia Book* (New York, 1986); *The Fourth Garfield Treasury* (New York, 1987); *A Garfield Christmas* (New York, 1987); *Garfield Goes to Hollywood* (New York, 1987); *Garfield Swallows His Pride* (New York, 1987). T. Kahn and S. Moore-Hall, "Market Is Going to the Cats," *People* 14 (November 17, 1980): 106–109. J. F. Baker, "Interview," *Publishers Weekly* 219 (March 13, 1981): 6–7. "Those Catty Cartoonists," *Time* 118 (December 7, 1981): 78–79. M. Vespa, "Garfield Goes Hollywood," *People* 18 (November 1, 1982): 88–89. *Los Angeles Times*, November 14, 1982. *New Jersey Sunday Record*, February 20, 1983. *Forbes*, November 21, 1983. H. G. Miller, "Jim Davis: He's Got the World by the Tail," *Saturday Evening Post* 256 (November 1984): 52–53. "Garfield Gets in the Picture," *Saturday Evening Post* 256 (November 1984): 45–51. Bill Diamond, "The Seven Deadly Sins," *Us* 3 (July 11–25, 1988): 41–42. Dana Aronsen and Nancy Nicolelis, *Jim Davis* (New York, 1988).

Phil Davis 1906–1964

Artist Phil Davis, best known for his illustration of *Mandrake the Magician*, was born in St. Louis in 1906. He graduated from Soldan High School in St. Louis, and afterward attended Washington University. Before beginning *Mandrake* in 1934 with creator Lee Falk (q.v.), Davis did commercial artwork for the *St. Louis Post-Dispatch*. During World War II Davis served as art director of the Curtiss-Wright Aircraft Plant in St. Louis. He died on December 16, 1964.

REFERENCES: Phil Davis and Lee Falk, *Mandrake the Magician* (New York, 1970). Couperie and Horn, pp. 71, 73, 91. Horn, p. 198.

Billy De Beck 1890–1942

The creator of *Barney Google*, William Morgan De Beck, was born in Chicago on April 15, 1890, the son of a meat-company executive. He graduated from Hyde Park High School and briefly attended the Chicago Academy of Fine Arts. De Beck's first job was that of staff artist for *Show World*, a Chicago theatrical weekly. He then worked at the *Youngstown Telegram* and in 1912 moved to Pittsburgh, where he became editorial cartoonist for the *Gazette Times*. In 1915 he began a cartoon correspondence course, the lessons for which were published as *De Beck Cartoon Hints*. On December 7, 1915, he joined the staff of the *Chicago Herald*, for which he created a two-column cartoon, *Married Life*, which appeared on December 9, 1915, and — anonymously — *Tom Rover* and *Haphazard Helen*. After Hearst acquired the *Chicago Herald* in 1918 he merged it with the *Examiner* to create the *Herald-Examiner*, where *Married Life* appeared thereafter. In June 1919 De Beck began *Barney Google*, which King Features syndicated from October 1 of that year. The strip was immediately popular, and in 1923 the Remick Music Corporation published the song "Barney Google," written by Billy Rose and Con Conrad. Through the strip De Beck added many phrases to the American vernacular, among them "horse feathers," "time's a' wastin'," and "heebie jeebies." De Beck died in New York City on November 11, 1942.

REFERENCES: Billy De Beck and Carter Feature Services, *De Beck Cartoon Hints* (Pittsburgh, 1915); Billy De Beck, *Barney Google: A Complete Compilation, 1919–1920* (Westport, Conn., 1977). "Comics and Their Creators," *Literary Digest* 117 (February 17, 1934): 13. W. E. Berchtold, "Men of Comics," *New Outlook* 165 (May 1935): 46. "Barney Google's Birthday," *Newsweek* 16 (October 14, 1940): 59–60. Sheridan, pp. 36–38. Obituary, *New York Times*, November 12, 1942, p. 25. *CB*, 1943, p. 162. *Who Was Who* 2 (1943–50): 149. Horn, pp. 198–199.

Kim Deitch 1944–

Comic artist Kim Deitch, the son of film-cartoon animator Gene Deitch, was born in Los Angeles on May 21, 1944. After graduation from high school, Deitch spent two years at Pratt Institute. At the end of his sophomore year, he shipped out as a deckhand with the Norwegian Merchant Marine, an adventure that lasted six months. Later jobs included those of Macy's stock boy, hardware warehouse worker, and psychiatric aide at New York Hospital in White Plains, New York. Deitch created his low-down "Waldo the Cat" for the *East Village Other* in 1966. Deitch described Waldo to *Comics Journal* interviewer Monte Beauchamp as a "negative, wise-guy personality" inspired by "all of those anonymous black cats that are running around by the dozens in those early Aesop's fables cartoons they used to show on TV." He met car-

toonist Trina Robbins (q.v.) in 1968. In 1969 the couple moved to San Francisco, where their daughter, Casey, was born in 1970. As part of the underground-comics movement, Deitch created Hector Perez, the Boy Vivisectionist. His relationship with Robbins ended in 1970, and in 1971 Deitch moved to Portland, Oregon, with animator Sally Cruikshank. There he created *Corn-Fed Comics*, no. 1. This was followed, in 1973, by *Corn-Fed Comics*, no. 2. *Hollywoodland*, Deitch's comic-strip saga of urban decay and spiritual growth, was created in Los Angeles in 1983. Deitch describes his distinctive style as "an attempt at trying to draw as realistically as possible, and, being basically a primitive artist, that is just what comes out." Deitch lives in seclusion in Dutton, Virginia.

REFERENCES: Kim Deitch, *Hollywoodland* (Westlake Village, Calif., 1987); "Kim Deitch: Interviewed by Monte Beauchamp," *Comics Journal* 123 (July 1988): 56–80; "Scenes from Wagandi Island," *Blab!* 3 (Fall 1988): 57–65; "Comments on Crumb," *Blab!* 3 (Fall 1988): 80–85.

Tony Di Preta 1921–

Tony Di Preta, who took over Ham Fisher's (q.v.) *Joe Palooka* in 1959, was born in Stamford, Connecticut, and educated in the Stamford public schools. His first job as a cartoonist, which he obtained while a senior in high school, entailed doing the lettering for Lyman Young's strip *Tim Tyler's Luck*. After high school, Di Preta did freelance work for comic books and took courses at Columbia University and the University of Connecticut. He later became Land Leonard's assistant on the comic strip *Mickey Finn*. In 1959 McNaught Syndicate hired him to continue *Joe Palooka*. Since 1985, Di Preta has drawn *Rex Morgan, M.D.*

REFERENCES: R. H. Boyle, "Champ for all Time!!! Joe Palooka," *Sports Illustrated* 22 (April 19, 1965): 120. Newspaper Comics Council, *Tony Di Preta: Profile* (New York, n.d.). Horn, pp. 70, 196, 344.

Rudolph Dirks 1877–1968

Rudolph Dirks was born in Heide, Germany, in 1877, the son of John Henry and Margaret Buenz Dirks. His father was a wood-carver. When Dirks was seven, the family moved to Chicago. At age seventeen Dirks was selling cartoons to *Judge* and *Life* magazines. In 1896 he left Chicago for Manhattan, and in 1897 editor Rudolph Block of William Randolph Hearst's *New York Journal* enlisted his services in the publication battle with Joseph Pulitzer's *Sunday World*, which had in 1896 begun publication of a color comic by R. F. Outcault (q.v.), *The Yellow Kid*. In response, Block urged Dirks to create a strip in conscious imitation of Wilhelm Busch's *Max und Moritz*, a series of cartoons that had been known in translation in the United States since 1871. The *Katzenjammer Kids* first appeared on December 12, 1897. At first, the cast consisted of Mama, Hans, and Fritz. "Der Captain" made his first appearance on August 31, 1902, the Inspector, on March 19, 1905. During the Spanish-American War the strip was discontinued while Dirks served as a corporal in the army. Dirks later took *The Katzenjammer Kids* to the *New York World*. A court battle over publication rights began. The judgment of the court was that Hearst retain rights to a strip entitled *The Katzenjammer Kids* and that Dirks could continue the characters he had created under a different title. Accordingly, in 1914 Harold Knerr (q.v.) drew the strip for Hearst while Dirks at the *World* continued the strip under the title *Hans and Fritz*, later changed to *The Captain and the Kids* because of anti-German hostility during World War I, and, from 1918 to 1920, *The Shenanigan Kids*. In addition to being a comic-strip artist, Dirks was associated with many artists' movements, including the Ash Can School, and, together with Walt Kuhn and Yasuo Kuniyoshi, was one of the founders of the Ogunquit, Maine, artists' colony. Dirks died at his New York home on April 20, 1968. After his death *The Captain and the Kids* was continued by his son, John.

REFERENCES: Rudolph Dirks, *The Cruise of the Katzenjammer Kids* (New York, 1907); *The Katzenjammer Kids: Early Strips in Full Color* (New York, 1974). Portrait, *Current Literature* 45 (December 1908): 631. "Saufenstein and Grouchensheim, a Christmas Legend of the Rhine," *Cosmopolitan* 46 (January 1909): 229–232. "In Darkest Africa," *Cosmopolitan* 46 (February 1909): 355–358. Sheridan, pp. 58, 83, 293. Jim Walsh, "Classics of the Comics," *Hob-*

bies 58 (April 1953): 146–149. "Dirks's Bad Boys: Katzenjammer Kids," *Time* 68 (March 4, 1957): 48. Obituary, *New York Times*, April 22, 1968, p. 47. Francis Russell, "Farewell to the Katzenjammer Kids," *National Review* 20 (July 16, 1968): 703–705. Couperie and Horn, author index. Nye, p. 217. Horn, pp. 11, 17, 156, 209, 421.

Walt Disney 1901–1966

Walter Elias Disney, best known for his animated cartoon features, was born in Chicago on December 5, 1901, one of five children of Elias and Flora Call Disney. He attended public schools in Marceline, Illinois, where his father was a farmer, and in Kansas City. In 1918 he enrolled at Chicago's McKinley High School and studied in the evenings at the Chicago Academy of Fine Arts. He drove a Red Cross ambulance during World War I and after the war was employed with the Gray Advertising Company of Kansas City, where he met Ubbe Iwerks, the artist who would later draw Disney's Mickey Mouse. In the evenings Disney experimented with an animated feature, *Kansas City Laugh-O-Grams*, which he showed at local theaters in 1922. In 1923 he moved to Hollywood, where he continued work on *Alice in Cartoonland*, a feature that combined cartoon and live characters, distributed by Margaret Winkler. In 1926 he made a series of animations starring Oswald the Rabbit, distributed by Universal. In 1928 Disney, his brother Roy, and Ubbe Iwerks released *Steamboat Willie*, the first animated cartoon to use sound effects successfully, starring the character that was to become Mickey Mouse. Because of the success of the animation, Disney decided to do a comic-strip version of the mouse. *Mickey Mouse* was first published in 1930. Originally drawn by Iwerks, the strip was then penned by Floyd Gottfredson. By 1956 seven Disney strips were appearing regularly in newspapers. Disney died in Hollywood in 1966.

REFERENCES: "Cartoon Characters," *Science* 39 (April 12, 1941): 229–230. "Disney Cartoons Spur Combat Flyers," *Popular Science* 144 (April 1944): 104–105. Sheridan, pp. 25, 62, 282. Robert Field, *The Art of Walt Disney* (New York, 1942). J. M. Brown, *Seeing Things* (London, 1946). Frank Nugent, "That Million Dollar Mouse," *New York Times Magazine*, September 21, 1947, p. 22. Irving Wallace, "Mickey Mouse and How He Grew," *Collier's* 123 (April 9, 1949): 20–21. *CB*, 1952, pp. 148–150. Diane Disney Miller, *The Story of Walt Disney* (New York, 1957). Obituary, *New York Times*, December 16, 1966, p. 49. Bosley Crowther, "Dream Merchant," ibid. *Who Was Who* 4 (1961–68): 252. Robert Benayoun, *Le Dessin animé après Walt Disney* (Paris, 1961). Richard Schickel, *Walt Disney* (London, 1968). Couperie and Horn, author index. Christopher Finch, *The Art of Walt Disney* (New York, 1973). Leonard Maltin, *The Disney Films* (New York, 1973). Bob Thomas, *Walt Disney* (New York, 1976). Greta Walker, *Walt Disney* (New York, 1977). Christopher Finch, *Walt Disney's America* (New York, 1978). Richard Schickel, *The Disney Version* (New York, 1985). Nye, pp. 233–234, 383. Horn, p. 210.

Edward Benton Dodd 1902–

Born in 1902 in Lafayette, Georgia, Edward Benton Dodd was the son of a Baptist minister and a music teacher. After working as a ranger in Glacier National Park and as driver of a mule train in Yellowstone, Dodd on April 15, 1946, pioneered the environmentalist strip *Mark Trail*. Upon Dodd's retirement in 1979, the strip was continued by Jack Elrod (q.v.). Dodd lives in Gainesville, Georgia.

REFERENCE: Mike Toner, "Mark Trail: Comic With a Cause," *National Wildlife* 26 (February–March 1988): 14–17.

William Donahey 1883–1970

Born on October 19, 1883, in Westchester, Ohio, the son of John C. and Catherine Letetia Chaney Donahey, William Donahey attended public schools and later the Cleveland School of Art. In 1903 Donahey began his career as an artist with the *Cleveland Plain Dealer*. Syndication of his strip *The Teenie Weenies* by the *Chicago Tribune* began in 1914. The strip has been anthologized in book form and translated into French, Portuguese, and Spanish.

160

REFERENCES: William Donahey, *Adventure of the Teenie Weenies* (Chicago, 1920); *The Teenie Weenies Under the Rose Bush* (Chicago, 1922); *The Teenie Weenies in the Wildwood* (Chicago, 1923); *Alice and the Teenie Weenies* (Chicago, 1927); *Teenie Weenie Town* (New York, 1942); *Teenie Weenie Days* (New York, 1944); *Teenie Weenie Neighbors* (New York, 1945); *The Teenie Weenie Man's Mother Goose* (Chicago, 1946). Josef Marino, *Hi! Ho! Pinocchio!*, illus. by William Donahey (Chicago, 1940). *Who's Who* 34 (1966–67): 557.

Tad Dorgan 1877–1929

Cartoonist Thomas Aloysius Dorgan, born in San Francisco on April 29, 1877, the son of Thomas and Anna Tobias Dorgan, lost three fingers from his right hand in a factory accident at age thirteen. He was hired in 1891 by the art department of the *San Francisco Bulletin*. Dorgan also worked for the *San Francisco Chronicle*. In 1902 he adopted the pen name "Tad." From 1902 to 1905 he was political cartoonist for the *New York Journal*. During the notorious trial of Harry K. Thaw, he began his comic strip *Judge Rummy's Court*. In addition to *Judge Rummy's Court* Dorgan drew a syndicated sports cartoon, *Indoor Sports*. Dorgan took over another strip, *Silk Hat Harry*, in 1907. Together with Ring Lardner and George Ade, Dorgan is credited with introducing such expressions as "Twenty-three, Skidoo," "Dumb Dora" (later to inspire two plays and a comic strip by Chic Young), "Yes, We Have No Bananas," "Benny" (meaning hat), and "Dogs" (feet). In 1920 Dorgan developed heart disease and retired. He died at his home in Great Neck, Long Island, on May 2, 1929.

REFERENCES: Obituary, *New York Times*, May 3, 1929, p. 25. Sheridan, pp. 32, 33, 140, 181, 220, 287. *Who Was Who* 4 (1961–68): 258. Horn, pp. 220–221, 294.

Stan Drake 1921–

Stan Drake, originator of *The Heart of Juliet Jones*, was born on November 9, 1921, the son of Allen and Josephine Drake. Drake was raised in River Edge, New Jersey, where he attended high school. Later he studied under William McNulty and George Bridgman at the Art Students League of New York. In 1949 he opened his own studio as a commercial artist. He created *The Heart of Juliet Jones*, which premiered on March 9, 1953. On May 20, 1989, Drake retired from *Juliet Jones*. He now serves as Dean Young's (q.v.) collaborator on *Blondie*. Since Drake's departure, *Juliet Jones* has been drawn by Frank Bolles.

REFERENCES: Stan Drake, *Juliet Jones* (Greenfield, Wis., 1986). King Features Syndicate, *Stan Drake*, Biographical Series, no. 152 (New York, n.d.). Couperie and Horn, pp. 111, 167, 184. Nye, p. 231. Horn, pp. 222–223, 310.

Grace Gebbie Wiedersheim Drayton, 1877–1936

Artist and illustrator Grace Gebbie was born on October 14, 1877, the daughter of George and Mary Fitzgerald Gebbie. Her father was Philadelphia's first art publisher. In 1903 she developed for Hearst *Naughty Toodles*. Her well-known drawings of *The Campbell Kids* first appeared in 1905. For the *Philadelphia Press* Grace Gebbie created *Bobby Blake and Dolly Drake*, which ran from March 4 to October 28, 1906. She also illustrated Mother Goose nursery rhymes as well as a series of verses by her sister, Margaret G. Hays. Together with her sister, she produced a comic-strip series, *The Terrible Tales of Kaptain Kiddo*. Published in the *Philadelphia Sunday North American* from August 29, 1909, to January 19, 1913, the strip shares the theme of children's sea voyages popularized in 1907 by Dirks's (q.v.) *The Cruise of the Katzenjammer Kids* but initiated in 1906 by Lyonel Feininger's (q.v.) *The Kinder-Kids*, of which the central theme was the circumnavigation of the globe. In 1911 she divorced her first husband, Theodore E. Wiedersheim, Jr., and married W. Heyward Drayton III, from whom she was divorced in 1923. Grace Gebbie's work is characterized by a certain cuteness in combination with a strong moralizing strain. On March 10, 1935, her last work appeared. This was King Features' *Pussycat Princess*, written by Ed Anthony. Grace Gebbie died on January 31, 1936.

REFERENCES: G. G. Drayton, *Dolly Dimples and Bobby Bounce* (New York, 1931); *More Dolly Dingle Paper Dolls* (Rochester and Mineola, New York, 1979). *Who's Who* 9 (1916–17): 697. Obituary, *New York Times*, February 2, 1936, p. 9. *Who Was Who* 1 (1897–1942): 339. Horn, p. 223.

Jerry Dumas 1930–

For more than twenty years the collaborator of Mort Walker (q.v.) on such strips as *Beetle Bailey*, *Hi and Lois*, and *Sam and Silo*, Jerry Dumas holds a B.A. in English from Arizona State University. Dumas served in the U. S. Air Force, and is the author of *An Afternoon in Waterloo Park* and of — for children — *Rabbits Rafferty*. He lives in Greenwich, Connecticut, with his wife, Gail, and sons, Timothy, David, and John.

REFERENCE: Mort Walker, *Jerry Dumas: Sam and Silo* (New York: King Features Syndicate, 1989).

Edwina Dumm 1893–

Artist Frances Edwina Dumm was born in 1893 in Sandusky, Ohio, where her family owned a newspaper. Her art training consisted of a correspondence course in cartooning, after the completion of which she obtained a position as a political cartoonist for a Columbus paper. At the time she was the only woman so employed. She was subsequently recruited by the George Matthew Adams Syndicate to do a strip featuring a boy and his dog. This was *Cap Stubbs and Tippie* (1918), created while Dumm attended the Art Students League of New York. In addition to *Tippie* she drew a dog cartoon, *Sinbad*, for *Life* magazine and illustrated a one-column feature, *Alec the Great*, written by her brother, Robert. Original drawings for Dumm's comics are housed in the Ohio State University Library for Communication and Graphic Arts.

REFERENCES: Edwina Dumm, *Sinbad, A Dog's Life* (New York, 1930); *Sinbad Again!* (New York, 1932). Robert Dennis Dumm, *Alec the Great*, illus. by Edwina Dumm (Racine, Wis., 1933); *Alec the Great*, illus. by Edwina Dumm (New York, 1946). Sheridan, pp. 195–197. Horn, p. 226. Lucy Shelton Caswell, "Seven Editorial Cartoonists," *1989 Festival of Cartoon Art* (Columbus, Ohio, 1989), pp. 71–73.

Ralph Dunagin 1937–

Ralph Dunagin, with Dana Summers (q.v.) co-creator of North America Syndicate's *The Middletons*, has worked since 1961 for the *Orlando Sentinel*. In 1969 his cartoon panel, *Dunagin's People*, was first syndicated. In 1975, following the retirement of George Lichty, Dunagin became the artist of *Grin and Bear It. The Middletons*, a racially integrated strip, began syndication on November 3, 1986.

REFERENCE: North America Syndicate, *The Middletons* (New York, n.d.).

Bob Dunn 1908–1989

Bob Dunn, longtime author and artist of King Features Syndicate's *They'll Do It Every Time*, was born on March 5, 1908, in Newark, New Jersey. Dunn attended St. Anselm's College in Manchester, New Hampshire, and the Art Students League of New York. In 1933 he became a reporter for Hearst's International News Service. He later joined the art department of King Features Syndicate. In 1948 he invited Al Scaduto (q.v.) to assist him on Jimmy Hatlo's (q.v.) *They'll Do It Every Time*. Following Hatlo's death in 1963, Dunn and Scaduto continued the strip. Dunn died on January 31, 1989.

REFERENCE: King Features Syndicate, *Bob Dunn, Award-Winning Cartoonist, Dies at Eighty* (New York, 1989).

Bil Dwyer

Dwyer was the creator of *When Mother Was a Girl*. After the departure of Paul Fung (q.v.), Dwyer continued *Dumb Dora* from around 1932 to 1935.

REFERENCE: Horn, p. 226.

Carl Ed 1890–1959

Carl Frank Ludwig Ed was born in Moline, Illinois, on July 16, 1890. When Ed was thirteen his father, John, died, leaving his mother, Eva, with the care of their three children. After high school, Ed took a degree at Augustana College in Rock Island, Illinois. Ed's first job was with the World Color Syndicate in St. Louis, where he drew a baseball strip, *Big Ben*. In 1910 he became sports reporter and editor for the *Rock Island Argus* and drew *Luke McGluke, the Bush League Bearcat*. In 1917 he took a job as sports cartoonist for the *Chicago American*, and later worked on the *Chicago Tribune*, where he supplemented his income by teaching at the Chicago Academy of Fine Arts. About 1918 Ed submitted drawings for a strip entitled *Seventeen* to Joseph Medill Patterson, co-owner of the *Tribune*. Patterson changed the name to *Harold Teen*, and the strip was published in 1919. In 1928 *Harold Teen* was made into a silent film by Warner Brothers, and in 1933 the strip was made into a sound film. *Harold Teen*, in which adults are portrayed either as ridiculous or thwarting, was the first strip to deal with adolescent subculture. Ed died of an unspecified illness on October 10, 1959 in Evanston, Illinois.

REFERENCES: Carl Ed, *Harold Teen*, 2 vols. (New York, 1929, 1931). "Comics and Their Creators," *Literary Digest* 118 (October 13, 1934): 10. Sheridan, pp. 55–56, 288. Obituary, *New York Times*, October 11, 1959, p. 86. *Who Was Who* 3 (1951–60): 250. Couperie and Horn, p. 45. Nye, p. 223. Horn, p. 229, 304.

Gus Edson 1901–1966

Cartoonist Gus Edson, heir to Sidney Smith's *The Gumps*, was born in Cincinnati, Ohio, on September 20, 1901, the son of Max and Emma Jeanette Simon Edson. After attending public schools in Florida and New York, Edson enrolled at Pratt Institute, where, according to Sheridan, Edson spent but four months. He enlisted in the army in 1917, serving in the chemical warfare division. He later attended the Art Students League of New York, where he met Gladys Cedar, whom he married on February 4, 1922. From 1925 to 1928 Edson worked as a sports cartoonist for the *New York Evening Graphic*. He then worked at the *New York Evening Post*, King Features Syndicate, and the *New York Daily News*. In 1933 he created his first strip, *Streaky* for the *Daily News*. Following the death of Sidney Smith (q.v.), Edson was chosen by Joseph Medill Patterson of the Chicago Tribune–New York News Syndicate to take over *The Gumps*. *Dondi* originated in 1955 after a trip to Italy. Edson wrote the strip for *Dondi*, but the drawing was done by Irwin Hasen. *The Gumps* was discontinued in 1959. In 1961 *Dondi*, the motion picture, was released by Allied Artists, with a screenplay by Edson. He died of heart failure in Stamford, Connecticut, on September 26, 1966.

REFERENCES: Sheridan, pp. 11, 35, 101–104, 150, 154. "Why Bertie! *Chicago Tribune* Evicted the Gumps!" *Time* 56 (July 17, 1950): 62. Obituary, *New York Times*, September 28, 1966, p. 47. *Who's Who* 34 (1966–67): 606. *Who Was Who* 4 (1961–68): 279. Horn, pp. 217, 229, 297.

Hy Eisman 1927–

Hy Eisman, artist of King Features Syndicate's *Katzenjammer Kids* and of *Archie* comic books, was born in Paterson, New Jersey, on March 27, 1927, the son of Hilda and Harry Eisman. He began his career as a cartoonist as the ghost artist for *Kerry Drake*. From March 1967 to 1983 he drew *Little Iodine*. Since 1986 he has drawn *The Katzenjammer Kids*. He received the Comic Book Humor Award from the National Cartoonists Society in 1975 and in

1984. Eisman is an instructor at the Joe Kubert School of Cartoon and Graphic Art in Dover, New Jersey. He and his wife, Adri, whom he married on December 4, 1955, reside in Glen Rock, New Jersey. States Eisman, "Cartooning has been a passion with me since I was five . . . it hasn't abated!"

REFERENCES: King Features Syndicate, *Hy Eisman* (New York, n.d.). Phil Love, "Love on Life," *Washington Star*, September 22, 1975. *Contemporary Authors* (1977). Andrew Grover, "CSPA," *Columbia Today* (June 1977). Tom Toolen, "Today," *Bergen* (N.J.) *Record*, April 25, 1984. Chip Deffaa, "Starting Over," *Cartoonist PROfiles* 67 (September 1985) 70–75.

Will Eisner   1917–

The influential creator of *The Spirit*, William Erwin Eisner was born in New York City in March 1917 and educated in the Bronx. Eisner's father, an Austrian immigrant, was a set painter for the Yiddish theater. Upon graduation from high school, Eisner entered the Art Students League of New York, where he became a student of George Bridgman. After a stint with the *New York American*'s advertising department, Eisner in 1936 became a contributor to John Henle's *Wow*, one of the first publishers to issue original comic books rather than newspaper reprints. In 1937, following *Wow*'s demise, Eisner and former *Wow* editor Jerry Iger became comic-book packagers. In 1939 they dissolved their union and Eisner went to Quality Comics. On June 2, 1940, Eisner produced for the *Des Moines Register and Tribune Syndicator* a sixteen-page Sunday comic supplement that included *The Spirit*, his own groundbreaking crime feature. Among *The Spirit*'s innovations were the use of the "splash page," an ever-changing, dramatic logo resembling a stage set; a self-doubting superhero; and the emergence of the strip's urban setting as a character in its own right. Drafted, Eisner was from 1942 to 1945 a warrant officer in the Pentagon. After World War II, Eisner extended his artistic influence by consistently employing such talented young creators as Jules Feiffer (q.v.) and Jack Cole of *Plastic Man* fame. Among the predominant forces contributing to Eisner's own development are, according to cultural historian Michael Barrier, short-story formulas, Yiddish theater, and radio programs. "I grew up on short stories," recounted the artist at the July 9, 1983, Comic Expo in Philadelphia, ". . . on literary works of the Dickens magnitude. . . . I was a fan of Ambrose Bierce's stories, I loved O. Henry, and for me this was an opportunity to do short stories in the great, classic tradition." *The Spirit* ceased publication in October 1952, and Eisner turned his attention to a series of autobiographical graphic novels exploring the rich ethnic life of the Bronx. In 1978 he published the touching *A Contract with God;* in 1987, *The Dreamer*. Kitchen Sink Press has issued comprehensive reprints of *The Spirit* and of Eisner's 1930s adventure strip, *Hawks of the Sea*. The vigor of Eisner's line, his formulas for characterizing hero and villain, his cinematic narration, and his brisk dialogue are all reflected in the style and stories of contemporary graphic novels.

REFERENCES: Will Eisner, "Comic Books in the Library," *Library Journal* 99 (October 15, 1974): 2703–2707; *Outer Space Spirit* (Princeton, Wis., 1983); "Eisner Interviews Chris Claremont, Frank Miller, and Wendy Pini," *Comics Journal* 89 (March 1984): 87–97; "Reminiscences and Hortations," *Comics Journal* 89 (March 1984): 73–85; "Getting the Last Laugh: My Life in Comics," *New York Times Book Review*, January 14, 1990, pp. 1, 26–27. Horn, pp. 230–231. Gary Groth, "Editorial," *Comics Journal* 89 (March 1984): 6. Dana Jennings, "Will Eisner in France," *Comics Journal* 89 (March 1984): 98–101. Dale Luciano, "Three From Eisner: Past, Present, and Future," *Comics Journal* 89 (March 1984): 41–46. *Who's Who* 45 (1988–89) 882. Michael Barrier, "Comic Master: The Art and Spirit of Will Eisner," *Print* 42: (November–December 1988): 88–97, 196–203.

Jack Elrod   1924–

Jack Elrod, artist of the child strip *Winky Ryatt*, is a native of Georgia. The strip, originated in 1959 by artist Cal Alley, was later taken over by Elrod, who developed it to its present form. The adventures of the Ryatts incorporated the activities of Elrod's own large family of three boys, a girl, and a Siamese cat. In addition to *Winky Ryatt* (now called *The Ryatts*), Elrod

since 1979 has drawn *Mark Trail*, originated by Ed Dodd (q.v.) in 1946.

REFERENCES: Ada Biehl, "Comic Strip Family," *Atlanta Neighbor*, April 24, 1969, p. 13. Mark Toner, "Mark Trail: Comic With a Cause," *National Wildlife* 26 (February–March 1988): 14–17. Horn, p. 478.

Ken Ernst   1918–

Kenneth Frederic Ernst was born in Illinois, where he began an early career as a magician. In 1941 he became one of a number of Martha Orr's (q.v.) successors on *Apple Mary*, the precursor of today's *Mary Worth*. Writer Allen Saunders (q.v.), a professor of French at Wabash College, liked Ernst's work and soon the two were producing a radically revised strip in which they sought to show the emotional and romantic problems of women in the more or less glamorous professions — artists, actors, musicians, advertising writers, business executives.

REFERENCES: Ken Ernst and Allen Saunders, "Mary Worth and Us," *Collier's*, 123 (January 8, 1949): 45. Allen Saunders, "Mary Worth and the Affluent Society," in *The Funnies: An American Idiom*, ed. by D. M. White and Robert Abel (London, 1963), pp. 274–283. Couperie and Horn, p. 109. Nye, p. 231. Horn, pp. 219, 235, 483, 600.

George Evans   1920–

Best known for King Features Syndicate's *Secret Agent Corrigan*, an adaptation of Dashiell Hammet and Alex Raymond's *Secret Agent X-9* (1934), George Evans was born on February 5, 1920, in a small town in Pennsylvania. In 1943 he joined the air force. After the war, Evans studied at the Art Students League of New York. He later worked at Fiction House, a publisher. As a freelance comics illustrator, he ghosted such strips as *Terry and the Pirates* and *Flash Gordon*, as well as *Secret Agent Corrigan*. Evans lives in Mount Joy, Pennsylvania.

REFERENCE: King Features Syndicate, *George Evans* (New York, n.d.).

Greg Evans   1947–

Greg Evans, creator of *Luann*, was born in the Los Angeles area on November 13, 1947, the son of Herman and Virginia Evans. He received a B.A. from California State University in Northridge in 1970. After graduation, Evans taught from 1970 to 1974 in California high schools. He has also worked as promotions manager and graphic artist for a television station. His first comics include *Stu Dance* and *Fogarty*, which he distributed to over twelve hundred high-school newspapers. North America Syndicate now distributes *Luann*, Evans's teenage-girl strip, created in 1985, to over 250 papers. Evans lives in San Marcos, California. States Evans about his work, "When it's fun, it's fun, which is most of the time."

REFERENCE: North America Syndicate, *Luann* (New York, n.d.).

Lee Falk   1905–

Born in St. Louis, writer Lee Falk, best known for his *Mandrake the Magician* and *The Phantom*, graduated from the University of Illinois, after which he spent some time as a writer and director of radio shows for a St. Louis advertising agency. In 1934 he moved to New York, intending to write for comic strips. There he created *Mandrake* in 1934, which was drawn by Phil Davis (q.v.) from 1934 until his death in 1964. It is now drawn by Fred Fredericks (q.v.). *The Phantom* was first drawn by Ray Moore, later by Wilson McCoy, and since 1962 by Seymour Barry. In addition to scripting comic strips, Falk has produced more than three hundred dramas, starring such talents as Marlon Brando, Karl Malden, and Charlton Heston.

REFERENCES: Lee Falk, *The Phantom, The Prisoner of the Himalayas* (New York, 1969); *Mandrake the Magician* (New York, 1970); *Mandrake the Magician in Hollywood* (New York, 1977); *The Phantom* (New York, 1977). Dale Robertson, *Son of the Phantom*, illus. by Ray Moore, adapted from the famous newspaper strip by Lee Falk (Racine, Wis., 1946). Couperie and Horn, pp. 71, 73. King Features Syndicate, *Lee Falk*, Biographical Series, no. 2-S (New York, n.d.). Horn, pp. 22, 198, 240, 475, 551.

Jules Feiffer 1929–

Satirist Jules Feiffer was born in the Bronx on January 26, 1929, the son of David Feiffer, a sometime salesman and dental technician, and Rhoda Davis Feiffer, a fashion designer. Feiffer spent a "miserable four years" in James Monroe High School, and after graduation in 1946 attended the Art Students League of New York. From 1947 to 1951 Feiffer attended Pratt Institute, supporting himself as an assistant to Will Eisner (q.v.), originator of the strip *The Spirit*. He also managed to begin his own Sunday feature, *Clifford*. In 1951 Feiffer was drafted and spent two years in the signal corps doing cartoon animation. About this time he created *Munro*, a strip featuring a four-year-old who had been mistakenly drafted. After his discharge in 1953 Feiffer did various odd jobs, finally beginning his long association with the *Village Voice* in 1956. Since 1958 Feiffer's cartoons have appeared weekly in the *London Observer*. Feiffer's cartoon characters went onstage in a revue, *The Explainers*, which opened on May 9, 1961, at Chicago's Playwrights Cabaret. On June 27, 1961, Feiffer's play *Crawling Around* was staged at Menotti's Festival of the Two Worlds in Spoleto, Italy. An accomplished playwright as well as comic-strip artist, Feiffer is best known for *Carnal Knowledge*.

REFERENCES: Jules Feiffer: *Sick, Sick, Sick* (New York, 1958); *Passionella and Other Stories* (New York, 1959); *The Explainers* (New York, 1960); *Boy, Girl, Boy, Girl* (New York, 1961); *Feiffer's Album* (New York, 1963); *Harry* (New York, 1963); *Hold Me!* (New York, 1963); *The Great Comic Book Heroes* (New York, 1965); *The Unexpurgated Memoirs of Bernard Mergendeiler* (New York, 1965); *Feiffer on Civil Rights* (New York, 1966); *The Penguin Feiffer* (Harmondsworth, England, 1966); *Feiffer's Marriage Manual* (New York, 1967); *Little Murders* (New York, 1968); *Feiffer's People, Sketches, and Observations* (New York, 1969); *The White House Murder Case* (New York, 1970); *Dick and Jane* (New York, 1970); *Feiffer on Nixon* (New York, 1974); *Jules Feiffer's America* (New York, 1982); *Ronald Reagan in Movie America* (New York, 1988). Portrait, *Time* 73 (February 9, 1959): 36. *CB*, 1961, pp. 155–156; Eve Auchincloss and Nancy Lynch, "Interview with Jules Feiffer," *Mademoiselle* 52 (January 1961): 64–65; Amory, p. 203. David Segal, "Feiffer, Steinberg, and Others," *Commentary* 32 (November 1961): 431–435. *Who's Who* 34 (1966–67): 660. Horn, p. 244. Gary Groth, "Jules Feiffer," *Comics Journal* 124 (August 1988): 36–95.

Lyonel Feininger 1871–1956

Lyonel Feininger, painter and graphic artist, was born on July 17, 1871, in New York City, the son of Frederick and Elizabeth Cecilia Lutz Feininger, both professional musicians. In 1886 he went to Germany to study music, but his interests shifted to art. For a time Feininger studied at Hamburg's Kunstgewerbeschule. In 1891 he continued his studies at the Berlin Academy of Art. In Berlin he joined his mother, who had recently separated from Feininger's father. He was a student in Paris at the Colarossi Academy in 1892 but returned to Berlin, where he worked as a cartoonist on various papers, including *Ulk*, *Karikatur*, and *Lustige Blätter*, where he was employed from 1895 to 1900. In 1906 the *Chicago Sunday Tribune* syndicated two of his comic strips, *The Kin-der-Kids*, from April 29 to November 18, 1906, and *Wee Willie Winkie's World*, from August 19, 1906, to January 20, 1907. Feininger exhibited with the Berlin Secession in 1910. In 1913 he was included with Marc and Kandinsky in a show of the *Blaue Reiter*. During World War I the artist continued to reside in Berlin, although according to German law, his status was that of an enemy alien. In 1919 he was invited to become an instructor at the recently established Weimar Bauhaus. In 1926 he became artist-in-residence at the newly completed Dessau facilities. After his art had been classified as "decadent" by the National Socialists, Feininger returned to the United States. For two summers he taught at Mills College in Oakland, California, after which he took up residence in New York City. Splendid examples of his comic-strip material are in the Feininger archive at the Busch-Reisinger Museum of Germanic Culture at Harvard University. Also at Harvard are photographs of a collection of small wooden figures carved by Feininger to represent the characters of his *Kin-der-Kids* comic strip. Feininger died on January 13, 1956.

REFERENCES: Lyonel Feininger, *The Ruin by the Sea* (New York, 1968); *Lyonel Feininger: A Definitive Catalogue of His Graphic Work* (Cleveland, 1972); *Lyonel Feininger* (New York, 1974); *Feininger* (Paris, 1974); *Two Masters of the Weimar Bauhaus* (Sydney, 1974); *Lyonel Feininger* (London, 1975); *Lyonel Feininger, 1871–1956* (Palm Beach, 1976); *Lyonel Feininger, Drawings and Watercolors* (New York, 1979). *The Kin-der-Kids* (New York, 1980); *Exhibition Lyonel Feininger* (New York and Washington, D.C., 1985). Charlotte Teller, "Feininger-Fantasist," *International Studio*, 63 (November 1917): 25–30. Museum of Modern Art, New York, *Lyonel Feininger* (New York, 1944). Institute of Contemporary Art, Boston, *Jacques Villon, Lyonel Feininger* (New York, 1949). Cleveland Print Club, *The Work of Lyonel Feininger*, (Cleveland, 1951). *Who's Who in American Art*, 1953. Pasadena Art Museum, *The Blue Four: Feininger, Jawlensky, Kandinsky, Paul Klee* (Pasadena, 1954). Bayerische Akademie der schönen Künste, *Lyonel Feininger* (Hanover, 1954). *CB*, 1955, 1956. Obituary, *New York Times*, January 14, 1956, p. 19. Archivarion-Kunstbibliothek, *Aus der Werkstatt Lyonels: fünfundzwanzig Zeichnungen und Holzschnitte* (Berlin, 1958). Alfred Hentzen, *Feininger: Aquarelle* (Munich, 1958). Stephen Becker, *Comic Art in America* (New York, 1959) p. 29. Hans Hess, *Lyonel Feininger* (Stuttgart, 1959). *Who Was Who* 3 (1951–60): 274. Eberhard Ruhmer, *Lyonel Feininger: Zeichnungen, Aquarelle, Graphik* (Munich, 1961). Hans Hess, *Lyonel Feininger* (New York, 1961). Johannes Langner, *Lyonel Feininger: Segelschiffe* (Stuttgart, 1962). Ernst Scheyer, *Lyonel Feininger: Caricature and Fantasy* (Detroit, 1964). Detroit Institute of Arts, *Lyonel Feininger: the Formative Years* (Detroit, 1964). Wenzel Nachbaur, ed., *Gemälde, Aquarelle, Zeichnungen, Graphik, [von] L. Feininger* (Lugano, 1965). T. Lux Feininger, *Lyonel Feininger: City at the Edge of the World* (New York, 1965). Pasadena Art Museum, *Lyonel Feininger, 1871–1956: A Memorial Exhibition* (Pasadena, Calif., 1966). Couperie and Horn, p. 27. Horn, pp. 244–245. Ulrich Luckhardt, *Lyonel Feininger* (Hamburg, 1981). Ulrich Luckhardt, *Lyonel Feininger, die Karikaturen und das Zeichnerische Fruhwerk* (Munich, 1987). T. Lux Feininger and Ralph R. Colin, *Lyonel Feininger* (Seattle, 1987). T. Lux Feininger and Ralph Colin, *Lyonel Feininger* (Seattle, 1987).

Bud Fisher 1885–1954

Harry Conway (Bud) Fisher, who originated *Mutt and Jeff*, was born in Chicago on April 3, 1885. He attended public schools, and spent three years at the University of Chicago. His first job was that of layout man at the *San Francisco Chronicle*, where *A. Mutt*, the forerunner of *Mutt and Jeff*, first appeared on November 15, 1907. The hero Mutt was drawn from racetrack types observed by Fisher, later popularized by Damon Runyon. In 1908 Fisher took the strip to Hearst's *San Francisco Examiner*. In 1909, at Hearst's *New York American*, it was retitled *Mutt and Jeff*. After Fisher's contract with Hearst expired in 1915 the strip was syndicated by Wheeler, later by Bell Syndicate, and finally by Fisher's own corporation. Fisher died of cancer in New York on September 7, 1954. His funeral oration was delivered by Rube Goldberg (q.v.), and the strip was continued by Al Smith (q.v.), who had been Fisher's assistant since 1922. As Stephen Becker has said, "Mutt and Jeff are of course part of the American mythology."

REFERENCES: H. C. Fisher, *The Adventures of Mutt and Jeff* (New York, 1920); *The Mutt and Jeff Cartoons*, 12 vols. (Boston, 1910–1932); "Seven Tips I Have Picked Up on the Way," *American Magazine* 89 (May 1920): 19–20; "Confessions of a Cartoonist," *Saturday Evening Post* 201 (July 28, 1928): 10–11; 201 (August 4, 1928): 26–28; 201 (August 11, 1928): 28–30; 201 (August 18, 1928): 31; *Mutt and Jeff* (New York, 1929); *The Mutt and Jeff Cartoons* (Greenfield, Wis., 1987). "Comic-ers," *Everybody's Magazine* 33 (July 1915): 71. John Wheeler, "Captain of Comic Industry," *American Magazine* 81 (May 1916): 48–50. H. S. Fullerton, "Highest Paid Newspaper Cartoonist in the World," *American Magazine* 89 (May 1920): 18–19. Sheridan, pp. 17, 75, 203, 295. Obituary, *New York Times*, September 8, 1954, p. 31. Stephen Becker, *Comic Art in America* (New York, 1959) pp. 36–37. *Who Was Who* 3 (1951–60): 238–239. Heinz Politzer, "From Little Nemo to Little Abner," in *The Funnies: An American Idiom*, ed. by D. M. White and Robert Abel (London, 1963), p. 49. Couperie and Horn, pp. 29, 30, 219. Nye, pp. 218, 230. Horn, pp. 251–252.

Dudley Fisher 1890–1951

Cartoonist Dudley Fisher was born in Columbus, Ohio, in 1890. Fisher began his newspaper career in 1911 when, a student at Ohio State University, he was hired by the art department of the *Columbus Dispatch*. He began *Right Around Home*, a kid strip starring a girl named Myrtle, in 1937; it was later syndicated by King Features. On May 26, 1941, *Myrtle*, a strip based on the exploits of Fisher's teenage daughter, began syndication. Fisher died of a heart attack on July 10, 1951, while vacationing in Rockport, Massachusetts.

REFERENCES: Sheridan, p. 263. Obituary, *New York Times*, July 11, 1951, p. 23.

Ham Fisher 1901–1955

Hammond Edward Fisher, creator of *Joe Palooka*, was born in Wilkes-Barre, Pennsylvania, in 1901. He attended public schools, and spent two weeks at Pennsylvania State University. Fisher became cartoonist and reporter for the *Wilkes-Barre Record;* later he worked for the *Wilkes-Barre Times-Leader*. Fisher got the idea for *Joe Palooka* from a conversation with "an especially dumb but good-natured prize fighter" (*Literary Digest*). The strip appeared in 1927, distributed by McNaught Syndicate. On December 27, 1955, Fisher was found dead in a friend's studio following his expulsion from the National Cartoonists Society. The expulsion resulted from the ghosting of an obscene *Li'l Abner* episode during the comic-strip controversy stimulated in the fifties by Wertham's *Seduction of the Innocent*. *Joe Palooka* was continued after Fisher's death by Tony Di Preta (q.v.).

REFERENCES: Ham Fisher, *Joe Palooka* (New York, 1933); "Joe Palooka and Me," *Collier's* 122 (October 16, 1948): 28. "Comics and Their Creators," *Literary Digest* 118 (November 17, 1934): 11. "Joe Palooka, Public Hero," *Newsweek* 14 (December 18, 1939): 42. "Palooka and Ann? Yes!" *Newsweek* 31 (June 7, 1948): 56. "Mr. and Mrs. Joe Palooka," *Time* 53 (June 27, 1949): 45–46. Obituary, *New York Times*, January 5, 1956, p. 8. *Who Was Who* 3 (1951–60): 284. D. M. White and Robert Abel, "Comic Strips and American Culture," in *The Funnies: An American Idiom* (London, 1963), p. 4. R. H. Boyle, "Champ for all Time!!!," *Sports Illustrated* 22 (April 19, 1965): 120–124. Sheridan, pp. 130–136. Couperie and Horn, pp. 65, 71, 83. Nye, pp. 227, 230. Horn, pp. 154, 211, 250–51, 343–44.

Mary Fleener 1951–

Born in Los Angeles on September 14, 1951, Mary Fleener is the daughter of Cecil and Virginia Fleener. Since attending California State University at Long Beach, where she majored in printmaking, Fleener has published in such underground organs as *Weirdo*, *Wimmen's Comix*, and *Snarf*. Her critically acclaimed *Hoodoo* (Ray Zone, 1988) brilliantly adapts in comic-book form African-American writer Zora Neale Hurston's studies of folklore and black magic. Fleener resides in Encinatas, California, from which she proclaims: "Being an underground cartoonist is the coolest thing in the world!!!"

REFERENCES: *Comics F/X* 7 (February 1989). *Comics Journal* 127 (March 1989): 38. *Seattle Star* 20 (May 1989): 8. *Amazing Heroes* 166 (June 1989): 54, 58. *Forced Exposure* 15 (Summer 1989): 118. *Sound Choice* 11 (1989): 45.

Max Fleischer 1888–1972

One of the founding fathers of the animated cartoon, Max Fleischer was born in Vienna, Austria. When Fleischer was four years old his parents came to the United States. He studied at Cooper Union, the Mechanic's and Trademan's School, and the Art Students League of New York. His first job was with the *Brooklyn Daily Eagle*, as a photoengraver. In 1915, while working on *Popular Science* magazine, Fleischer was urged by editor Waldemar Kaempffert to research problems in motion-picture animation. In 1916, while working for Bray, Fleischer created *Out of the Inkwell*. In 1919, according to Fleischer's biographer, Leslie Cabarga, Fleischer formed Out of the Inkwell Films, Inc. Koko the Clown and Betty Boop, two of the

better known Fleischer cartoon stars, were later adapted as comic strips. But Fleischer is perhaps best known for his *Popeye* animations, which were released from July 14, 1933, to July 3, 1942.

REFERENCES: Max Fleischer, *Noah's Shoes* (Detroit, 1944). Ruth F. Kneitel, "Max Fleischer: Out of the Inkwell," *World of Comic Art* 1 (Fall 1966): 40–46. Leslie Cabarga, *The Fleischer Story* (New York, 1976). Horn, pp. 110, 255.

Frank Fletcher 1919–

Fletcher drew *Bringing Up Father* after the death of George McManus (q.v.).

REFERENCES: Horn, pp. 132, 255.

Harold Foster 1892–1982

Canadian artist Harold R. Foster was born in Nova Scotia in 1892. His family moved to Winnipeg in 1906, and for a time Foster was a professional boxer. At eighteen he quit school to support his family. After the Canadian depression of 1913, Foster became a guide in western Ontario and northern Manitoba. He tried prospecting, but a claim he located in 1917 was jumped in 1920. Later Foster attended the Art Institute of Chicago, then the National Academy of Design and the Chicago Academy of Fine Arts. While working for Detroit's Campbell-Ewald Advertising Agency in 1928, he was introduced to Edgar Rice Burroughs by Joseph H. Neebe, who had suggested to the writer the idea of a comic-strip adaptation. On January 7, 1929, *Tarzan* appeared in cartoon form, syndicated by Metropolitan Newspaper Service, which later became part of United Feature Syndicate. On March 15, 1931, *Tarzan* appeared as a Sunday color strip, and Rex Maxon (q.v.) took over the drawing for the daily. Foster continued to do the Sunday feature until 1937, when he began his own strip, *Prince Valiant in the Days of King Arthur*. Strips related to *Prince Valiant* include Cornell Greening's *Prince Errant*, which Stephen Becker cites as one of the sources of *Prince Valiant*, and Ralph Fuller's (q.v.) *Oakey Doakes*, begun in 1925 as a conscious satire of the knightly strip. Foster retired in 1979. *Prince Valiant* was then drawn by John Cullen Murphy (q.v.), his assistant since May 23, 1971.

REFERENCES: Harold Foster, *Prince Valiant in the Days of King Arthur* (New York, 1951); *Prince Valiant Fights Attila the Hun* (New York, 1952); *Prince Valiant on the Island Sea* (New York, 1952); *Prince Valiant in the Days of King Arthur* (New York, 1954); *Prince Valiant's Perilous Voyage* (New York, 1954); *Prince Valiant and the Golden Princess* (New York, 1955); *Prince Valiant in the New World* (New York, 1956); *The Medieval Castle* (New York, 1957); *Prince Valiant and the Three Challenges* (New York, 1960); *Prince Valiant's Perilous Voyage* (New York, 1976); *Prince Valiant: Adventures in Two Worlds* (New York, 1978); *Prince Valiant: Queen of the Misty Isles* (New York, 1978); *Prince Valiant*, vols. 1–4, 29–31 (Thousand Oaks and Westlake Village, Calif., 1985–). E. R. Burroughs, *The Illustrated Tarzan*, illus. by Harold Foster (New York, 1929). Stephen Becker, *Comic Art in America* (New York, 1959), p. 26. R. S. Craggs, "Harold Foster, Father of the Adventure Strip," *World of Comic Art* 1 (Fall 1966): 4–11. Couperie and Horn, author index. Nye, pp. 225, 229. Horn, pp. 21, 259–60, 487, 507, 565, 649, 650.

Fontaine Fox 1884–1964

The creator of *Toonerville Folks*, Fontaine Fox was born in Louisville, Kentucky, the son of Fontaine and Mary Pitkin Fox. After graduation from high school Fox worked on the *Louisville Herald*. He then spent two years at Indiana University but left because of financial difficulties, returning to the *Herald* and later joining the staffs of the *Louisville Times* and *Chicago Post*. At the *Post* he drew boys' cartoons from 1910 to 1915, when he joined Wheeler Syndicate and created *Toonerville Folks*. The strip's cast of characters included the Powerful Katrinka, the Terrible Tempered Mr. Bang, Auntie Eppie Hogg, the Toonerville Cop, and Mickey (Himself) McGuire. Most of the Toonerville personalities were based on characters from Fox's hometown. The personality of the Toonerville Trolley, however, was a composite of two streetcar companies with which Fox was familiar, the Louisville Line and the Pelham Manor (New York) Company. In 1955 the Toonerville Trolley made its last run. Fox died at the age of eighty on August 9, 1964, in Greenwich, Connecticut.

REFERENCES: Fontaine Fox, *Funny Folk* (New York, 1917); *Cartoons* (New York, 1918); *Toonerville Trolley and Other Cartoons* (New York, 1921); "Queer Way to Make a Living," *Saturday Evening Post* 200 (February 11, 1928): 6–7. Sheridan, pp. 89, 293. Obituary, *New York Times*, August 10, 1964, p. 31. *Who Was Who* 4 (1961): 325–26. Horn, p. 260.

Ramona Fradon 1926–

Since 1980 the artist for the Tribune Media Services' *Brenda Starr*, Ramona Fradon was raised in Westchester County, New York, and attended the Art Students League of New York. In 1952 she was hired by a comic-book publisher — a remarkable achievement for a woman at the time — and in this capacity drew numerous superheroes, including Superman, Batman, and Plastic Man. Fradon lives in Greenwich Village, and is the mother of a grown daughter.

REFERENCE: Tribune Media Services, *Ramona Fradon Biography*, 1986.

Fred Fredericks 1929–

Artist Harold Fredericks, Jr., of *Mandrake the Magician* fame was born in Atlantic City, New Jersey, on August 9, 1929, and educated at the Atlantic City Friends School. From 1947 to 1949 Fredericks worked for the *Atlantic City Press*. After joining the marine corps in 1950, he became a cartoonist for the *Camp Lejeune Globe*, where he drew *Salty Ranks*. In 1953 the artist was discharged and enrolled at the School of Visual Arts in New York. At the same time he drew a historical strip, *Atlantic City History Sketches*. This was followed by another historical strip, *New Jersey's Patriots*, based on the revolutionary war and syndicated throughout New Jersey from 1957 to 1959. In 1960 Fredericks originated two more historical strips, *The Late Late War* and *Under the Stars and Bars*. When artist Phil Davis (q.v.) died in 1964, Fredericks joined creator Lee Falk (q.v.) as artist for *Mandrake the Magician*. Since 1972 Fredericks has lived in Cape Cod.

REFERENCES: King Features Syndicate, *Fred Fredericks*, Biographical Series, no. 230 (New York, n.d.); *Fred Fredericks: Mandrake the Magician* (New York, n.d.). Horn, pp. 264–265. Rich Margopoulos, *A Monster Among Us* (Racine, Wis., 1986).

Drew Friedman 1958–

Raw contributor Drew Friedman was born in New York in 1958. Among the books upon which he has collaborated with his brother, Josh Alan Friedman (q.v.), is *Any Similarity to Persons Living or Dead Is Purely Coincidental* (Fantagraphics, 1986). Friedman's finely executed work has also appeared in the *National Lampoon*, the *Village Voice*, *Heavy Metal*, and *Blab*. Friedman has sometimes collaborated with author Harvey Pekar (q.v.).

REFERENCE: "Raw Data" in Art Spiegelman and Françoise Mouly, *Read Yourself Raw: The Graphix Anthology for Damned Intellectuals* (New York, 1987).

Josh Alan Friedman 1956–

Josh Alan Friedman was born in New York City in 1956. A frequent contributor to alternative publications, including *Raw*, Friedman's work includes *Tales of Times Square* (Delacorte, 1986).

REFERENCE: "Raw Data" in Art Spiegelman and Françoise Mouly, *Read Yourself Raw: The Graphix Anthology for Damned Intellectuals* (New York, 1987).

Michael Fry 1959–

Michael Fry, creator and author of King Features Syndicate's *When I Was Short*, was born in

1959 in Minneapolis. He attended Baylor University and the University of Texas at Austin, receiving a B.A. in history. In January 1984 Fry's comic strip *Scotty* appeared in the *Houston Post*. Between 1985 and 1987 Fry created *Cheeverwood*, a tale of suburbia. In August 1989 King Features first distributed *When I Was Short*, written by Fry and drawn by Guy Vasilovich (q.v.). Fry, his wife, Kim, and daughter, Sarah, live in Houston.

REFERENCE: King Features Syndicate, *Michael Fry* (New York, 1989).

R. B. Fuller 1890–1963

Ralph Briggs Fuller was born in Michigan in 1890. Among the magazines to which he contributed humorous cartoons were *Life*, *Judge*, *Liberty*, and the *Saturday Evening Post*. In 1935 he created for Associated Press the comic strip *Oakey Doakes*, a mild satire on knighthood. The strip was discontinued in 1961. Fuller died while on vacation in Boothbay Harbor, Maine, on August 16, 1963. *Oakey Doakes*, begun some time after Cornell Greening's *Prince Errant*, marks a further refinement in the adventure strip — a cartoon that makes ironic reference to its prototype.

REFERENCES: *AAA* 30 (1933). Mallett, p. 149. Obituary, *New York Times*, August 17, 1963, p. 19. Fielding, p. 131. Horn, p. 525.

Paul Fung 1897–1944

Chinese-American artist Paul Fung was born in Seattle in 1897. Before going to New York, Fung was sports cartoonist at the *Seattle Post-Intelligencer*. Later he was Billy De Beck's (q.v.) assistant for *Barney Google*, and in the twenties took over *Bughouse Fables*, which he produced with Jack Lait. In April 1925 Fung began *Gus and Gussie*. In 1930 he continued Chic Young's (q.v.) *Dumb Dora*, and — later — Cliff Sterrett's (q.v.) *Polly and Her Pals*. Fung died in New York on October 16, 1944.

REFERENCES: Sheridan, pp. 83, 97. Obituary, *New York Times*, October 17, 1944, p. 23. Horn, pp. 226, 269.

William Gaines 1922–

Pioneering comic-book publisher William M. Gaines, best known for his collaboration with Harvey Kurtzman (q.v.) on *Mad* magazine, was born on March 1, 1922, the son of comic-book magnate M. C. Gaines, creator of E. C. Publications. Introduced to a new generation of comics fans through the 1988 documentary *Comic Book Confidential*, Gaines is well known to civil libertarians for his spirited defense of comic books before the Kefauver Senate subcommittee to investigate juvenile delinquency on April 21, 1954. Following the demise of his E. C. empire in 1956, Gaines turned his energies to the promotion of *Mad*, begun by Kurtzman in 1952. This legendary magazine is now a property of Time Warner Inc.

REFERENCE: Horn, pp. 273, 741–789.

Randy Glasbergen 1957–

Randy Glasbergen, who under the pen name "Harris" creates King Features Syndicate's *The Better Half*, began his career as a full-time cartoonist in 1976. Since then, over 6,500 Glasbergen cartoons have appeared in such publications as *Good Housekeeping*, *Cosmopolitan*, *Woman's World*, the *Saturday Evening Post*, *Woman*, *New Woman*, the *Wall Street Journal*, the *National Enquirer*, *Reader's Digest*, *Playgirl*, the *Christian Science Monitor*, and the *Los Angeles Times*. Glasbergen and his wife live in upstate New York.

REFERENCE: King Features Syndicate, *Randy Glasbergen* (New York, n.d.).

Phoebe Gloeckner 1960–

Best known for her work for *Wimmen's Comix*, underground cartoonist Phoebe Gloeckner was born in Philadelphia on December 22, 1960, the daughter of Mary Louise Adams and David Gloeckner. Gloeckner received her master's degree from the University of Texas in biomedical communications in 1988. She has also studied at San Francisco State University (1980–85), the Université D'Aix-Marseille, Aix-en-Provence, France (1983–84), and Charles University, Prague, Czechoslovakia (1986). Since 1979 Gloeckner has worked as a freelance artist and medical illustrator. Exhibitions of her paintings and illustrations include *Twisted Sisters*, a forthcoming show of comic-book art and painting featuring, in addition to her own work, that of Diane Noomin (q.v.), Carol Tyler (q.v.), Kristine Kryttre (q.v.), and Aline Kominsky-Crumb (q.v.), scheduled for May 1990 at the Himowitz Gallery in Sacramento, California; *Modern Primitives*, a show at the Center on Contemporary Art Gallery in Seattle, Washington (1989); *Medical Illustration*, an exhibit at the Southwestern University, Georgetown, Texas (1987); The Association of Medical Illustrators' Salon (1986); and *Comic Book Art*, an exhibit at San Francisco State University (1983). Her comics have appeared in *Young Lust*, no. 6; *Weirdo*, nos. 3, 25, 27; *Wimmen's Comix*, nos. 8, 9, 14, 15; and *Pox* (1985–86). Gloeckner's films *Nuit Blanche* and *Science in Action* won awards at the 1985 San Francisco Art Institute Film Festival. States Gloeckner, "My comics are generally autobiographical. They've been getting 'funnier' as I grow older, humorous in a black sort of way, but making people laugh has been my primary motivation. . . . I am fascinated by the possibilities of the visual/verbal narrative, and expressing feelings about my life in comic-book stories has acted as an emotional catharsis for me." Gloeckner lives in San Francisco.

REFERENCES: Phoebe Gloeckner, *A Semiotic Analysis of Medical Illustration* (Austin, Tex., 1987); "Comics: A Medium Deserving Another Look," *Et cetera, the Journal of the International Society of General Semantics* (Fall 1989): 246. "The Real Toonville," in *Pacific Film Archive Film Festival Catalogue* (Berkeley, Calif., 1989): 18.

Rube Goldberg 1883–1970

Satirist Reuben Lucius Goldberg was born in San Francisco on July 4, 1883. Following his father's wishes he attended the College of Mining Engineering at the University of California, from which he received his B.S. in 1904. Three months after graduation, according to an autobiography published in *Literary Digest*, Goldberg had "fled" his "chosen profession" and become the *San Francisco Chronicle*'s sports cartoonist. In October 1907 he went to New York, where, for the *New York Evening Mail*, he created in 1909 *Foolish Questions*, and in 1915 *Boob McNutt*, a strip syndicated by Hearst, from 1918 to 1933, whose hero Goldberg described as "a simple young man whose sympathetic interest in other people is constantly getting him into trouble." Goldberg is also famous for the inventions of his Professor Lucifer Gonzaga Butts, interpreted by Goldberg as "a bewhiskered child of my brain, but a subconscious offspring of my engineering career." Other humorous creations by Goldberg include *Boobs Abroad, I'm the Guy, They All Look Alike When You're Far Away*, and *The Weekly Meeting of the Tuesday Ladies' Club*. Goldberg was awarded the Pulitzer Prize in 1948. In his later years Goldberg's interests shifted to sculpture. He died on December 7, 1970.

REFERENCES: Reuben Goldberg, *Foolish Questions* (Boston, 1909); *Chasing the Blues* (Garden City, N.Y., 1912); *Is There a Doctor in the House?* (New York, 1929); *The Rube Goldberg Plan For the Post War World* (New York, 1944); *Rube Goldberg's Guide to Europe* (New York, 1954); *Famous Artists Cartoon Course* (Westport, Conn., 1956); *How to Remove Cotton from a Bottle of Aspirin* (Garden City, N.Y., 1959); *I Made My Bed*, by Kathy O'Ferrell, as told to Rube Goldberg (New York, 1960); *Rube Goldberg Versus the Machine Age* (New York, 1968); *Bobo Baxter, the Complete Daily Strip, 1927–1928* (Westport, Conn., 1977); *The Best of Rube Goldberg* (Englewood Cliffs, N.J., 1979); *Rube Goldberg* (New York, 1983); "My Answer to the Question: How Did You Put It Over?" *American Magazine* 93 (March 1922): 33–39; "It Happened to a Rube," *Saturday Evening Post* 201 (November 10, 1928): 20–21; "Comics, New Style and Old," *Saturday Evening Post* 201 (December 15, 1928): 12–13; "What Do I Do After Forty?" *Saturday Evening Post* 205 (December 3, 1932): 26; "Thankless Children," *Saturday Evening Post* 205 (March 25, 1933): 30; "Nobody Listens," *Saturday Evening Post* 206 (November 4, 1933): 23; "Comics and Their Creators," *Literary Digest* 116 (December 2, 1933): 11.

"Old Man Takes His Boy Back Home," *Scholastic* 26 (May 18, 1935): 7. "Rube Goldberg's New Leaf," *Newsweek* 12 (December 5, 1938): 27. Sheridan, pp. 39–40. Stephen Becker, *Comic Art in America* (New York, 1959), pp. 52–53. *Who's Who* 34 (1966–67): 793. Couperie and Horn, author index. Peter Marzio, *Rube Goldberg: His Life and Work* (New York, 1973). Horn, pp. 17, 20, 124–126, 284–285, 492.

Larry Gonick 1946–

Internationally acclaimed author and illustrator Larry Gonick was born on August 24, 1946, in San Francisco, the son of Emanuel and Mollie Rebhun Gonick. Gonick received his A.B. and M.A. in mathematics from Harvard University. His voluminous publications include *The Cartoon History of the Universe*, Volumes 1–7 (Rip Off Press, 1978–85); *The Cartoon Guide to Genetics* (Harper & Row, 1981); *Computer Science* (Harper & Row, 1983); and *U.S. History*, Volumes 1–2 (Harper & Row, 1987–88). His comics include *The Cartoon Kitchen*, which has been syndicated since 1978; *Yankee Almanack*, which appeared in the *Boston Globe* from 1975 to 1976; and *Boston Comics*, which appeared in *Boston After Dark* from 1972 to 1975. Queries Gonick, "Comics + Information = What?" Gonick lives in San Francisco.

Chester Gould 1900–1985

Chester Gould, creator of *Dick Tracy*, was born in Pawnee, Oklahoma, on November 20, 1900, the son of Gilbert R. and Alice Miller Gould. From 1919 to 1921 Gould attended Oklahoma A & M University; he graduated in 1923 from Northwestern University. From 1924 to 1929 he was a cartoonist for Hearst publications, where he created the daily *Fillum Funnies*. He joined the staff of the *Chicago Tribune* in 1931, where he originated a detective strip originally entitled *Plainclothes Tracy*, described by White and Abel as consisting of a cast of "grotesques in [a] morality play," and by Russel Nye as centering about "a kind of idealized J. Edgar Hoover." *Dick Tracy* was conceived by Joseph Medill Patterson in response to the then-current gangster era. Its publication in 1931, as Nye points out, "marked the first appearance in the comics of real violence, although the dime-novel and the pulp had dealt in it for years." The character of Dick Tracy changed over the years. Over the years Tracy become more bourgeois, and the strip focused increasingly on the grotesque and vulgar, the latter strikingly exemplified by B. O. Plenty. The physical appearance of the early Tracy is very close to Capp's (q.v.) satiric *Fearless Fosdick*.

REFERENCES: Chester Gould, *Dick Tracy and Dick Tracy Junior, and How They Captured "Stooge" Viller* (New York, 1933); *How Dick Tracy and Dick Tracy Junior Caught the Racketeers* (New York, 1934); *Dick Tracy Meets the Night Crawler* (Racine, Wis., 1945); *Dick Tracy and the Mad Killer*, adapted by Helen Berke (Racine, Wis., 1947); *The Celebrated Cases of Dick Tracy, 1931–1951* (New York, 1970); *Dick Tracy, the Thirties, Tommy Guns, and Hard Times* (New York, 1978); *Dick Tracy, Dailies and Sundays, 1940* (Long Beach, Calif., 1983); *Dick Tracy, Books One to Twenty* (El Cajon, Calif., 1986–); *Dick Tracy* (Secaucus, N.J., 1987). "Are Comics Bad for Children?" *Rotarian* 56 (March 1940); 18–19; *Reply* 56 (May 1940): 2. Sheridan, pp. 16, 121–122, 258. John Bainbridge, "Chester Gould," *Life* 17 (August 14, 1944); 43–46. "Sparkle Plenty," *Life* 23 (August 25, 1947): 42. "Dick Tracy and Me," *Collier's* 122 (December 11, 1948): 54. R. M. Yoder, "Dick Tracy's Boss," *Saturday Evening Post* 222 (December 17, 1949): 22–23. "Bonny Braids," *The New Yorker* 27 (July 7, 1951): 14–15. "Dick Tracy in Orbit," *Newsweek* 61 (January 14, 1963): 47. Richard Oaks, "Chester Gould: Sanguinary Squire from Pawnee," *The World of Comic Art* 1 (Winter 1966–67): 28–31. *Who's Who* 34 (1966–67): 809. Couperie and Horn, author index. "Too Harsh in Putting Down Evil: Violence in the Dick Tracy Strips," *Time* 91 (June 28, 1968): 42. Nye, pp. 226–227. Horn, pp. 22, 289. Obituary, *Chicago Tribune*, May 13, 1985. Obituary, *Los Angeles Times*, May 12, 1985. Obituary, *Newsweek*, May 20, 1985. Obituary, *New York Times*, May 12, 1985. Obituary, *Time*, May 20, 1985.

Bud Grace

Bud Grace, creator of King Features Syndicate's *Ernie*, was born in Chester, Pennsylvania. At the age of five he moved with his family to Florida. There he later attended Florida State University, from which he received in 1971 a Ph.D. in atomic physics. From 1971 to 1973, Grace taught at the University of Georgia; from 1973, at Florida State University. In 1979 Grace began his career as a cartoonist; on February 1, 1988, he launched the daily *Ernie*, "a comedy of low manners." *Ernie* became a Sunday feature on February 7, 1988. Among *Ernie*'s cast are Ernie, "Mr. Nice Guy," "Ernie's would-be girlfriend," Doris Husselmeyer, "Ernie's husband-hungry landlady," Mrs. Effie Munyon; and "the fast-talking bamboozler, Ernie's Uncle," Sid Fernwilter. Grace lives in Silver Spring, Maryland, with his wife and son.

REFERENCE: King Features Syndicate, *Ernie by Bud Grace* (New York, n.d.).

Alexander Graham 1917–

Alexander Graham, creator of Tribune Media Services' *Fred Bassett*, was born in Glasgow, Scotland, where he attended the Dumfries Academy and the Glasgow School of Art. In 1945 he began his career as a cartoonist, eventually publishing his work in numerous British periodicals and in *The New Yorker*. In 1963 he began his enormously popular dog strip, *Fred Bassett*. Graham resides in Sussex, England.

REFERENCE: Tribune Media Services, *Alexander Graham Biography*, January 1988.

Dave Graue 1926–

After the retirement of V. T. Hamlin (q.v.) in 1973, *Alley Oop* was continued by Hamlin's assistant, Dave Graue. A high-school friend of Hamlin's daughter, Graue served in the air force during World War II. After the war, Graue joined the staff of the *Pittsburgh Post-Gazette* as an editorial cartoonist. In 1950 he became Hamlin's assistant. Graue and his wife, Eliza, reside in Brevard, North Carolina.

REFERENCES: Jane Bryant, " 'Alley Oop' Celebrates Its 50th Birthday," NEA News Release (New York, 1983). April Zion and Nancy Nicoledis, "Alley Oop by Dave Graue," NEA News Release (New York, n.d.). Horn, p. 76.

Clarence Gray 1902–1957

Clarence Gray was born in Toledo, Ohio, in 1902. He was first employed on the art staff of the *Toledo News-Bee*, and later was employed by papers in Cleveland. Together with William Ritt, Gray began *Brick Bradford* in 1933 for the Central Press Association of Cleveland. After Central Press's acquisition by Hearst, the strip was circulated by King Features. The association between Gray and Ritt, who wrote the strip's continuity, ended with Ritt's death in 1950. Artist Paul Norris drew the dailies beginning in 1952. Gray died in Cleveland on January 5, 1957, and the feature passed to Norris. Couperie and Horn cite the strip for its "poetry and festive atmosphere." Together with *Buck Rogers* and *Flash Gordon*, *Brick Bradford* was part of the general escape from the present represented by the space-age comics of the thirties. The last daily *Brick Bradford* appeared on April 25, 1987; the Sunday, May 10, 1987.

REFERENCES: Clarence Gray and William Ritt, *Brick Bradford in the City Beneath the Sea* (Akron, Ohio, 1934). Obituary, *New York Times*, January 7, 1957, p. 25. Couperie and Horn, author index. Horn, pp. 290–291.

Harold Gray 1894–1968

Harold Lincoln Gray was born in Kankakee, Illinois, on January 20, 1894, the son of Ira Lincoln Gray and Estella Rosencranz Gray. In his article "One Shade of Gray" Robert Abel reports that Gray took great pride in tracing his ancestors' early roots in America, one forefather supposedly emigrating from England in 1640. Gray received his B.S. in 1917 from Pur-

due. His first marriage was to Doris C. Platt, who died on November 22, 1925. On July 17, 1929, Gray was remarried to Winifred Frost, with whom he coauthored *My Folks*, Little Orphan Annie's autobiography. Gray joined the staff of the *Chicago Tribune* in 1917. In May 1918 he enlisted in the army and was discharged as a second lieutenant in November of that year, returning a month later to the *Tribune*. For a time, Gray was Sidney Smith's (q.v.) assistant on *The Gumps*. In 1924 Gray responded to Joseph Medill Patterson's request for a child strip featuring a girl by creating *Little Orphan Annie*. As Abel points out, Gray's specific innovation was the use of the strip to express a personal political philosophy in an aggressive way, without reference to his audience. The strip has stimulated tremendous political controversy. A comprehensive collection of Gray's drawings are preserved in the Mugar Library, Boston University. The strip, after Gray's death in 1968, was taken over by Philip Blaisdell.

REFERENCES: Harold Gray: *Little Orphan Annie* (New York, 1926); *My Folks, As Told by Little Orphan Annie*, in collaboration with H. W. F. Gray (Racine, Wis., 1940); *Little Orphan Annie and the Gila Monster Gang* (Racine, Wis., 1944); *Little Orphan Annie and the Gooneyville Mystery*, adapted by Helen Berke (Racine, Wis., 1947); *The Life and Hard Times of Little Orphan Annie, 1935–1945* (New Rochelle, N.Y., 1970); *Little Orphan Annie and Little Orphan Annie in Cosmic City* (New York, 1974); *Little Orphan Annie in the Great Depression* (New York, 1979); "Little Orphan Annie," *Nemo* 8 (August 1984): 49–66; "The Am That Was," *Nemo* 23 (December 1986): 5–32. R. L. Neuberger, "Hooverism in the Funnies," *New Republic* 79 (July 11, 1934): 234. "Fascism in the Funnies," *New Republic* 84 (September 18, 1935): 147. "Little Orphan Annie," *Nation* 141 (October 23, 1935), 454. Sheridan, pp. 69, 259. Marshall McLuhan, *The Mechanical Bride* (Boston, 1951), pp. 64–65. "Little Orphan Delinquent," *Time* 67 (March 19, 1956): 70. "Orphan in a Storm," *Newsweek* 47 (March 17, 1956): 80. S. P. Ryan, "Orphan Annie Must Go!" *America* 96 (December 8, 1956): 293–295; *Discussion* 96 (January 19, 1957): 437. "Little Orphan Annie," *New Republic* 136 (February 25, 1957): 6. Robert Abel, "One Shade of Gray: the Art of Personal Journalism," in *The Funnies: An American Idiom*, ed. by D. M. White and Robert Abel (London, 1963) pp. 114–27. "Tougher than Hell with a Heart of Gold," *Time* 84 (September 4, 1964): 71–72. "Censoring Orphan Annie," *Time* 85 (February 26, 1965): 52. "Odds and Ends," *World of Comic Art* 1 (Fall 1966): 50. *Who's Who* 34 (1966–67): 821. Obituary, *New York Times*, May 10, 1968, p. 47. Couperie and Horn, author index. R. B. Gehman, "But What Goes After the Third Line?" *Saturday Review* 52 (July 12, 1969): 4. Nye, pp. 221–222. Horn, p. 291. Kenneth Barker, "The Life and Loves . . . of Little Orphan Annie," *Nemo* 8 (August 1984): 8–31. Harry McCracken, "Annie's Real 'Daddy,' " *Nemo* 8 (August 1984): 40–47. Donald Phelps, " 'Who's That Little Chatterbox?' " *Nemo* 8 (August 1984): 33–38.

Roberta Gregory 1953–

Roberta Gregory, best known as the creator of the underground *Sheila and the Unicorn*, was born in Los Angeles on May 7, 1953, the daughter of Betty and Bob Gregory. Gregory's father was a cartoonist for Walt Disney; between 1960 and 1988, he drew *Donald Duck* and *Donald & Daisy*. Gregory received her B.A. from California State University at Long Beach. Between 1983 and 1988 she worked for Creative Age Publications. Her work has appeared in *Wimmen's Comix* (1974–76, 1986, 1988) and *Gay Comix* (1980–88). Separate publications exclusively by Gregory include: *Dynamite Damsels* (1976); *Winging It* (1988); and *Sheila and the Unicorn* (1988). States the artist, "Comics are a wonderfully rich means of self-expression, and with self-publishing, everyone can share their creations with the world. I try to do work that is very different and very personal, even if it looks like pure fantasy. My work doesn't get wide circulation, but I get some excellent feedback from individuals who relate very strongly to what I do. It's a lot of work, but I love it." Gregory lives in Seattle, Washington.

Bill Griffith 1944–

Born in Brooklyn on January 20, 1944, Bill Griffith, the son of Barbara and James Griffith, is best known as the creator of *Zippy the Pinhead*. In 1952 the Griffiths moved to Levittown, New York. After attending Pratt Institute, Griffith in 1967 began his career as a cartoonist, moving to San Francisco in 1970. Griffith's work has appeared in *Yellow Dog*, *Young Lust*, *Real Pulp*, *Arcade*, and *National Lampoon*. Originally conceived as an underground satire, *Zippy* is now distributed by King Features Syndicate to more than seventy-five newspapers. Compilations of Griffith's work can be found in *Yow* and *Zippy*, both publications of Last Gasp (Berkeley, Calif.). Griffith is now working on *Zippyvision* (*The Movie*), a production of Pacific Arts. Griffith lives in San Francisco. He is married to comic-strip artist Diane Noomin (q.v.), creator of *Didi Glitz*. Of his achievements, Griffith states, "In my own way, I try to bring a little confusion into people's lives. By being consistently inconsistent, 'Zippy' helps keep me sane. My major contribution to Western Civilization: the phrase, 'Are we having fun yet?' "

REFERENCES: Bill Griffith, *Pointed Behavior* (Berkeley, Calif., 1984); *Are We Having Fun Yet?* (New York, 1985); *Pindemonium* (Berkeley, Calif., 1986); *Kingpin* (New York, 1987); *Pinhead's Progress* (New York, 1989). "Raw Data," in Art Spiegelman and Françoise Mouly, *Read Yourself Raw: The Graphix Anthology for Damned Intellectuals* (New York, 1987). Richard Woodward, "Comics As Inspiration," *New York Times*, April 23, 1989. "Pinhead's Progress," *People* 31 (May 1, 1989). David Armstrong, "Bringing Up Zippy," *San Francisco Examiner*, July 2, 1989, p. E-4 David Elliott, "Lowdown on Comic Books Leaves Us High," *San Diego Union*, August 4, 1989.

Matt Groening 1954–

Matt Groening, creator of the weekly *Life in Hell*, grew up in Portland, Oregon, the third of five children of a cartoonist. In Portland, the Groenings lived next door to an abandoned zoo. As a child, recounted the cartoonist to *Washington Post* writer Richard Harrington, the young Groening created "The Creature Club." The motto of this grade-school association was "I'm Peculiar," its mandate, to draw monsters. "My friends and I tried to draw Batman, but it didn't work, and I realized the whole enterprise of cartooning was ridiculous so I started drawing little animals. . . ." The cast of Groening's childhood strip, *The Enchanted Forest*, included Rotten Rabbit. Later, Rotten Rabbit was to become Binky of *Life in Hell*. Groening attended Evergreen State College in Olympia, Washington, where, with fellow students Lynda Barry (q.v.) and Charles Burns (q.v.), he first published his strips in the *Copper Point Journal*, the college paper. Upon graduation, Groening migrated to Los Angeles, where he obtained employment as — in turn — a chauffeur, a dishwasher, and a distributor for the *Los Angeles Reader*, in which he first published his comics in 1980. "My strip started running when Reagan was running for president in 1980, so 'Life in Hell' was an appropriate title," Groening told the *Washington Post*. Influences on the strip include those of Dr. Seuss, *Mad* magazine, Walt Kelly (q.v.), Charles Schulz (q.v.), and R. Crumb (q.v.). Groening is married to Deborah Caplan, a former head of the *Los Angeles Reader*'s advertising department. Groening's animated situation comedy, *The Simpsons*, premiered in fall 1989.

REFERENCES: J. Foote "A Doodle God Makes Good," *Newsweek* 110 (September 28, 1987): 70. T. Hamilton, "Rabbit Punch," *Rolling Stone* (September 22, 1988): 81–82. Richard Harrington, "The Cartoon Hell of Matt Groening," *Washington Post*, December 18, 1988. Robert Lloyd, "Cartoon From Hell," *American Film* 15 (October 1989): 112.

Milt Gross 1895–1953

Father of *Nize Baby*, Milt Gross was born in New York in 1895. He attended high school in Kearney, New Jersey, and became copy boy on the *New York American*. From the *American*, he moved to the art department of the *New York World*, where he began his first strip, *Banana Oil*. Later, *Gross Exaggerations* was done as a filler for the Sunday page of the *World*, and featured Anglo-Yiddish dialect; the strip was later published in book form under the title *Nize Baby*. In 1935 Gross described another of his strips, *Count Screwloose of Toulouse* as "the direct result of the Mah Jong, Flag Pole Sitting, and Happy Days in Wall Street Era." Other features by Gross included *Looie* and *The Speckled Wonder*. Gross joined the staff of the *Daily Mirror* in October 1934, and produced an illustrated prose column "Grossly Exaggerated" in addition to *That's My Pop* and *Joe Runt*. Gross's strips were syndicated by King Features until

his retirement following a heart attack in 1945. Gross died on November 28, 1953, aboard the liner *Lurline* while returning from a vacation in Hawaii.

REFERENCES: Milt Gross, *Nize Baby* (New York, 1926); *Hiawatta* (New York, 1926); *De Night in de Front from Chreesmas* (New York, 1927); *Dunt Esk!* (New York, 1927); *He Done Her Wrong* (New York, 1930); "Comics and Their Creators," *Literary Digest*, 119 (February 16, 1935): 10; *What's This?* (New York, 1936); *I Shoulda Ate the Eclair* (Chicago, 1946); *Hiawatta and De Night in de Front from Chreesmas* (New York, 1950); *He Done Her Wrong* (New York, 1971); *Nize Baby* (New York, 1971); *Hearts of Gold* (New York, 1983). Margaret Linden, *Pasha the Persian*, illus. by Milt Gross (New York, 1936). Sheridan, pp. 87–88, 174. Obituary, *New York Times*, December 1, 1953, p. 2. Couperie and Horn, pp. 23, 38, 39. Horn, pp. 17, 20, 94, 181, 196, 294, 522.

Cathy Guisewite 1950–

Cathy Guisewite, who in 1976 originated Universal Press Syndicate's *Cathy*, is a native midwesterner. One of the first women to pen a nationally syndicated "working-girl" strip, Guisewite is a former Detroit advertising executive. Born on September 5, 1950, in Dayton, Ohio, she was educated at the University of Michigan, from which she received a B.A. in English in 1972. Her mother, Anne, and father, Bill, former stand-up comedian and retired advertising executive, are major characters in Guisewite's strip. The artist resides in Los Angeles.

REFERENCES: Cathy Guisewite, *The Cathy Chronicles* (Kansas City, Kans., 1978); "*What Do You Mean, I Still Don't Have Equal Rights?*" (Kansas City, Kans., 1980); "*I Think I'm Having a Relationship With a Blueberry Pie*" (Toronto, 1981); *Another Saturday Night of Wild and Reckless Abandon* (Kansas City, Kans., 1983); *Cathy's Valentine Day Survival Book* (Kansas City, Kans., 1983); *Climb Every Mountain, Bounce Every Check* (Kansas City, Kans., 1983); *Eat Your Way to a Better Relationship* (Kansas City, Kans., 1983); *How To Get Rich, Fall in Love, Lose Weight, and Solve All Your Problems by Saying "No"* (Kansas City, Kans., 1983); *A Mouthful of Breath Mints and No One To Kiss* (Kansas City, Kans., 1983); *Men Should Come with Instruction Booklets* (Kansas City, Kans., 1984); *Wake Me When I'm a Size Five* (Kansas City, Kans., 1985). Dan Sterling, "Cathy Guisewite," *USA Today*, October 30, 1986, p. D 4. David Hinkley, "Like Mother, Like Daughter: Life Imitates Comics for Real Cathy and Her Mom," *New York Daily News*, May 10, 1987, p. 4. Claudia Lapin, "Cathy on Cathy," *Savvy* (January 1988): 50–53.

V. T. Hamlin 1900–

Vincent T. Hamlin, creator of *Alley Oop*, was born in Perry, Iowa, in 1900. At the age of seventeen he enlisted in the army and was part of the American Expeditionary Force in France. In 1918 he returned to Perry, attended high school, and later studied journalism at the University of Missouri. From reporting jobs at the *Des Moines Register and Tribune* and *Des Moines News* Hamlin went on to the *Fort Worth Record*, where he was both artist and photographer. After a short term on the *Fort Worth Star-Telegram* Hamlin worked for various oil companies. While making layouts and maps in the Texas oil fields, Hamlin became interested in prehistoric life. He went back to working as a photographer, and also did a "girl" strip, but Hamlin's wife insisted that he combine his artistic and paleontological interests in a comic strip. *Alley Oop* first appeared in 1929, distributed by the NEA Syndicate. In 1938, a likely borrowing from Jules Verne, a "time machine" was added to the strip, enabling *Alley Oop* to travel into the modern and future worlds and providing Hamlin with greater narrative and pictorial possibilities. In 1960 *Alley Oop* inspired a popular song of the same name. Nye refers to the strip as an "anti-*Tarzan*."

REFERENCES: V. T. Hamlin, "Alley Oop and Me," *Collier's* 123 (March 19, 1949): 28. "Comics and Their Creators," *Literary Digest* 118 (July 28, 1934): 11. Sheridan, pp. 223–235. Couperie and Horn, pp. 69, 75. Nye, p. 228. Horn, pp. 76, 301.

Chris Harmon 1964–

Born on June 3, 1964, in Huntsville, Alabama, underground-comics creator Chris Harmon is the son of David and Pat Harmon. Harmon was raised in Atlanta, Georgia. In 1988 he received his B.F.A. in graphic design from the University of Georgia in Athens, where he was staff artist for the student newspaper, *The Red and Black*, for which he created two daily strips: *The Big Stall* (1987–88) and *Chester* (1983–86). Harmon's Rip Off Press comics include *A Visit From Uncle Walt* (1989), *Billy the Barbarian* (1989), and *Danger Vacation* (1989). States Harmon, "Being a cartoonist is the most surefire way to avoid becoming a responsible adult." Harmon lives in Alamo, California.

Johnny Hart 1931–

Cartoonist John Hart, creator of *B.C.* and *The Wizard of Id*, was born on February 18, 1931, in Endicott, New York, the son of Grace Ann and Irwin James Hart. In 1949 he graduated from Union-Endicott High School. Later, he met cartoonist Brant Parker (q.v.), with whom he would eventually collaborate. He joined the air force, and while in Korea produced cartoons that appeared in the *Pacific Stars and Stripes*. In 1953 Hart was discharged, and he and his wife, Bobby, whom he had married in 1952, moved to his mother-in-law's farm in Georgia. Hart circulated his cartoons, and eventually they began to appear in the *Saturday Evening Post*, *Collier's*, and *Bluebook*. Hart and his wife moved to New York, where he worked for two years in the art department of General Electric. Inspired by Charles Schulz's (q.v.) *Peanuts*, Hart originated *B.C.*, which was rejected by five major syndicates before it was accepted for publication by the New York Herald Tribune Syndicate in 1958. It is now distributed by Creators Syndicate to over eleven hundred newspapers. In 1960 Hart conceived the idea for *The Wizard of Id*, and during a visit with Brant Parker in 1963 Hart asked Parker to illustrate the strip. On November 9, 1964, *The Wizard of Id* was published. First syndicated by Publishers-Hall, it is now distributed by North America Syndicate to more than eleven hundred newspapers.

REFERENCES: Johnny Hart, *Hey! B.C.* (New York, 1959); *Back to B.C.* (New York, 1961); *B.C. Strikes Back* (New York, 1962); *The Sunday Best of B.C.* (New York, 1964); *B.C. Rides Again* (Kansas City, Kans., 1988). Publishers-Hall Syndicate, *Profile: Johnny Hart* (New York, 1968). Horn, p. 305.

James Hatlo 1893–1963

Best known as the creator of *Little Iodine* and *They'll Do It Every Time*, James Hatlo was born in Providence, Rhode Island, but raised in Los Angeles. Among the papers with which the artist was associated are the *Los Angeles Times*, the *San Francisco Bulletin*, the *San Francisco Call*, the merged *San Francisco Call-Bulletin*, and the *Los Angeles Herald Express*. For Hearst Hatlo created *They'll Do It Every Time*, a strip occasioned, according to Sheridan, by the void created by Tad Dorgan's (q.v.) death in 1929. King Features Syndicate began syndication of *They'll Do It Every Time* in 1936. Hatlo's second major feature, the irascible *Little Iodine*, was created in 1943. Hatlo died on December 1, 1963. After his death, *They'll Do It Every Time* was written by Bob Dunn (q.v.) and drawn by Al Scaduto (q.v.). Upon Dunn's death in 1989, Scaduto took over the cartoon in its entirety. *Little Iodine*, similarly, was written by Dunn and drawn by Scaduto from 1966 to 1967, and from 1967 until its demise in 1983 written by Dunn and drawn by Hy Eisman (q.v.).

REFERENCES: Sheridan, pp. 275–276. Horn, p. 307.

A. E. Hayward 1885–1939

Born in Camden, New Jersey, the son of an English painter, Alfred E. Hayward, the creator of the *Philadelphia Ledger*'s *Somebody's Stenog*, began his career as a cartoonist in 1906. Features originated by Hayward include *Great Caesar's Ghost* (1913–14) and *Kernel Corn* (1917–18), which were produced for the *New York Herald*. For the *Ledger* he created *The Padded Cell*

(1916) and *Somebody's Stenog* (December 1918), which became a Sunday feature on April 30, 1922. Hayward was a faculty member at the Pennsylvania Academy of the Fine Arts. In 1924 he originated Art Week in Philadelphia, one of the first programs involving the community with the fine arts. Hayward died on July 25, 1939, in his New York apartment. After Hayward's death, the daily *Somebody's Stenog* was continued by Sam Nichols until 1941.

REFERENCES: *AAA* 28 (1931): 569. Obituary, *New York Times*, July 27, 1939, p. 19. Mallett, p. 86. Fielding, p. 163.

John Held, Jr. 1889–1958

John Held, Jr., the artist who visually defined the Jazz Age, was born in Salt Lake City on January 10, 1889. In 1904 he sold his first cartoon to *Life* magazine and the following year became sports cartoonist for the *Salt Lake City Tribune*. His only art training was with the sculptor Mahonri Young. In 1910 the young Held moved to New York, where he worked for the Collier's agency. During 1915 and 1916 he contributed drawings, signed "Myrtle Held," to *Vanity Fair*. In 1918 he began drawing the women who were to evolve into the flappers of the twenties. It was in *The New Yorker* during the twenties that, according to Stephen Becker, Held "elegantly butchered . . . the sacred cows of Traditional Emotion and Lachrymose History" and helped to create the era later referred to as that of "the lost generation." A series of cartoons, including *Merely Margy* (1927–30) (splash pages, 1931–36), was done by Held for King Features Syndicate. By 1939 Held had become interested in sculpture, and that year an exhibition of his bronze horses was held at the Bland Gallery, New York. During 1940 Held became artist-in-residence, in turn, at Harvard University and the University of Georgia. Interest in the artist was revived in the fifties. Held died on March 2, 1958.

REFERENCES: John Held, Jr., *Frankie and Johnny* (New York, 1930); *Outlines of Sport* (New York, 1930); *Dog Stories* (New York, 1930); *Grim Youth* (New York, 1930); *Women Are Necessary* (New York, 1931); *The Works of John Held, Jr.* (New York, 1931); *The Flesh Is Weak* (New York, 1931); *A Bowl of Cherries* (New York, 1932); *Crosstown* (New York, 1933); *I'm the Happiest Girl in the World* (New York, 1935); *The Gods Were Promiscuous* (New York, 1937); *Danny Decoy* (New York, 1942); *John Held, Jr.: Prints* (Hastings-on-Hudson, N.Y., 1964). Stephen Becker, *Comic Art in America* (New York, 1959), p. 125. The Smithsonian Institution, *The Art of John Held, Jr.* (Washington, D.C., n.d.). Horn, p. 312.

George Herriman 1880–1944

On August 22, 1880, George Joseph Herriman was born in New Orleans, Louisiana, the son of George Herriman, Jr., and Clara Morel Herriman. Sometime about 1886, the family — now consisting of George and his younger siblings, Henry, Ruby, and Pearl — moved to Los Angeles. From 1891 to 1897 George attended St. Vincent's College, a Catholic secondary school. In 1897 Herriman obtained his first newspaper job — that of assistant in the *Los Angeles Herald*'s engraving department. In 1900 the artist moved to New York, where, for a time, he painted billboards for a Coney Island sideshow. In 1901 his first New York cartoons appeared in *Judge* (June 15–October 26, 1901), Pulitzer's papers (September 29), the Philadelphia North American Syndicate (September 29–April 27, 1902), and the McClure Syndicate (October 20). On February 16, 23, and March 9, *Musical Mose*, a comic-strip satire of a good-hearted African American who attempts to assume various ethnic identities, appeared in the Pulitzer papers, as did *Professor Otto and His Auto* (March 20–December 28, 1902) and *Acrobatic Archie* (April 13, 1902–January 25, 1903). On July 7, 1902, Herriman married Mabel Lillian Bridge. From January 11 to November 15, 1903, *Two Jollie Jackies* was published, again in the Pulitzer papers. In June 1903 Herriman joined the staff of the *New York World*. From January 2 to July 10, 1904, he created *Major Ozone's Fresh Air Crusade* for the World Color Printing Company. On January 3, 1904, he switched employers, this time becoming a member of the *New York Daily News* team. On February 22, 23, 26, and March 4 he published *Home Sweet Home*. Herriman began his lifelong association with his patron, William Randolph Hearst, on April 22, 1904, becoming a staff artist for the *New York American*. On June 2, 1905, Herriman returned to California, where he revived *Major Ozone* (September 10–October 20, 1906) and published *Bud Smith* (October 29–November 19, 1905) and *Grandma's Girl — Likewise Bud Smith* (November 26–May 12, 1906). On January 8, 1906, he joined the staff of the *Los Angeles Times*, which he left on August 21 for the *Los Angeles Examiner*. Strips from 1906 include *Rosy Posy — Mama's Girl* (May 19–September 15); 1907, the *Examiner*'s *Mr. Proones the Plunger* (December 10–26). Among Herriman's 1909 strips are *Baron Mooch* (October 12–December 19), *Alexander the Cat* (November 7–January 9, 1910), *Daniel and Pansy* (November 21, 28, and December 4), *Mary's Home from College* (December 20), and *Gooseberry Sprigg* (December 23–January 24, 1910). In 1910 — a critical year in his development — Herriman returned to New York as an employee of the *Evening Journal*. There on June 20 appeared the seminal cartoon, *The Dingbat Family*, from which Krazy Kat was to derive. Originally a substrip in *The Dingbat Family* (renamed *The Family Upstairs* on August 1, 1910), *Krazy Kat* became a strip in its own right on October 28, 1913. On April 23, 1916, the first *Krazy Kat* Sunday page was published. From January 5, 1916, to January 22, 1919, Herriman published his second major strip, *Baron Bean*. Other strips include *Stumble Inn* (October 30, 1922–May 12, 1923), *Us Husbands* (January 16–December 18, 1926), and *Embarrassing Moments* (April 28, 1928–December 3, 1932). Herriman died on April 25, 1944. *Krazy* appeared for the last time on June 25, 1944. In 1972 the University of Arizona Art Gallery mounted a Herriman retrospective, as did the Graham Gallery in 1983. In 1986 Harry Abrams published the first comprehensive study of Herriman — Patrick McDonnell, Karen O'Connell, and Georgia Riley de Havenon's *Krazy Kat: The Comic Art of George Herriman*. Publication of such seminal studies as that of Dr. Thomas Inge, Blackwell Professor of Humanities at Randolph-Macon College, in Ashland, Virginia, is eagerly awaited.

REFERENCES: George Herriman, *Krazy Kat*, introd. by e. e. cummings (New York, 1946); *Krazy Kat* (New York, 1969); *Krazy Kat* (New York, 1975); *Baron Bean*, introd. by Thomas Inge (Westport, Conn., 1977); *The Family Upstairs*, introd. by Bill Blackbeard (Westport, Conn., 1977); Patrick McDonnell, Karen O'Connell, Georgia Riley de Havenon, *Krazy Kat: The Comic Art of George Herriman* (New York, 1986). Gilbert Seldes, *The Seven Lively Arts* (New York, 1924), pp. 231–248. Arthur Asa Berger, *The Comic Stripped American* (New York, 1973). Portrait, *Collier's* 79 (February 12, 1927): 13. Sheridan, pp. 64–65, 293. Obituary, *New York Times*, April 27, 1944, p. 23. W. E. Berchtold, "Men of Comics," *New Outlook* 165 (May 1935): 45. "Comics and Their Creators," *Literary Digest* 119 (April 20, 1935): 25. Bill Blackbeard, "The Forgotten Years of George Herriman," *Nemo* 1 (June 1983): 50–60. Couperie and Horn, author index. Nye, pp. 218, 219, 223, 233–235. Horn, p. 314.

Harry Hershfield 1885–1974

The first comic-strip artist to do a specifically Jewish cartoon, Harry Hershfield was born in Cedar Rapids, Iowa, on October 13, 1885, the son of Russian immigrants. He attended public schools in Chicago and spent a few months at the Chicago School of Illustration. He later joined the art staff of the *Chicago Daily News*, where he did a dog strip, *Homeless Hector*. In 1907 Hershfield was fired, supposedly for mistakenly straightening an accurate photograph of the Leaning Tower of Pisa. He went to San Francisco, where he drew sports cartoons for the *San Francisco Chronicle*. There Hershfield came to the attention of Arthur Brisbane, who recruited him to work on the *New York Journal*. In 1909 Hershfield published a second dog strip, *Rubber*, for Hearst's *Chicago Examiner*. In 1910 Hershfield began the melodramatic *Desperate Desmond*, which featured a then-popular cannibal chief, this one named Gomgatz, who spoke Yiddish. Eventually retitled *Dauntless Durham of the U.S.A.*, the strip ceased publication in 1914. In 1914 Hershfield created *Abie the Agent*, the hero of which was a likable Jewish businessman. The strip was distributed by King Features Syndicate until Hershfield's departure in 1931. Taking a vacation from *Abie*, Hershfield did a series of radio broadcasts including *Meyer the Buyer* and *One Man's Opinions*. *Abie* returned in 1935, and ran intermittently until 1940. In 1938 Hershfield took charge of Metro-Goldwyn-Mayer's animation department, from which he later resigned. During the forties, Hershfield was a regular on the radio show *Can You Top This?* Hershfield died in New York City in 1974.

REFERENCES: Harry Hershfield: *Super-City* (New York, 1930); *Jewish Jokes* (New York, 1932); *Now I'll Tell One* (New York, 1938); *The Sin of Harold Diddlebock* (New York, 1947); *Abie the Agent*, introd. by Peter Marzio (Westport, Conn., 1977); *Dauntless Durham of the U.S.A.*, introd. by Bill Blackbeard (Westport, Conn., 1977). Camillo Berg, *The Perpetual Comedy*, illus. by Harry Hershfield (Boston, 1943). Edward Ford, *Can You Top This?* illus. by Harry Hershfield (New York, 1946); *Cream of the Crop*, illus. by Harry Hershfield (New York, 1947). J. L. Hochman, *The Sergeant Speaks to a Harvard Man*, illus. by Harry Hershfield (New York, 1948). *AAA* 28 (1931): 573. Sheridan, pp. 31–35, 274. Wife's obituary, *New York Times*, June 13, 1960, p. 27. Couperie and Horn, p. 29. Nye, pp. 218, 220. Horn, p. 315. Obituary, *New York Times*, December 16, 1974.

Walt Hoban 1890–1939

Walter C. Hoban was born in Philadelphia in 1890. His father was Peter J. Hoban, founder of the *Catholic Standard and Times*. Hoban studied at St. Joseph's College and at the School of Industrial Art. His first job was that of office boy at the *Philadelphia North American*, for which he created *Jerry MacJunk* (1910–14) and *Waffles the Crook* (1913–14). In 1912 Hoban joined the staff of the *New York Journal*, where in 1914 he created *Jerry on the Job*, a master strip syndicated by King Features. During World War I Hoban continued cartooning while serving as a second lieutenant of artillery. In 1924 he married Marie Lamson, another *Journal* employee. In 1932 he created *Noodlehead Noonan* for the *Daily Mirror*. He died in New York's Post Graduate Hospital on November 22, 1939.

REFERENCES: Obituary, *New York Times*, November 24, 1939, p. 23. Horn, pp. 319–320.

Dick Hodgins, Jr. 1931–

Dick Hodgins, Jr., who continues for King Features Syndicate Carl Anderson's (q.v.) 1932 *Henry*, was born in Binghamton, New York. After stints in television and at the Associated Press, Hodgins in 1969 became the artist for *Half-Hitch*, a strip created by Hank Ketcham (q.v.). Among Hodgins's numerous awards are two Best Editorial Cartoon accolades bestowed by the National Cartoonists Society. In addition to *Henry*, Hodgins has created artwork for the European editions of Dik Browne's (q.v.) *Hagar the Horrible*. Hodgins and his sons, Richard and Jonathan, live in Wilton, Connecticut.

REFERENCE: King Features Syndicate, *Dick Hodgins, Jr.* (New York, 1989).

Bill Hoest 1926–1988

Bill Hoest, best known as the creator of King Features Syndicate's *The Lockhorns*, *Agatha Crumm*, and *What A Guy!*, was born on February 7, 1926, in Newark, New Jersey. After graduating from Montclair High School, Hoest joined the U.S. Navy. Upon his discharge, he studied at the Cooper Union. After three years with Norcross Greeting Card Company, Hoest became a freelance cartoonist in 1951. On September 9, 1968, he created *The Lockhorns*, which in 1976 and 1980 received the National Cartoonists Society's award for Best Syndicated Panel. In 1974 he created the panel *Bumper Snickers* for *The Enquirer*. On August 24, 1977, King Features began distribution of Hoest's strip *Agatha Crumm*. In 1979 Hoest became cartoon editor of *Parade*, for which he created *Laugh Parade* (1980) and *Howard Huge* (1981). His last strip, *What A Guy!*, began syndication in 1986. Hoest died of complications from lymphoma on November 7, 1988, in Lloyd Neck, Long Island. His work is continued by his wife and co-creator, Bunny Hoest (q.v.).

REFERENCE: King Features Syndicate, *Bill Hoest, Award-Winning Cartoonist, Is Dead at Sixty-two* (New York, 1988).

Bunny Hoest 1932–

Following the death of her husband, Bill Hoest (q.v.), in 1988 Bunny Hoest succeeded him as head of William Hoest Enterprises. Enlisting the services of John Reiner (q.v.), Hoest's assistant, Bunny continues to produce the strips created by her husband. These include *The Lockhorns*, *Agatha Crumm*, and *What a Guy!* for King Features; *Laugh Parade* and *Howard Huge* for *Parade*; and *Bumper Snickers* for *The Enquirer*. Bunny Hoest was born Madeline Mezz in New York City on November 12, 1932, the daughter of a surgeon and an opera singer. She received her B.A. from Adelphi College in English literature, and her M.A. from C. W. Post College in 1962. From 1963 to 1973 she taught English in secondary schools, while continuing to pursue a lifelong interest in theater. In 1973 she married Bill Hoest. Hoest is the mother of three children, the stepmother of two, and the grandmother of five. She lives in Lloyd Neck, Long Island.

REFERENCE: King Features Syndicate, *Bunny Hoest* (New York, 1989).

Burne Hogarth 1911–

Artist Burne Hogarth was born on December 25, 1911, in Chicago. Before attending the Art Institute of Chicago, Hogarth studied art history at Crane College, Northwestern University, and Columbia University. In 1929 he began his first strip for the Barnet Brown Company, *Ivy Hemmanhaw*. For Leeds Features Syndicate he did *Odd Jobs and Weird Accidents*. Hogarth taught art history on the WPA in 1933, and the following year worked as an artist's assistant at King Features. In 1935 he was hired by the McNaught Syndicate to do a pirate strip, *Pieces of Eight*. When Hal Foster (q.v.) gave up *Tarzan* to do *Prince Valiant* in 1937, Hogarth took over the strip, which he continued until 1950, when he left United Feature Syndicate. In 1945 Hogarth did an original strip for the Robert Hall Syndicate entitled *Drago*. The strip's plot centered on the activities of an unreformed ex-Nazi, Baron Zodiac, whose antagonists are Drago and his comic sidekick, Tabasco. The strip was discontinued in 1947. That same year Hogarth began for United Feature Syndicate his only humorous strip, *Miracle Jones*, the main character of which, as Maurice Horn points out, is of the Walter Mitty variety. This strip ended in November 1948. Departing from the comics in 1950, Hogarth together with Silas Rhodes founded the School of Visual Arts in New York. Today, this living legend teaches analytical figure drawing at the Art Center College of Design in Pasadena, California.

REFERENCES: Burne Hogarth, "About Those Comics," *Design* 51 (January 1950): 23; *Dynamic Anatomy* (New York, 1958); *Drawing the Human Head* (New York, 1965); "Jack Potter," *American Artist* 31 (December 1968): 38–43; "Outline of American Painting," *American Artist* 25, 26 (September 1961–June 1962); *Tarzan: Seigneur de la Jungle*, introd. and biography by Maurice Horn (Paris, 1967); *Dynamic Figure Drawing* (New York, 1970); *Tarzan of the Apes* (New York, 1972); *Tarzan of the Apes* (New York, 1973); *Jungle Tales of Tarzan* (New York, 1976); *Golden Age of Tarzan* (New York, 1979); *Dynamic Light and Shade* (New York, 1981); *Life of King Arthur* (Carmel, Calif., 1984). Couperie and Horn, author index. Horn. pp. 22, 27, 222, 320, 650–651, 664. Thomas Pendleton, "Tarzan of the Papers," *Journal of Popular Culture* 12 (Spring 1979): 691–701.

Bill Holbrook 1958–

Bill Holbrook, creator of King Features Syndicate's *On the Fastrack*, was born in Los Angeles on October 17, 1958, the son of engineer William W. Holbrook and Joyce Holbrook. In 1963 his family moved to Huntsville, Alabama. Holbrook attended Auburn University, from which he graduated in 1980, having been art director of the *Auburn Plainsman*. In June of 1981, Holbrook joined the staff of the *Atlanta Journal and Constitution* as an editorial cartoonist. His first comic strip, created in 1982, was *Winston Lewsome*, a wistful tale of a displaced college graduate working in a sandwich shop. His second strip, *On the Fastrack*, was an immediate success, syndicated by King Features on March 19, 1984. His most recent strip, *Safe Havens*, began publication on October 3, 1988. The artist and his wife, writer Teri Jill Peitso-Holbrook, live in Tucker, Georgia. States Holbrook, "I attempt to create an alternate universe in which the follies and foibles of mankind are rendered ridiculous through exaggeration. . . . It pays the bills."

REFERENCES: Bo Emerson, "Illustrator and His Characters Ride Fastrack," *Atlanta Constitution*, March 19, 1984. *Cartoonist PROfiles* 61 (March 1984). David Astor, "A Fast Start for 'On the Fastrack,' " *Editor and Publisher* 25 (August 1984): 30. *Cartoonist PROfiles* 82 (June 1989).

Nicole Hollander 1940–

Chicago artist Nicole Hollander in 1978 created *Sylvia*, described by the *Village Voice* as "the toughest woman in America." Seated by the *Voice* "three bar stools to the left of Garry Trudeau [q.v.] and Jules Feiffer [q.v.]," Hollander's heroine is a middle-aged, middle-class, cynical single parent, the bane of her faddish daughter, Rita; the companion of Gerniff, an alien from Venus; a regular at Harry's Bar; the confidante of Grunella the Fortune Teller; and critic of Ramon the Playboy. The Devil is also a strip regular. Performing the role of detached observer, he caustically comments on the contemporary American scene, dishing up a trivialized hell in which to annoy yuppies. Hollander, a graduate of Chicago public schools, after receiving an M.F.A., began her professional life as a Cook County social worker. Later occupations included those of art teacher, graphic designer, and book illustrator. In 1976 she did the artwork for *The Spokeswoman*, a feminist periodical. Created in 1978, *Sylvia* was distributed by United Press Syndicate in 1979 and by Field Enterprises in 1981. In 1983 Hollander was the recipient of the Warner Communications Wonder Woman Award for her controversial creations.

REFERENCES: Nicole Hollander, *I'm in Training to Be Tall and Blonde* (New York, 1979); *Ma, Can I Be a Feminist and Still Like Men?* (New York, 1980); *That Woman Must Be on Drugs* (New York, 1981); *Mercy, It's the Revolution and I'm in My Bathrobe* (New York, 1982); *My Weight Is Always Perfect for My Height, Which Varies* (New York, 1982); *Hi, This Is Sylvia* (New York, 1983); *Drawn Together* (New York, 1983); *Sylvia on Sundays* (New York, 1983); *Okay, Thinner Thighs for Everyone* (New York, 1984); *Never Tell Your Mother This Dream* (New York, 1985); *The Whole Enchilada* (New York, 1986); *Never Take Your Cat to a Salad Bar* (New York, 1987); *You Can't Take It With You So Eat It Now* (New York, 1989). *Washingtonian Magazine* (November 1983): 248. Judy Klemesrud, " 'Wonder Women' Cited for Gifts to American Life," *New York Times*, November 15, 1983. Jan Hoffman, "The Toughest Woman in America," *Village Voice* 27 (December 27, 1983): 55–56. Kim Upton, "The Wit Behind the Wisdom of 'Sylvia,' " *Chicago Sun-Times*, January 1, 1984.

Bill Holman 1903–1987

Creator of *Smokey Stover* Bill Holman was born in Crawfordsville, Indiana. He studied at the Chicago Academy of Fine Arts, and later became an office boy in the art department of the *Chicago Tribune*. Holman later traveled to New York, where in 1923 he did a child strip, *G. Whizz, Junior*, for the *New York Herald Tribune*. By 1932 Holman's cartoons were appearing in *Collier's*, *Life*, *Judge*, and the *Saturday Evening Post*. Holman was recruited by the Chicago Tribune–New York News Syndicate to do a Sunday gag comic, *Smokey Stover*, which first appeared on March 10, 1935.

REFERENCES: Chicago Tribune-New York News Syndicate, *Bill Holman* (New York, n.d.). Leslie Moneypenny, "Smokey Stover," *Chicago Tribune*, January 28, 1952. Sheridan, pp. 225, 268, 289. Mallett, p. 199. Couperie and Horn, p. 75. Nye, p. 224. Horn, pp. 246, 322, 627, 632.

Greg Howard 1944–

Attorney and artist Greg Howard was born on April 16, 1944, in St. Paul, Minnesota, the son of Robert B. Howard and Lorraine L. Howard. He attended the University of Minnesota, from which he received a degree in psychology in 1966 and a law degree in 1969. Upon graduation Howard became an associate with Faegre and Benson in Minnesota, becoming a partner in 1976. In October 1978 Howard launched his comic-strip career. His *Sally Forth* began syndication under the aegis of North America Syndicate on January 4, 1982. Howard and his wife reside in Minneapolis.

REFERENCES: *Editor and Publisher* 22 (December 19, 1981). *St. Petersburg Times*, January 4, 1982. *Finance and Commerce*, January 8, 1982. *Minneapolis Star*, January 8, 1982. *National Law Journal* (January 18, 1982). *Minneapolis Tribune*, January 24, 1982. *Twin Cities Magazine*, February 1982. *San Diego Tribune*, February 8, 1982. *St. Petersburg Evening Independent*, April 24, 1982. *St. Louis Post Dispatch*, April 26, 1982. *Baton Rouge* (La.) *State-Times*, July 19, 1982. *New York Times*, February 28, 1983. *Meriden* (Conn.) *Record-Journal*, March 19, 1983; January 6, 1984. *Minneapolis/St. Paul Magazine*, March 1985. *Minnesota Women's Press*, April 1, 1986. *Austin* (Minn.) *American Statesman*, April 12, 1987. *Editor and Publisher* 28 (April 25, 1987). *Ford Times*, May 1987. *National Law Journal*, August 10, 1987. *Capital Times* (Madison, Wis.), February 6, 1988. *Minnesota Magazine*, March 1988. *Vancouver Sun*, April 9, 1988. *Alameda* (Calif.) *Times-Star*, August 15, 1988. *New York Times*, September 1, 1988. *Miami Herald*, December 1, 1988. King Features Syndicate, *Greg Howard* (New York, 1988).

Jack Jackson   1941–

Best known for *Comanche Man*, underground-comics creator Jack Jackson ("Jaxon") was born on May 15, 1941, in Pandora, Texas, the son of Ellie Jay and Cynthia Jackson. In 1961 Jackson received a B.A. in accounting from Texas A&I; in 1963 an M.A. in psychology from the University of Texas; and in 1966 a Ph.D. in physics from Waco Tech. Between 1962 and 1964 Jackson was employed as a comptroller. His underground comics, which appeared as early as 1964, include *God Nose, Happy Endings, Slow Death, The Leather Nun*, and *Death Rattle*. *The Secret of San Saba* (Kitchen Sink, 1989) compiles Jackson's serialized "horror-fantasy novel," which first appeared in *Death Rattle*, nos. 3–6 and 12–18, to tell the tale of an alien god who empowers a tribe of Texas Apaches. Jackson has also authored and illustrated numerous historical works, including *Long Shadows: Indian Leaders Standing in the Path of Manifest Destiny, 1600–1900* (Paramount Publishing Co., 1989). States Jackson, "I like comics that grab you and bite you on the ass." Jackson lives in Austin, Texas.

Ferd Johnson   1905–

After the death in 1957 of Frank Willard (q.v.), the creator of *Moon Mullins*, the strip was taken over by Willard's longtime assistant, Ferd Johnson. Johnson was born in Erie, Pennsylvania, and educated at the Chicago Academy of Fine Arts. A frequent visitor to the art department of the *Chicago Tribune*, Johnson soon became acquainted with Harold Gray (q.v.), Sidney Smith (q.v.), Frank King (q.v.), and Willard, whose assistant he became in 1923. In 1925 Joseph Medill Patterson had an idea for a western strip, *Texas Slim*, which Johnson did from 1925 to 1928. At the same time he drew the Sunday strip *Lovey Dovey*. In his article "Moon Mullins Today," Raymond Fisher points out that Johnson modernized the strip, "simplifying the pen technique from the rough lines, cross-hatching, and loose style to his own crisp, clearly defined, firm pen outline with just a minimum of shading." Johnson was later assisted in drawing the strip by his son.

REFERENCES: Ferd Johnson, "Waifs of the Sunday Page," *World of Comic Art* 1 (Fall 1966): 47–49. Clive Howard, "Moon Mullins: Magnificent Roughneck," *Saturday Evening Post* 220 (August 9, 1947): 20–21. Raymond Fisher, "Moon Mullins Today," *World of Comic Art* 1 (June 1966): 6–9. Horn, pp. 345–346, 504, 655, 700. *Who's Who* 44 (1986): 1425.

Frank B. Johnson   1931–

Born in Miami, Florida, on April 13, 1931, Frank B. Johnson is the son of Gene and Marjorie Johnson. Strips undertaken by Johnson include *Amy* (inking), *Beany* (writing and art), *Beetle Bailey* (inking), *Hubert* (inking), *Moose* (inking), *Mutt and Jeff* (Sunday page, art), *Boner's Ark* (writing and art), *Bringing Up Father* (writing and art), and *Hi and Lois* (inking). He began working on Mort Walker's (q.v.) creation *Boner's Ark* in 1969; *Bringing Up Father* in 1980. Johnson and his wife, Millie, live in Fairfield, Connecticut. Johnson is the recipient of two National Cartoonists Society awards.

REFERENCE: King Features Syndicate, *Frank Johnson* (New York, n.d.).

Lynn Franks Johnston   1947–

Lynn Johnston, creator of Universal Press Syndicate's *For Better or for Worse* (1975), was born in Collingwood, Ontario, and raised in North Vancouver. Educated in art at the Vancouver Art Gallery and the Vancouver School of Art, she first worked as a medical illustrator for the McMaster Medical School in Ontario. An early marriage was to CBC cameraman Doug Franks; the couple had one son, Aaron. Her second marriage was to dentist Rod Johnston; the couple has one daughter, Katie. The first woman to receive the coveted Reuben, awarded by the National Cartoonists Society, Johnston lives near Corbeil, Ontario.

REFERENCES: Lynn Johnston, *Hi Mom, Hi Dad* (Toronto, 1977); *I've Got the One More Washload Blues* (Kansas City, Kans., 1981); *Is This "One of Those Days," Daddy?* (Kansas City, Kans., 1982); *More Than a Month of Sundays* (Kansas City, Kans., 1983); *David, We're Pregnant* (Deephaven, Minn., 1983); *Do They Ever Grow Up?* (Deephaven, Minn., 1983); *It Must Be Nice to Be Little* (Kansas City, Kans., 1983); *Just One More Hug* (Kansas City, Kans., 1984); *Our Sunday Best* (Kansas City, Kans., 1984); *The Last Straw* (Kansas City, Kans., 1985); *Keep the Home Fries Burning* (Kansas City, Kans., 1986); *It's All Downhill From Here* (Kansas City, Kans., 1987); *Pushing Forty* (Kansas City, Kans., 1988). N. Geeslin, "For Better or for Worse," *People* 26 (September 15, 1986): 121 Owen Findsen, "Are the Funnies Funny?," *Cincinnati Enquirer*, October 12, 1986, I1, 4. Susan Baxter, "Drawing on the Past," *Easy Living* 8 (November 3–December 1, 1986): 29. "B-T Comics Survey," *Blade-Tribune*, April 3, 1988, p. B3.

Ralston (Bud) Jones   1927–

Ralston Jones, with Frank Ridgeway (q.v.) co-creator of King Features Syndicate's *Mr. Abernathy*, was born in Salem, Ohio. He attended school in Euclid, Ohio, and went to Kenyon College. After a stint as a salesman for a Cleveland art studio, Jones moved to New York City. There, with Ridgeway, he created *Mr. Abernathy*, which was introduced by King Features Syndicate on October 14, 1959. Ridgeway is the strip's author, Jones its artist. Jones also assists cartoonist Mort Walker (q.v.) on *Boner's Ark*.

REFERENCES: King Features Syndicate, *Frank Ridgeway* (New York, n.d.). Horn, p. 496.

Bob Kane   1916–

Born in New York City on October 24, 1916, Kane attended Cooper Union and the Art Students League of New York. In 1939 he created *Batman* for National Comics. The strip made its first appearance in *Detective* 27 (May 1939). Kane lives in Los Angeles, California.

REFERENCES: *Who's Who in American Art* (1973, 1976, 1978); Horn, pp. 101, 249, 419, 586.

Bill Kavanaugh   1905–1981

Kavanaugh wrote *Bringing Up Father* from 1960, his scripts accompanying Frank Fletcher's (q.v.) drawings.

Bil Keane   1922–

Artist Bil Keane, creator of *The Family Circus*, was born in Philadelphia on October 5, 1922, the son of Aloysius W. Keane, an ironworks manufacturer, and Florence R. Bunn Keane. He graduated in 1940 from Northeast Catholic High School in Philadelphia. Keane soon obtained employment as a messenger at the *Philadelphia Bulletin*. From 1942 to 1945 Keane served in the U.S. Army, drawing for *Yank* and *Pacific Stars and Stripes*. After his discharge, Keane returned to the *Philadelphia Bulletin*, doing cartoons for the news art department and caricatures for the entertainment section. For the *Bulletin* he created the Sunday comic *Silly Philly*.

On October 23, 1948, Keane married Thelma Carne, an Australian whom he met during the war; their domestic life was to inspire *The Family Circus*, first syndicated on February 29, 1960, by the *Des Moines Register and Tribune*, and later by Cowles Syndicate. In 1954 he created the cartoon *Channel Chuckles*. Its success enabled him to move to Paradise Valley, Arizona, in 1959. Fawcett has published over fifty compilations of Keane's comics, which appear in over thirteen hundred newspapers. In 1983 Keane was named Cartoonist of the Year by the National Cartoonists Society.

REFERENCE: King Features Syndicate et al., *The Family Circus* (New York, 1989).

Walt Kelly 1913–1973

Walt Kelly, originator of *Pogo*, was born in Philadelphia on August 25, 1913, the son of William Crawford and Genevieve MacAnnulla Kelly. He attended public schools in Bridgeport, Connecticut, and from 1928 to 1935 worked on the *Bridgeport Post*. Kelly was an animator in Disney's studios from 1935 to 1941. From 1941 to 1948 he was a commercial artist in New York City. In 1948 Kelly became art director for the *New York Star*, where he satirized presidential candidate Thomas E. Dewey as a mechanical man. *Pogo* appeared as a comic strip in May 1949, syndicated by Publishers-Hall. During the McCarthy purge in the fifties Kelly caricatured the senator in *Pogo*, and in 1954 presented to the Library of Congress the original drawings for a *Pogo* "Alice in Wonderland" in which the senator enacted the role of the Red Queen ("Off with their heads!"). In June 1954 *Newsweek* quoted Kelly as saying, "Good cartoonists are subversive. They are against things." One of the *Pogo* innovations was the use of the balloon to express character: each character speaks in an appropriate script. Kelly's work is collected at the Ohio State University Library for Communication and Graphic Arts, Columbus, Ohio.

REFERENCES: Walt Kelly, *Pogo* (New York, 1951); *I Go Pogo* (New York, 1952); *Uncle Pogo's So So Stories* (New York, 1953); *The Pogo Stepmother Goose* (New York, 1954); *The Incompleat Pogo* (New York, 1954); *The Pogo Peek-a-Book* (New York, 1955); *Potluck Pogo* (New York, 1955); *The Pogo Sunday Book* (New York, 1956); *The Pogo Party* (New York, 1956); *Songs of Pogo* (New York, 1956); *Pogo's Sunday Punch* (New York, 1957); *Positively Pogo* (New York, 1957); *Go Fizzickle Pogo* (New York, 1958); *The Pogo Sunday Parade* (New York, 1958); *The Pogo Sunday Brunch* (New York, 1959); *Ten Ever-lovin' Blue Eyed Years with Pogo* (New York, 1959); *Pogo Extra* (New York, 1960); *Beau Pogo* (New York, 1960); *Pogo à la Sundae* (New York, 1961); *Gone Pogo* (New York, 1961); *Instant Pogo* (New York, 1962); *The Jack Acid Society Book* (New York, 1962); *The Pogo Papers* (New York, 1963); *Pogo Puce* (New York, 1963); *Deck Us All with Boston Charlie* (New York, 1963); *The Return of Pogo* (New York, 1965); *The Pogo Poop Book* (New York, 1966); *Prehysterical Pogo* (New York, 1967); *Pogo, Prisoner of Love* (New York, 1969); *Impollutable Pogo* (New York, 1970); *We Have Met The Enemy And He Is Us* (New York, 1972); *Pogo Re-Runs* (New York, 1974); *Pogo Revisited* (New York, 1974); *The Pogo Candidate* (Kansas City, 1976); *Pogo's Body Politic* (New York, 1976); *Pogo's Bats and Bellies Free* (New York, 1976); *A Pogo Panorama* (New York, 1977); *Pogo's Will Be That Was* (New York, 1979); *The Best of Pogo* (New York, 1982); *Pogo Even Better* (New York, 1984); *Outrageously Pogo* (New York, 1985); *Walt Kelly's Pluperfect Pogo* (New York, 1987). "Pogo Looks at the Abominable Snowman," in *The Funnies: An American Idiom*, ed. by D. M. White and Robert Abel (London, 1963), pp. 284–292. "Pogo's Progress," *Newsweek* 33 (May 30, 1949): 57. "Possum Time," *Time* 58 (December 18, 1950): 81–82. Murray Robinson, "Pogo's Papa," *Collier's* 129 (March 8, 1952): 20–21. "Speaking of Pictures," *Life* 32 (May 12, 1952): 12–14. "Pogo, Dennis, Star at Lunch Club Meeting," *Publishers Weekly* 162 (December 20, 1952): 237–238. "Our Archives of Culture: Enter the Comics and Pogo," *Newsweek* 43 (June 21, 1954): 60; *Discussion* 44 (July 12, 1954): 6. "Pogo for President," *Newsweek* 48 (July 2, 1956): 48–49. "Pogo Problem: Khruschchev-Castro Satire," *Commonwealth* 76 (June 8, 1962): 267–268. *Who's Who* 34 (1966–67): 1128. Couperie and Horn, author index. Nye, pp. 234–235. Obituary, *New York Times*, October 19, 1973. Obituary, *Washington Post*, October 19, 1973. Obituary, *Time*, October 29, 1973. Obituary, *Newsweek*, October 29, 1973. Obituary, *New York Times*, November 1, 1973. Daniel Mishkin, "Pogo: Walt Kelly's American Dream," *Journal of Popular Culture* 12 (Spring 1979): 681–690. Horn, pp. 422–423. The Ohio State University Libraries, *Walt Kelly*

(Columbus, 1988). Amory, p. 331. Mark Burstein, *Much Ado* (Richfield, Minn., 1988). Steve Thompson, *The Walt Kelly Collector's Guide* (Richfield, Minn., 1988).

Hank Ketcham 1920–

Henry King Ketcham was born in Seattle, Washington, on March 14, 1920, the son of Weaver Vinson and Virginia Emma King Ketcham. In 1938 he attended the University of Washington, and on June 13, 1942, married his first wife, Alice Louise Mahar. The couple had one child, Dennis, the prototype for *Dennis the Menace*. His first wife having died, Ketcham married JoAnne Stevens on July 1, 1959. Ketcham was trained as a cartoonist at Lantz Productions of Universal Studios in Hollywood, where he worked until 1940. From 1941 to 1945 Ketcham was chief photographic specialist in the U.S. Naval Reserve. He worked as a freelance cartoonist until 1951, when *Dennis the Menace* appeared, syndicated by Hall. Distributed by North America Syndicate, the panel now appears in more than a thousand newspapers. Ketcham received the Billy De Beck Award for outstanding cartooning in 1952. From 1959 to 1963, CBS-TV ran a hit situation comedy featuring Ketcham's character. A Japanese series of animated cartoons featuring Dennis is now in syndication.

REFERENCES: Hank Ketcham, *Dennis the Menace* (New York, 1952); *More Dennis the Menace* (New York, 1953); *Baby Sitter's Guide* (New York, 1954); *Dennis the Menace Rides Again* (New York, 1955); *Dennis the Menace versus Everybody* (New York, 1956); *Wanted: Dennis the Menace* (New York, 1956); *Dennis the Menace, Household Hurricane* (New York, 1957); *In This Corner, Dennis the Menace* (New York, 1958); *Dennis the Menace, Teacher's Threat* (New York, 1959); *Ambassador of Mischief* (New York, 1960); *Dennis the Menace, Happy Half-Pint* (New York, 1961); *Dennis the Menace, Who Me?* (Greenwich, Conn., 1963); *Dennis the Menace, Make-Believe Angel* (Greenwich, Conn., 1963); *I Wanna Go Home!* (New York, 1965); *Dennis the Menace, Where the Action Is* (Greenwich, Conn., 1971); *Someone's in the Kitchen with Dennis* (New York, 1978); *Dennis the Menace Hopes You Will Get Well* (Boulder, Colo., 1979); *Dennis the Menace Sheds Some New Light on Friendship* (Boulder, Colo., 1979); *Dennis the Menace Shows Us New Ways to Say Happy Birthday* (Boulder, Colo., 1979); *Dennis the Menace Talks About Love Stuff* (Boulder, Colo., 1979); *Dennis the Menace* (New York, 1987); *Dennis the Menace Takes the Cake* (Racine, Wis., 1987). "Pogo, Dennis, Star at Lunch Club Meeting," *Publishers Weekly* 162 (December 20, 1952): 237–238. "Ketcham's Menace: Billy De Beck Award," *Newsweek* 41 (May 4, 1953). "Menace Gets Dressed," *Look* 17 (October 6, 1953): 87. Betty Wilson, "Menace Pays Off," *Americas* 5 (June 1953): 7–9. "From Cartoon to Big Business," *Publishers Weekly* 179 (January 9, 1961): 34–35. Amory, p. 338. *Who's Who* 34 (1966–67): 1141–1142. Couperie and Horn, pp. 113, 114, 131. Nye, p. 221. Horn pp. 201, 301, 424.

Ted Key 1912–

The creator of the beloved cartoon maid, *Hazel*, Ted Key was born in Fresno, California, on August 25, 1912, the son of Simon Leon and Fanny Key. Key attended the University of California at Berkeley. He graduated in 1933, having served as art editor of the *Daily Californian* and as associate editor of the humor journal *California Pelican*. After a brief stint with the Walt Disney organization, Key moved to New York City, where his cartoons soon appeared in such distinguished organs as *The New Yorker*, *Ladies' Home Journal*, *Good Housekeeping*, *McCall's*, and *Mademoiselle*. In 1943 he created *Hazel*, which for many years ran in the *Saturday Evening Post*. E. P. Dutton has published numerous compilations of the artist's cartoons, including *Hazel* (1946); *Here's Hazel* (1949); *Many Happy Returns* (1950); *If You Like Hazel* (1952); *So'm I* (1953); *Hazel Rides Again* (1955); *Fasten Your Seat Belts* (1956); *All Hazel* (1958); *The Hazel Jubilee* (1959); *Hazel Time* (1962); *Life With Hazel* (1965); and *Hazel Power* (1971). Key is also the creator of the cartoon *Diz and Liz* (1960); the television series *Hazel*, which ran on NBC from 1961 to 1964 and on CBS from 1965 to 1966; the screenplay for *The Cat from Outer Space* (Walt Disney Productions); and the stories for Disney's *Million Dollar Duck* and *Gus*. States the artist, "Once, in a TV interview, I was asked: 'What one word comes to mind when you think of Hazel?' I said, 'Humanity.' I try to attain some feeling of compassion in my work." Key lives in Wayne, Pennsylvania, with his wife, the former Bonnie Williams-Cohen.

REFERENCES: Max Wylie, *Best Broadcasts of 1939–40* (New York, 1940). Frederic Birmingham, "A Gift of Laughter: Ted Key," *Saturday Evening Post* (Fall 1971). George Beiswinger, "Hazel's Here! — and Everywhere," *Media History Digest* 5 (Fall 1985). "Ted Key, Creator of Hazel," *Syracuse University Courier* 23 (Fall 1988).

Frank O. King 1883–1969

Frank O. King was born in Cashton, Wisconsin, on April 9, 1883, the son of John J. and Caroline I. Harris King. He attended public schools in Tomah, Wisconsin, where he graduated from high school in 1901. From 1905 to 1906 he was a student at the Chicago Academy of Fine Arts. He married Delia Drew on February 7, 1911. King was a cartoonist for the *Minneapolis Times* (1901–1905), the *Chicago Examiner* (1906–1909), and from 1909, the Chicago Tribune–New York News Syndicate. King's early cartoons include *Motorcycle Mike, Bobby Make-Believe,* and *The Rectangle.* In 1919 he began *Gasoline Alley,* which capitalized on the popularity of the automobile. On February 14, 1921, a baby was left on the doorstep of Walt, the strip's protagonist, and the interest of the strip shifted from the automobile to the family. King was the first comic-strip artist to age his characters with exact reference to the time progression of everyday life. The strip, a celebration of the cyclical nature of human existence, was later coauthored by Dick Moores (q.v.) and Bill Perry (q.v.). Today, *Gasoline Alley* is drawn by Jim Scancarelli (q.v.).

REFERENCES: Frank King, *Skeezix and Uncle Walt* (Chicago, 1924); *Skeezix and Pat* (Chicago, 1925); *Skeezix at the Circus* (Chicago, 1926); *Skeezix Out West* (Chicago, 1928); *Gasoline Alley* (Chicago, 1929); *Nina and Skeezix* (Racine, Wis., 1942). "Comics and Their Creators," *Literary Digest* 116 (December 16, 1933): 13. "Twenty Years of Skeezix," *Newsweek* 17 (February 17, 1941): 74. Sheridan, pp. 20, 49, 109. Mallett, p. 229. H. N. Oliphant, "Skeezix: King of the Comics," *Coronet* 25 (February 1949): 77–80. *Who's Who* 34 (1966–67): 1152. Couperie and Horn, author index. Obituary, *New York Times*, June 25, 1969. Obituary, *Time*, July 4, 1969. Obituary, *Newsweek*, July 7, 1969. Nye, p. 220. Horn, pp. 275, 427, 470.

Harold Knerr 1883–1949

The second artist to draw *The Katzenjammer Kids,* Harold Knerr, born in Bryn Mawr, Pennsylvania, worked for both the *Philadelphia Record* and *Ledger.* He began doing the strip in 1912 after a court decision gave Hearst the rights to the title *Katzenjammer Kids* and Rudolph Dirks (q.v.) the rights to the strip under a different title. Knerr's strip was syndicated by King Features; Dirks's, retitled *Hans and Fritz* then *The Captain and the Kids,* by United Feature. Knerr died of a heart ailment in New York City on July 8, 1949. The strip then passed into the hands of Doe Winner, and was later drawn by Joe Musial.

REFERENCES: Sheridan, pp. 61, 287, 293. Obituary, *New York Times*, July 9, 1949, p. 13. Couperie and Horn, author index. Horn, pp. 17, 156, 208, 421, 432.

Aline Kominsky-Crumb 1948–

Born in Long Beach, New York, on August 1, 1948, Aline Goldsmith Kominsky-Crumb attended the State University of New York at New Paltz, Cooper Union, and the University of Arizona in Tucson, from which she received her B.A. in 1971. That same year she moved to San Francisco, where she became a founding contributor to *Wimmen's Comix,* with which she has long been associated. In October 1971 she met comic creator R. Crumb (q.v.), whom she married in January 1978. Interviewed by columnist Patrick Grizzell, Kominsky-Crumb enumerated the greatest influences on her richly autobiographical work, including those of "German Expressionism, Woody Allen, and Jewish stand-up comedians in the Catskills." In addition to Aline, husband Bob, and daughter Sophie, the stock characters featured in her *Power Pack* comics are parents Blabette and Arnie; the entrepreneurial Rick Smitnarf; the promiscuous

Valerie Feldman; and her demoniac alter ego, Mr. Bunch. The Crumbs live in seclusion in Winters, California. In 1990 Fantagraphics Books will publish an anthology of Kominsky-Crumb's work, *Love That Bunch!*

REFERENCES: Aline Kominsky-Crumb, *The Bunch's Power Pack Comics* (Princeton, Wis., 1979); *The Bunch's Power Pack Comics,* no. 2 (Princeton, Wis., 1981). Patrick Grizzell, "The Bunch: Wine, Cheese and Self-Hatred — An Interview with Aline Kominsky-Crumb," *On the Wing* (Sacramento, Calif.), April 1985. J. Ashburn, "Aline's Comic Art," *Suttertown* (Calif.) *News*, April 18–25, 1985, p. 5.

Alex Kotzky 1923–

Alex Kotzky, best known for the magic realism of *Apartment 3-G,* was born in the Bronx on September 11, 1923, the son of fur manufacturer Theodor Kotzky and Helen Kotzky. Kotzky attended Music and Art High School, Pratt Institute, and the Art Students League of New York. During World War II, he saw service with the Fourth Division. On September 21, 1946, Kotzky married his wife, Emma. After a long artistic apprenticeship, during which he ghosted such strips as *Big Ben Bolt* and *The Heart of Juliet Jones,* Kotzky on May 8, 1961, saw publication of the masterfully drawn *Apartment 3-G,* a creation of Dr. Nicholas Dallis (q.v.).

REFERENCES: King Features Syndicate, *Alex Kotzky* (New York, n.d.). Horn, pp. 434–435.

Krystine Kryttre 1958–

Underground cartoonist Krystine Kryttre, best known for her scratchboard comics, was born October 9, 1958, in St. Luke's Hospital, San Francisco, California, the daughter of Richard and Ruth Lankenau. She attended Benjamin Bubb Elementary School, Graham Junior High School, and Awalt High School in Mountain View, California. From 1976 to 1986 Kryttre (a pen name pronounced "critter") worked as a jewelry and sign engraver. Since 1986 she has worked in a neon-sign shop. Her numerous comic creations have appeared in *Viper* (Rip Off Press, 1985); *Wimmen's Comix,* nos. 1–3 (1985, 1987, 1988); *Cannibal Romance* (Last Gasp, 1986); *Weirdo,* nos. 17, 22, 25, 26 (1986, 1988, 1989); *Tits & Clits,* no. 7 (Last Gasp, 1987); *Rip Off Comics* (1987); *Centrifugal Bumble-Puppy,* nos. 7, 8 (Fantagraphics, 1988); *Heck!* (Rip Off Press, 1989); and *Raw,* vol. 2, no. 1 (Penguin Books, 1989). Kryttre also contributed to the *Jonestown Memorial Death Cult Card Set* (Carnage Press, 1989), and participated in the U.S.–U.S.S.R. Cartoon Art Exchange that took place in 1989. States Kryttre, "I've been attracted to the romance, outrageousness, and freedom of underground comix since age eleven. This is not normal for young girls, but it is true, however. Comics are the most socially acceptable way I've found with which to express myself." Kryttre lives in San Francisco.

REFERENCES: "Krystine Kryttre," (*kar-ton'*) *new comic arts journal* 1 (1988): 10. Susan Harrow, "Controlled Chaos," *San Francisco Comical* (April 1989): 20–21.

Joe Kubert 1926–

In 1965 artist Joe Kubert began *Tales of the Green Beret* as part of the comic-strip coverage of the Vietnamese conflict. The strip was based on writer Robin Moore's (q.v.) novel about the U.S. Special Forces. By September 1966 *Tales of the Green Beret* was appearing in seventy-five newspapers, but it was soon dropped by some, including the *Charlotte Observer,* because of what *Newsweek* magazine described as its "paramilitary bloodthirstiness." *Newsweek* also reported that artist Kubert considered the strip apolitical. In September 1966 *Tales of the Green Beret* was published as a Dell comic book.

REFERENCES: "Pop Goes the War!" *Newsweek* 68 (September 12, 1966): 66. Horn, pp. 439–440.

Harvey Kurtzman 1924–

Born in New York on October 3, 1924, Harvey Kurtzman is best known as the father of the influential and iconoclastic *Mad* magazine. Educated at New York's Cooper Union, Kurtzman in 1952 began *Mad*, which was to inspire generations of cartoonists. In 1957 the artist began his second comic periodical, the short-lived *Trump*, which was followed by *Humbug* and *Help!* The range and diversity of Kurtzman's influence can be seen in the encyclopedic variety of associates whom he enumerates in the *National Cartoonists Society Album:* "Could never make it without associates, i.e., Willy Elder, Jack Davis, Wally Wood, Bill Gaines, Terry Gilliam, Gloria Steinem, Bob Crumb, Gilbert Shelton, Sarah Downs, Phil Felix, Arnold Roth and others." An instructor at the School of Visual Arts, Kurtzman lives in Mount Vernon, New York, with his wife, Adele. He has four children: Meredith, Pete, Liz, and Nell.

REFERENCES: National Cartoonists Society, *National Cartoonists Society Album* (Greenwich, Conn., 1988), p. 104. Horn, p. 442.

Gary Larson 1950–

Gary Larson, creator of the anthropomorphized *Far Side*, grew up in Tacoma, Washington. Larson attended Washington State University in Pullman, from which he graduated in 1973 with a degree in communications. That year he moved to Seattle, obtaining employment as a music-store clerk. In 1976 Larson sold his first cartoons to what is now *Pacific Northwest* magazine. In 1977 Larson went to work for the Humane Society, coinciding with publication that same year of his cartoon *Nature's Way* in the *Seattle Times*. The *Times* canceled *Nature's Way* in 1979, and Larson took the cartoon to the *San Francisco Chronicle*. In 1984, Larson moved to Universal Press Syndicate, which now distributes *The Far Side* to more than seven hundred daily newspapers. Among the numerous *Far Side* anthologies published by Andrews and McMeel are *The Far Side* (1982); *Beyond the Far Side* (1983); *The Far Side Gallery* (1984); *Bride of the Far Side* (1985); *In Search of the Far Side* (1985); *It Came from the Far Side* (1985); *Valley of the Far Side* (1985); *The Far Side Gallery II* (1986); *The Far Side Observer* (1987); *Hound of the Far Side* (1987); and *Night of the Crash-Test Dummies* (1988).

REFERENCE: Peter Richmond, "Creatures From the Black Cartoon," *Rolling Stone* (September 24, 1987): 79–80, 83, 149–150. Fred Bernstein, "Loony 'Toonist Gary Larson," *People* 23 (February 4, 1985): 103. C. Bond, "The Far Side of the National Museum of Natural History," *Smithsonian* 18 (April 1987): 168. "Taking a Break from 'The Far Side,' " *Newsweek* 112 (October 10, 1988): 81. Steve Weiner, "Funny Money," *Forbes* 142 (December 12, 1988): 272. Thomas Miller, "The Far Side of Science," *Natural History* 5 (May 1989): 78.

Fred Lasswell 1916–

Artist Fred Lasswell, Billy De Beck's (q.v.) heir to *Barney Google*, was born in Kennett, Missouri, in 1916. His family later moved to Gainesville, Florida, then to Tampa, Florida. After high school, Lasswell became a cartoonist for the *Tampa Times*. When he was seventeen he was discovered by De Beck, and became his assistant. De Beck died in 1942, and in 1943 Lasswell joined the navy. He drew a service cartoon, *Hashmark*, for the U.S. Marine's magazine *Leatherneck* from 1943 to 1945. After his discharge Lasswell continued *Barney Google* for King Features. Lasswell was later engaged in the production of comic strips in braille for the blind. In 1984, Lasswell received the Elzie Segar Award from the National Cartoonists Society.

REFERENCES: King Features Syndicate, *Fred Lasswell*, Biographical Series, no. 34 (New York, n.d.); *Barney Google and Snuffy Smith Comic Strip Celebrates 70 Successful Years* (New York, 1989). Horn, pp. 88, 143, 199, 446. B. Young, "Snuffy Smith's Pappy," *Southern Living* 22 (July 1987): 106.

Carol Lay 1952–

Best known for her underground comic *Good Girls*, Carol Lay was born on September 15, 1952, in Whittier, California, the daughter of Aldyth Evans Lay and Robert Herman Lay. Lay received her B.F.A. from the University of California at Los Angeles in 1975. Since 1977 Lay

has been self-employed. Her work includes cartoons, illustrations, storyboards for live-action films, and comics featured in rock videos. Her comics include *Good Girls*, nos. 1–4 (Fantagraphics, 1986–89); *Raw*, no. 5; *Weirdo*, no. 10; *DC Comics*; *Viper*; and *Heck*. States Lay, "I try to do the unusual. My drawing style tends to vary according to whatever story I tackle but I always inject a strong, positive, feminine perspective to the goings on." Lay lives in Los Angeles.

REFERENCE: Stan Bobrof, "Grab Bag," *Paper Magazine* (June 1988).

Mell Lazarus 1927–

Artist Mell Lazarus, creator of *Miss Peach*, was born and educated in Brooklyn. Before originating *Miss Peach* in 1957, Lazarus was a contributor to the *Saturday Evening Post* and *Collier's*, and served as art director of a small magazine. His 1970 strip, *Momma*, is a sympathetic portrayal of the Jewish mother stereotype made notorious by Philip Roth's novel *Portnoy's Complaint* (1969).

REFERENCES: Mell Lazarus, *Miss Peach* (New York, 1960); *Miss Peach, Are These Your Children?* (New York, 1964); *Momma* (New York, 1970). Publishers Newspaper Syndicate, *Mell Lazarus* (Chicago, n.d.). Couperie and Horn, pp. 107, 180. Horn, pp. 447, 495.

Harold LeDoux 1926–

Cartoonist Harold LeDoux, best known for his drawing of Nicholas Dallis's (q.v.) *Judge Parker*, was born in Louisiana in 1926, the son of French colonists. He left home when he was eighteen and joined the merchant marine; during his three years of service he traveled to Europe, Africa, and South America. After attending the Chicago Academy of Fine Arts, LeDoux went to New York, where he obtained a position as a comic-book illustrator for *Famous Funnies*, for whom he specialized in the series *Movie Love*. In 1953 he became an assistant on the year-old *Judge Parker*, then drawn by Dale Heilman. In July 1965 LeDoux took over the artwork of *Judge Parker*.

REFERENCES: Publishers Newspaper Syndicate, *Harold LeDoux* (Chicago, n.d.). King Features Syndicate, *Harold LeDoux* (New York, 1989). Couperie and Horn, p. 111. Horn, pp. 193, 346.

Joe Lee 1953–

Joe Lee, perhaps the only underground cartoonist clown, was born on August 4, 1953, in Olney, Illinois, the son of Ronald and Jean Lee. He received his B.A. in 1975 from Indiana University, where he majored in medieval history. He then matriculated at Ringling Brothers Clown College, from which he graduated in 1976. From 1976 to 1981, Lee was employed as a clown by — in turn — Ringling Brothers Barnum and Baily Circus World, King Brothers Circus, and Hoxie Brothers Circus. Between 1981 and 1986 Lee worked as an assistant instructor of printmaking at the Art Students League of New York. Since 1986 he has been a freelance illustrator. His illustrations include those for Henry Carlisle's *The Jonah Man* (Alfred A. Knopf, 1984) and *Four Seasons of Brownies* (Harriet's Kitchen, 1986). His work has been exhibited at the Ruschman Gallery in Indianapolis (1987, 1988, 1989), the American States Insurance Show in Indianapolis (1988), the Alan Stone Gallery (New York, 1988), the Crucial Gallery (London, 1987), the Art Students League of New York (1984, 1985, 1986), and the Rockland Center for the Arts (West Nyack, N.Y., 1984). Appearing in Rip Off Comics are his *Lectures of the Space Academy* (1989) and *Perchance Ta Canasta* (1977). Lee explains, "The comic book is the last refuge of all those messiahs who know that 'it' (the big omniscIT) means nothing but still believe in the crackle of a page covered with ink and a simple story, no matter how absurd, with a beginning, middle, and an end. And, Lord, I know I'm one (yes, Lord, the one with the lampshade chapeau)." Lee lives in Bloomington, Indiana.

Stan Lee 1922–

Stan Lee, best known as the legendary creator of *The Amazing Spider-Man*, was born in New York City in 1922. In 1939, at age seventeen, Lee became a copywriter and assistant to the editor at Timely Comics, the predecessor of Atlas and Marvel comics. Lee soon became editor, art director, and — eventually — executive editor, head writer, and publisher. In 1962 Lee created the character which was to ensure his fame — Spider-Man. Other Lee creations include *The Hulk* (1962), written by Lee and drawn by Jack Kirby; *The Fantastic Four* (1961), also with Kirby; *Doctor Strange*, with artist Steve Ditko; and *The Silver Surfer* (1966). In addition to his comics, Lee is an accomplished screenwriter who has collaborated with such giants of cinema as director Alain Resnais. Lee is also the executive producer of filmmaker George Lucas's feature *Howard the Duck*. And he has collaborated with the Children's Television Workshop's *Electric Company* on the production of *Spidey Super Stories*. Lee is the founder and first president of the Academy of Comic Book Arts and a member of the Academy of Television Arts and Sciences and the National Cartoonists Society.

REFERENCES: Stan Lee, *Origins of Marvel Comics* (New York: Simon & Schuster, 1974). King Features Syndicate, *Stan Lee* (New York, n.d.). Horn, pp. 447–448.

John J. Liney 1912–

John J. Liney, who continued *Henry* after the death of Carl Anderson (q.v.) in 1948, was born in South Philadelphia. He sold his first cartoon to the *Philadelphia Bulletin* when he was fourteen, and later won a cartoon contest sponsored by the *Philadelphia Public Ledger*. When his father was injured in an accident he quit his studies at South Philadelphia High School and went to work to support his family. He met Anderson in 1940, and became his assistant. After World War II Liney taught cartooning at Temple University.

REFERENCES: Dorothy McGreal, "Silence Is Golden," *World of Comic Art* 1 (Winter 1966–67): 10–18. Horn, pp. 79, 312.

Dick Locher 1929–

Artist Dick Locher, who now draws Tribune Media Service's *Dick Tracy*, was born on June 4, 1929, in Dubuque, Iowa. He graduated from Dubuque's Loras Academy and attended Loras College, the University of Iowa, the Chicago Academy of Fine Art, and the Art Center of Los Angeles. After serving in the U.S. Air Force as a pilot and aircraft designer, he was from 1957 to 1961 Chester Gould's (q.v.) assistant on *Dick Tracy*. The recipient of a 1983 Pulitzer Prize for his editorial cartooning, Locher took over *Dick Tracy* that same year. He resides in Naperville, Illinois, with his wife, Mary. The couple has two children: a daughter, Jana, and a son, Steve.

REFERENCE: Tribune Media Services, *Dick Locher Biography*, 1986.

Bobby London 1950–

Bobby London, since February 1986 the artist and author of King Features Syndicate's daily *Popeye*, was born in New York City and attended Adelphi University. In 1969 he began his career as a cartoonist in the underground papers of Chicago and New York. In 1971 the *Los Angeles Free Press* began publication of his *Dirty Duck*. From 1972 to 1977 the *National Lampoon* carried the strip; from 1977 to 1987, *Playboy*. London's work has appeared in numerous publications, including *Rolling Stone*, the *New York Times*, *Esquire*, the *Washington Post*, and the *Village Voice*. An accomplished songwriter as well as artist, London wrote *White Guy's Rap*, which was performed by Jim Belushi on *Saturday Night Live*. London was given the Yellow Kid Award for Best Artist-Writer at the 1978 International Salon of Comics.

REFERENCE: King Features Syndicate, *Bobby London* (New York, n.d.).

John Long 1950–

John Long, creator of King Features Syndicate's *Long Overdue*, was for fifteen years senior sergeant in the Lincoln Park, Michigan, fire department. *Long Overdue* was created in 1983 for the *Detroit News;* in September 1988, King Features launched the panel nationally.

REFERENCE: King Features Syndicate, *King Features Announces "Long Overdue" Syndication* (New York, August 15, 1988).

Harold MacGill 1877–1952

Creator of *The Hall Room Boys* and *Percy and Ferdie* Harold MacGill was best known for his cartoons in the *New York Evening Journal*. A collection of *Percy and Ferdie* strips was published in 1926 by Cupples and Leon. MacGill died in 1952 at the age of seventy-six, survived by his wife, Dorothy, and his son, Leighton.

REFERENCES: Harold MacGill, *Percy and Ferdie* (New York, 1926). Obituary, *New York Times*, December 3, 1952, p. 33.

James Ruel MacNaughton III 1961–

Born on April 12, 1961, in Portland, Maine, Jim MacNaughton — with co-creator Shannon Hamilton — in April 1988 began publication of *The Cosmic Steller Rebellers*. The artist lives in Oakland, Maine, where he directs Hammac Publications.

Jeff MacNelly 1947–

Jeff MacNelly, creator of the Tribune Media Service's *Shoe*, is the son of portrait artist and *Saturday Evening Post* publisher C. L. MacNelly. *Shoe* made its debut in 1977. MacNelly has received the Pulitzer Prize for editorial cartooning in 1972, 1978, and 1985. He has also twice received the Reuben, the highest award of the National Cartoonists Society. From 1970 to 1982, MacNelly worked as an editorial cartoonist for the *Richmond News Leader*. In 1982 he joined the staff of the *Chicago Tribune*.

REFERENCE: Tribune Media Services, *Jeff MacNelly Biography*, May 1987.

Gus "Watso" Mager 1878–1956

Born in Newark, New Jersey, in 1878, Charles Augustus Mager created his famous *Sherlocko the Monk* in 1910, and *Hawkshaw the Detective* in 1913. Mager died on July 17, 1956, in Murraysville, Pennsylvania.

REFERENCES: Gus Mager, *Sherlocko the Monk* (Westport, Conn., 1977). Horn, pp. 308–309, 473.

Jerry Marcus 1924–

Jerry Marcus, creator of King Features Syndicate's *Trudy*, which began daily distribution on March 18, 1963, and Sunday on June 5, 1966, attended the School of Visual Arts in New York City. Marcus's work has appeared in the *Saturday Evening Post*, *The New Yorker*, *McCall's*, *Ladies' Home Journal*, *Playboy*, and *Paris Match*. In addition to being a cartoonist, Marcus is also an actor who has appeared in several feature films and over a dozen television commercials.

REFERENCE: King Features Syndicate, *Trudy* (New York, 1989).

William Moulton Marston 1893–1947

The creator of one of two widely distributed comics to feature superheroines, William Moulton Marston, is best known for his invention of the polygraph. A psychologist, Marston joined forces with artist H. G. Peter to create *Wonder Woman*, which first appeared in December 1941 in *All-Star*, no. 8 (National Comics). The counterpart of Superman, Wonder Woman also had a secret identity — that of Diana Prince. Following Marston's death in 1947, the comic's focus changed from exultation of feminine superiority to routine adventure.

REFERENCES: William Moulton Marston, *Wonder Woman* (New York, 1972). Michael L. Fleisher, *Wonder Woman* (New York, 1976). *Wonder Woman* (New York, 1980). Horn, p. 706.

Henry Martin 1925–

Henry Martin, creator of Tribune Media Services' *Good News, Bad News*, graduated in 1948 from Princeton University. Martin's art subsequently appeared in such important periodicals as *The New Yorker*, the *Saturday Evening Post, Look*, the *Saturday Review*, the *Ladies' Home Journal, Good Housekeeping*, and *Punch*. Martin resides in Princeton, New Jersey, with his wife, Edie Matthews, and children, Ann and Jane.

REFERENCE: Tribune Media Services, *Henry Martin Biography* (November 1988).

Joe Martin 1945–

Joe Martin, creator of North America Syndicate's *Willy 'n' Ethel*, was for many years a successful executive, running a large Chicago employment agency before launching his cartoon career. Among his panels are *Willy 'n' Ethel* (1981) and *Porterfield*. Martin and his wife, Marie, reside in Oak Park, Illinois.

REFERENCE: King Features Syndicate, *Joe Martin* (New York, 1989).

Fran Matera 1924–

Fran Matera, who has drawn the North America Syndicate–distributed *Steve Roper and Mike Nomad* since 1984, was born in Connecticut. As a high-school student he assisted Alfred Andriola (q.v.). Matera attended the School of the Art Institute of Chicago for one year. He served in the U.S. Marines. After his discharge in 1947, Matera worked for Associated Press, serving as the artist of *Dickie Dare*, a strip created by Milton Caniff (q.v.) and later drawn by Coulton Waugh. Matera also draws *Bruce Lee*. In 1964 Matera moved to Florida; he resides in Safety Harbor.

REFERENCE: King Features Syndicate, *Fran Matera* (New York, 1989).

Paul Mavrides 1963–

Best known for his work with Gilbert Shelton (q.v.) on *The Fabulous Furry Freak Brothers*, Paul Mavrides was born on November 22, 1963, in Dallas, Texas, the son of Bob and Connie Mavrides. His published comics include *The Idiots Abroad: The Fabulous Furry Freak Brothers* (with Gilbert Shelton; Rip Off Press, 1987); *The Fabulous Furry Freak Brothers*, nos. 6–10 (with Gilbert Shelton; 1980–87); *Cover-Up Lowdown* (with Jay Kinney; Rip Off Press, 1978); *Anarchy Comics*, nos. 1–4 (Last Gasp, 1978, 1979, 1981, 1987); and features in *Real War Stories* (Eclipse Comics, 1987); *American Splendor*, nos. 13–14 (with Harvey Pekar; 1988–89); *"Bob" 's Favorite Comics* (Rip Off Comics, 1989); and *The Adventures of Dinoboy* (with Hal Robins), which has appeared in *Viper* (Auburn, Calif.: Rip Off Press, 1985), *Cannibal Romance* (Last Gasp, 1987), and *Rip Off Comics* (1982, 1983, 1984, 1987). Mavrides's paintings, drawings, and graphics have been exhibited at San Diego State University (*Cheap Lurid Images*, May 1983) and at Installation in San Diego (*No Signs of a Struggle*, August 1982). Mavrides has also conceived, produced, designed, and directed multimedia stage events, including *Atomic Seance and Devival: West Coast SubGenius Prophecy Crusade* (with Doug Wellman and Doug Smith, November 5, 1985, The Stone, San Francisco, and November 15–16, 1985, Alexandria Hotel, Los Angeles); *Night of Slack* (with Doug Wellman, January 21–22, 1984, Victoria Theater, San Francisco); *The Post-Science Fair* (with Doug Wellman, September 17–18, 1983, YMCA Theater, San Francisco); *The Pill-Chainsaw Festival* (September 11–

14, 1983, The Mega-FisTemple, Little Rock, Ark.); *SubCon One* (November 20–24, 1981, The SubGenius Foundation, Dallas, Texas); and Cover-Up Blow Out (November 22, 1979, Jetwave, San Francisco). Mavrides lives in San Francisco.

Rex Maxon 1892–1973

One of several artists to draw *Tarzan*, Rex Maxon was born in Lincoln, Nebraska. After his family moved to St. Louis, Maxon worked on the art staff of the *St. Louis Republic*. He also did feature drawings for the *New York Evening Mail*, the *Evening World*, and the *Globe*. In 1931 he took over drawing the daily *Tarzan;* Hal Foster (q.v.) continued doing the Sunday page until 1937. In 1937, Maxon's assistant, Burne Hogarth (q.v.), took over the Sundays.

REFERENCES: Sheridan, pp. 226, 236. Couperie and Horn, p. 131. Horn, pp. 486, 650.

Winsor McCay 1871–1934

In 1871 Winsor Z. McCay was born in Spring Lake, Michigan, where his father was a lumberman. McCay did not complete grade school. In his teens he journeyed to Chicago, where he took art lessons and made woodcuts for traveling vaudeville shows, painted street signs, and designed posters. Later, in Ohio, he prepared the murals for Cincinnati's Vine Street Dime Museum. He worked as a reporter and illustrator for the *Cincinnati Commercial Tribune* and the *Cincinnati Enquirer*. In 1891 McCay married Maude Dufour; the couple had two children, Marian and Robert Winsor, who served as the model for Little Nemo. In 1903 McCay moved to New York, where he became a cartoonist for the *Telegram* and the *Herald*, originating many comic strips, including *Little Nemo in Slumberland, Dream of the Rarebit Fiend, Sammy Sneeze, Hungry Henrietta, The Man from Montclair*, and *Poor Jake*. McCay created the first sophisticated animated cartoons, among them *Little Nemo* (1911), the 1912 *Story of a Mosquito (How a Mosquito Operates)*, *Gertie* (1914), *The Sinking of the Lusitania* (1918), and — from 1918 to 1921 — *Gertie on Tour, Flip's Circus, The Centaurs, Bug Vaudeville, The Pet*, and *The Flying House*. After World War I he turned from the comic strip to editorial cartooning, although he revived *Nemo* for Hearst under the title *In the Land of Wonderful Dreams*. McCay died on July 26, 1934. In 1966 his work was shown with that of Herbert Crowley in the Metropolitan Museum of Art's exhibition *Two Fantastic Draftsmen*. Blanchard notes a similarity between the line of McCay and that of Beardsley, and McCay is often credited with anticipating surrealism. Significant collections of McCay's original artwork are housed at the Ohio State University Library for Communication and Graphic Arts, Columbus, Ohio, and at the Library of Congress.

REFERENCES: Winsor McCay, *Dreams of the Rarebit Fiend* (New York, 1905; *Little Sammy Sneeze* (New York, 1905); *Little Nemo in Slumberland* (New York, 1945); *Dreams of the Rarebit Fiend* (New York, 1973); *Little Nemo in the Palace of Ice and Further Adventures* (New York, 1976); *Winsor McCay's Dream Days* (Westport, Conn., 1977). Claude Bragdon, "Mickey Mouse and What He Means," *Scribner's* 96 (July 1934): 40–43. Obituary, *New York Times*, July 27, 1934, p. 17. Edna Levine, *Little Nemo* (Chicago, 1941). Georges Sadoul, *Les Pionniers du cinéma* (Paris, 1947), p. 485. Mallett, p. 283. Stephen Becker, *Comic Art in America* (New York, 1959), pp. 22–24, 97–99. Heinz Politzer, "From Little Nemo to Little Abner," in *The Funnies: An American Idiom*, ed. by D. M. White and Robert Abel (London, 1963), pp. 39–54. René Jeanne, *Cinéma 1900* (Paris, 1965). "And a Merry Christmas from Little Nemo," *Redbook* 126 (December 1965): 70–71. "Two Fantastic Draftsmen," *Arts* 40 (April 1966): 54. John Canaday, "Little Nemo at Met," *New York Times*, February 13, 1966, p. 21. Judith O'Sullivan, "In Search of Winsor McCay," *AFI Report* 5 (Summer 1974): 3–10. Will Eisner, "Little Nemo and the Great McCay," *Changes* 86 (1974): 18. John Canemaker, "Winsor McCay," *Film Comment* (January–February 1975): 44–48. Thomas Inge, "Little Nemo," *Crimmer's: The Journal of the Narrative Arts* 3 (Spring 1976): 44–49. Judith O'Sullivan, "The Art of Winsor McCay: From Illustration to Animation." Ph.D. diss., University of Maryland, 1976. Thomas W. Hoffer, "From Comic Strips to Animation: Some Perspective on Winsor McCay," *Journal of the University Film Association* 27 (Spring 1976): 23–32. John Canemaker, *Winsor McCay*,

His Life and Art (New York, 1987). Couperie and Horn, author index. Nye, pp. 218–233. Horn, pp. 12, 17, 38, 223, 458, 467–468.

Darrell McClure 1903–1987

Darrell McClure, of *Little Annie Rooney* fame, was born on February 25, 1903, in Ukiah, Mendocino County, California. McClure's father was a hardware-store clerk. While in his early teens he studied at the California School of Fine Arts, and later at a school for cartoonists. In 1923 James Swinnerton (q.v.) got McClure a job at King Features as an artist's apprentice. *Little Annie Rooney* first appeared in the *New York Journal* on February 24, 1930; McClure took over the strip on October 6, 1930. The script was written by Brandon Walsh. Unlike Harold Gray's (q.v.) Orphan Annie, Annie Rooney is an outlaw, a fugitive from an orphanage, and the supposedly benevolent institutions that pursue her are presented by McClure as agents of a malevolent world force.

REFERENCES: Mel Heimer, *Darrell McClure*, King Features Syndicate Biographical Series, no. 89 (New York, n.d.). Couperie and Horn, p. 75. Horn, pp. 454, 468–469, 684.

Walt McDougall 1858–1938

Walter Hugh McDougall was born on February 10, 1858, in Newark, New Jersey, the son of a painter, John McDougall. He attended a military academy until 1874, when he quit school. On October 30, 1884, in the *New York World*, McDougall introduced the daily editorial cartoon to the American newspaper. McDougall began his career as a comic-strip artist for the *Philadelphia North American*, creating between 1901 and 1908 such strips as *Peck's Bad Boy* and — with L. Frank Baum — *Mysterious Visitors from the Land of Oz*. Other comic strips, such as *The Radio Buggs*, appeared in the *New York World*. McDougall was also the author of *The Hidden City* (1886), *Number Eleven* (1890), *History of Christopher Columbus* (1892), and *The Rambilicus and His Friends*. In 1926 McDougall published an extensive autobiography, *This Is the Life*. At the time of his suicide in 1938 McDougall was employed by the *Philadelphia North American*.

REFERENCES: Walt McDougall, *Fun and Fancy* (New York, 1885); *This Is the Life* (New York, 1926); "Last Conflict," *American Magazine* 73 (November 1911): 75–82; *American Magazine* 78 (November 1914): 32–34; "Old Days on the World," *American Mercury* 4 (January 1925): 20–28; "Pictures in the Papers," *American Mercury* 6 (September 1925): 67–73. Stephen Becker, *Comic Art in America* (New York, 1959), p. 8. Horn, p. 469.

George McManus 1884–1954

Born in St. Louis on January 23, 1884, George McManus, creator of *Bringing Up Father*, was the son of a theater manager. He began his newspaper career during his sophomore year at high school when he became janitor in the *St. Louis Republic*'s art department. When he was promoted to fashion editor McManus began his first comic strip, *Alma and Oliver*. Later, at the *New York World*, he originated *Panhandle Pete*, *Let George Do It*, *Snoozer*, *Nibsy the Newsboy in Funny Fairyland*, and *Cheerful Charlie*. Perhaps his most important strip at the *World* was *The Newlyweds*. In 1910 McManus married Florence Berger, and in 1912 he joined the Hearst publications, where, the same year, he began *Their Only Child* and *Bringing Up Father*, the latter based on a play from the turn of the century called *The Rising Generation*. The strip, conversely, was frequently dramatized, one example being Wilbur Braun's 1936 comedy. Radio programs were also based on the strip, as were films by Christie Brothers, Metro-Goldwyn-Mayer, Vitagraph, and Monogram. In four of the movies McManus himself played Jiggs. McManus died on October 23, 1954, in Santa Monica, California, the victim of hepatitis. The strip was then continued by Frank Fletcher (q.v.) and Vernon Greene. McManus's mastery of the art nouveau line was *Bringing Up Father*'s most appealing feature.

REFERENCES: George McManus, *The Newlyweds* (New York, 1907); *Bringing Up Father*, 14 vols. (New York, 1919–1932); *Fun for All* (Cleveland, 1947); *Bringing Up Father* (New York,

1973); *Bringing Up Father* (Westport, Conn., 1977); *Jiggs Is Back* (Berkeley, Calif., 1986). "Literature and Art: Sounding the Doom of the Comics," *Current Literature* 45 (November 1908): 6321. "Portrait," *Current Literature* 45 (December 1908): 632. "Comics and Their Creators," *Literary Digest* 117 (March 1934): 13. W. E. Berchtold, "Men of Comics," *New Outlook* 165 (April 1935): 37–38. "Jiggs: the Twenty-fifth Birthday of Corned Beef and Cabbage Craze," *Newsweek* 6 (November 16, 1935): 29. Wilbur Braun, *Bringing Up Father* (New York, 1936). E. W. Murtfeldt, "Making of a Funny," *Popular Science* 136 (June 1940): 84–88. Sheridan, pp. 42–48. George McManus and Henry La Cossitt, "Jiggs and I," *Collier's* 129 (January 19, 1952): 9–11; 129 (January 26, 1952): 24–25; 129 (February 2, 1952): 30–31. Obituary, *New York Times*, October 23, 1954, p. 15. Stephen Becker, *Comic Art in America* (New York, 1959), pp. 43–45. *Who Was Who* 3 (1951–60): 585. Couperie and Horn, author index. Nye, pp. 219, 224. Horn, p. 471.

Dale Messick 1906–

Creator of *Brenda Starr*, Delia Messick was born in South Bend, Indiana, in 1906, the daughter of sign painter and vocational-school teacher Cephas Messick. After graduating from high school in 1926, she spent one summer at the Art Institute of Chicago. For a time she designed greeting cards in New York, and she changed her name to Dale because of the prejudice that denied employment to women cartoonists. She applied for a job with Joseph Medill Patterson of the *New York Daily News* and the Chicago Tribune–New York News Syndicate, who told her that he would not hire a woman artist. Patterson's assistant, Mollie Slott, however, liked her work, and together Slott and Messick worked out the plot of *Brenda Starr*. Dale Messick had originally intended Brenda to be a lady bandit, but Mollie Slott decided that a female reporter would have wider appeal. The strip first appeared on June 30, 1940, as a Sunday page. In October 1945 it became a daily as well. The strip was produced by a staff, each member of which had a particular specialty. In 1960, for example, John Olson did backgrounds and lettering, and Jim Mackey did architecture and cars. It was one of Dale Messick's assistants, moreover, who provided the model for Basil St. John, Brenda's long-lost lover. "Authenticity," Dale Messick has said, "is something I always try to avoid." The strip has recently been made into a motion picture starring Brooke Shields. Messick lives in Santa Rosa, California.

REFERENCES: Dale Messick, *Brenda Starr* (Racine, Wis., 1943). Norma Lee Browning, "First Lady of the Funnies," *Saturday Evening Post* 233 (November 19, 1960): 34–35. "A Pretty Nose for News," *World of Comic Art* 1 (Fall 1966): 20–23. *Who's Who* 34 (1966–67): 1452. Couperie and Horn, pp. 119, 184. Nye, pp. 229, 231. Horn, p. 488.

Frank Miller 1898–1949

On October 2, 1898, Frank Miller was born in Sheldon, Iowa. His aviator strip, *Barney Baxter*, was created in 1936 for King Features. From 1942 to 1948 he served in the U.S. Coast Guard. He died on December 3, 1949.

REFERENCE: Horn, pp. 98, 493–494.

Frank Miller 1957–

Raised in New England, comic-book artist Frank Miller is best known for his graphic novels *Daredevil*, *Ronin*, and *Batman: The Dark Knight Returns*. Continuing the practice of depicting the city as protagonist established by Will Eisner (q.v.), Miller in *The Dark Knight* created an aggressive urban hell, populated by bloodthirsty punks, against which is pitted a cynical, middle-aged superhero. As brilliantly illuminated as its vision is bleak, *The Dark Knight* resplendently combines cinematic depiction of action and vibrant color in an illustrator's tour de force.

REFERENCE: "Will Eisner Interviews Chris Claremont, Frank Miller, and Wendy Pini," *Comics Journal* 89 (May 1984): 87–97; "Return of the Dark Knight: Kim Thompson Interviews Frank Miller," *Comics Journal* 101 (August 1985): 58–79.

Robin Moore 1925–

In 1965 writer Robin Moore, together with artist Joe Kubert (q.v.), created the short-lived comic strip *Tales of the Green Beret*. Robert Lowell (Robin) Moore was born in Boston on October 31, 1925, the son of Eleanor Turner and Robert Lowell Moore. He attended the Middlesex School in Concord, Massachusetts, and graduated from Belmont High School in 1944. He earned his A.B. at Harvard in 1949. In 1947 he was European correspondent for the *Boston Globe*. From 1949 to 1952 he was a television producer in New York City. Moore worked in public relations until 1965, when he wrote the book (*The Green Berets*) that served as basis for the later comic strip.

REFERENCES: Robin Moore and Jack Youngblood, *The Devil to Pay* (New York, 1961). Robin Moore: *The Green Berets* (New York, 1965); *The Country Team* (New York, 1967); *Fiedler* (Boston, 1968); *The French Connection* (Boston, 1969). "Pop Goes the War!" *Newsweek* 68 (September 12, 1966): 66. *Who's Who* 34 (1966–67): 1498.

Dick Moores 1909–1986

Dick Moores, author and artist of the daily *Gasoline Alley*, was born in Lincoln, Nebraska, on December 12, 1909. Moores's family later moved to Omaha, where he attended Omaha Central High School, and then to Fort Wayne, Indiana, where Moores graduated from South Side High School in 1926. After a year at Chicago's Academy of Fine Arts, Moores went to work as an assistant to Chester Gould (q.v.) on *Dick Tracy*, a position he held for five years. He later drew the *Jim Hardy* strip, subsequently retitled *Windy and Paddles*. At the same time he shared a Chicago studio with Frank King (q.v.), originator of *Gasoline Alley*. From 1942 to 1956 Moores worked for Walt Disney Studios, where he drew *Uncle Remus* and *Scamp*. In 1956 he moved to Florida, where he did the daily *Gasoline Alley* strips for Frank King.

REFERENCES: Dick Moores, *Gasoline Alley* (New York, 1976); *The Smoke from Gasoline Alley* (Kansas City, Kans., 1976); *Jim Hardy* (Westport, Conn., 1977). Chicago Tribune–New York News Syndicate, *Dick Moores and Bill Perry, Producers of "Gasoline Alley,"* (New York, 1969). Horn, pp. 276, 341, 427.

Gray Morrow 1934–

Since 1983 cartoonist Gray Morrow and author Don Kraar have created *Tarzan* for United Feature Syndicate.

REFERENCE: United Feature Syndicate, *Tarzan, Seventy-five Years Old and Still Swinging* (New York, September 22, 1987).

Zack Mosley 1906–

The creator of *Smilin' Jack*, Zack Terrell Mosley, was born on December 12, 1906, in Hickory, Oklahoma, the son of Zack Taylor and Irah Corinna Aycock Mosley. In 1925 he graduated from high school in Shawnee, Oklahoma. He attended the Chicago Academy of Fine Arts from 1926 to 1927, and studied at the Art Institute of Chicago until 1928. Mosley began flying lessons in 1932, and the following year created *Smilin' Jack*, later distributed by the Chicago Tribune–New York News Syndicate. The last *Smilin' Jack* appeared on April 1, 1973. Mosley makes his home in Stuart, Florida.

REFERENCES: Zack Mosley, *Smilin' Jack and the Daredevil Girl Pilot* (Racine, Wis., 1942); *Brave Coward Zack* (St. Petersburg, Fla., 1976). Sheridan, p. 148. Bruce Deutsch, "Smilin' Zack," *Flying* 45 (October 1949): 24–25. *Who's Who* 34 (1966–67): 1518. Horn, pp. 505, 623, 624.

Françoise Mouly 1955–

Françoise Mouly, since 1977 the publisher, coeditor, and designer of Raw Books and Graphics, was born in Neuilly, France, in 1955. She is married to cartoonist Art Spiegelman (q.v.).

REFERENCE: "Raw Data," in Art Spiegelman and Françoise Mouly, *Read Yourself Raw: The Graphix Anthology for Damned Intellectuals* (New York, 1987).

Cullen Murphy 1953–

Cullen Murphy, who often contributes stories to his father John Cullen Murphy's (q.v.) *Prince Valiant*, graduated in 1974 from Amherst College, where he studied medieval history. The managing editor of *The Atlantic* since 1985, Murphy has also served as senior editor at the *Wilson Quarterly*, and is a frequent contributor to such distinguished periodicals as *Harper's*.

REFERENCE: King Features Syndicate, *Prince Valiant Celebrates Fifty Years of High Adventure* (New York, n.d.).

Jimmy Murphy 1891–1965

Cartoonist James Edward Murphy, Jr., was born in Chicago on November 20, 1891, the son of James Edward and Clara Laura Burand Murphy. He studied at Creighton University in Omaha. From June to December of 1906 Murphy was a cartoonist for the *Omaha Examiner;* earlier that year he had worked for the *Omaha Bee* and the *Omaha World Herald*. In 1910 he moved to Washington, where he was a cartoonist for the *Spokane Inland Herald*. Before joining the *San Francisco Call and Post* on October 1, 1915, Murphy also worked on the *Oregon Daily Journal*. At the *Call and Post* he created his famous cartoon strips, including *Toots and Casper*, which was created in 1919 and ceased publication in 1956, and *It's Papa Who Pays*, which began in 1926. Murphy retired in 1958 and died in Beverly Hills, California, on March 9, 1965.

REFERENCES: *Who's Who* 9 (1916–17): 1781. Sheridan, pp. 20, 111. Stephen Becker, *Comic Art in America* (New York, 1959), p. 58. *Who Was Who* 4 (1961–68): 690. Couperie and Horn, p. 45. Nye, p. 221. Horn, pp. 506–507, 668, 669.

John Cullen Murphy 1919–

John Cullen Murphy, best known for *Big Ben Bolt* and *Prince Valiant*, was born on May 3, 1919, in New York City, the son of Doubleday executive Robert F. Murphy and Jane Finn Murphy. A protégé of next-door-neighbor artist Norman Rockwell, Murphy studied at the Chicago Art Institute, the Phoenix Art Institute, and the Art Students League of New York, where he worked with the legendary instructor George Bridgman. Murphy saw military service in the U.S. Army from 1941 to 1946, spending three years in the Pacific. After his discharge, Murphy began his career as an illustrator. His work has appeared in such magazines as *Collier's*, *Look*, *Esquire*, *Reader's Digest*, and *Sport*. In 1950 he created *Big Ben Bolt*, a comic strip authored by Elliot Caplin, brother of Al Capp (q.v.). In 1970 Murphy began his collaboration with Hal Foster (q.v.), taking over *Prince Valiant* upon Foster's retirement in 1979. Murphy has been president of the prestigious National Cartoonists Society, and is the recipient of the Elzie Segar prize for cartooning. He lives with his wife, the former Joan Byrne, in Cos Cob, Connecticut.

REFERENCES: King Features Syndicate, *John Cullen Murphy* (New York, n.d.); *Royal Celebration: Fifty Years of High Adventure with Prince Valiant* (New York, n.d.).

Russell Myers 1938–

On April 19, 1970, Russell Myers launched *Broom-Hilda*, his Tribune Media Services masterwork. Born in Pittsburg, Kansas, Myers was the son of a member of the business faculty at the University of Tulsa. Following his graduation from the University of Tulsa in 1960, Myers worked as a writer and illustrator for Hallmark Greeting Cards in Kansas City, Missouri, while in the evening experimenting with comic-strip concepts. "I was the world's most accomplished failure," stated Myers in a biography published by Tribune Media Services in October 1986. "Every year, almost on a schedule, I would do a strip, take it to New York, and fail. I became so adept that I could get the plane at 8 A.M., get to New York, get rejected by the six major syndicates, and be home in Kansas City by midnight. I got it down to a one-day experience. That only comes from years of practice." Myers's break came when he was contacted by Elliott Caplin, Al Capp's (q.v.) brother. "Elliott called me," recounted Myers, "and said he had an idea for a strip about a witch called Broom-Hilda and asked if I would send along some samples of greeting cards. . . . Caplin, who is a playwright and author of comic strips [*Dr. Kildare* and *The Heart of Juliet Jones*, among others], took the six strips to the Chicago Tribune–New York News Syndicate . . . and got a contract." Among the influences on his work numbered by Myers are W. C. Fields, Carl Barks (q.v.), Chester Gould (q.v.), Jack Benny, Edgar Bergen, and Fred Allen.

REFERENCES: Tribune Media Services, *Broom-Hilda's Scrapbook: Fifteen Years of Cherished Memories*, n.d.; *Russell Myers Biography*, October 1986. Horn, p. 509.

Mark Newgarden 1959–

Born in Brooklyn, New York, Mark Newgarden is a frequent contributor to *RAW*. With Art Spiegelman (q.v.) he created the *Garbage Pail Kids* for Topps Chewing Gum, Inc. An instructor at the New York School of Visual Arts, Newgarden has published in such diverse organs as *Spy*, *High Times*, and the *East Village Eye*.

REFERENCE: "Raw Data," in Art Spiegelman and Françoise Mouly, *Read Yourself Raw: The Graphix Anthology for Damned Intellectuals* (New York, 1987).

Diane Noomin 1947–

Diane Noomin, creator of the cynical underground heroine *Didi Glitz*, was born on May 13, 1947, in Brooklyn, New York, the daughter of Sam and Nessa Rosenblatt. She graduated in 1965 from the High School of Music and Art, and subsequently attended Brooklyn College and Pratt Institute. Since 1973 she has lived in San Francisco, where she is a driving force in underground comics. In 1980 she married cartoonist Bill Griffith (q.v.), creator of *Zippy the Pinhead*. In 1981 she collaborated with Les Nickelettes, a women's theater group, to produce *The Didi Glitz Story*, a musical comedy featuring her cartoon character. Her work has appeared in *Wimmen's Comix*, nos. 2, 3, 4, 8, 9, 10, 11, 12, 14, 15 (1973–74, 1980–86, 1988–89); *Twisted Sisters Comix* (1976); *Young Lust*, no. 6 (1980); *Lemme Outta Here* (1978); *Arcade, the Comics Revue* (1975–76); and *Weirdo*, nos. 17–18, 26 (1986, 1989). States Noomin: "Comics, to me, are a place for social commentary, satire, and personal revelations using a graphic narrative. I use scratchboard primarily because I enjoy the strong black and white 'woodcut' effect."

REFERENCES: *Titters, the First Collection of Humor by Women* (New York, 1976). *After Shock* (San Francisco, 1980). Dan Turner, "Stage: The Glitz Story," *Bay Area Reporter*, August 13, 1981. Alexandra Provence, "Didi Glitz Struts Her Campy Stuff," *San Francisco State Phoenix*, November 19, 1981.

Phil Nowlan 1888–1940

Writer Philip Francis Nowlan, who together with Richard Calkins (q.v.) created *Buck Rogers* in 1929, was born in Philadelphia in 1888. In 1910 Nowlan graduated from the University of Pennsylvania, and later was married to Teresa Marie Junker. He worked on the *Philadelphia Public Ledger*, the *North American*, and the *Retail Ledger*. He died of a stroke in Philadelphia on February 1, 1940.

REFERENCES: Obituary, *New York Times*, February 4, 1940, p. 41. Couperie and Horn, p. 60. Horn, pp. 21, 137, 523–524.

Paul Andrew Ollswang 1945–

Underground creator Paul Andrew Ollswang, best known for his *Dream of a Dog* comics, was born on May 24, 1945, in Manhattan, the son of Arthur Howard Ollswang and Pearl Silvers

Ollswang. Ollswang received a B.A. in philosophy from St. John's College in Annapolis, Maryland, and a B.F.A. from the University of Oregon in Eugene, Oregon, where he now resides. From 1967 to 1968 Ollswang was a salesman at Chrystalship; from 1968 to 1972 a salesman at the Sunshop; from 1972 to 1974 a salesman and buyer at the Buy and Sell Center; from 1972 to 1979 a classical music disc jockey at KZEL; from 1985 to 1986 a talk show host called "Mr. Nice Guy" at KRXX-AM 1450; and from 1986 to 1988 marketing director for the Genesis Juice Co-op. His publications include *The Song of Tom o' Bedlam* (1977), *Dreams of a Dog* (Rip Off Press, 1989), and *Tales of McEarth, Fast Food Planet* (Fantagraphics 1990). His comics have appeared in *Centrifugal Bumble-Puppy*, nos. 6, 8; *Primecuts*, no. 10; *The Whole Earth Review* (Fall 1987); and *Rip Off Comics*, nos. 19, 21, 22, 23. Ollswang observes, "Many people, many cartoonists, feel that philosophers should be the butt of jokes; I place philosophers in the middle of muddle-thinking 'normal people' and make 'normal people' the butt of my jokes. My central character — 'Rube' — is a philosopher, a socialist, a Marxist. He reacts to the racism, sexism, and sheer unthinking slothful ignorance of America. I only hope that 'normal people' will finally see the humor in *their own* ideas . . . through the eyes of Rube, dog, philosopher, and political animal." Ollswang's *Bartalk Duets* will be syndicated by the *Eugene* (Oreg.) *Comic News*. Ollswang lives in Eugene, Oregon, with his dog, Rosa Luxemburg.

REFERENCES: Fred Crafts, "The Mad, Mad, Mad World of Paul Ollswang," *Eugene* (Oreg.) *Register-Guard*, September 22, 1977, pp. D1–3. *The Open Gallery, A Cultural Guide to Lane County* (Eugene, Oreg., 1979).

Rose O'Neill 1874–1944

Familiar to all Americans as the inventor of the Kewpie, Rose O'Neill was born on June 24, 1874, in Wilkes-Barre, Pennsylvania, and raised in Battle Creek, Nebraska. In 1893 she moved to New York, where the artist found immediate success, selling her cartoons and illustrations to such important periodicals as *The Bookman*. In 1894 she joined her family in Bonniebrook, Missouri. In 1896 she returned to New York, where she married Gray Latham. In 1897 she became a staff artist for *Puck*, divorcing Latham in 1901. In 1902, she married *Puck*, editor Harry Leon Wilson, whom she divorced in 1907. She created *The Kewpies* in 1909, which was first published in the *Ladies' Home Journal*. *The Kewpies* was popularized by a doll of the same name, manufactured in 1912 in Waltershausen, Thuringia, Germany. In 1917 O'Neill syndicated *The Kewpies*, revived in 1935 for King Features Syndicate. She died in Springfield, Missouri, on April 6, 1944. In September 1989 the Brandywine River Museum at Chadds Ford, Pennsylvania, mounted a major retrospective of her work. Helen Goodman of the Fashion Institute of Technology served as guest curator of this monumental exhibition.

REFERENCES: Helen Goodman, *The Art of Rose O'Neill* (Chadds Ford, Pa., 1989). Horn, p. 529.

Frederick Burr Opper 1857–1937

Frederick Burr Opper was born on January 2, 1857, in Madison, Ohio, the son of an Austrian immigrant, Lewis Opper. When he was fourteen, he went to work on the *Madison Gazette*. His early cartoons were published in *Century*, *Scribner's*, *Saint Nicholas*, and *Wild Oats* magazines. In May 1899 he was hired by William Randolph Hearst's *New York Journal*, where his most famous strips, *Her Name Was Maud!* and *Happy Hooligan*, first appeared. In 1937 the *New York Times* said of Happy Hooligan that "although his metamorphosis from a pudgy tramp to a lank outcast was marked, he never lost his tin-can hat nor his healthy vulgarity." A thirty-first-birthday celebration for *Happy Hooligan* was attended by Herbert Hoover, Calvin Coolidge, and Alfred E. Smith. Opper was well known for his editorial cartoons, as well as for his comic strips. He died in New Rochelle, New York, of a heart ailment on August 28, 1937.

REFERENCES: F. B. Opper, *A Museum of Wonders* (New York, 1884); *Puck's Opper Book* (New York, 1888); *The Funny World* (New York, 1890); *The Folks of Funnyville* (New York, 1902); *Our Antediluvian Ancestors* (New York, 1903); *Happy Hooligan Home Again!* (New York, 1907); *Maud the Matchless* (New York, 1907); *Mother Goose* (New York, 1916); *Aesopus*

(Philadelphia, 1917); *Happy Hooligan: A Complete Compilation, 1904–1905* (Westport, Conn., 1977). Emma Opper, *Slate and Pencil People*, illus. by F. B. Opper (New York, 1885). Marion Kinnaird, *The Story of Happy Hooligan*, illus. by F. B. Opper (Springfield, Mass., 1932). Eugene Field, ed., *The Complete Tribune Primer*, illus. by F. B. Opper (Minneapolis, 1967). "Cartoons of Opper," *Bookman* 12 (November 10, 1900): 207. "Caricature Country and Its Inhabitants," *Independent* 53 (April 4, 1901): 778–781. B. O. Flower, "Cartoonist of Democracy," *Arena* 33 (June 1905): 583–593. R. L. McCardell, "Opper, Outcault, and Company," *Everybody's Magazine* 12 (June 1905): 763–772. Portrait, *Current Literature* 45 (December 1908): 631. *Who's Who* 16 (1930–31): 1692. Obituary, *New York Times*, August 28, 1937, p. 15. *Who Was Who* 1 (1897–1942): 917–918. Sheridan, p. 16. "Speaking of Pictures," *Life* 31 (July 30, 1951): 2–4. *World of Comic Art* 1 (June 1966): 30–33. Couperie and Horn, author index. Nye, pp. 217–218, 223. Horn, pp. 11, 77, 80–81, 160, 302, 530–531.

Martha Orr

Martha Orr created the strip *Apple Mary* in 1934. In 1938 she married and decided not to continue the strip. Publishers Syndicate then asked Allen Saunders (q.v.) to continue *Apple Mary*. He did so, but with significant changes, transforming the heroine into the wealthy widow Mary Worth.

REFERENCE: John Saunders, interviewed by Mark Johnson, November 29, 1989.

R. F. Outcault 1863–1928

Richard Felton Outcault, originator of *The Yellow Kid*, was born in Lancaster, Ohio, on January 14, 1863, the son of J. P. and Catherine Davis Outcault. After graduating from McMicken University in Cincinnati, Outcault married Mary Jane Martin on December 25, 1890. In 1894 he joined the staff of the *New York World*, where he produced the first well-known color cartoon in American newspapers, *Hogan's Alley*. Outcault drew *The Yellow Kid* for the *New York Journal* from 1895 to 1897. In 1901 he created *Pore Li'l Mose*, and in 1902 he produced *Buster Brown* for the *New York Herald*, a strip that became a model of fashion for children's clothes in the first decade of the twentieth century. In 1905 Outcault returned to the *New York Journal*, where he remained until his retirement in 1918. He continued to draw *Buster Brown* from 1906 to 1920. He died in Queens on September 5, 1928.

REFERENCES: R. F. Outcault, "Li'l Mose and the Beasts," *Current Literature* 30 (May 1901): 593; *Pore L'il Mose* (New York, 1902); *Buster Brown and His Resolutions* (New York, 1903); *Buster Brown Abroad* (New York, 1904); *Buster Brown's Pranks* (New York, 1905); *Tige, His Story* (New York, 1905); *My Resolutions: Buster Brown* (New York, 1906) *Buster and Mary Jane's Painting Book* (New York, 1907); *Buster Brown's Autobiography* (New York, 1907); *Outcault's Buster Brown* (New York, 1907); *Buster Brown's Fun and Nonsense* (New York, 1911); *Buster Brown, the Fun Maker* (New York, 1912); *Buster and Tige Here Again* (New York, 1914). Rick Marschall, *Buster Brown, 1906* (Westport, Conn., 1977). R. L. McCardell, "Opper, Outcault, and Company," *Everybody's Magazine* 12 (June 1905): 763–772. Portrait, *Current Literature* 45 (December 1908): 630. *Who's Who* 9 (1916–17): 1858–1859. Obituary, *New York Times*, September 26, 1928, p. 27. *Who Was Who* 1 (1897–1942): 924. Sheridan, pp. 16–17, 57, 217. Mallett, p. 323. "Buster Brown: Merchandising's Oldest Comic Trademark," *World of Comic Art* 1 (June 1966): 41. Couperie and Horn, author index. Nye, pp. 216–217, 223. Horn, pp. 11, 145, 533–534, 711.

Gary Panter 1950–

Born in Durant, Oklahoma, in 1950, Gary Panter is best known as the production designer for *Pee Wee's Playhouse* (CBS-TV). His graphic work has appeared in *Rolling Stone*, *Time*, and *Raw*.

REFERENCES: Gary Panter: *Jimbo* (New York, 1981); *Invasion of the Elvis Zombies* (New York, 1985); *Pee Dog*, with Jay Cotton (self-published, 1986); *Jimbo* (New York, 1986). "Raw

Data," in Art Spiegelman and Françoise Mouly, *Read Yourself Raw: The Graphix Anthology for Damned Intellectuals* (New York, 1987).

Brant Parker 1920–

Brant Parker, best known for his collaboration with Johnny Hart (q.v.) on *The Wizard of Id*, was born on August 26, 1920, in Los Angeles. After some training at the Otis Art Institute, Parker began his career as a cartoonist for the *Los Angeles Daily News*. He later worked for the Walt Disney Studios. From 1942 to 1945 Parker served in the U.S. Navy. He later became an employee of the *Binghamton Press* in New York. In this capacity, he served as judge of a local art contest, the winner of which was Johnny Hart (q.v.), Parker's future collaborator. *The Wizard of Id*, the result of their teamed efforts, began syndication on November 9, 1964. Parker received the coveted Reuben Award in 1984. He resides in Centreville, Virginia.

REFERENCES: King Features Syndicate, *Johnny Hart and Brant Parker* (New York, 1989). Horn, p. 539.

Russell Patterson 1894–1977

Illustrator, costume, stage-, and cinema-set designer Russell Patterson was born on December 26, 1894, in Omaha, Nebraska, the son of attorney William Francis and Kathleen Callahan Patterson, and raised in Newfoundland, Toronto, and Montreal. He studied at St. Patrick's School and McGill University, in Montreal, Canada, and at the Art Institute of Chicago. His comic strips included the French *Pierre et Pierrette*, which appeared in *La Patrie*, a Montreal paper, about 1913; *Film Flam;* and *Mamie* (1951–56). From 1920 to 1925 Patterson lived in France, where he studied under the aging Impressionist master Claude Monet. Upon his return from Europe Patterson studied architecture in Canada. He became best known for his popular drawings of women but also experimented with a puppet theater, worked as a costume designer, staged the production numbers for the Zeigfield Follies and designed costumes and sets for the movies. Patterson's works were exhibited at the Delaware Art Museum from June 24 to July 24, 1977.

REFERENCES: Russell Patterson, *A View From the Pit* (Kansas City, Kans., 1987). *AAA* 30 (1933): 658. "Puppets Invade Mickey Mouse's Domain," *Literary Digest* 119 (April 27, 1935): 20. Mallett, p. 331. Stephen Becker, *Comic Art in America* (New York, 1959), pp. 84–85. *Who's Who* 34 (1966–67): 1641. Horn, pp. 540–541.

Lute Pease 1869–1966

Lucius Curtis Pease, editor and cartoonist, was born on March 27, 1869, in Winnemuca, Nevada, one of the five children of Lucius Curtis and Mary Isabel Hutton Pease. Orphaned at the age of five, he became the ward of his paternal grandfather, a farmer in Charlotte, Vermont. Pease graduated from the Franklin Academy in Malone, New York, in 1887. After a series of odd jobs he became political cartoonist on the *Portland Oregonian* in 1895, a position he held until he joined the 1897 Klondike gold rush. From 1901 to 1902 he was the first resident U.S. commissioner in Nome, Alaska. In 1902 Pease returned to the *Oregonian*, and in 1905 became editor of the *Portland Pacific Monthly*. At the *Pacific Monthly* he accepted for publication Jack London's novel *Martin Eden*, which he illustrated. In 1913 Pease came East and became political cartoonist on the *Newark Evening News* in June 1914. He was awarded the Pulitzer Prize for a 1948 cartoon of John L. Lewis. Pease retired in 1952; he died in Maplewood, New Jersey, on August 16, 1966, at age ninety-four. Pease's best-known comic strip was *Powder Pete*.

REFERENCES: Lute Pease, "Cartoonists As They See Themselves," *Literary Digest* 116 (November 4, 1933): 11. *CB*, 1949, pp. 475–477. Obituary, *New York Times*, August 17, 1966, p. 19.

Harvey Pekar 1939–

Born in Cleveland, Ohio, on October 8, 1939, the son of grocery-store owner Saul Pekar and

Dora Pekar, Cleveland comic-book author and playwright Harvey Pekar began his autobiographical *American Splendor* in 1976. "By then," related Pekar to *Washington Post* correspondent Henry Allen, "I had a hell of a lot of influences, like novelists and short-story writers and comedians like Lenny Bruce and movies like 'The Bicycle Thief,' stuff like that. . . . Dostoyevsky, I remember reading that 'Notes From Underground' and being real impressed with it, but I was also impressed with . . . George Orwell's 'Down and Out in Paris and London.' " *Newsweek* has described Pekar as "the high priest of comic-book naturalism." Pekar's saga, which celebrates the humble preoccupations of ordinary people, is illustrated by numerous underground artists, including R. Crumb (q.v.). On May 16, 1983, Pekar married cartoonist Joyce Brabner (q.v.). States Pekar, "Because the potential of the comic form has scarcely been explored, it is particularly interesting to me. . . . I have access to the same words as any novelist, poet, or dramatist and can arrange them in any order I choose. My primary influences have been prose fiction, comedy (stand-up and on radio and TV) and film. My work is autobiographical and deals with everyday events, which writers throughout history have ignored but which ultimately influence human behavior far more than seldom-occurring 'big' or traumatic events. There are acts of heroism and great comedy happening around us every day."

REFERENCES: Harvey Pekar, *American Splendor* (Garden City, N.Y., 1986); *More American Splendor* (Garden City, N.Y., 1987). "How I Quit Reading Dreiser and Found Neo-Realism in a Comic from Cleveland," *Village Voice*, (December 31, 1979). "Interview," *Comics Journal* 97 (April 1985). "Harvey Pekar," *Cleveland Plain Dealer*, April 20, 1986; "The Cosmic Meets the Ordinary," *New York Times Book Review*, May 11, 1986; "Comics and Genre Literature," *Comics Journal* 130 (July 1989); Henry Allen, "The Not-Ready-for-Prime-Time Pekar," *Washington Post*, November 2, 1987, pp. C1–3; Peter S. Prescott with Ray Sawhill, "The Comic Book (Gulp!) Grows Up," *Newsweek* (January 18, 1988): 70–71; Joseph Witek, *Comic Books As History* (University of Mississippi Press, 1989/1990).

Bill Perry 1905–

Bill Perry, Frank King's (q.v.) longtime assistant, began doing the complete drawing for the Sunday *Gasoline Alley* in April 1951. Born William M. Perry on September 26, 1905, in Chicago, he attended public schools and graduated from Carl Schurz High School in 1924. Before working for King, Perry was Carl Ed's (q.v.) assistant on *Harold Teen*. From 1945 to 1951 he drew *Ned Handy, Adventures in the Deep South*, a *Chicago Tribune* Sunday feature he gave up in 1951 when he began *Gasoline Alley*.

REFERENCE: Chicago Tribune–New York News Syndicate, *Dick Moores and Bill Perry, Producers of "Gasoline Alley"* (New York, 1969). *Who's Who in American Art* (1978).

Mike Peters 1943–

Mike Peters, creator of Tribune Media Services' *Mother Goose and Grimm*, is a native of St. Louis, Missouri. After graduating from Washington University in 1965, Peters went to work for the *Chicago Daily News* as a political cartoonist. Peters later served as a military artist for the Seven Psychological Operations Group, in Okinawa. After completing his tour of duty, Peters returned to the *Daily News*. In 1969, at the suggestion of cartoonist Bill Maudlin, Peters joined the staff of *The Dayton* (Ohio) *Daily News*, where his cartoons first enjoyed national syndication. Bantam has published three compilations of Peters's work: *The Nixon Chronicles* (1976), *Clones, You Idiot* (1978), and *Win One for the Geezer* (1982). In 1985 Peters created his popular strip *Mother Goose and Grimm*. He is the recipient of the Pulitzer Prize (1981) and the Reuben Award (1982). Peters resides in Beaver Creek, Ohio, with his wife, Marian, an English teacher, and daughters Marci, Tracy, and Molly.

REFERENCE: Tribune Media Services, Inc., *Mike Peters Biography*, October 28, 1985.

Daniel Pinkwater 1941–

Award-winning author and National Public Radio commentator Daniel Pinkwater is, with artist Tony Auth (q.v.), the creator of *Norb* (1989).

REFERENCE: King Features Syndicate, *Norb* (New York, 1989).

John Prentice 1920–

John Prentice, best known for his precisionist rendering of *Rip Kirby*, was born on October 17, 1920, in Whitney, Texas. From 1940 to 1946 Kirby served in the U.S. Navy, surviving the bombing of Pearl Harbor and eight military campaigns. After his discharge, Prentice briefly attended the Art Institute of Pittsburgh. In 1947 he moved to New York City. Following the tragic death of Alex Raymond (q.v.) on September 6, 1956, Prentice was selected to continue Raymond's *Rip Kirby*. The strip has thrice (most recently in 1987) been accorded the National Cartoonists Society's silver plaque for "Best Story Strip of the Year." Prentice and his wife, Antonia, live in Westport, Connecticut.

REFERENCES: King Features Syndicate, *John Prentice* (New York, n.d.). Horn, pp. 564–565.

Joshua Quagmire 1952–

Joshua Quagmire, the creator of *Cutey Bunny*, was born in Peoria, Illinois, in 1952. From 1972 to 1976 Quagmire served in the U.S. Marine Corps Air Wing. In 1978 he was a switchman for General Telephone. His publications include *Army Surplus Komikz Featuring Cutey Bunny* (Eclipse, 1982–), *Fantasy Book, Featuring the Nasty Naughty Nazi Ninja Nudnik Elves* (Fantasy Book Enterprises, 1985–87), and comics in *Grunts*, no. 1; *Launch*, no. 1; *Critters*, no. 1; *Telegraph Wire*, no. 14; *Cerebus*, nos. 51–52; *California Girls*, nos. 4, 6; and *Rip Off Comics* (1988–). Reflects Quagmire, "I suppose my Comix pretty much have to speak for themselves. . . . I suppose the main thing is to entertain. . . . And possibly [one] might be able to sneak in a li'l education without the readers realizing it. . . . I learned long ago that No One wants to be preached to by a Bunny Rabbit!" Quagmire lives in Hollywood, California.

REFERENCE: Dennis Wepman, "Joshua Quagmire," in *Contemporary Graphic Artists*, vol. 2.

Mac Raboy 1914–1967

Emanuel Raboy was born on April 9, 1914, in New York, the only child of Isaac and Sarah Raboy. He attended P.S. 44 and DeWitt Clinton High School in the Bronx. After graduation he worked with the WPA and his wood engravings were included in traveling exhibitions. Raboy later worked at Fawcett Publications, where he produced the *Captain Marvel, Jr.*, comic books. In 1948 he was recruited by King Features Syndicate to do the *Flash Gordon* Sunday strips.

REFERENCES: Mel Heimer, *Mac Raboy*, King Features Syndicate Biographical Series, no. 107 (New York, n.d.). Horn, pp. 141, 158, 254, 327, 499, 571.

Sam C. Rawls

Sam C. Rawls, creator of King Features Syndicate's *Pops Place*, was born in Clarksville, Mississippi. He attended Florida State University. Rawls has been a rodeo rider, a bulldozer operator, and a sportswriter. Formerly the editorial cartoonist for the *Atlanta Constitution*, Rawls is the illustrator of *How to Speak Southern* and *The Great American Moon Pie Handbook*. In 1986 *Pops Place* began syndication. The past president of the Association of American Editorial Cartoonists, Rawls is the recipient of numerous honors, including Florida Cartoonist of the Year and Florida Press Club Best Illustrator.

REFERENCE: King Features Syndicate, *Sam C. Rawls* (New York, n.d.).

Alex Raymond 1909–1956

Alex Raymond, best known as the creator of *Flash Gordon*, was born in New Rochelle, New York, on October 2, 1909, the son of Alexander Gillespie and Beatrice Wallaz Crossley Raymond. He studied at Iona Preparatory School, in New Rochelle, between 1925 and 1928 on an athletic scholarship, and the following year was a student at the Grand Central School of Art, New York. From 1930 to 1932 he was an artist's apprentice at King Features Syndicate, where he assisted Lyman Young in drawing *Tim Tyler's Luck*. Raymond originated the strips *Jungle Jim* and *Flash Gordon* in 1934, and collaborated with mystery writer Dashiell Hammett on *Secret Agent X-9*. In 1946 he began his final strip, *Rip Kirby*. He was recipient of the De Beck Award for excellence in cartooning in 1949, and served as president of the National Cartoonists Society from 1950 to 1952. Although his paintings were exhibited at the National Gallery of Art after World War II, Raymond, according to the *New York Times*, preferred the comic strip as an art form. Raymond died in an auto accident in Westport, Connecticut, on September 6, 1956.

REFERENCES: Alex Raymond, *Flash Gordon in the Caves of Mongo* (New York, 1937); *Flash Gordon* (New York, 1967); *Flash Gordon into the Water World of Mongo* (New York, 1971); *Flash Gordon* (New York, 1974); *Flash Gordon Escapes to Arboria* (New York, 1977); *Flash Gordon Versus Frozen Horrors* (New York, 1978); *Flash Gordon Joins the Power Men* (New York, 1978); *Flash Gordon* (New York, 1983); Alex Raymond and Dashiell Hammett, *Secret Agent X-9* (Philadelphia, 1934); *Secret Agent X-9* (New York, 1976); *Dashiell Hammett's Secret Agent X-9* (New York, 1983). Marion Ryder, *Secret Watches*, illus. by Alex Raymond (New York, 1941). Sheridan, pp. 160, 230–232. Obituary, *New York Times*, September 7, 1956, p. 24. *Who Was Who* 3 (1951–60): 714. Obituary of Dashiell Hammett, *New York Times*, January 11, 1961, p. 47. "Where Are They Now? Creators of *Buck Rogers* and *Flash Gordon*," *Newsweek* 74 (August 4, 1969): 8. Couperie and Horn, author index. Nye, pp. 228–229. Horn, pp. 573–574.

Bill Rechin 1930–

Best known for his rendering of *Crock*, Bill Rechin is a graduate of the State University of New York at Buffalo. During the Korean War, Rechin served in the U.S. Army, creating training materials, including film strips and animated cartoons. After his discharge, Rechin worked in Washington, D.C., at a graphics studio whose clients included government agencies. In 1975 he joined forces with author Don Wilder (q.v.) to create the comic strip *Crock*, which began distribution through Field Enterprises on October 26. In 1987 *Crock* syndication was taken over by North America Syndicate.

REFERENCE: King Features Syndicate, *Bill Rechin and Don Wilder* (New York, 1989).

John Reiner 1956–

John Reiner, artist's assistant to the late Bill Hoest (q.v.), was born in 1956 in New York City and raised on Long Island. In 1974 he graduated from Smithtown High School. He attended the State University of New York at Stony Brook, from which he graduated in 1978 with a degree in psychology. In 1974 Reiner met the legendary Mort Drucker (q.v.) of *Mad* magazine fame, who encouraged his interest in cartooning. In 1975 he was hired by Joe Simon, creator of *Captain America*. He also worked for Marvel Comics. In 1984 he was hired by Drucker to work on King Features Syndicate's strip *Benchley*, which he did until 1986, when he was employed by Hoest to assist with *The Lockhorns*, *Agatha Crumm*, and *What a Guy!*

REFERENCE: King Features Syndicate, *John Reiner* (New York, 1989).

Frank Ridgeway 1930–

Cartoonist-writer Frank Ridgeway, the co-creator with illustrator Ralston Jones (q.v.) of *Mr. Abernathy*, was born on April 7, 1930, in Danbury, Connecticut. Ridgeway attended Danbury public schools, the Art Students League of New York, and the Cartoonists' and Illustrators' School of New York City. Ridgeway served as an instructor at the Famous Artists School in Connecticut. On October 14, 1959, *Mr. Abernathy* began syndication by King Features.

REFERENCES: King Features Syndicate, *Mr. Abernathy* (New York, n.d.). Horn, p. 496.

Frank Robbins 1917–

Frank Robbins was born in Boston on September 9, 1917. When he was fifteen his family moved to New York, where he met muralist Edward Trumbull, then color director for the Rockefeller Center project. Through Trumball, Robbins met the Rockefellers, from whom he would receive a grant to study and paint. For a time Robbins did commercial illustration for RKO Pictures. In 1938 he became the artist of *Scorchy Smith*, originated by Noel Sickles and later drawn by Bert Christman. In 1944 Robbins created his own strip, *Johnny Hazard*, the adventures of a flyer.

REFERENCES: Sheridan, p. 120. Couperie and Horn, author index. Mel Heimer, *Frank Robbins*, King Features Syndicate Biographical Series, no. 12 (New York, n.d.). Horn, pp. 101, 278, 344, 528, 584, 604, 610. *Who's Who in American Art* (1978).

Trina Robbins 1938–

Cartoonist Trina Robbins, long associated with the feminist movement, was born in Brooklyn on August 17, 1938, the daughter of Max Perlson and Elizabeth Rosenman Perlson. She attended Cooper Union. Married in 1960, Robbins moved to Los Angeles. The marriage ended in 1966, and Robbins returned to New York. There she opened a boutique and created the comic strip *Suzy Slumgoddess* for the fledgling *East Village Other*. In 1969 she moved to San Francisco with artist Kim Deitch (q.v.); their daughter Casey was born in 1970. Robbins's work was prominently featured in the feminist paper *It Ain't Me Babe*, published in Berkeley, and in a comic book of the same name that appeared in 1971. Robbins was one of the founders of *Wimmen's Comix*. States Robbins: "I've never really fit into the small world of comics; too slick for the undergrounds, not grey and fussy enough for the Marvel/D.C. crowd. If that weren't enough, I don't *say* the same things they do. I continue to object to the extremely graphic violence (all too often directed at women) gleefully exhibited in *both* comics worlds, and have a growing desire to do something *meaningful* with my work, rather than simply to amuse. This desire has been partly satisfied by the AIDS benefit book *Strip AIDS USA*, which I co-edited, and by the pro-choice benefit book (a benefit for NOW) which I am currently putting together. The Europeans, who define my style as 'la ligne claire,' seem to accept me more readily than their American counterparts."

REFERENCES: Trina Robbins and Ronald Levitt Lanyi, "Trina, Queen of the Underground Cartoonists — An Interview," *Journal of Popular Culture* 12 (Spring 1979): 737–754; *The Silver Metal Lover* (New York, 1985); Trina Robbins and Catherine Yronwode, *Women and the Comics* (Forestville, Calif., 1985); "Trina Robbins," *(kar-ton') new comic arts journal* 1 (1988): 6–8; "Comments on Crumb," *Blab!* 3 (Fall 1988): 92–94.

Harry S. Robins 1950–

Harry S. Robins, best known as the co-creator of *Dino Boy*, was born on November 28, 1950, in Lebanon, Indiana, the son of Harry Franklin Robins and Mary Louise Scifres Robins. In 1972 Robins graduated from the University of Arizona, where he majored in English and minored in history. Robins has worked as a truck driver and construction worker, actor and playwright, film inspector, file clerk, and freelance artist, illustrator, writer, screenwriter, film actor, and radio broadcaster. His powerful illustrations have appeared in *The Fringes of Reason*, a *Whole Earth Catalog* (1989), *The Book of the Sub-Genius* (Simon & Schuster, 1987), and Arthur Conan Doyle's *The Poison Belt* (Easton Press, forthcoming). Robins is also an accomplished author, whose work has appeared in *Gnosis* magazine since 1985. His comics have appeared in *Coverup Lowdown* (1977), *Food Comics/Comix* (1980), *Weirdo*, nos. 2, 5, 24 (1981, 1982, 1988), *Rip Off Comix*, nos. 10, 11, 12, 13, 20, 23, *Fat Freddy's Comics and Stories*, no. 1 (1983), *Dr. Wertham's Comix and Stories* (1987), *Anarchy Comics*, no. 4 (1987), *Viper* (1985), *Cannibal Romance* (1986), *"Bob's" Favorite Comics* (Rip Off Press, 1989), *Heck!* (Rip Off Press, 1989), and *Dinoboy Comics* (Rip Off Press, 1990). States Robins, "Comics are to me principally a vehicle for the expression of satire. In an overview of my own work, the one theme which perennially appears seems to be the pronounced distance between expressed intentions and aspirations on the one hand, and on the other, the rather pathetic events which are born from such once noble plans. One could summarize the subject as: *the failure of intention to make good.*" Robins lives in San Francisco.

Paul Robinson 1898–1974

Artist Paul Robinson, originator of *Etta Kett*, was born in Ohio in 1898, the son of a farmer. His youth was spent in Ohio, at Sandusky, Findlay, and Cedar Point. In 1918 he moved to New York, where he worked as an animator for the Bray Studios. Robinson claimed creation of the first color animation in 1920, a distinction also credited to Max Fleischer (q.v.) and Walt Disney (q.v.). In 1925 Robinson started his teen strip, *Etta Kett*, for King Features Syndicate. *Etta Kett* ceased publication in 1974.

REFERENCES: Paul Robinson, *ASC Cartooning Course* (Sandusky, Ohio, 1922). Mel Heimer, *Paul Robinson*, King Features Syndicate Biographical Series, no. 24 (New York, n.d.). Horn, p. 237.

Sharon Rudahl 1947–

Wimmen's Comix creator Sharon Rudahl was born on August 4, 1947, in Arlington, Virginia, the daughter of Ruth and Norman Kahn. A National Merit Scholar, Rudahl attended Cooper Union, from which she received her B.F.A. in 1969. From 1972 to 1975 Rudahl worked at the University of Wisconsin in Madison, where she illustrated educational materials. From 1982 to 1985 she was a writer and cartoonist for *Playgirl* magazine. Her publications include *Acid Temple Ball* (Olympia Press, 1969); *Take Over* (1971–72); and *Crystal Night* (Kitchen Sink, 1979). Since 1972 her work has appeared regularly in *Wimmen's Comix*. She has also contributed to *Ms*, *National Lampoon*, *WomenSports*, and *Chess Life*. States Rudahl, "Comics seemed like honest work to me, like illuminating manuscripts or building furniture, a need that was unsatisfied by modern art." Rudahl lives in Los Angeles.

Tom K. Ryan 1926–

Born in Anderson, Indiana, on June 6, 1926, the son of Francis Ryan and Katherine Ryan, Tom K. Ryan was raised in Muncie. He attended Notre Dame University and the University of Cincinnati. In 1965 Ryan created the comic strip *Tumbleweeds*, twenty compilations of which have been published by Fawcett. First distributed by Lew Little, *Tumbleweeds* is now a North America Syndicate feature. Ryan and his wife, Joanne, live in Boca Raton, Florida.

REFERENCES: King Features Syndicate, *Tom K. Ryan* (New York, n.d.). Horn, pp. 594, 673. P. Pinella, "Rolling Along with Tumbleweeds," *Saturday Evening Post* 251. (November 1979): 70–77.

Bud Sagendorf 1915–

Since 1958 the cartoonist for *Popeye*, Forrest Cowles Sagendorf was born in Wenatchee, Washington, on March 22, 1915, the son of engineer Philip Sagendorf and Evelyn Cowles Sagendorf. While a student at Santa Monica High School, Sagendorf became an apprentice to *Popeye*'s creator, the legendary Elzie Segar (q.v.), whom he assisted from 1932 to 1938. From 1939 to 1945 he edited *Popeye*. He then became King Features Syndicate's assistant comic-art director, a post he held until he became *Popeye*'s author and artist in 1959. Sagendorf has also since 1945 created *Popeye* comic books, books, toys, and games. He also wrote and drew the Famous Artists School's cartooning curriculum. In 1986 Sagendorf relinquished the daily *Popeye*. Sagendorf lives in Connecticut and Sarasota, Florida, with his wife, Nadia, who serves as curator of Nadia Sagendorf's Miniature Popeye Museum.

REFERENCES: Bud Sagendorf, *Popeye, The First Fifty Years* (New York: King Features Syn-

dicate and Workman Publishing Company, 1979). King Features Syndicate, *Bud Sagendorf* (New York, n.d.).

Richard Sala 1956–

Underground-comics creator Richard Sala was born on June 2, 1956, in Oakland, California, the son of Vincent J. Sala, an antique dealer, and Nancy Rogers Sala, a housewife. Sala received his B.F.A. in 1979 from Arizona State University, in Tempe, and his M.F.A. in 1982 from Mills College, in Oakland, California. Among his numerous comics creations are *Night Drive* (1984), and strips in *Raw*, no. 8 (1986); *Escape*, no. 9 (1986); *Prime Cuts*, nos. 1, 2, 4, 7, 8 (1987–88); *Twist*, nos. 2, 3 (1988); *Blab*, nos. 3, 4 (1988–89); *Street Music*, nos. 1, 3 (1988–89); *Taboo*, no. 2 (1989); and *Heck* (Rip Off Press, 1989). His work has also appeared in *Glamour*, *New York Woman*, *Savvy*, *New York*, *Premiere*, and *Mother Jones*. States Sala, "My drawings and stories often convey the anxiety of living in a seemingly irrational, threatening world — a world filled with phantoms and mysterious shadows, where fear breeds suspicion and violent impulses. Quirky and absurd, with elements of pulp culture — fragments of detective thrillers and old-time horror films — the resulting work is often a dark-humored burlesque of mystery and danger." Sala lives in Berkeley, California.

REFERENCES: *Comics Journal* 100 (July 1985): 208; *Comics Journal* 102 (September 1985): 47. Steve Bissette, Introduction to "Hate Mail," *Taboo* 2 (September 1989).

Art Sansom 1920–

Art Sansom, creator of the Newspaper Enterprise Association's Reuben Award–winning *Born Loser*, was born in Cleveland, Ohio. After graduating from Ohio Wesleyan University, Sansom in 1945 joined the staff of the Newspaper Enterprise Association. There he worked as an illustrator in the comic-art department, for twenty years penning works originated by others, until, in 1965, he created his own strip, *The Born Loser*. Sansom resides in Lakewood, Ohio.

REFERENCES: "The Born Loser Comes Up a Winner — Again!," *AM & PM*, "Profile," Summer 1988. April Zion and Nancy Nicolelis, *The Born Loser by Art Sansom*; *The Born Loser Is a Winner in Reader Surveys*; *The Born Loser Wins Another Comics Poll*; *The Born Loser Wins Reuben Award for Best Humor Strip*, news releases (Newspaper Enterprise Association, n.d.).

Allen Saunders 1899–1986

Best known for the comic strip *Mary Worth*, writer Allen Saunders was at one time a professor of French at Wabash College, his alma mater. He then became drama critic for the *Toledo News-Bee*, after which he wrote the continuity for Elmer Waggon's *Big Chief Wahoo*, which first appeared in 1936. In 1940 Saunders and female cartoonist Dale Connor took over Martha Orr's (q.v.) *Apple Mary*, which had begun in 1932 as a commentary on the Depression. The strip was retitled *Mary Worth's Family* and produced under the pseudonym Dale Allen. In 1947 Dale Connor was replaced by Ken Ernst (q.v.), who continues to draw *Mary Worth*. The only strip actually drawn by Saunders was an early work, *Miserable Moments*. Saunders retired in 1979, succeeded by his son John (q.v.) on *Mary Worth*.

REFERENCES: Allen Saunders, *Three Taps at Twelve* (New York, 1933); *Standard Equipment* (New York, 1937); *A Crown on the Hall Tree* (New York, 1940). Sheridan, pp. 193–194. Ken Ernst and Allen Saunders, "Mary Worth and Us," *Collier's* 123 (January 8, 1949): 45. Allen Saunders, "Mary Worth and the Affluent Society," in *The Funnies: An American Idiom*, ed. by D. M. White and Robert Abel (London, 1963), pp. 274–283. Couperie and Horn, pp. 109, 113. Nye, p. 231. Horn. p. 600.

John Saunders 1924–

Born in Crawfordville, Indiana, on September 9, 1924, author John Saunders has worked as producer for television and newspaper chains and as a news anchorman. A graduate of Northwestern University, Saunders married Alice Jean Shelley in 1947. In 1950 he joined forces with his father, Allen Saunders (q.v.), to produce the script for *Steve Roper*. In 1955 he became *Roper*'s primary scriptwriter. In 1965 he created the racially integrated *Dateline: Danger* with artist Alden MacWilliams. Following his father's 1979 retirement, Saunders took over *Mary Worth*. The Saunders reside in Waterville, Ohio, and Naples, Florida.

REFERENCE: King Features Syndicate, *John Saunders Biography* (New York, n.d.).

Al Scaduto 1928–

Best known for his work on King Features Syndicate's *They'll Do It Every Time*, artist Al Scaduto was born in the Bronx on July 12, 1928. He was educated at the School of Industrial Art and at the Art Students League of New York. In 1946 he was hired by King Features Syndicate. There, in 1948, he became cartoonist Bob Dunn's (q.v.) assistant on Jimmy Hatlo's (q.v.) *They'll Do It Every Time*. Upon Hatlo's death in 1963, Scaduto became the artist of both the Sunday and the daily version of the strip. From 1966 to 1967 Scaduto worked on *Little Iodine*. In 1979 Scaduto received the award for Best Panel Strip from the National Cartoonists Society. He lives in Jericho, New York, with his wife, Joyce.

REFERENCE: King Features Syndicate, *Al Scaduto* (New York, n.d.).

Jim Scancarelli 1941–

Jim Scancarelli, best known for his rendering of *Gasoline Alley*, was born in the Bronx on August 24, 1941, but raised in Charlotte, North Carolina. After serving in the U.S. Navy, where, stated the artist, "during the Cuban crises . . . [I] prepared secret slide art of Soviet missile silos," Scancarelli became art director for the *Johnny Cash* and *Bill Anderson* television shows. After serving as Dick Moores's (q.v.) assistant on *Gasoline Alley* and as George Breisacher's assistant on *Mutt and Jeff*, Scancarelli took over *Gasoline Alley* in 1986. In addition to his work as an artist, Scancarelli is a fiddler and comic-strip collector.

REFERENCE: National Cartoonists Society, *National Cartoonists Society Album* (Greenwich, Conn., 1988).

Mary Theresa Schmich 1954–

Mary Theresa Schmich, who scripts Tribune Media Services' *Brenda Starr*, was born in Georgia and raised in Phoenix, Arizona, graduating from Gerard High School. She graduated from Pomona College in Claremont, California, and was the recipient of a Rotary International Foundation fellowship for foreign study. In 1979, after her sojourn in France, Schmich enrolled at Stanford University as a graduate student in journalism. Among the papers for which she has worked are the *Los Angeles Times*, the *Peninsula Times Tribune* (Palo Alto, Calif.), the *Orlando Sentinel*, and the *Chicago Tribune*. Schmich resides in Chicago.

REFERENCE: Tribune Media Services, *Mary Theresa Schmich Biography*, October 21, 1985.

"Bunny" Schultze 1866–1939

Carl Emil Schultze, the originator of *Foxy Grandpa*, was born in Lexington, Kentucky, on May 25, 1886, the son of Charles and Jane Delph Schultze. He attended public schools in Cassel, Germany, and Lexington, Kentucky. In January 1900 he began drawing cartoons for newspapers, using the pseudonym Bunny. *Foxy Grandpa*, the strip that was to rival *Buster Brown* and *The Katzenjammer Kids* in popularity, first appeared in the *New York Herald* on January 7, 1900. It was taken over by the *New York American* on February 17, 1902. When Hearst dropped the strip, it was distributed by the C. J. Mar Syndicate (1912–13). Although *Foxy Grandpa* continued until 1922, it declined in popularity after World War I, intermittently appearing in such papers as the *Philadelphia Evening Ledger* and the *New York Press*. In 1935, through the Association for Improving the Condition of the Poor, the destitute Schultze found work with the German American Relief Conference. He was working with the WPA

when he died of heart failure on January 18, 1939.

REFERENCES: Carl Schultze, *The Adventures of Foxy Grandpa* (New York, 1900); *Foxy Grandpa's Mother Goose* (New York, 1903); *New Adventures of Foxy Grandpa* (New York, 1903); *Foxy Grandpa Up to Date* (New York, 1904); *Foxy Grandpa's Surprise* (New York, 1905); *The Merry Pranks of Foxy Grandpa* (Chicago, 1905); *Foxy Grandpa's Triumphs* (New York, 1907). Portrait, *Current Literature* 45 (December 1908): 630. *Who's Who* 9 (1916–17). Obituary, *New York Times*, January 19, 1939, p. 42. *Who Was Who* 1 (1897–1942): 1091. Horn, pp. 261, 602.

Charles Schulz 1922–

Cartoonist Charles Schulz was born in Minneapolis, Minnesota, on November 26, 1922, the son of Carl and Dena Halverson Schulz. He attended high school in St. Paul. His artistic training was limited to enrollment in a correspondence course given by Art Instruction, Incorporated, of Minneapolis. Schulz was drafted in 1943 and served in France and Germany. He returned to St. Paul after the war, where he worked at lettering cartoons for a religious magazine. In 1948 the artist sold some cartoons to the *Saturday Evening Post*, and the United Feature Syndicate bought a Schulz strip entitled *Li'l Folks*, distributed as *Peanuts*. Schulz was named Cartoonist of the Year by the National Cartoonists Society in 1955. *Peanuts* has since been animated for television, anthologized, and made the subject of numerous articles. In 1985, a major retrospective of Schulz's work curated by Christina Orr-Cahall was mounted by the Oakland Museum, subsequently traveling to the Albuquerque Museum, the Art Institute of Chicago, the Norton Gallery and School of Art, the Evansville Museum, the Palm Springs Desert Museum, the Brooklyn Children's Museum, the Huntsville Museum of Art, the San Antonio Museum of Art, and the University of Minnesota Art Museum. The show was complemented by Schulz's *You Don't Look Thirty-five, Charlie Brown!* (New York, 1985). In 1990 the Louvre's Museum of Decorative Arts hosted a major Schulz retrospective on the occasion of Snoopy's fortieth birthday.

REFERENCES: Charles Schulz: *A Charlie Brown Christmas* (Cleveland, 1965); *Charlie Brown's All-Stars* (Cleveland, 1966); *Home Is on Top of a Dog House* (New York, 1966); *Snoopy and the Red Baron* (New York, 1966); *It's the Great Pumpkin, Charlie Brown* (Cleveland, 1967); *You're in Love, Charlie Brown* (Cleveland, 1968); *"He's Your Dog, Charlie Brown"* (Cleveland, 1968); *Who Do You Think You Are, Charlie Brown?* (London, 1968); *Suppertime* (San Francisco, 1968); *Adelante, Charlie Brown* (New York, 1969); *A Boy Named Charlie Brown* (New York, 1969); *Charlie Brown's Yearbook* (New York, 1969); *Snoopy and His Sopwith Camel* (New York, 1969); *Peanuts Cook Book* (San Francisco, 1969); *It Was a Short Summer, Charlie Brown* (New York, 1970); *You're Out of Sight, Charlie Brown* (New York, 1970); *Play It Again, Charlie Brown* (New York, 1971); *Snoopy and "It Was a Dark and Stormy Night"* (New York, 1971); *Snoopy's Secret Code Book* (New York, 1971); *You've Come a Long Way, Charlie Brown* (New York, 1971); *Ha Ha Herman* (New York, 1972); *The "Snoopy, Come Home" Movie Book* (New York, 1972); *Snoopy's Grand Slam* (New York, 1972); *The Charlie Brown Dictionary* (New York, 1973); *Thompson Is in Trouble, Charlie Brown* (New York, 1973); *You're the Guest of Honor, Charlie Brown* (New York, 1973); *The Snoopy Festival* (New York, 1974); *Win a Few, Lose a Few, Charlie Brown* (New York, 1974); *There's No Time for Love, Charlie Brown* (New York, 1974); *A Charlie Brown Thanksgiving* (New York, 1974); *Peanuts Jubilee* (New York, 1975); *It's a Mystery, Charlie Brown* (New York, 1975); *Speak Softly and Carry a Beagle* (New York, 1975); *Charlie Brown's Super Book of Things to Do and Collect* (New York, 1975); *Be My Valentine, Charlie Brown* (New York, 1976); *"I Never Promised You an Apple Orchard"* (New York, 1976); *It's the Easter Beagle, Charlie Brown* (New York, 1976); *You're a Good Sport, Charlie Brown* (New York, 1976); *Don't Hassle Me with Your Sighs, Chuck* (New York, 1976); *Charlie Brown's Super Book of Questions and Answers about All Kinds of Animals . . . from Snails to People* (New York, 1976); *It's Arbor Day, Charlie Brown* (New York, 1977); *There Goes the Shutout* (New York, 1977); *Always Stick Up for the Underbird* (New York, 1977); *It's Hard Work Being Bitter* (New York, 1977); *How Long, Great Pumpkin, How Long?* (New York, 1977); *A Charlie Brown Christmas* (New York, 1977); *Char-*

lie Brown's Second Super Book of Questions and Answers (New York, 1977); My Anxieties Have Anxieties (New York, 1977); It's Great to Be a Superstar (New York, 1977); Stop Snowing on My Secretary (New York, 1977); Sandlot Peanuts (New York, 1977); Summers Fly, Winters Walk (New York, 1977); Race for Your Life, Charlie Brown (New York, 1978); Charlie Brown's Third Super Book of Questions and Answers (New York, 1978); It's Your First Kiss, Charlie Brown (New York, 1978); The Beagle Has Landed (New York, 1978); What a Nightmare, Charlie Brown (New York, 1978); Happiness Is . . . a Warm Puppy (New York, 1979); Love Is Walking Hand-in-Hand (San Francisco, 1979); Snoopy's Tennis Book (New York, 1979); The Snoopy's Doghouse Cook Book (San Francisco, 1979); Charlie Brown's Fourth Super Book of Questions and Answers (New York, 1979); Snoopy's Facts and Fun Book about Boats (New York, 1979); Snoopy's Facts and Fun Book about Planes (New York, 1979); Snoopy's Facts and Fun Book about Houses (New York, 1979); Snoopy's Facts and Fun Book about Seasons (New York, 1979); And a Woodstock in a Birch Tree (New York, 1979); You're the Greatest, Charlie Brown (New York, 1979); Snoopy's Facts and Fun Book about Nature (New York, 1980); Snoopy's Facts and Fun Book about Seashores (New York, 1980); Snoopy's Facts and Fun Book about Trucks (New York, 1980); Snoopy's Facts and Fun Book about Farms (New York, 1980); Bon Voyage, Charlie Brown, and Don't Come Back (New York, 1980); Charlie Brown, Snoopy and Me, and All the Other Peanuts Characters (New York, 1980); Here Comes the April Fool (New York, 1980); Charlie Brown's Fifth Super Book of Questions and Answers (New York, 1981); She's a Good Skate, Charlie Brown (New York, 1981); Life Is a Circus, Charlie Brown (New York, 1981); Christmas Is Together-Time (San Francisco, 1981); Dr. Beagle and Mr. Hyde (New York, 1981); Charlie Brown's 'cyclopedia (New York, 1980–81); Things I Learned After It Was Too Late (And Other Minor Truths) (New York, 1981); It's Magic, Charlie Brown (New York, 1982); Charlie Brown's Encyclopedia of Energy (New York, 1982); Someday You'll Find Her, Charlie Brown (New York, 1982); The Snoopy Collection (New York, 1982); Home Is on Top of a Doghouse (San Francisco, 1982); Classroom Peanuts (New York, 1982); You're Weird, Sir (New York, 1982); Through the Seasons with Snoopy (New York, 1983); Security Is a Thumb and a Blanket (San Francisco, 1983); Kiss Her, You Blockhead (New York, 1983); And the Beagles and the Bunnies Shall Lie Down Together (New York, 1984); Things I've Had to Learn Over and Over and Over (New York, 1984); I'm Not Your Sweet Babboo (New York, 1984); Is This Goodbye, Charlie Brown? (New York, 1984); Big League Peanuts (New York, 1985); You Don't Look Thirty-five, Charlie Brown! (New York, 1985); Snoopy's Getting Married, Charlie Brown (New York, 1986); The Way of the Fussbudget Is Not Easy (New York, 1986); Happy New Year, Charlie Brown (New York, 1986); The Peanuts Trivia and Reference Book (New York, 1986); Dogs Don't Eat Dessert (New York, 1987); Snoopy's ABC's (New York, 1987); Snoopy's One, Two, Three (New York, 1987); Snoopy's Book of Colors (New York, 1987); Snoopy's Book of Shapes (New York, 1987); Snoopy's Book of Opposites (New York, 1987); Let's Fly a Kite, Charlie Brown (New York, 1987); Come Back, Snoopy (New York, 1987); Sally (New York, 1988); By Supper Possessed (New York, 1988); Charlie Brown, This Is Your Life (New York, 1988); Schroeder, Music Is My Life (New York, 1988); Snoopy, My Greatest Adventures (New York, 1988). "Linus in Love," Senior Scholastic 75 (November 4, 1959): 1. "Linus Gets a Library Card," Wilson Library Bulletin 35 (December 1960): 312–313. "Success of an Utter Failure," Saturday Evening Post 229 (January 12, 1957): 34–35. Gerald Weales, "Good Grief, More Peanuts!" Reporter 20 (April 30, 1959): 45–46. CB, 1960, pp. 363–365. "Good Grief; Curly Hair; Peanuts," Newsweek 57 (March 6, 1961): 68. Amory, p. 556. C. R. Jennings, "Good Grief, Charlie Schulz!" Saturday Evening Post 237 (April 25, 1964): 26–27. R. L. Short: "Peanuts and the Bible," Americas 16 (April 1964): 16–20. The Gospel According to Peanuts (London 1966). "Woes of a Baseball Manager," Sports Illustrated 24 (June 20, 1966): 46–50. "Peanuts, The Thinking Man's Diet," The World of Comic Art 1 (June 1966): 43–48. Jon Borgzinner, "Inept Heroes," Life 62 (March 17, 1967): 74–78. Barnaby Conrad, "You're a Good Man, Charlie Schulz," New York Times Magazine, April 16, 1967, pp. 32–35; reprinted, Reader's Digest 91 (July 1967): 168–172. Who's Who 34 (1966–67): 1890. J. H. Loria, What's It All About, Charlie Brown? (New York, 1968). Robert Short, The Parables of Peanuts (New York, 1968). Fritz Ridenour, I'm a Good Man . . . (Glendale, Calif., 1969). John Tebbel, "Not So Peanuts World of Charles Schulz," Saturday Review 52 (April 12, 1969): 72–74. "You're an Adman's Dream,

186

Charlie Brown," Business Week, December 20, 1969, pp. 44–46. Jane Dutton, Peanuts Lunch Bag Cook Book (San Francisco, 1970). Lee Mendelson, Charlie Brown and Charlie Schulz (New York, 1970). Marion Vidal, M. Schulz et Ses Peanuts (Paris, 1976). Lee Mendelson, Happy Birthday, Charlie Brown (New York, 1979). Jane Dutton, Snoopy and the Gang Out West (San Francisco, 1982). Monica Bayley, The Snoopy Omnibus of Fun Facts (San Francisco, 1982). The Oakland Museum, The Graphic Art of Charles Schulz (Oakland, Calif., 1985). Marilyn Mascola, Charles Schulz: A Great Cartoonist (Vero Beach, Fla., 1988). Couperie and Horn, author index. Nye, pp. 52, 232–233, 235. Horn, pp. 602–603.

Jerry Scott 1955–

Jerry Scott, since 1983 the creator of United Feature Syndicate's Nancy, was born in 1955 in South Bend, Indiana. His cartoons have appeared in such prominent national periodicals as Good Housekeeping and the Saturday Evening Post. Other comics by Scott include Gumdrop and Copps & Roberts. Scott and his wife reside in Phoenix, Arizona.

REFERENCES: "Lifeline," USA Today, April 27, 1988. Thomas P. Wyman, "Nancy To Fall in Love With Sluggo," Valley News Dispatch, "Lifestyles," May 2, 1988. Big Brothers/Big Sisters of America, The Correspondent, October 21, 1988. Jennifer Donnelly and Nancy Nicolelis, Nancy — Past and Present: Five Compilation Books Due Out, news release (United Feature Syndicate, n.d.). April Zion and Nancy Nicolelis, Nancy by Jerry Scott, news release (United Feature Syndicate, n.d.).

Dori Seda 1951–1988

A frequent contributor to Wimmen's Comix, Dori Seda died in 1988 at age thirty-seven, a victim of alcoholism and occupational disease. Pursuing the darkly destructive course frequently followed by male artists, Seda traced in her self-referential strips her journey from countercultural experimentation to isolation. Her work has appeared in such underground organs as Cannibal Romance, Lonely Nights, Prime Cut, no. 1, Yellow Silk, no. 17, Rip Off Comix, nos. 14, 16, and 17, Sexy Stories From the World's Religions, San Francisco Comic Book, no. 7, Tits and Clits, no. 7, Viper, Weirdo, nos. 2, 4, 7, 8, 9, 18, 20, and 22, Wimmen's Comix, nos. 8, 9, 10, 11, 12. Seda, who supported her comic-strip habit by working as a bookkeeper, has been described by R. Crumb (q.v.) as "the wacko broad that she is in person" but also a "highly skilled, sharply humorous" comic artist, two conflicting identities that "don't connect up that well." "But if you look real close," observed Crumb, "you see that her comics are all about this very puzzle. . . . She is her own best cartoon character."

REFERENCES: Dori Seda, Lonely Nights (Berkeley, Calif., 1986), Introduction by R. Crumb. (kar-ton') new comic arts journal 1 (1988): 1.

Elzie Segar 1894–1938

Artist Elzie Crisler Segar, creator of Popeye, was born in Chester, Illinois, on December 8, 1894. After high school, Segar took a correspondence course in cartooning. With the help of R. F. Outcault (q.v.) Segar later got a job on the Chicago Herald, where he did a strip adaptation, Charlie Chaplin's Comic Capers. He began Looping the Loop for the Chicago Evening American on June 1, 1918. In 1919 King Features Syndicate hired Segar to draw The Thimble Theatre, which had as its theme the trials of the Oyl family, and which first appeared in the New York Journal on December 25, 1919. Popeye was recruited by Olive Oyl's brother to sail their ship in 1929. The sailor made his first appearance on January 17, 1929. Segar died in Santa Monica, California, on October 13, 1938. After his death the strip was drawn, in turn, by Tom Sims, Bela Zaboly, Bud Sagendorf (q.v.) and Bobby London (q.v.). Max Fleischer (q.v.) and subsequent studios animated Popeye. Other strips by Segar include The Five-Fifteen, a commuter strip which began publication on December 24, 1920, and was renamed Sappo on March 6, 1926.

REFERENCES: Elzie Segar, Thimble Theatre Starring Popeye (New York, 1931); Popeye *among the White Savages* (New York, 1934); *Popeye Cartoon Book* (Akron, 1937); *Popeye and the Pirates* (New York, 1945); *Thimble Theatre, Starring Popeye the Sailor* (New York, 1971); *Thimble Theatre, Introducing Popeye* (Westport, Conn., 1977); *The Complete E. C. Segar Popeye: Sundays, 1930–1932* (Westlake Village, Calif., 1984). Obituary, *New York Times*, October 14, 1938, p. 25. Sheridan, pp. 46, 196, 210–211. Couperie and Horn, author index. Nye, pp. 223–224. Horn, pp. 606–607. R. C. Harvey, "The Comics Library: Graphic Story Reviews," *Comics Journal* 101 (August 1985): 44–49.

Gilbert Shelton 1940–

In 1968, Gilbert Shelton created three characters who were to embody the counterculture — the Fabulous Furry Freak Brothers — Freewheelin' Franklin, Fat Freddy, and Phineas. First published in the *Los Angeles Free Press*, the Fabulous Furry Freak Brothers were to become the best-known fruits of Rip Off Press. Established in San Francisco in 1969 by Texans Gilbert Shelton, Jack Jackson, Dave Moriarty, and Fred Todd, Rip Off Press consistently introduced young Americans to the best in underground cartooning. Among the influential artists published there were R. Crumb (q.v.) and Bill Griffith (q.v.). Of the *Freak Brothers* Shelton related to author Diana Schutz, "The first Freak Brothers strip was an advertisement for a little film I did, a 16 mm black-and-white called 'Texas Hippies March on Capitol' — the only print of which we later lost. . . . The advertisement for the film featuring the Freak Brothers was better received than the film itself, so I just kept doing the comic strip and forgot about being a film director." Among the innovations of Shelton's strip was its regionalism. "There's another thing about so-called 'underground' comix," continued Shelton, "the fact that they emphasized a *regional* aspect of whatever it was. They were personal and regional — whereas before everything had been published in New York, the center of the publishing industry." Other strips drawn by Shelton include *Wonder Wart Hog*, created as a satire of *Superman* by the artist and author Bill Killeen while both were undergraduate contributors to the *Texas Ranger*, the University of Texas periodical.

REFERENCES: Gilbert Shelton, *The Fabulous Furry Freak Brothers Library*, Vol. 1 (Auburn, Calif., 1988); with Dave Sheridan, *The Fabulous Furry Freak Brothers in "The Idiots Abroad"* (Auburn, Calif., 1987). with Paul Mavrides, *The Fabulous Furry Freak Brothers Library*, Vol. 2 (Auburn, Calif., 1988); Diana Schutz, "Rip Off Press," *Comics Journal* 92 (August 1984): 69–86. Horn, p. 612.

Joe Shuster 1914–

Superman, which provided pop artist Jean-Louis Brau with one of his major themes, was created in 1938 by two Cleveland high-school students, artist Joe Shuster and writer Jerome Siegel (q.v.). *Superman* originally appeared in comic-book form and was adapted to a newspaper strip distributed by the McClure Syndicate in 1939. *Superman* became a radio show on February 12, 1940, and Paramount Pictures later commissioned Max Fleischer (q.v.) to do a series of animations. In the fifties *Superman* became a television series; in the seventies, a popular film series began.

REFERENCES: Jerry Siegel and Joe Shuster, "Of Supermen and Kids with Dreams," *Nemo* 2 (August 1983): 6–19. E. J. Kahn, "Why I Don't Believe in Superman," *The New Yorker* 16 (June 29, 1940): 64–66. Sheridan, pp. 233, 279. George Lowther, *Superman*, illus. by Joe Shuster (New York, 1942). "Supersuit," *Newsweek* 29 (April 14, 1947): 65. "Superman and the Atom Bomb," *Harper's* 196 (April 1948): 355. "Superman Adopted," *Time* (May 31, 1948): 72. "Superceding Superman," *Newsweek* 32 (July 19, 1948): 51–53. R. B. Gehman, "Deadwood Dick to Superman," *Science Digest* 25 (June 1949): 52–57. Geoffrey Wagner, "Superman and His Sister," *New Republic* 132 (January 17, 1955): 17–19. "Superman Goes to College," *Esquire* 62 (September 1964): 106–107. Roderick Nordell, "Superman Revisted," *Atlantic Monthly* 217 (January 1966): 104–105. George Lowther, *Superman* illus. by Joe Shuster (Los Angeles, 1979). Couperie and Horn, author index. Nye, pp. 229–230, 237–240, 277, 402. Horn, pp. 615–616.

Jerome Siegel 1914–

With artist Joe Shuster (q.v.) the co-creator of *Superman*, writer Jerome Siegel was born in Cleveland on October 17, 1914. Inspired by novelist Philip Wylie's *Gladiator* (1930), Siegel and Shuster's superhero first appeared in Action Comics in June 1938.

REFERENCES: Horn, pp. 616–617.

Donald Simpson 1961–

Donald Simpson, creator of Kitchen Sink Comix's *Megaton Man*, was born in Garden City, Michigan, on December 3, 1961, the son of James and Elizabeth Simpson. He graduated from Stevenson High School in Livonia, Michigan, in 1980, and that same year completed the Commercial Art Program at Livonia Career Center. From September 1980 to May 1981 he studied graphic design at the Detroit College of Art and Design. Simpson received an associate's degree in visual communication from The Art Institute of Pittsburgh in 1989. In 1984 he created *Megaton Man*, fourteen issues of which have been published by Kitchen Sink. Kitchen Sink has also published seven issues of Simpson's *Border Worlds*. Since 1986 Simpson's illustrations have appeared in DC Comics's *Wasteland*. Simpson's work has appeared in *National Lampoon*, the *Cleveland Plain Dealer*, the *Comics Journal*, and Harvey Pekar's (q.v.) *American Splendor*. He lives in Pittsburgh, Pennsylvania.

Al Smith 1902–

After Bud Fisher's (q.v.) death in 1954, *Mutt and Jeff* was continued by Al Smith, who had been Fisher's assistant on the strip since 1932. Smith, whose real name was Albert Schmidt, was born in Brooklyn on March 21, 1902, the son of Henry and Josephine Dice Schmidt. On May 25, 1921, he married Erna Anna Strasser. From 1920 to 1930 Smith was art editor at the *New York World*. He was a comic-strip artist for United Feature Syndicate between 1930 and 1932. After 1932 he was ghostwriter for several strips, as well as Fisher's assistant on *Mutt and Jeff*. Smith has also drawn *Rural Delivery*, *Remember When*, and *Life in the Suburbs*.

REFERENCES: *Who's Who* 34 (1966–67): 1973. Nye, p. 218. Horn, pp. 120, 251, 509, 625.

Sidney Smith 1877–1935

Sidney Smith, who originated *The Gumps* and *Old Doc Yak*, was born in Bloomington, Illinois, on February 13, 1877, the son of T. H. and Frances A. Shafer Smith. Smith's father was a physician. His first job was that of cartoonist with the *Bloomington Sunday Eye* in 1895. He was later employed by the *Indianapolis News*, the *Indianapolis Press*, the *Philadelphia Inquirer*, the *Pittsburgh Post*, the *Pittsburgh Press*, the *Indianapolis Sentinel*, the *Toledo News-Bee*, and the *Chicago Tribune*. Smith died on October 20, 1935. After his death *The Gumps* was continued by Gus Edson (q.v.), and, for a time, by Harold Gray (q.v.).

REFERENCES: Sidney Smith: *Sidney Smith's the Gumps* (New York, 1974). M. M. Clark, "Sidney Smith and His Gumps," *American Magazine* 95 (September 1924): 50–51. *Who's Who* 16 (1930–31): 2053. F. M. Meek, "Sweet Land of Andy Gump," *Christian Century* 52 (May 8, 1935): 605–607. Obituary, *Time* 26 (October 28, 1935): 45. "Gumps: Andy, Min, and Chester Carry on Without Sidney Smith," *Newsweek* 6 (November 2, 1936): 35. Sheridan, pp. 11, 35, 70, 101–102, 108, 109. *Who Was Who* 1 (1897–1942): 1149. Mallett, p. 411. "Why Bertie! *Chicago Tribune* Evicted the Gumps," *Time* 56 (July 17, 1950): 62. Couperie and Horn, pp. 44, 49. Nye, p. 224. Horn, pp. 625–626.

Reggie Smythe 1917–

Born in Hartlepool, Yorkshire, in 1917, cartoonist Reggie Smythe is best known as the creator of *Andy Capp*. The son of a boat builder, Smythe attended Galleys Field School until 1931, going "directly from school to the relief rolls." Smythe served for eleven years with the British

Army's Northumberland Fusiliers, during World War II surviving the siege of Tobruk. After the war, Smythe became a postal employee, then a cartoonist for the *Daily Mirror* (London). His best-known comic strip, *Andy Capp*, first appeared in the *Daily Mirror* on August 5, 1957; in the United States, where it is distributed by North America Syndicate, *Andy Capp* debuted on September 16, 1963. Smythe lives in London.

REFERENCES: King Features Syndicate, *Reggie Smythe* (New York, n.d.). Horn, pp. 82–83.

Otto Soglow 1900–1975

Artist Otto Soglow, famous for his *Little King*, was born in New York on December 23, 1900. He attended public schools before enrolling at the Art Students League, where he studied from 1919 to 1925. While a student he also worked as a dishwasher, machinist's helper, and painter of baby rattles. On October 11, 1928, he married Anna Rosen, a graphic artist. *The Little King* first appeared in *The New Yorker*, on September 9, 1934. King Features first syndicated it as a strip, along with *Sentinel Louie*. Soglow's work also appeared in *Life*, *Judge*, *Collier's*, and *Harper's Bazaar*. He died on April 3, 1975.

REFERENCES: Otto Soglow, *Pretty Pictures* (New York, 1931); *Everything's Rosy* (New York, 1932); *The Little King* (New York, 1933); *Wasn't the Depression Terrible?* (New York, 1934); *A Confidential History of Modern England* (New York, 1937). Norman Anthony, *The Drunk's Blue Book*, illus. by Otto Soglow (New York, 1933). Cornelia Otis Skinner, *Excuse It, Please!*, illus. by Otto Soglow (New York, 1936). Richard Hyman, *It's Against the Law*, illus. by Otto Soglow (New York, 1936). Annie Fisher, *Live with a Man and Love It!*, illus. by Otto Soglow (New York, 1939). Myra Mae Haas, *Recipes for Allergies*, illus. by Otto Soglow (New York, 1939). Groucho Marx, *Many Happy Returns*, illus. by Otto Soglow (New York, 1942). Frank Case, *Do Not Disturb*, illus. by Otto Soglow (New York, 1943). Richard Hyman, *Looney Laws*, illus. by Otto Soglow (New York, 1946). Richard Arndt, *Liberated Latin*, illus. by Otto Soglow (New York, 1951). "Comics and Their Creators," *Literary Digest* 1 (September 1934): 10. "Most Overrated People in America," *Scribner's* 104 (September 1938): 22–23. *CB*, 1940, p. 748. Sheridan, pp. 206–208. *Who's Who* 34 (1966–67): 1999. Couperie and Horn, p. 73. Horn, pp. 627–628. Obituary, *New York Times*, April 4, 1975; *Current Biography* (May 1975). *Who's Who in American Art* (1976, 1978).

Art Spiegelman 1948–

Born in Stockholm, Sweden, in 1948, Art Spiegelman is the son of Holocaust survivors Vladek and Anja Spiegelman. Since 1978 Spiegelman has taught at the School of Visual Arts in New York. He is the cofounder and coeditor of *Raw* magazine, and the creator of Topps Chewing Gum's Garbage Pail Kids, Wacky Packs, and Garbage Candy. His illustrations have appeared in the *New York Times*, *Playboy*, and the *Village Voice*. In 1986 Pantheon Books published his seminal work, *Maus: A Survivor's Tale*, to immediate critical acclaim. Alternately set in present-day Rego Park, New York, and in war-torn Poland, *Maus* — utilizing comic-strip conventions — documents the Holocaust through the remembered experiences of Spiegelman's aging father, Vladek. *Maus* was the recipient of Europe's prestigious Yellow Kid Award. Cartoonist Edward Sorel proclaimed "Spiegelman's passionate pen has stretched the boundaries of the comic-strip form and created a work of immense power," and David Levine stated that *Maus* "in its effect on the reader, [is on] par with Kafka" (back cover, *Maus*). Spiegelman is married to editor and designer Françoise Mouly.

REFERENCES: Art Spiegelman, *Whole Grains: A Book of Quotations* (New York, 1973); *Breakdowns* (New York, 1977); *Maus* (New York, 1986); ed., with Françoise Mouly, *Read Yourself Raw: The Graphix Anthology for Damned Intellectuals* (New York, 1987). Dale Luciano, "Trapped by Life: Pathos and Humor among Mice and Men," *Comics Journal* 113 (December 1986): 43–45. Harvey Pekar, "Maus and Other Topics," *Comics Journal* 113 (December 1986): 54–57. "Mauschwitz," *Esquire* 107 (March 1987): 67–69. Adam Gopnik, "Comics and Catastrophe," *New Republic* 196 (June 22, 1987): 29–33. Peter S. Prescott with Ray Sawhill, "The Comic Book (Gulp!) Grows Up," *Newsweek* 111 (January 18, 1988): 70–71.

Frank Stack 1937–

University professor Frank Stack, known to the world of underground comics as "Foolbert Sturgeon," was born in Houston, Texas, on October 31, 1937, the son of Maurice and Norma Huntington Stack. Stack attended public schools in Houston, Corpus Christi, and Midland, Texas. In 1959 he received his B.F.A. from the University of Texas, where he edited the *Texas Ranger*. After graduation, Stack worked as a reporter and graphic designer for the *Houston Chronicle;* between 1960 and 1962 Stack served in the U.S. Army. From 1960 to 1961 he studied at the School of the Art Institute of Chicago. In 1963 he received his M.A. from the University of Wyoming. Stack then joined the faculty of the University of Missouri in Columbia, eventually becoming chair of the art department, a position he held from 1981 to 1984. Stack's numerous comics include *New Adventures of Jesus*, nos. 1, 2, 3 (1968, 1969, 1971); *Feelgood Funnies*, nos. 1, 2 (1971, 1984); *Amazon Comics* (1972); *Dorman's Doggie* (1979); *The Collected New Adventures of Jesus* (1979); and *Classics of the Underground Comix: The New Adventures of Jesus*, nos. 1, 2, 3, 4 (1989), all from Rip Off Press. Stack has also published a book on *John Sloan's Etchings* (1967) and *Etchings and Lithographs by Frank Stack* (1976). His work has appeared in *National Lampoon* (October 1981); *American Splendor*, no. 12 (1987); and *Snarf*, no. 12 (1989). States Stack, "The form itself fascinates me; I've loved what artists have done in comic strips: Roy Crane, V. T. Hamlin, Hal Foster, Chester Gould, Elzie Segar; but with my own art I don't like to work 'for' institutions like corporations with their precious 'properties' (like *Batman*) or to reflect credit on a political group. Through the sixties I'd given up on the idea of being a professional cartoonist (I'd almost become *The Chronicle*'s editorial cartoonist before the Army got me in 1960). Cartoons were a medium of protest and satire for me. I drew them without expecting them to be published. A principle all my cartoonist friends agreed on, though, was 'If it's not funny, it's not good.' "

Mark Alan Stamaty 1947–

Born in Brooklyn, New York, on August 1, 1947, Mark Alan Stamaty was raised in Elberon, New Jersey, the son of professional cartoonists. Stamaty graduated in 1969 from The Cooper Union, and quickly gained distinction for his graphic art. His work, for example, is in the collection of the State Museum of New Jersey, in Trenton. From 1971 to 1977 he authored and illustrated children's books, including *Yellow Yellow* (McGraw-Hill, 1971), *Who Needs Donuts?* (Dial Press, 1973), *Small in the Saddle* (Windmill Books, 1975), *Minnie Maloney and Macaroni* (Dial, 1976), and *Where's My Hippopotamus?* (Dial, 1977), in 1974 winning a Gold Medal from the Society of Illustrators. From 1977 to 1981 Stamaty was a member of the faculty of the Parsons School of Design, where he taught a course on writing and illustrating children's books. In 1977 his centerfold cartoons, posters, and first comic strips appeared in the *Village Voice*, where from 1978 to 1979 *MacDoodle Street*, a popular comic strip celebrating the weird vitality of New York City, appeared weekly. The comic strip *Carrrttooooonn* ran in the *Voice* from 1980 to 1981. Since 1981 *Washingtoon*, Stamaty's satire of power politics in the nation's capital, has appeared in the *Washington Post* and the *Voice*. Today, *Washingtoon* is syndicated to over twenty papers, including the *Boston Globe* and the *Philadelphia Inquirer*. *Washingtoon* is now syndicated by the Washington Post Writers' Group. Two anthologies of Stamaty's comic strips have been published: *MacDoodle Street* (1980) and *Washingtoon* (1983). In addition to his roles of graphic artist, author of experimental fiction, and comic-strip artist, Stamaty is an Elvis impersonator.

REFERENCES: Mark Alan Stamaty, *Biography*, 1988, files of the Library for Communication and Graphic Arts, The Ohio State University Libraries. *New York Times Book Review*, October 14, 1973. *Saturday Review* (May 4, 1974). *New York Times Book Review*, May 25, 1975. *Newsweek* 98 (December 15, 1975). *Saturday Review* (November 27, 1976). *Newsweek* 100 (July 18, 1977). *Publishers Weekly* (February 27, 1978). *Washington Post Book World*, August 12, 1979. *New York Times Book Review*, December 28, 1980. *Washington Post Book World*, January 4, 1981. *Washington Post Book World*, October 30, 1983. *Village Voice Literary Supplement*, November 1983.

Leonard Starr 1925–

Artist Leonard Starr, creator of *Mary Perkins, On Stage*, was born in Manhattan on October 25, 1925. He was a student at New York's High School of Music and Art and later attended Pratt Institute. In 1957 he began the strip *On Stage*, highly praised by Couperie and Horn as "one of the best of the contemporary comic strips." Since 1979 Starr has drawn the revived *Orphan Annie*. Starr lives in Westport, Connecticut.

REFERENCES: Couperie and Horn, author index. Chicago Tribune–New York News Syndicate, *Leonard Starr: On Stage* (New York, 1968); *Leonard Starr Biography* (Chicago, 1986). Horn, pp. 68, 310, 529, 634.

Leslie Sternbergh 1960–

Artist and model Leslie Sternbergh was born on June 29, 1960, in York, Pennsylvania, the daughter of Maureen Ruth McGready and D. Dexter Sternbergh. She attended Kutztown University in Kutztown, Pennsylvania, and Bucknell University in Lewisburg, Pennsylvania. From 1982 to 1985 Sternbergh worked in Manhattan as a model for the Art Students League of New York, the Parsons School of Design, the School of the Visual Arts, and for artists David Levine, Harvey Dinerstein, and Burton Silverman. Photos of Sternbergh have appeared in the *Village Voice* and *Hawgs*, a bikers' magazine. Her illustrations and underground comics have been published in *Screw* (1985), *Wimmen's Comix*, nos. 9, 11 (1985, 1987), *Weird Smut* (1986), *Viper* (1986), *Borderland* (1986), *Cannibal Romance* (1987), *Tits and Clits*, no. 7 (1988), *Marvel Comics* (1988), *Wonder Woman Annual* (DC Comics, 1989), *Weirdo*, no. 26 (1989), and *High Times* (1989). States Sternbergh, "Comix as a form is capable of producing a reaction equivalent to spontaneous thought combustion; the storytelling forms which persist do so because they speak to, and evolve with, individual consciousness. My comix aim [is] to transcend the readers' indoctrinated aversion to empathy. In an age when cultural comprehension is transmitted primarily through visual media, it is imperative that comix receive the recognition due them as tools for the transmission of the mythic building blocks of cultural currents." Sternbergh is married to toy inventor Adam Alexander; the couple lives in Manhattan.

REFERENCES: Bryan Denson, "Ingenuous Native's Now a Cover Girl," *York* (Pa.) *Daily Record*, January 22, 1987. Carol Leggett, "Baby Blue," *Spin* (July 1989): 104.

Cliff Sterrett 1883–1964

Cliff Sterrett, whose *Polly and Her Pals* is credited with being the first "girl" strip, was born in Fergus Falls, Minnesota, on December 12, 1883, the son of Samuel O. and Virginia Johnson Sterrett. Sterrett attended public schools and spent a year studying art at the Chase School in Manhattan. From 1904 to 1908 he was a cartoonist for the *New York Herald*. He was with the *New York Times* from 1908 to 1910. Before beginning *Positive Polly* (later *Polly and Her Pals*) for the *New York Journal* on December 4, 1912, he also worked for the *Herald*, the *Rochester* (N.Y.) *Democrat* and *Chronicle*, and the *New York Telegram*. Begun in 1912, *Polly* ran until Sterrett's retirement in 1958. Couperie and Horn note that the strip reflected in style Sterrett's interest in cubism. Sterrett's other strips included *For This We Have Daughters*, *When a Man's Married*, and *Before and After*. The best known of the many girl strips influenced by Sterrett were Martin Branner's (q.v.) *Winnie Winkle, the Breadwinner*, which first appeared in 1920, and Russ Westover's (q.v.) *Tillie the Toiler*, which began publication in January 1921.

REFERENCES: Cliff Sterrett, *Polly and Her Pals* (New York, 1934); *Polly and Her Pals: A Complete Compilation, 1912–1913* (Westport, Conn., 1977). "Comics and Their Creators," *Literary Digest* 117 (June 16, 1934): 11. *Who's Who* 16 (1930–31): 2098. Sheridan, pp. 60, 80, 293. Mallett, p. 420. King Features Syndicate, *Famous Artists and Writers: Cliff Sterrett* (New York, 1949). Stephen Becker, *Comic Art in America* (New York, 1959), pp. 40–41. Couperie and Horn, pp. 43, 49, 205. Nye, p. 222. Horn, pp. 635–636.

Heidi Stetson 1957–

Born in New Hampshire, Heidi Stetson, creator of United Feature Syndicate's *Ophelia and Jake*, was raised in Lexington, Massachusetts, and attended Massachusetts College of Art, where she concentrated on sculpture. After stints as a mail clerk, copier operator, and company librarian, Stetson married. Her husband, Christopher, is a restorer of organs. They have two children, Thomas and Katie, and live in Easthampton, Massachusetts. In 1983 Stetson began her career as a professional artist, creating cartoons for magazines. In 1985 she created *Ophelia and Jake*, which began publication on January 25, 1988. The strip's youthful protagonist, Ophelia, loves ballet, baseball, and her pet rabbit, Jake. "I wanted to do a strip about a girl who was happy doing traditional 'girl' things but who also did 'boy' things. I also wanted to do a strip about a rabbit since we have one. I couldn't decide which to do, so I combined the two."

REFERENCES: David Astor, "Avoiding Stereotypes in Girl/Rabbit Strip," *Editor and Publisher* (March 12, 1988). United Feature Syndicate, *Heidi Stetson*, n.d.; *Ophelia and Jake*, n.d.

Pat Sullivan 1888–1933

Pat Sullivan, originator of *Felix the Cat*, was born in Australia in 1888. In 1908 he worked in London on the cartoon *Ally Sloper*, moving to the United States the following year, where he set up a studio in New York. He created an animated *Felix* in 1917, and in 1923 distributed *Felix* as a strip through King Features Syndicate. Blanchard credits Sullivan with innovations in depicting motion, Couperie and Horn with bringing to the comic strip "the poetry of its strange landscapes, its flights into the world of the dream, the melancholy of deserted forests and roads in which the skinny black cat wanders under the low-hanging full moon."

REFERENCES: Pat Sullivan, *Félix le chat* (Paris, 1931); *Félix au pays de l'ogre* (Paris, 1931); *Félix au cinéma* (Paris, 1932); *Félix chez les sauvages* (Paris, 1932); *Félix en l'an 2000* (Paris, 1933); *Félix dans la jungle* (Paris, 1933); *Félix et Riri* (Paris, 1934); *Félix au travail* (Paris, 1934); *Félix et Zizi* (Paris, 1939); *Félix patine* (Paris, 1940); *Felix the Cat* (New York, 1953); *Pat Sullivan's a Surprise for Felix* (New York, 1959). Gerard Blanchard, *La Bande dessinée* (Verviers, 1969) p. 196. Couperie and Horn, pp. 35, 37, 183. Horn, p. 641.

Dana Summers 1950–

Best known as the co-creator, with Ralph Dunagin (q.v.), of North America Syndicate's *The Middletons*, Dana Summers was born in Lawrence, Massachusetts. Summers attended the Art Institute of Boston, later becoming a freelance editorial cartoonist whose work appeared in Massachusetts weeklies and college dailies. In 1977 he joined the *Fayetteville* (Ark.) *Times* as staff artist. In 1980 he moved to the *Dayton* (Ohio) *Journal Herald;* in 1982, to the *Orlando* (Fla.) *Sentinel*. On November 3, 1986, *The Middletons* debuted.

REFERENCE: North America Syndicate, *The Middletons* (New York, n.d.).

James Guilford Swinnerton 1875–1974

In 1966 the *World of Comic Art* celebrated the eighty-ninth birthday of one of the fathers of the comic strip, James Swinnerton. His first important strip, *Little Jimmy*, was created in 1905 for the *New York American* and ran until 1941, when Swinnerton began *Rocky Mason, Government Agent*. Couperie and Horn credit Swinnerton as "the first to simplify draftsmanship, eliminate pen scribbling, and depict his characters with a clean outline supported by the carefully delineated black areas of their clothing."

REFERENCES: J. G. Swinnerton, *Jimmy, a Series of Comic Pictures* (New York, 1905); *Canyon Country Kiddies* (New York, 1923); *Hosteen Crotchetty: or, How a Good Heart Was Born* (Palm Desert, Calif., 1965). Portrait, *Current Literature* 45 (December 1908): 633. Harold G. Davidson, *Jimmy Swinnerton* (New York, 1985). Sheridan, pp. 67, 244, 293. Mallett, p. 428. Fielding, p. 358. *World of Comic Art* 1 (June 1966): 50. Couperie and Horn, pp. 19, 21, 205.

Nye, pp. 216, 223. Horn, pp. 11, 454–455, 645–646.

Joseph George Szabo 1950–

The former graphics editor of the Hungarian publication *Magyar Nemzet*, immigrant cartoonist and publisher Joseph Szabo was born on February 4, 1950. In 1979 Szabo came to the United States, where he began *Witty World*, a journal of international comic and cartoon art, in 1987.

REFERENCE: Carol Burbank, "The King of Cartooning," *Philadelphia City Paper* 260 (August 4–11, 1989): 8.

Bob Thaves 1924–

Industrial psychologist Bob Thaves, creator of Newspaper Enterprise Association's *Frank and Ernst*, was raised in Burt, Iowa, where his father published the local newspaper. While an undergraduate at the University of Minnesota, Thaves began publishing his cartoons in the student newspaper. In 1972 he began *Frank and Ernst*, which received the Reuben Award for Best Syndicated Panel in 1983, 1984, and 1986. Thaves and his wife, Katie, live in Manhattan Beach, California, with their children, Sara and Tom.

REFERENCES: Newspaper Enterprise Association: *Gibson Launches Frank and Ernst Greeting Card Line*, n.d.; *Frank and Ernst by Bob Thaves*, n.d.; *Frank and Ernst in America's Top Five Favorite Comics*, n.d.; *Frank and Ernst Help Increase Voter Registration*, n.d.

Jack Tippit 1923–

Born in Texas, Jack Tippit received his B.F.A. from Syracuse University in 1949. From 1941 to 1974, Tippit served in the U.S. Air Force Reserve, retiring in 1974 as a full colonel. Tippit was on active duty during World War II, the Korean War, and the Vietnamese conflict. From 1966 to 1973 he chaired the National Cartoonists Society's Overseas Entertainment Committee, which organized tours to hospitals in Vietnam and the Far East. From 1971 to 1973 he was president of the National Cartoonists Society. His panel comic, *Amy*, first distributed by the Register-Tribune Syndicate, received the society's award for Best Syndicated Panel in 1970.

REFERENCE: King Features Syndicate, *Jack Tippit* (New York, 1989).

Lawrence Stickle Todd 1948–

Underground creator Lawrence Stickle Todd was born on April 6, 1948, in Buffalo, New York, the son of Ruth Ann Pfieffer Stickle and George Stickle. He attended Syracuse University. Since 1982 Todd has owned and operated *Proto Prints*, a T-shirt printing company in Willits, California. Todd's work has appeared in Last Gasp Publishing's *Dr. Atomic Comics*, nos. 1–6 (1972–81); *It's a Dog's Life* (1982); and, with Harlan Ellison, *The Chocolate Alphabet* (1978). "Being principally a story writer," states Todd, "I've stayed in the comic-book field, where daily gags aren't needed. My objective has been to create those comics I would most like to read as a kid."

Don Trachte 1915–

Don Trachte, best known for his rendition of King Features Syndicate's *Henry*, was born in Madison, Wisconsin. In 1935 Trachte, who had studied with *Henry*'s creator, Carl Anderson (q.v.), became Anderson's assistant. From 1941 to 1945 Trachte served in the U.S. Army. Upon his discharge, Trachte took over the Sunday *Henry*. Trachte and his wife, Betty, reside in Arlington, Vermont.

REFERENCE: King Features Syndicate, *Don Trachte* (New York, n.d.).

G. B. Trudeau 1948–

The first comic-strip artist to receive the Pulitzer Prize for editorial cartooning, Garretson Beekman Trudeau was born into a physician's family in New York City. Trudeau was raised in Saranac, New York, and attended St. Paul's preparatory school in New Hampshire and Yale University. While a junior at St. Paul's, he created the character that was to become his phenomenally popular Doonesbury. This was Weenie Man, conceived to encourage hot-dog consumption at school football games. In a November 12, 1986, interview with *Washington Post* correspondent Lloyd Grove, Trudeau recalled the character's genesis as the prototype for Mike Doonesbury. "He was very Feifferesque in look, and in temperament he greatly resembled Bernard Mergendeiler, the Feiffer character." Weenie Man appeared, rechristened Michael Doonesbury, in *Bull Tales*, Trudeau's undergraduate strip, which ran in the *Yale Record* and in the *Yale Daily News*. Soon Trudeau's strip had captured the imagination of undergraduate America. In October 1970 Universal Press Syndicate distributed it — as *Doonesbury* — to twenty-eight newspapers. In 1975, Trudeau received the Pulitzer. By 1980, *Doonesbury* was appearing in approximately nine hundred newspapers, regularly placing as both the "best loved" and "most hated" of strips in reader surveys.

REFERENCES: G. B. Trudeau, *Doonesbury* (New York, 1971); *Still a Few Bugs in the System* (New York, 1971); *But This War Had Such Promise* (New York, 1973); *Call Me When You Find America* (New York, 1973); *The President Is a Lot Smarter Than You Think* (New York, 1973); *Guilty, Guilty, Guilty* (New York, 1974); *Joanie* (New York, 1974); *Dare To Be Great, Ms. Causus* (New York, 1975); *The Doonesbury Chronicles* (New York, 1975); *We'll Take It from Here, Sarge* (New York, 1975); *"What Do We Have for the Witnesses, Johnnie?"* (New York, 1975); *Wouldn't a Gremlin Have Been More Sensible?* (New York, 1975); *"Speaking of Inalienable Rights, Amy . . ."* (New York, 1976); *You're Never Too Old for Nuts and Berries* (New York, 1976); *An Especially Tricky People* (New York, 1977); *As the Kid Goes for Broke* (New York, 1977); *"Any Grooming Hints for Your Fans, Rollie?"* (New York, 1978); *Doonesbury's Greatest Hits* (New York, 1978); *John and Faith Hubley's "A Doonesbury Special"* (New York, 1978); *Stalking the Perfect Tan* (New York, 1978); *But the Pension Fund Was Just Sitting Here* (New York, 1979); *A Tad Overweight, But Violet Eyes To Die For* (New York, 1979); *We're Not Out of the Woods Yet* (New York, 1979); *And That's My Final Offer* (New York, 1980); *He's Never Heard of You Either* (New York, 1981); *In Search of Reagan's Brain* (New York, 1981); *The People's Doonesbury* (New York, 1981); *Ask for May, Settle for June* (New York, 1982); *Unfortunately, She Was Also Wired for Sound* (New York, 1982); *The Wreck of the "Rusty Nail"* (New York, 1983); *You Give Great Meeting, Sid* (New York, 1983); *Doonesbury Dossier* (New York, 1984); *Check Your Egos at the Door* (New York, 1985); *Death of a Party Animal* (New York, 1986); *That's Doctor Sinatra, You Little Bimbo* (New York, 1986); *Calling Doctor Whoopee* (New York, 1986); *Doonesbury Deluxe* (New York, 1987); *Downtown Doonesbury* (New York, 1987); *Talkin' About My G-G-Generation* (New York, 1988). Nicholas von Hoffman, *The Fireside Watergate* (New York, 1973); *Tales From the Margaret Mead Tamproom* (Kansas City, Kans. 1976). Elizabeth Swados, *Doonesbury* (New York, 1984); *Doonesbury* (New York, 1986). Allan Satin, *A Doonesbury Index* (Metuchin, N.J., 1985). Lloyd Grove, "Trudeau Speaks," *Washington Post*, November 12, 1986, pp. D1, 14–15.

Morrie Turner 1923–

Born on December 11, 1923, in Oakland, California, Morrie Turner, creator of the first integrated kid strip of the sixties, *Wee Pals*, began his comic-strip career during World War II as a cartoonist for an army air corps base newspaper. For a time, Turner worked for the Oakland police department. Inspired by Charles Schulz's (q.v.) gentle *Peanuts*, Turner in 1965 began syndication of *Wee Pals*, which has been distributed by Lew Little, the Register and Tribune Syndicate, King Features Syndicate, News America Syndicate, and North America Syndicate. In addition to *Wee Pals*, which has appeared in more than a hundred newspapers, Turner is the creator of *Soul Corner*, a Sunday panel coauthored with his wife, Letha, which presents African-American history in comic-strip format, and of *Prophet of Peace*, an animated biography of Martin Luther King, Jr., distributed by the University of California Extension Media

Center. The Turners reside in Berkeley, California.

REFERENCES: *Biography: Morrie Turner*, n.d., files of The Library for Communication and Graphic Arts, Ohio State University Libraries. The University of California Extension Media Center, *Prophet of Peace: The Story of Dr. Martin Luther King, Jr.*, 1986. Horn, p. 674. National Cartoonists Society, *National Cartoonists Society Album* (Greenwich, Conn., 1988).

Carol Tyler 1951–

Best known for her tender tales of familial and employment conflict, Carol Tyler was born on November 20, 1951, in Chicago, Illinois, one of five children of Chuck and Hannah Tyler, a pipe fitter and executive secretary whom Tyler describes as "fun, generous, salt of the earth people." Tyler received her M.F.A. in 1983 from Syracuse University. She is employed as an exhibition designer/coordinator at the Sacramento History Center in Old Sacramento, California. Her marvelous underground comics have appeared in *Weirdo*, nos. 8, 20, 21, 22, and 24 (Last Gasp, 1986–89); *Street Music*, nos. 1–6 (Fantagraphics, 1989–90), *Heck* (Rip Off Press, 1989), *Wimmen's Comix*, nos. 13, 14, 15 (Rip Off Press, 1987, 1989), and *Strip AIDS USA* (Last Gasp, 1988). States Tyler, "I turn to comics to resolve my emotional pain and to record the general weirdness I see in the world. Many times comics have saved my life. Not just because of let's say the therapeutic value of safely cussing out an old employer in print, but mainly because in the process of doing a story, I'm able to surrender to this wonderful magical thing within myself . . . and before you know it, it's not even me drawing the panels anymore. I guess that's why I sacrifice my housework so much to draw comics. Yep, the dishes aren't done but my life seems like a miracle." Tyler lives in Sacramento with her husband, cartoonist Justin Green, and their daughter.

REFERENCES: Carol Tyler, "Interview," *Comics F/X* (August 1989). "Interview," *Comics Journal* (November–December 1989).

Jim Unger 1937–

Jim Unger, creator of Universal Press Syndicate's Reuben Award–winning *Herman*, was born in poverty in London and attended grammar school in Wimbledon. After working as a policeman, driving-school instructor, and automobile repossessor, Unger emigrated to Ottawa in 1968. In 1971 he became art director of the *Mississauga Times*. In 1974 he was recruited as a cartoonist by Universal Press Syndicate. Andrews and McMeel has published seven *Herman* anthologies. In 1982 Unger moved to the Bahamas; he lives in Nassau.

REFERENCES: Andy Juniper, "Striving For the Perfect Goof," *Globe and Mail* (Nassau), April 14, 1984. Seymour Rothman, "Jim Unger, The Man Behind," *The Blade*, January 5, 1986. "We Want Our Comics Back," *Washington Post*, March 8, 1986. Ronald Roy, "Cartooning Serious Work to Creator of 'Herman'," *Norwich Bulletin*, n.d. Kathryn Massman, *Herman Cartoonist Jim Unger Wins "Best Syndicated Panel"* (Universal Press Syndicate, n.d.).

Jerry Van Amerongen 1940–

Jerry Van Amerongen, creator of *The Neighborhood*, attended Ferris State College in Michigan, graduating in 1963 with a degree in commercial art. For five years he worked in Denver for design studios and advertising agencies. He moved to Minneapolis, where in 1968 he joined the staff of Josten's Inc., eventually becoming director of marketing. In 1978 he began his career as a cartoonist in a small, volunteer, neighborhood newspaper. His creation, *The Neighborhood*, was acquired by the *Minneapolis Tribune* and syndicated first by the Register and Tribune Syndicate, and then by the Cowles Syndicate.

REFERENCE: King Features Syndicate, *The Neighborhood* (New York, 1988).

Guy Vasilovich 1955–

Guy Vasilovich, artist of *When I Was Short*, was born in 1955 in Oak Park, Illinois. In 1972 he moved to Wisconsin. There he attended the University of Wisconsin. In 1979, he entered the California Institute of Arts, from which he received a scholarship. Vasilovich became an artist for The Walt Disney Company, working as a journeyman layout artist on *The Black Cauldron*, as art director of *The Great Mouse Detective*, and as senior show designer for Walt Disney Imagineering. In August 1989 *When I Was Short* began syndication by King Features. Vasilovich lives in the Los Angeles area with his wife, Linda.

REFERENCE: King Features Syndicate, *Guy Vasilovich* (New York, August 1989).

Mort Walker 1923–

Born in El Dorado, Kansas, in 1923, Addison Morton Walker was the son of an architect-author father and an artist mother. During World War II, Walker served with the U.S. Army in Italy as a first lieutenant in charge of German prisoner-of-war camps. Walker drew upon his army experiences to create his most successful strip, *Beetle Bailey*, which he began in 1950 for King Features Syndicate. Originally a college strip, *Beetle* soon became an army saga. Among Walker's other creations are *Hi and Lois* (1954), *Boner's Ark* (1968), *Sam and Silo* (1977), and *Gamin and Patches* (1987). In 1963 Walker conceived the Museum of Cartoon Art, which became a reality in Port Chester, New York, in 1974. Now located in Rye Brook, New York, the museum includes a library and research center and numbers among its extensive collections more than fifty thousand original cartoons from 1850 to the present. Walker's numerous publications include *Most* (Windmill Books, 1972), *Land of Lost Things* (Windmill Books, 1972), *Backstage at the Strips* (Mason/Charter, 1975), *The Lexicon of Comicana* (Comicana, 1980), and *The Best of Beetle Bailey* (Comicana, 1984). His collaborators have included Dik Browne (q.v.) and Jerry Dumas (q.v.) — on *Hi and Lois* and *Sam's Strip*, respectively — Johnny Sajem (*The Evermores*), and his sons Brian, Greg, Neal, and Morgan (*Betty Boop and Felix*). He lives in Stamford, Connecticut, with his wife, Catherine Carty Prentice.

REFERENCE: Rick Marschall, "Man Bites Dog," *Comics Journal* 116 (July 1987): 134–144. National Cartoonists Society, *National Cartoonists Society Album* (Greenwich, Conn., 1988).

Reed Waller 1949–

Best known, with author Kate Worley (q.v.) for the underground strip *Omaha, the Cat Dancer*, artist Reed Waller was born on August 3, 1949, in Albert Lea, Minnesota, the son of hatchery owner Mercer Douglas Waller and upholsterer Dorothea Jane Waller. He attended Lea College. Since then, Waller has been a rock vocalist, guitarist, and bandleader; an applications supervisor; a word processing supervisor; a business-machine repairman; a cook; and an "office bum." His work includes comics in *No Ducks* (Last Gasp, 1977); *Bizarre Sex*, nos. 9–10 (Kitchen Sink, 1982); and *Dope Comics*, no. 5. He is most familiar to the countercultural community, however, for *Omaha*, which began serial publication in 1985. In 1988 and 1989 Kitchen Sink Press published collections of the *Omaha* comics. States Waller, "*Omaha* is mostly storyboard work rather than flashy illustrative art. I like to do the work with an animator's attitude, concerned with bringing characters to life, and make the style unobtrusive so as not to distract from the storytelling. Funny animals are a great medium for dramatizing human personalities and foibles. Aesop liked them too."

Bill Watterson 1959–

Bill Watterson, creator of the phenomenally popular *Calvin and Hobbes*, is the son of a Cleveland attorney. Watterson spent his boyhood in Chagrin Falls, Ohio. He attended Kenyon College, where he majored in political science, graduating in 1980. After stints as an editorial cartoonist for the *Cincinnati Post* and as a layout artist for a tabloid shopper, on November 18, 1985, Watterson began publication of *Calvin and Hobbes*, the saga of a six-year-old boy and his stuffed tiger, distributed by Universal Press Syndicate. Reflecting Watterson's academic interests, the protagonists' names are derived from those of the theologian John Calvin and philosopher Thomas Hobbes. In an interview with *Detroit Free Press* editor John Smyntek,

Watterson described the origin of his popular characters: "They were originally two minor characters in another strip I proposed to syndicate. . . . The syndicate suggested I try again and build a strip revolving around them. It worked." Describing Calvin, Watterson confided to *Editor and Publisher*, "There's a dark undercurrent of nastiness to him . . . he's got a little dark side." Among the influences Watterson acknowledges are those of Charles Schulz's *Peanuts* and Walt Kelly's *Pogo*. Watterson resides in Hudson, Ohio, with his wife, Melissa, and three cats.

REFERENCES: Bill Watterson, *Calvin and Hobbes* (Kansas City, Mo., 1987). John Smyntek, "You Picked Em," *Detroit Free Press*, January 13, 1986; David Astor, "An Overnight Success After Five Years," *Editor and Publisher* (February 8, 1986). "Calvin and Hobbes a Hit," *The Province*, September 26, 1986; Richard Ellers, "Calvin Has His Cartoonist by the Tail," *Cleveland Plain Dealer*, October 25, 1986; Michael Milstein, "Comic Relief Elected," *Duke University Chronicle*, November 7, 1986; Evelyn McCormack, "The Winners," *Gannett Westchester Newspapers*, March 22, 1987; "A Boy and His Toy Tiger," *Sacramento Bee*, April 23, 1987; Ken Tucker, "On the Making of a Standout Comic," *Philadelphia Inquirer*, April 28, 1987; Philip Herrera, "The Delightful Secret of Calvin and Hobbes," *Connoisseur* 9 (June 1987): 126; Michael Grant, "And the Winner Is," *San Diego Union*, November 1, 1987; Susan Bischoff, "Calvin Tops Readers Poll," *Houston Chronicle*, January 31, 1988; Lynn Arave, "Calvin and Hobbes Most Popular Strip," *Salt Lake City Desert News*, April 6, 1988; "Calvin a Hero for the '80s," *USA Today*, June 6, 1988.

Bob Weber 1934–

Bob Weber was born in Baltimore on June 26, 1934. He graduated from the New York School of the Visual Arts in 1953. In 1959 he moved to New York, where his cartoons soon became a popular feature in the *Saturday Evening Post*. In 1965 he created his popular *Moose Miller*. Weber and his wife, Jean, live in Westport, Connecticut.

REFERENCE: King Features Syndicate, *Moose Miller* (New York, n.d.).

Bob Weber, Jr. 1957–

Bob Weber, Jr., creator of King Features Syndicate's 1986 children's feature, *Comics for Kids*, was born on January 21, 1957, in Baltimore, Maryland, the son of comic-strip artist Bob Weber (q.v.), creator of *Moose Miller*. From 1976 to 1977 he attended the University of Maryland, where he majored in biology. In 1978 he began working as assistant to his father. He sold his first cartoon to *Good Housekeeping* in 1981. Weber later became a staff artist at King Features Syndicate. He lives in Westport, Connecticut, with his wife, Lisa.

REFERENCE: King Features Syndicate, *Bob Weber, Jr.* (New York, n.d.).

Larry Welz 1948–

Born on November 21, 1948, in Bakersfield, California, underground-comics creator Larry Welz is the son of Edward and Louise Welz. Welz attended junior college in Bakersfield, and, later, the California College of Arts and Crafts, in Oakland. Welz's employment has included stints as a fruit picker in the summers of 1964 and 1965 and as a designer of gym clothing, bowling shirts, cheerleader emblems, and Econoline signs. From 1973 to 1980 Welz was copartner in Grafix, a sign/art shop. Since 1980 he has been a carnival-ride painter. Welz's numerous comics have appeared in *Yellow Dog Comix*, nos. 13, 14, 17, 19 (1969–70); *Captain Guts*, nos. 1, 2, 3 (1969–71); *The San Francisco Comic Book*, nos. 2, 3 (1970); *American Flyer Funnies*, nos. 1, 2 (1971–72); *Slow Death*, no. 3 (1971); *Aquarian Age Magazine*, vol. 2, no. 1 (1971); *Funnybook*, no. 1 (1971); *Tuff Shit* (1971); *The Kids' Liberation Coloring Book* (1971); *Bakersfield Kountry Comics* (1973); *Weird Smut*, no. 2 (1987); and *Cherry Poptart*, nos. 1–8 (1982, 1985–1989). He lives in Santa Rosa, California.

Russ Westover 1886–1966

Cartoonist Russell Channing Westover was born in Los Angeles on August 3, 1886, the son of Channing Clissen and Alice Aldrich Westover. He attended public schools in Oakland and studied for a year at the Mark Hopkins Institute of Art in San Francisco. On August 2, 1908, Westover married Genesta Grace De Lancey, later the model for his strip *Tillie the Toiler*. From 1904 to 1908 he worked on the *San Francisco Bulletin;* he later was a cartoonist for the *Oakland Herald*, the *San Francisco Chronicle*, the *San Francisco Post*, and the *New York Herald*. Between 1918 and 1921 he frequently contributed cartoons to *Life* and *Judge*. *Tillie the Toiler* was syndicated by King Features beginning in January 1921, continuing the "girl" strip originated in 1912 by Cliff Sterrett's (q.v.) *Polly and Her Pals*. *Tillie* differed from *Polly* in that the strip emphasized Tillie's role as employee, in much the same manner as Martin Branner's (q.v.) *Winnie Winkle, the Breadwinner*, begun a year prior to *Tillie*. The strip ran from 1921 until 1956. Westover died of heart failure on March 5, 1966, and is buried in Oakland's Mount View Cemetery. In addition to *Tillie* he created many other strips, among them *Betty, Daffy Dan, Fat Chance, Rose of the Office*, and the *Van Swaggers*, which appeared in conjunction with *Tillie the Toiler* on Sundays.

REFERENCES: Russell Westover, *Tillie the Toiler*, 6 vols. (New York, 1928–33); *Tillie the Toiler and the Masquerading Duchess* (New York, 1943). *Who's Who* 16 (1930–31): 2324. Arthur Baer, "Comics and Their Creators," *Literary Digest* 117 (April 28, 1934): 13. Sheridan, pp. 11, 179–182, 230, 234. Mallett, p. 471. Stephen Becker, *Comic Art in America* (New York, 1959), pp. 77–78. Obituary, *New York Times*, March 7, 1966, p. 27. *Who Was Who* 4 (1961–68): 999. Couperie and Horn, p. 45. Nye, p. 222.

Ed Wheelan 1888–1966

Edgar Stow Wheelan, originator of *Minute Movies*, was born in San Francisco. After graduating from Cornell University, he went to work for the *San Francisco Examiner*. In 1922 he began a series of sixty-day continuities that he titled *Minute Movies*. These movies gave pictorial plot summaries of such classics as *Ivanhoe, Treasure Island*, and *Hamlet*. The series was published by the George Matthew Adams Service. Couperie and Horn note that it "utilized the 'camera viewpoint' in the treatment of subjects from adventure novels . . . as well as the close-up in the depiction of the characters, thus paving the way for future innovations."

REFERENCES: Edgar Stow Wheelan, *Minute Movies: A Complete Compilation, 1927–1928* (Westport, Conn., 1977). Sheridan, pp. 19, 139. Couperie and Horn, pp. 49, 53. Horn, p. 697.

Don Wilder 1934–

Don Wilder, best known as the author of North America Syndicate's *Crock* — created with artist Bill Rechin (q.v.) in 1975 — holds a B.S. in art from East Tennessee State University. Wilder has worked as a technical illustrator, visual-media coordinator, and publications specialist at Lockheed Aircraft, R.C.A., and General Electric. He has also been a visual-information specialist for the C.I.A.

REFERENCE: King Features Syndicate, *Bill Rechin and Don Wilder* (New York, 1989).

Frank Willard 1893–1958

Artist Frank Willard was born in Anna, Illinois, on September 21, 1893, the son of Francis William and Laura Kirkham Willard. Willard's father was a doctor. Willard graduated from the Union Academy of Fine Arts. His newspaper experience included a position with the *Chicago Herald* from 1914 to 1918 and a job as cartoonist with King Features Syndicate from 1920 to 1923. Willard joined the staff of the *Chicago Tribune* on June 19, 1923, and was recruited by Joseph Medill Patterson to do a strip about a roughneck, *Moon Mullins*. The first name "Moon" (derived from *moonshine*) was suggested for the character by Patterson. The last name was selected from the listings of plumbers in a Bronx phone book. After Willard's death on January

12, 1958, the strip was continued by his longtime assistant, Ferd Johnson (q.v.), who introduced cosmetic modifications in the characters, making Emma less ugly and Mamie slimmer. Other strips by Willard include *Mrs. Pippin's Husband*, *The Outta Luck Club*, and *Tom, Dick, and Harry*.

REFERENCES: Frank Willard, *Moon Mullins*, 4 vols. (New York, 1929–32); "Moon Mullins and Me," *Collier's* 123 (May 7, 1949): 68. *Who's Who* 16 (1930–31): 2361. Sheridan, pp. 16, 17, 274. Clive Howard, "Moon Mullins: Magnificent Roughneck," *Saturday Evening Post* 220 (August 9, 1947): 20–21. Mallett, p. 476. Obituary, *New York Times*, January 13, 1958, p. 29. John Lardner, "King of the Lowdowns, Moon Mullins," *Newsweek* 51 (January 27, 1958): 67. Raymond Fisher, "Moon Mullins Today," *World of Comic Art* 1 (June 1966): 6–9. Couperie and Horn, pp. 46, 49. Nye, p. 223. Horn, p. 700.

S. Clay Wilson 1941–

Born in Lincoln, Nebraska, on July 25, 1941, S. Clay Wilson is the son of John and Ione Wilson. After serving in the U.S. Army as a medic, Wilson worked in a New York City wallet factory. In February 1968, Wilson moved to San Francisco, where, on the pages of *Zap*, with poster artists Victor Moscoso and Rick Griffin and underground cartoonists R. Crumb (q.v.) and Gilbert Shelton (q.v.), he was to father a comics renaissance. Best known for his violent *Checkered Demon*, Wilson combines in his "comix" sadistic sexuality and rabid iconoclasm. States the artist, "I find it very moralistic. . . . I'm depicting hell." Wilson's work has been exhibited at The Whitney Museum (1969), The Corcoran Gallery (1971), The And/Or Gallery in Seattle (1974), The Simon Lowinsky Gallery in San Francisco (1981), The Museum of the Surreal and Fantastique in New York City (1982), and The Psychedelic Solution in New York (1989). His classic comics have appeared in *Snatch Comix*, nos. 1–4 (1968–69); *Zap Comix*, nos. 2–9 (1968–78); *Yellow Dog Comix*, nos. 3, 5, 7, 8, 9, 10, 13, 14 (1968–69); *Gothic Blimp Works*, nos. 1, 2, 4, 6, 7 (1969); *Jiz Comix* (1969); *King Bee* (1969); *Laugh in the Dark* (1969); *Radical America Comix* (1969); *Insect Fear*, nos. 1–3 (1970–72); *San Francisco Comix Book*, nos. 1–3 (1970), *Pro Junior Comix* (1971), *Thrilling Murder* (1971) *Douglas Comix* (1972), *Zam Zap Comix* (1974); *Arcade*, nos. 1, 3, 4, 6, 7 (1975–76); *Comix Book*, nos. 1, 2, 5 (1975–76); *Felch Comix* (1975); *Barbarian Women*, no. 2 (1977); *Missoula Comix* (1979); *Raw* (1980); *Cocaine Comix*, no. 3 (1981); *Commies From Mars* (1981), *Maggotzine* (1981); and *Yama Yama/Ugly Head Comix* (1981). Wilson has illustrated and designed German editions of author William Burroughs's *Wild Boys* and *Cities of the Red Night*. Wilson lives in San Francisco, where a permanent installation of his work can be seen at Dick's Bar.

REFERENCE: S. Clay Wilson, *S. Clay Wilson: Selected Works* (New York, 1982).

Dick Wingert 1919–

Creator of *Hubert*, artist Dick Wingert was born in Cedar Rapids, Iowa. Wingert attended the Herron School of Art in Indianapolis for three years. Drafted, he was assigned to the Thirty-fourth Infantry Operations Division, and in 1942 saw combat in the European theater. Wingert's first cartoons were published in *Stars and Stripes*, for which he created *Hubert*. While still in uniform, Wingert met William Randolph Hearst, Jr. After Wingert's discharge, King Features began syndication of a civilian *Hubert* in 1945.

REFERENCE: King Features Syndicate, *Dick Wingert* (New York, n.d.).

Kate Worley 1958–

Kate Worley, author of *Omaha, the Cat Dancer*, was born on March 16, 1958, in Belleville, Illinois, the daughter of Charles D. Worley, U.S. Air Force staff sergeant, and Aurelia Emma Klemme Worley, a civil servant. Worley attended college in Belleville in 1976. In 1982, she attended the University of Minnesota. Worley describes her work history as that of an "erratic clerical worker while pursuing music and writing careers . . . also worked as a freelance calligrapher, keyliner, and radio scriptwriter." In 1986 she began scripting *Omaha*. Her work has

also appeared in *Wimmen's Comix*, no. 14 (1989); *The Best of Rip Off Press Annual* (1989); *Critters*, nos. 12, 20 (1987); and in *Strip AIDS USA* (Last Gasp, 1988). States Worley, "I find comics a tremendously exciting medium. As a writer I have all the storytelling capacity available in any other visual medium, plus the possibility to completely transcend (or avoid) the limitations of reality. It's great fun — whether I'm doing something serious or something comic."

George Wunder 1912–1989

George Wunder, stepfather to Milton Caniff's (q.v.) *Terry and the Pirates*, was born in New York City on April 24, 1912, the son of August and Mary Powell Wunder. On April 16, 1938, Wunder married Mildred A. Smith. He worked for the Associated Press as a cartoonist from 1936 until 1946, when he took over Caniff's *Terry*. Couperie and Horn credit Wunder with pioneering the experimental use of color in the comic strip, using it to "help to create a psychological mood, and especially to reinforce the psychological and dramatic effects of the picture or the narrative by frequently daring applications." Another notable aspect of Wunder's work is the use of personal mannerisms to create engaging national stereotypes. Wunder's own army experiences in World War II furnished him with the basis for some *Terry* episodes. In 1963 Wunder was honored with the U.S. Air Force's Service Award.

REFERENCES: "Terry's Wunder Penman," *Newsweek* 28 (October 7, 1946): 68. *Who's Who* 34 (1966–67): 2360. Couperie and Horn, author index.

Rick Yager

Legendary comic-strip author and artist Rick Yager, best known for *Buck Rogers* and *Grin and Bear It*, was born in Alton, Illinois, the son of Charles M. Yager, publisher of *Modern Miller*, a grain-and-flour weekly. The family later moved to Oak Park, Illinois, where neighbors included Ernest Hemingway and Edgar Rice Burroughs. During the Depression, Yager attended the Chicago Academy of Fine Arts, where he was later to become an instructor. He also studied with *Chicago Tribune* political cartoonist Carey Orr. In 1931 he began his work on *Buck Rogers*, which he continued until 1958. In 1960 he created *Little Orvy*, which ran until 1965. Since 1962 he has penned North America Syndicate's *Grin and Bear It*. Yager lives in Douglas, Michigan, with his wife, the former Jane Horder. States Yager, "Sick or well, you must meet your deadlines. If you're going to die, don't die until your work is out! That is the hard part of cartooning — and yet it has been a career of many rewards as well as extremely difficult work, though anyone not in the business might think it a snap job!"

REFERENCES: Ronald Emondson, "Buck Rogers' Creator Visits Baldwin," *The Independent*, April 18, 1984. "The Hand Behind Buck Rogers," *Grand Rapids Press*, January 27, 1985. Kristen Roberts, "Artist's Busy Life," *Waves of West Michigan*, June 21–28, 1986. Ben Beversluis, " 'Buck Rogers' Cartoon Creator to Figure Prominently in Libertyfest Celebration," *Grand Rapids Press*, June 30, 1986. King Features Syndicate, *Rick Yager* (New York, n.d.).

Bill Yates 1921–

Bill Yates was born on July 5, 1921, in Samson, Alabama. He studied cartooning through the W. L. Evans Correspondence School. Yates attended the University of Texas, where he edited the campus humor magazine. In 1950 he moved to New York City and obtained employment with Dell Publishing. In 1960 Yates created the strip *Professor Phumble*, which ended daily syndication in 1978. (The strip still appears in approximately seven hundred weekly newspapers around the country.) He became comics editor for King Features Syndicate in 1978. Yates succeeded Morrie Brickman (q.v.) as cartoonist of *the small society* in 1985, and in May 1988 began scripting *Redeye*. At the close of 1988, Yates retired from King Features.

REFERENCE: King Features Syndicate, *Floyd Buford ("Bill") Yates* (New York, August 1989).

Chic Young 1901–1973

Murat Bernard Young was born in Chicago on January 9, 1901, the son of James Luther and Martha Techen Young. He was educated in the public schools of St. Louis and attended art schools in Chicago, New York, and Cleveland. He married Athel L. Lindorff on October 4, 1927. Young worked as a cartoonist for the Newspaper Enterprise Association from 1920 to 1921. He was then employed by Bell Syndicate until 1923, when he joined the King Features Syndicate. There, in 1924, he created *Dumb Dora*. The strip, later drawn by Bil Dwyer (q.v.) and Paul Fung (q.v.), inspired a play the following year, and continued as a strip until 1930, when Young began *Blondie*, which has enjoyed larger circulation than any other strip. As Nye states, this "most widely syndicated of all comics" (*Blondie* appears in more than two thousand newspapers) has inspired a forty-picture movie series, a radio series, a television series, and two network animated television specials.

REFERENCES: Murat Young, *Blondie and Dagwood's Secret Service* (Racine, Wis., 1942); *Blondie and Dagwood's Snapshot Clue* (Racine, Wis., 1943); *Blondie from A to Z* (Philadelphia, 1943); *Blondie* (Philadelphia, 1944); *Blondie and Dagwood's Adventure in Magic* (Racine, Wis., 1944); *Blondie and Dagwood's Marvelous Invention* (Racine, Wis., 1947); *Blondie's Soups, Salads, and Sandwiches Cook Book* (Philadelphia, 1947); *Blondie's Family* (New York, 1954); *Twenty-five Years with Blondie* (New York, 1958); *Blondie and Dagwood's America* (New York, 1981). Helga Lund, *Blondie and Dagwood: A Novel of the Great American Family*, illus. by Chic Young (New York, 1944). Joseph Musial, *Learn How Dagwood Splits the Atom!* (New York, 1949). F. G. Johnson, *Dumb Dora, a Comedy in One Act* (Minneapolis, 1932). "Comic Strip Blondie," *Newsweek* 17 (June 23, 1941): 64. Sheridan, pp. 20, 95–97, 162, 232. Jack Alexander, "Dagwood and Blondie," *Saturday Evening Post* 220 (April 10, 1948): 15–17. "Dagwood Splits the Atom," *Popular Science* 153 (September 1948): 146–149. "Blondie's Pop," *Newsweek* 32 (November 1, 1948): 48. "Blondie's Father," *Time* 53 (May 9, 1949): 80–81. *Who's Who* 34 (1966–67): 2370. Couperie and Horn, author index. Nye, pp. 77, 223–225, 388. Obituary, *New York Times*, March 16, 1973. Obituary, *Washington Post*, March 16, 1973. Obituary, *Newsweek*, March 26, 1973. Horn, p. 714.

Dean Young 1938–

Dean Young was born in Flushing, New York, in 1938, the son of artist Chic Young (q.v.), the creator of *Blondie*. He graduated from La Grange College, later working as an advertising account executive. In 1963 Young began his collaboration with his famous father. Following his father's death in 1973, Young collaborated with Jim Raymond, then Stan Drake (q.v.), to continue the strip. Young has worked with King Features Entertainment to produce two prime-time animated specials for CBS.

REFERENCES: Dean Young and Rick Marschall, *Blondie and Dagwood's America* (New York, 1981). King Features Syndicate, *Blondie* (New York, 1988).

Bill Ziegler 1925–

Since 1954 an artist on *Mary Worth*, Bill Ziegler was born on July 7, 1925, in Portland, Oregon, and raised in Berkeley, California. In 1943 he was drafted. After his discharge, Ziegler attended the Portland School of Art and the Schouinard Art Institute in Los Angeles. In 1950 he launched his career as a cartoon artist when he won a contest sponsored by the Los Angeles Mirror Syndicate, becoming the illustrator of *Annie Oakley*. A second strip penned by Ziegler was *Dragnet*. In 1954 he went to work with Ken Ernst (q.v.) on *Mary Worth*, becoming the strip's lead artist in 1985. He resides in Santa Barbara, California, with his wife, Norma.

REFERENCE: King Features Syndicate, *Bill Ziegler* (New York, 1989).

NOTES

CHAPTER ONE

1. Marshall McLuhan, *The Mechanical Bride: Folklore of Industrial Man*, rev. ed. (New York: Vanguard, 1969), p. 69.
2. Stephen Becker, *Comic Art in America* (New York: Simon & Schuster, 1959), pp. 2, 3. Such long-held views of the Yellow Kid's origins have recently been disputed by Richard Marschall — *America's Great Comic-Strip Artists* (New York: Abbeville Press, 1989), p. 22 — who asserts that the historical explanation for the character's yellowness remains obscure.
3. Clark Kinnaird, "Cavalcade of Funnies," in D. M. White and Robert Abel, eds., *The Funnies: An American Idiom* (New York: Free Press of Glencoe; London: Collier-Macmillan, 1963), pp. 88–89.
4. Becker, p. 10.
5. Martin Sheridan, *Comics and Their Creators* (Boston: Robert T. Hale & Co., 1942), pp. 69, 259.
6. Ray Bradbury, Introduction to Robert C. Dille, ed., *The Collected Works of Buck Rogers in the Twenty-fifth Century* (New York: Chelsea House, 1969), p. xiii.
7. Joe Queenan, "Drawing on the Dark Side," *New York Times Magazine* (April 30, 1989): 79.

CHAPTER TWO

1. Winsor McCay, "Movie Cartoons," *Cartoon and Movie Magazine* 31 (April 1927): 11; *New York Evening Journal*, July 27, 1934; John A. Fitzsimmons to author, February 8, 1974.
2. Ruth Wright to author, April 19, 1973; McCay, "Movie Cartoons," p. 11; Austin George, "John Goodison: In Memoriam," *Aurora 1893* (Yearbook of Eastern Michigan University), p. 47; E. R. Isbell, *A History of Eastern Michigan University, 1849–1965* (Ypsilanti, Mich.: Eastern Michigan University, 1966), pp. 69–70; Susan McCulloch to author, July 13, 1973; Montgomery Phister, "People of the Stage: Winsor McCay," *Cincinnati Commercial Tribune*, November 28, 1909, Dramatic Magazine, p. 1.
3. *New York American*, July 27, 1934.
4. "Winsor McCay: Artist, Inventor, and Prophet" (Manuscript, ca. 1938), collection of Richard Gelman, p. 5; *New York Herald Tribune*, July 27, 1934.
5. Phister, "People of the Stage: Winsor McCay," p. 1.
6. Ibid.
7. Ibid.
8. Ibid.
9. Ibid.
10. *Atlanta Constitution*, June 11, 1911.
11. *Variety*, July 1908.
12. "Winsor McCay: Artist, Inventor, and Prophet," p. 22.
13. Claude Bragdon, "Mickey Mouse and What He Means," *Scribner's* 96 (July 1934): 40–43.
14. "Winsor McCay: Artist, Inventor, and Prophet," p. 15.

CHAPTER THREE

1. Herriman, *Krazy Kat*, December 28, 1919, and November 17, 1916, collections of Dee Cox and Bea and Murray Harris; reproduced in Patrick McDonnell, Karen O'Connell, and Georgia Riley de Havenon, *Krazy Kat: The Comic Art of George Herriman* (New York: Harry N. Abrams, 1986), pp. 160, 111, and in George Herriman, *Krazy Kat* (New York: Grosset & Dunlap, 1969), p. 45.
2. e. e. cummings, Introduction to Herriman, *Krazy Kat*, pp. 10–16.
3. "The resemblance [of Krazy Kat's speech patterns to African-American idioms] suggests that Krazy Kat may be a 'black cat' — he is always drawn as a black cat — or that Herriman's youth in New Orleans may have brought him in touch with the black art of 'rappin.'" Judith O'Sullivan, *The Art of the Comic Strip* (College Park, Md.: University of Maryland, 1971), pp. 26–27.
4. Birth certificate of George Joseph Herriman, New Orleans Bureau of Vital Statistics; U.S. Census, 1880; McDonnell et al., *Krazy Kat: The Comic Art of George Herriman*, p. 30.
5. Pulitzer newspapers, February 16, 23 and March 9, 1902; McDonnell et al., *Krazy Kat: The Comic Art of George Herriman*, pp. 34, 36, 215, 223.
6. Tad Dorgan, "This Is about Garge [sic] Herriman," ca. 1920, in McDonnell et al., *Krazy Kat: The Comic Art of George Herriman*, p. 40. (An original copy of this article is in the collections of the Museum of Cartoon Art, Rye Brook, New York).
7. See the following *Krazy Kat* strips by George Herriman: June 22, 1919, collection of Al Ordover, reproduced in McDonnell et al., *Krazy Kat: The Comic Art of George Herriman*, p. 8; February 3, 1919, collection of Karen O'Connell, reproduced in ibid., p. 130; April 4, 1918, collection of Dee Cox, reproduced in ibid., p. 131; May 5, 1919, collection of Dee Cox, reproduced in ibid., p. 132; May 18, 1918, collection of Dee Cox, reproduced in ibid., p. 152; December 28, 1919, collection of Dee Cox, reproduced in ibid., p. 160; March 21, 1920, collection of Dee Cox, reproduced in ibid., p. 164; July 2, 1939, collection of Art Spiegelman, reproduced in ibid., p. 198.
8. Herriman, *Krazy Kat*, August 25, 1918, collection of Dee Cox, reproduced in ibid., p. 136.
9. Herriman, *Krazy Kat*, May 5, 1918, collection of Dee Cox, reproduced in ibid., p. 132.
10. Gilbert Seldes, "The Krazy Kat That Walks by Himself," in *The Seven Lively Arts* (New York: Harper and Brothers, 1924). Reprinted in McDonnell et al., *Krazy Kat: The Comic Art of George Herriman*, p. 17.
11. Dorgan, "This Is About Garge [sic] Herriman," reprinted in McDonnell et al., *Krazy Kat: The Comic Art of George Herriman*, p. 40.
12. Herriman, *Krazy Kat*, January 6, 1918, reproduced in ibid., p. 61.
13. Herriman, *Krazy Kat*, December 9, 1917, collection of Garry Trudeau, reproduced in ibid., p. 60.
14. Herriman, *Krazy Kat*, September 17, 1916, collection of Dee Cox, reproduced in ibid., p. 113.
15. Herriman, *Krazy Kat*, May 21, 1916, collection of Mr. and Mrs. Frank Daly, reproduced in ibid., p. 114.
16. Herriman, *Krazy Kat*, June 24, 1936, reproduced in Herriman, *Krazy Kat*, p. 94. The rap continues in the next episode: "I kwoff a kwatt of lightnin' for my brekfitz — / I dib my mug in

a gallon jug of thunda for my lunch — / An' for suppa I sib a silo full of cyclone soup —" (Herriman, *Krazy Kat*, June 26, 1936, reproduced in Herriman, *Krazy Kat*, p. 94).

17. E. Franklin Frazier, *The Negro in the United States* (New York: Macmillan, 1958), pp. 67–68.

18. O'Sullivan, *The Art of the Comic Strip*, p. 92; Charles Hardy, "A Brief History of Ethnicity in the Comics," *Nemo* 28 (December 1987): 8; Stephen Jones, "From 'Under Cork' to Overcoming: Black Images in the Comics," *Nemo* 28 (December 1987): 19.

19. McDonnell et al., *Krazy Kat: The Comic Art of George Herriman*, p. 30.

20. Martin Sheridan, *Comics and Their Creators* (Boston: Robert T. Hale & Co., 1942), p. 65; McDonnell et al., *Krazy Kat: The Comic Art of George Herriman*, p. 25.

21. Dorgan, "This Is about Garge [sic] Herriman," in McDonnell et al., *Krazy Kat: The Comic Art of George Herriman*, p. 40.

22. Collection of Garry Trudeau, reproduced in McDonnell et al., *Krazy Kat: The Comic Art of George Herriman*, p. 165.

23. Dorgan, "This Is about Garge [sic] Herriman," in McDonnell et al., *Krazy Kat: The Comic Art of George Herriman*, p. 40.

24. e. e. cummings, Introduction to Herriman, *Krazy Kat*, p. 11.

CHAPTER FOUR

1. Rosemary Gallick, "The Comic Art of Lyonel Feininger" (master's thesis, Pratt Institute, 1974), p. 3.

2. *Chicago Sunday Tribune*, May 6, 1906.

3. Gallick, "The Comic Art of Lyonel Feininger," p. 1.

4. Ibid., p. 9.

5. *Chicago Sunday Tribune*, June 24 and November 4, 1906.

6. T. Lux Feininger, *Lyonel Feininger: City at the Edge of the World* (New York: Frederick A. Praeger, 1965), p. 80.

7. Gallick, "The Comic Art of Lyonel Feininger," p. 18.

8. Ernest Scheyer, *Lyonel Feininger: Caricature and Fantasy* (Detroit: Wayne State University Press, 1964), p. 112.

9. Gallick, "The Comic Art of Lyonel Feininger," pp. 21–22.

10. Hans Hess, *Lyonel Feininger* (New York: Harry Abrams, 1955), p. 138.

11. Gallick, "The Comic Art of Lyonel Feininger," pp. 24–25.

12. Lyonel Feininger, 1896 letter to Alfred Vance Churchill, in Hans Hess, *Lyonel Feininger*, p. 22.

13. Bill Blackbeard, "Buster Brown," in Maurice Horn, ed., *The World Encyclopedia of Comics* (New York: Chelsea House, 1976), p. 145.

14. Philip Herrera, "The Delightful Secret of Calvin and Hobbes," *Connoisseur* 9 (June 1987): 126.

15. Martin Sheridan, *Comics and Their Creators* (Boston: Robert T. Hale & Co., 1942), p. 43; Herb Galewitz, Introduction to George McManus, *Bringing Up Father* (New York: Charles Scribner's Sons, 1973), p. v.

16. Sheridan, *Comics and Their Creators*, p. 43.

17. Ibid., p. 45; Coulton Waugh, *The Comics* (New York: Macmillan, 1947), p. 47; Judith O'Sullivan, *The Art of the Comic Strip* (College Park, Md.: University of Maryland, 1971), p. 89; Galewitz, Introduction to McManus, *Bringing Up Father*, p. v.

18. Sheridan, *Comics and Their Creators*, p. 45.

19. Waugh, *The Comics*, p. 45.

20. Sheridan, *Comics and Their Creators*, p. 44.

21. *New York American*, May 14, April 30, and August 27, 1933, reproduced in George McManus, *Jiggs Is Back* (Berkeley, Calif.: Celtic Book Company, 1986), p. 53.

22. *New York American*, November 4, 1933, reproduced in ibid., p. 19.

23. Galewitz, Introduction to McManus, *Bringing Up Father*, p. ix.

24. *New York American*, February 2, 1936, reproduced in McManus, *Jiggs Is Back*, p. 16.

25. *New York American*, December 3, 1939, to July 7, 1940, reproduced in ibid., pp. 26–49.

26. George McManus and Henry La Cossitt, "Jiggs and I," *Collier's* 129 (January 28, 1952): 39; O'Sullivan, *The Art of the Comic Strip*, pp. 22–23.

27. O'Sullivan, *The Art of the Comic Strip*, p. 23.

28. McManus and La Cossitt, "Jiggs and I," p. 39.

29. William Kennedy, Introduction to McManus, *Jiggs Is Back*, p. 7.

30. O'Sullivan, *The Art of the Comic Strip*, p. 80.

31. Sheridan, *Comics and Their Creators*, p. 45.

32. O'Sullivan, *The Art of the Comic Strip*, p. 40.

33. Russel Nye, *The Unembarrassed Muse: The Popular Arts in America* (New York: Dial Press, 1970), pp. 77, 233–235, 338.

34. Sheridan, *Comics and Their Creators*, p. 190; O'Sullivan, *The Art of the Comic Strip*, p. 13.

35. O'Sullivan, *The Art of the Comic Strip*, p. 13.

36. Susan Baxter, "Drawing on the Dark Side," *Easy Living* 12 (November 3–December 1, 1986): 30.

CHAPTER FIVE

1. Judith O'Sullivan, *The Art of the Comic Strip* (College Park, Md.: University of Maryland, 1971), pp. 73–74.

2. Ibid., p. 73; Martin Sheridan, *Comics and Their Creators* (Boston: Robert T. Hale & Co., 1942), p. 69.

3. McManus, *Bringing Up Father*, November 4, 1923, *New York American*, reproduced in George McManus, *Jiggs Is Back* (Berkeley, Calif.: Celtic Book Company, 1986), p. 69.

4. Books containing proofs of the daily strips can be found in the collections of the Mugar Memorial Library, Boston University. The 1931 strips have been reproduced in Harold Gray, *Little Orphan Annie in the Great Depression* (New York: Dover, 1979), and in Harold Gray, *Little Orphan Annie* (Agoura, Calif.: Fantagraphics Books, 1987).

5. Gray, *Little Orphan Annie*, p. 3.

6. Coulton Waugh, *The Comics* (New York: Macmillan, 1947), p. 83.

7. Gray, *Little Orphan Annie*, p. 83.

8. *Chicago Tribune*, August 7, 1935, reproduced in Harold Gray, *Arf! The Life and Hard Times of Little Orphan Annie,*

1935–1945 (New Rochelle, N.Y.: Arlington House, 1970), n.p.

9. *Chicago Tribune*, February 22, 1937, reproduced in Gray, *Arf!*, n.p.

10. *Chicago Tribune*, March 3, 1937, reproduced in Gray, *Arf!*, n.p.

11. *Chicago Tribune*, July 16, 1935, reproduced in Gray, *Arf!*, n.p.

12. *Chicago Tribune*, April 18–June 25, 1937, reproduced in Gray, *Arf!*, n.p.

13. Sheridan, *Comics and Their Creators*, p. 70.

14. Al Capp, Introduction to Gray, *Arf!*, n.p.

15. Waugh, *The Comics*, p. 83.

16. Chester Gould, *The Celebrated Cases of Dick Tracy* (New York: Chelsea House, 1970), p. xvi.

17. Art Spiegelman, *Print* 42 (November–December 1988): 68.

18. Gould, *The Celebrated Cases of Dick Tracy*, p. xi.

19. *Chicago Tribune*, December 28, 1941, reproduced in Chester Gould, *Dick Tracy: Book Fifteen* (El Cajon, Calif.: Blackthorne Publishing, 1987), pp. 7–8.

20. Art Spiegelman, *Print* 42 (November–December 1988): 68–69.

21. Gould, *The Celebrated Cases of Dick Tracy*, p. xv.

22. Waugh, *The Comics*, p. 215.

23. Al Capp, *From Dogpatch to Slobbovia* (Boston: Beacon Press, 1964); O'Sullivan, *The Art of the Comic Strip*, p. 64.

24. Al Capp, *Li'l Abner Dailies, Volume One: 1934–1935*, p. 7.

25. Al Capp, *The Best of Li'l Abner* (New York: Holt, Rinehart & Winston, 1978), p. 10.

26. United Feature Syndicate Press Book, "How Al Capp Came To Create Li'l Abner," reprinted in Capp, *Li'l Abner Dailies, Volume One: 1934–1935*, p. 6.

27. Capp, *Li'l Abner Dailies, Volume One: 1934–1935*, p. 4.

28. Al Capp, Introduction to Gray, *Arf!*, n.p.

29. Capp, *The Best of Li'l Abner*, p. 12.

30. Al Capp, "Li'l Abner: Fearless Fosdick by Lester Gooch." The original drawing for this 1943 episode (DLC/PP-1974: 232.1293) is part of the Swann Collection of Cartoon and Caricature, Prints and Photographs Division, the Library of Congress.

31. Charles Burns, *Hard-Boiled Defective Stories* (New York: Pantheon Books, 1988).

CHAPTER SIX

1. Alex Raymond, *Flash Gordon, Volume One, The Planet Mongo*, ed. Woody Gelman (New York: Nostalgia Press, 1974), n.p.

2. Ibid.

3. Ibid.

4. Hal Foster, "Interview with Bill Crouch," *Cartoonist PROfiles* (June 1974), reprinted in Hal Foster, *Prince Valiant, Volume Two* (New York: Nostalgia Press, 1974), n.p.

5. Ibid.

6. The original drawing for this 1967 episode (DLC/PP-1974: 232.1627) is part of the Swann Collection of Cartoon and Caricature, Prints and Photographs Division, the Library of

Congress.

7. Judith O'Sullivan, *The Art of the Comic Strip* (College Park, Md.: University of Maryland, 1971), p. 27.

8. Walter James Miller, "Burne Hogarth and the Art of Pictorial Fiction," *Jungle Tales of Tarzan* (New York: Watson-Guptill, 1976), pp. 7, 34.

9. Ibid., p. 11.

10. Martin Sheridan, *Comics and Their Creators* (Boston: Robert T. Hale & Co., 1942), p. 157.

11. O'Sullivan, *The Art of the Comic Strip*, pp. 60–61; Sheridan, *Comics and Their Creators*, p. 119.

CHAPTER SEVEN

1. Henry Brandon, "Interview," *London Sunday Times* (1959), reprinted in Walt Kelly, *Pluperfect Pogo*, eds. Mrs. Walt Kelly and Bill Crouch, Jr. (New York: Simon & Schuster, 1987), p. 96.

2. "Our Archives of Culture: Enter the Comics and Pogo," *Newsweek* 43 (June 21, 1954): 60; Judith O'Sullivan, *The Art of the Comic Strip* (College Park, Md.: University of Maryland, 1971), p. 77.

3. *Code of the Comics Magazine Association of America* (New York: Comics Magazine Association of America, Inc., n.d.).

4. Library for Communication and Graphic Arts, Ohio State University Libraries, *Walt Kelly: A Retrospective Exhibition To Celebrate the Seventy-fifth Anniversary of His Birth* (Columbus, Ohio: The Ohio State University Libraries, 1988), p. 7. Frederic Wertham's *Seduction of the Innocent* has been recently satirized by cartoonists Lloyd Llewellyn and Daniel Clowes in *Blab!* 3 (Fall 1988): 2–7.

5. Brandon, "Interview," in Kelly, *Pluperfect Pogo*, p. 96.

6. Kelly, *Pluperfect Pogo*, pp. 113–114.

7. Walt Kelly, Interview with WCRS-TV, July 15, 1962, transcribed in "WCBS-TV Views the Press," pp. 7–8; reprinted in Kelly, *Pluperfect Pogo*, pp. 193–94.

8. Brandon, "Interview," in Kelly, *Pluperfect Pogo*, p. 94.

9. Library for Communication and Graphic Arts, Ohio State University Libraries, *Walt Kelly*, p. 48.

10. O'Sullivan, *The Art of the Comic Strip*, p. 77.

11. Brandon, "Interview," in Kelly, *Pluperfect Pogo*, p. 94.

12. Steve Thompson, "Highlights of Pogo," in Library for Communication and Graphic Arts, Ohio State University Libraries, *Walt Kelly*, pp. 42–43.

13. Brandon, "Interview," in Kelly, *Pluperfect Pogo*, p. 95.

14. Will Eisner, "Reminiscences and Hortations," *Comics Journal* 89 (March 1984): 80.

15. Jules Feiffer, *Jules Feiffer's America* (New York: Alfred A. Knopf, 1982), p. 12.

16. Ibid., p. 10.

17. Ibid., p. 11.

18. Ibid.

19. Ibid., p. 15.

20. Ibid., p. 168.

21. Ibid.

22. Ibid., pp. 15, 168.

23. Ibid., p. 13.

24. Gary Groth, "Jules Feiffer; Memories of a Pro Bono Cartoonist," *Comics Journal* 124 (August 1988): 55.

25. Mark Jannot, "Can Breathed Be Taken Seriously?" *Comics Journal* 125 (October 1988): 93.

26. Ibid., p. 97.

27. Ibid., p. 98.

28. Feiffer, *Jules Feiffer's America*, p. 230.

CHAPTER EIGHT

1. Robert Hughes, "An X Cartoon," *Time* 99 (May 22, 1972): 101.

2. Ibid.

3. Ibid.

4. R. Crumb, *Cat Life*, September 1959–February 1960, reprinted in *The Complete Fritz the Cat* (New York: Belier Press, 1978), p. 15.

5. Ibid., p. 17.

6. R. Crumb, *The Complete Fritz the Cat*, p. 4.

7. R. Crumb, "Fred the Teen-Age Girl Pigeon," in *Help* 24 (May 1965): 39–40; reprinted in Crumb, *The Complete Fritz the Cat*, pp. 26–27.

8. R. Crumb, "Fritz the Cat in 'Fritz Bugs Out,'" reprinted in R. Crumb, *R. Crumb's Fritz the Cat: Three Big Stories!* (New York: Ballantine, 1969), in R. Crumb, *Fritz Bugs Out* (New York: Ballantine, 1972), and in R. Crumb, *The Complete Fritz the Cat*, pp. 29–50.

9. Ibid.

10. Ibid.

11. R. Crumb, "Fritz the Cat: Special Agent for the C.I.A.," reprinted in R. Crumb, *R. Crumb's Fritz the Cat: Three Big Stories!*, in Crumb, *Fritz the Cat: Special Agent for the C.I.A.* (New York: Ballantine, 1972), and in Crumb, *The Complete Fritz the Cat*, pp. 51–66.

12. Ibid.

13. Ibid.

14. Ibid.

15. Ibid.

16. Ibid.

17. Ibid.

18. Ibid.

19. R. Crumb, "Fritz the Cat Doubts His Masculinity," reprinted in Crumb, *The Complete Fritz the Cat*, p. 75; R. Crumb, "Fritz the Cat in 'Fritz the No-Good,'" reprinted in Crumb, *R. Crumb's Fritz the Cat: Three Big Stories!*, in Crumb, *Fritz the No-Good* (New York: Ballantine, 1972), and in Crumb, *The Complete Fritz the Cat*, pp. 88–103.

20. Ibid.

21. R. Crumb, "Fritz the Cat 'Superstar,'" in *The People's Comics* (Princeton, Wis.: Kitchen Sink Press, 1972), n.p.; reprinted in Crumb, *The Complete Fritz the Cat*, pp. 105–119.

22. Ibid.

23. Ibid.

24. R. Crumb, Introduction to *The Complete Fritz the Cat*, p. iv.

25. Thomas Albright, "Zap, Snatch, and Crumb," *Rolling Stone* 28 (March 1, 1969): 24–25; quoted in Don Fiene, *R. Crumb Checklist* (Cambridge, Mass.: Boatner Norton Press, 1981), p. 151.

26. Feine, *R. Crumb Checklist*, pp. 148–159.

27. R. Crumb, *Mr. Natural*, no. 1 (1970), *Mr. Natural*, no. 2 (1971), *Mr. Natural*, no. 3 (1977), *Home Grown Funnies*, no. 1 (1971), *Snoid Comics* (1980). Feine, *R. Crumb Checklist*, pp. 128, 151, 155.

28. Crumb, *Mr. Natural*, no. 2, front cover.

29. R. Crumb, "Mr. Natural Meets God," *East Village Other* (February 16–22, 1968): 10; reprinted in R. Crumb, *R. Crumb's Head Comix: Twenty Years Later* (New York: Simon & Schuster, 1988).

30. Crumb, *Mr. Natural*, no. 3.

31. Crumb, *Snoid Comics*, back cover, reprinted in R. Crumb, *R. Crumb's Snoid Comics* (Princeton, Wis.: Kitchen Sink Press, 1986); Crumb, *Mr. Natural*, no. 3.

32. Crumb, *Snoid Comics*.

33. Richard Krafsur, ed., *The American Film Institute Catalog, Feature Films 1961–1970* (New York: R. Bowker, 1976).

34. *R. Crumb's Snoid Comics*.

35. R. Crumb, "My Troubles With Women," in *Zap Comix*, no. 10 (Berkeley, Calif.: Last Gasp, 1982).

36. Gary Groth and Joe Sacco, "The Straight Dope from R. Crumb," *Comics Journal* 121 (April 1988): 104.

37. R. Crumb, "Joe Blow," in *Zap Comix*, no. 4 (Berkeley, Calif., Last Gasp, 1969); 316 N.Y.S. 2d 37 (Crim. Ct. of the City of New York), 1970.

38. Ibid.

39. 11 Md. App. at 230.

40. Thomas Maremaa, "Who Is This Crumb?" *New York Times Magazine* (October 1, 1972): 70, quoted in Feine, *R. Crumb Checklist*, pp. 153–154.

41. Trina Robbins, *Blab* (Fall 1988): 91.

CHAPTER NINE

1. Allen Saunders, "Playwright for Paper Actors," *Nemo* 18 (April 1986): 58–59.

2. Gilbert Shelton, "Little Orphan Amphetamine," reprinted in Gilbert Shelton, *The Collected Adventures of the Fabulous Furry Freak Brothers* (Auburn, Calif.: Rip Off Press, 1980), and in Gilbert Shelton, *The Fabulous Furry Freak Brothers*, Vol. 1 (Auburn, Calif.: Rip Off Press, 1988), p. 29.

3. Norma Lee Browning, "First Lady of Funnies," *Saturday Evening Post* 233 (November 19, 1960): 34–35.

4. Richard Marschall, "A Forgotten Landmark: Torchy Brown," *Nemo* 28 (January 1988): 56–66.

5. Kim Upton, "The Wit Behind the Wisdom of 'Sylvia,'" *Chicago Sunday Sun Times*, January 1, 1984, pp. 8–9.

6. Nicole Hollander, *Never Take Your Cat to a Salad Bar* (New York: Random House, 1987), pp. 23, 9, 113, 58, 57, 108.

7. Ibid., p. 102.

8. Ibid., p. 100.

9. Ibid., pp. 46, 16, 72, 78.

10. Jan Hoffman, "The Toughest Woman in America," *Village*

Voice, December 27, 1983, pp. 54–55.

11. Lynda Barry, *The Fun House* (New York: Harper & Row, 1987), n. p.

12. Ibid.

13. Ibid.

14. Ibid.

15. Ibid.

16. Ibid.

17. Ibid.

18. Chris McCubbin, " 'Lonely Nights' Artist Dori Seda Dead at Thirty-Seven," *Comics Journal* 121 (April 1988): 12.

19. Dori Seda, *Lonely Nights* (Berkeley: Last Gasp, 1986).

20. R. Crumb, Introduction to Seda, *Lonely Nights*, n.p.

21. Seda, *Lonely Nights*, n.p.

22. Aline Kominsky-Crumb, *The Bunch's Power Pac Comics* (Princeton, Wis.: Kitchen Sink Enterprises, 1979); Aline Kominsky-Crumb, *The Bunch's Power Pak Comics*, no. 2 (Princeton, Wis.: Kitchen Sink Enterprises, 1981).

CHAPTER TEN

1. Art Spiegelman and Françoise Mouly, "Raw Nerves," in *Read Yourself Raw* (New York: Pantheon Books, 1987), p. 5.

2. Ibid., pp. 5–6.

3. Ibid., p. 6.

4. R. Crumb, Introduction to *The Complete Fritz the Cat* (New York: Belier Press, 1978), p. iv.

5. Adam Gopnik, "Comics and Catastrophe," *New Republic* 25 (June 22, 1987): 29–33.

6. Spiegelman, *Maus: A Survivor's Tale* (New York: Pantheon Books, 1986), p. 5.

7. Chris McCubbin and Thom Powers, "Graphic Novel Explosion in '88," *Comics Journal* 121 (April 1988): 6.

8. The origins of the graphic novel are often disputed. Among the important publishing houses contributing to its development are Ballantine, Berkeley, Byron Press Visual Publications, the Donning Company, Doubleday/Dolphin, First Comics, Marvel Comics, NAL/Plume, New Society Publishers, Pantheon, Pocket Books/Archway, Simon & Schuster, and Warner Books.

9. Beth Levine, "Graphic Novels: The Latest Word in Illustrated Books," *Publishers Weekly* (May 22, 1987): 45–47.

10. Frank Miller, "Book Four" in *Batman: The Dark Knight Returns* (New York: DC Comics and Warner Books, 1986), p. 77.

11. Bill Griffith, *Yow*, no. 1 (Berkeley, Calif.: Last Gasp, 1978), reprinted in *Zippy Special Two-in-One Issue* (Berkeley, Calif.: Last Gasp, 1985).

12. Ibid.

13. Bill Griffith, *Yow*, no. 2 (Berkeley, Calif.: Last Gasp, 1980), reprinted in *Zippy Special Two-in-One Issue* (Berkeley, Calif.: Last Gasp, 1985).

14. "Kim Deitch: Interviewed by Monte Beauchamp," *Comics Journal* 123 (July 1988): 66.

15. Kim Deitch, Afterword to *Hollywoodland* (Westlake Village, Calif.: Fantagraphics, 1987), p. 65–66.

16. Kim Deitch, "Murder on the Midway," *Weirdo*, no. 15 (Winter 1985–86); "The Mystic Shrine," *Weirdo*, no. 16 (Spring 1986); "Young Ledicker," *Weirdo*, no. 19 (Winter 1987); and "Pong Wook-ee!" *Weirdo*, no. 23 (Summer 1988).

17. Charles Burns, *Hard-Boiled Defective Stories* (New York: Pantheon Books, 1988), back flap.

18. Kim Thompson, "Return of the Dark Knight," *Comics Journal* 101 (August 1985): 59.